CW01656338

Especially for

Umi

Congratulations

Barakallah in this world

& in the Hereafter ...

TAKE CARE !

Love Always

Mak Ros & family

A Gift for
Muslim Bride

By Muhammad Haneef Abdul Majeed

Published by
Dakwah Corner Bookstore (M) Sdn Bhd.

First Published 2009

A Gift for Muslim Bride by Muhammad Haneef Abdul Majeed
ISBN 978-983-44208-7-1

Typeface : Book Antiqua, Naskh, Emiri

Address all correspondence to:
Dakwah Corner Bookstore (M) Sdn Bhd
No. 34-1, Jalan 14/22, Section 14, 46100 Petaling Jaya,
Selangor Darul Ehsan. (*Near Masjid Bulat / Right Angle*)
Tel / Fax : +603 - 7956 4664
Website : www.dakwahbookstore.com.my

SAUDI ARABIA :
Dawah Corner Bookstore
Makkah Commercial Center
2nd Floor,Shop No.201 Hilton Tower , Holy Makkah
Tel: + 966 2 5311895

JEDDAH :
Al Salamah Dist.
Near Shiabi Mosque. Tel: 6989380 Fax: 6975012

Cover Design, Typesetting & Printed by:
Percetakan IWC Sdn. Bhd.
No. 78 Jalan 10/118B,
Desa Tun Razak, Cheras,
56000 Kuala Lumpur.
Tel : 603-9172 5803 Fax : 603-9172 1290
Email : admin@iwcprint.com

Contents

Publisher Note

All Praise is for Allah, Lord of the worlds. Peace and Blessing be upon Prophet Muhammad, His Family, His companions and all those who follow in their footsteps until the Last Day.

In your Hands is the English Translation of the book Tuhfa-e Dulhan by Brother Muhammad Haneef Abdul Majid.

It is really an ideal gift to our Muslim sisters (brides), as the Muslim Brides mainly deals with the concerned affairs of married life according to Qur'an and Sunnah; touching upon topics like the excellence of a righteous wife, her attributes and duties to her husband.

Prophet Muhammad (Peace be Upon Him) Said, "All of this world is a utility and the best utility is a righteous wife."

He (Peace be Upon Him) also said ,"Let one of you possess a heart which is thankful, a tongue which makes mention of Allah, and a Believing wife who helps one of you upon the affairs of the hereafter ."

So It gives us great Pleasure in presenting this book in its new revised edition to our English speaking community, due to the importance of the subject and the benefits that may be attained.

We would like to thank all brothers and sisters who helped in this project, particularly to Percetakan IWC Sdn Bhd Kuala Lumpur, for supporting us with all of his effort (Jazahulllahu Khairan).

All Praise and thanks are due to Allah, who enabled us to accomplish this work.

Farid Ullah Ahmed Hussin
Managing Director
25-01-2009
Kuala Lumpur

Foreword by Maulana Muhammed Yusuf Ludhyanwi

(May Allah shower His mercy on him)

Allah Ta'ala has created man and woman as couples so that they may effectively assist each other to lead their lives in a manner that pleases Allah Ta'ala. The blessing of leading such a life will be prosperity and happiness in this world coupled with delight when standing before Allah Ta'ala on the Day of Qiyamah. As a result of this, eternal happiness in Jannah will be secured. However, this can be achieved only when both husband and wife fulfil each other's rights with the intention of pleasing Allah Ta'ala. Furthermore, the basis for preserving love and affection between the couple depends more on the wisdom, tolerance and pleasant-naturedness of the wife. A pleasant and good-natured wife easily converts a home of this world into a garden of Jannah. On the contrary, a miserable and ill-natured wife can turn a home into a pit of Jahannam. Not only does she suffer the consequences of her behaviour, but so does the husband together with both their families.

My good friend, Moulana Mufti Muhammed Haneef (may Allah Ta'ala keep him in peace) has written this book so that married couples may glean from its light and create an atmosphere of love, compassion and serenity in their homes. In doing this, they will be blessed with the bounties of the Aakhirah. I have perused through some parts of the book and hope that the rest of the book is also as correct.

May Allah Ta'ala make the book beneficial to the Ummah.

How to read this book

This book deals with people's domestic life. Since one's domestic happiness has a direct bearing on one's happiness outside the home, we advise that the contents of this book should be read with great earnestness and that the failings cautioned against should be avoided. Although these failings may result from immaturity and inexperience, they are nevertheless extremely harmful. One should read this book with the intention of reforming oneself. One will be able to avoid these failings if one reads this book with the following advices in mind:

1. Before reading the book, make du'aa to Allah Ta'ala saying, "O Allah Ta'ala! Make this book a means for my guidance and make me the delight of my husband's eyes and make me his most valuable asset."
2. Set aside such time for reading this book, which is free from disturbances and worries, because a mind that is preoccupied with other concerns will soon become weary with the subject matter of any book.
3. An important advice is that this book should be read in sequence from cover to cover even though this may take months. In fact, one should never grow despondent even if it takes longer than a few months. An easy way to ensure that one completes the book is to calculate a specific number of pages that one will read daily, based on the total number of pages in the book. A book mark should always be used to mark the page where one stops.
4. Another extremely important advice is that one should keep a pencil handy to mark places that mention something especially pertinent to one. These parts should be read many times and du'aa should be made to Allah Ta'ala to grant one the ability to practise accordingly.

Another benefit of keeping a pencil handy is that when reading, it may occur to one that some subject matter which may satisfy the thirst of some Muslim sister has not been included in this book. It may be that this subject pertains to a woman's life as a Muslim woman or as a wife or as a mother, or it may even be something that could terminate disputes. Should such a though occur to one, one should make a note of it under the heading of

"Clarification" and bring it to the attention of the publisher or the compiler, specifying the page number and line number where it is to be added.

We advise you to read A Gift To Groom too because it is imperative to understand the psyche of husbands and be better able to maintain peace and tranquilityin family life. The book is available at Maktaba Baitul Ilm (www.mbi.com.pk). For information you can contact them at writers_panel@yahoo.com.

While reading the book, one should make du'aa to Allah Ta'ala that He creates love and affection between all married Muslim couples and that He makes them all a means of rearing pious children. One should make du'aa daily that Allah Ta'ala keeps them all happy together with all those getting married. Together with reading this book and progressing spiritually and morally, one should also pass these advices on to other women.

The final request to the reader is to make du'aa for the compiler of this book, the people who authored the books from which information was taken and all those who assisted in this publication in any way. Of course, the person making the du'aa will never be deprived of the good of the du'aa. May Allah Ta'ala reward you all tremendously.

Introduction

This book cites the sterling examples of six women during the time of Our beloved Prophet (Peace be on him). The lessons that this book teaches include:

- Obeying the husband
- True love for the husband
- Honouring and serving the husband
- Being loyal towards the husband
- Making one's husband a Muslim or a pious person
- Qualities of a good wife
- How to remain the beloved of one's husband
- Bad habits of women and ways of losing them
- How to live in harmony with one's in-laws The rights that women owe to their husbands
- Advice for the married couple
- Formulas to avoid disputes between a bride and her husband, mother-in-law and sisters-in-law, which often lead to premature separations and bitter feelings between entire families Besides the above there are many other subjects and solutions discussed. By practising the teachings of this book, a home can become a garden of Jannah and means of attaining success in this world and in the Aakhirah (Hereafter).

SAVE YOUR HUSBANDS FROM SIN

Our Muslim sisters are generally negligent of attracting their husbands to themselves sufficiently by beautification and by other means. As a result, even if they are physically close to the husband, it is as if they are not there at all. Whether the consequences of this are light or serious, it is unfortunate that the woman will have to bear the brunt of it all. Allah Ta'ala has made the wife a garment of her husband and vice versa. However, many women do not seem to give this enough thought. Whereas an important function of garments is to conceal the body, another very important purpose of clothing is to beautify a person.

Just as clothing wraps a person, a woman should beautify herself so that she wraps her husband's attention exclusively for herself. She should captivate his attention and imagination by fulfilling all his permissible desires. A person is open and unrestricted beneath his clothing, yet he appears well covered in front of people. Similarly, a married man's chastity is well protected in public because he has a wife. However, he is open and unrestricted to satisfy himself with her in a permissible manner. She therefore has an extremely important function to fulfil because she is the only means by which her husband can satisfy his sensual passions. Now if a woman has to be dressed like a street-sweeper and is careless about personal hygiene, her husband will have no interest in her. His eyes will then start roving and it should never occur that the poisonous arrows of infatuation penetrate his heart.

Is the cure for this situation not that a woman should keep herself attractive so that her husband's eyes stay riveted to her? If a wife neglects this, she will soon find her husband enamoured with the parading masqueraders adorned with the artificial beauty and false glitter all manufactured by beauty parlours. The evil effect of this will even distract him from remembering Allah Ta'ala. We therefore appeal to our Muslim sisters to ensure that their bodies, their clothing and their permissible means of beautification should all harness the complete attention of their husbands. In this manner, they will secure their dominion. It should be borne in mind that if they resort to impermissible means of beautification, they will drive their husbands further from them.

When the wife takes the time and effort to beautify herself, she will be saving her husband from major sins. In addition to this, she will also be saving herself from unnecessary grief.

Many women complain to the Ulama and Muftees that their husbands do not love them and have no feelings for them. They lament about how their husbands meticulously carry out the orders of their parents without any consideration for her feelings. These husbands have no time for their children and continuously scold their wives. The best "Ta'weez" (amulet) for this situation is that the wife should use whatever means of beautification she has at her disposal to ensure that she remains attractive. She should be grateful for the natural beauty that Allah Ta'ala has given her and do her best to captivate the husband's attention. When this is achieved, all her worries will disappear. She will then have her husband eating out of her hand and he will even ignore her major faults. He will then do nothing against her wishes and no other woman will appeal to him irrespective of her beauty and charm.

If a wife fails to charm her husband, the consequences will be devastating. When at his office or company, another woman needs only to affectionately ask, "What is the matter that you seem so sad today?" thereafter even a married man's heart melts. Then, she leads him into sin. It may even happen that the most unattractive prostitute is waiting on a side street for someone to pick her up. However, the passing man does not realise what she is hiding beneath the layers of make-up until after he has committed the most despicable sin and she has washed her face. In many cases, the man realises only after marrying a second wife that she was previously married and that he was foolish to cause grief to his first wife. All these situations may well have been averted if the man's wife did not dress like a maid-servant at home and if she had taken better care of herself.

This piece of advice to women is given with conviction based on the experiences of thousands of women. When a woman fails to maintain a high standard of personal hygiene and fails to adorn herself for her husband, the couple may face serious problems. You may try it for yourself. Whenever your husband looks at you, you should appear like a bride to him. In this manner, you will avert many difficulties and unpleasant situations that leave a bitter taste even though they may be permissible. May Allah Ta'ala grant all Muslim women the ability to take heed and to practise.

We will now present to you some advices that an Arab poetess gave to her daughter who was to be married. A brief explanation has been given in English. It is anticipated that if a woman in any age practises the teachings taught in these advices, Insha Allah Ta'ala her home will be like a garden of Jannah.

Foreword

All praises belong to Allah Ta'ala and may His choicest mercies and blessing be on His noble Messenger (Peace be upon him). We present to our Muslim sisters the lives of six exemplary Muslim ladies from the best era who displayed excellent qualities as wives and lifelong friends to their husbands. Islam has taught us perfect guidelines to lead our domestic lives and Messenger of Allah (Peace be upon him) and the Companion of the Prophet have displayed excellent examples for us to emulate. However, we have ignored these teachings and therefore instead of being happy, content and successful, we have become miserable, dissatisfied and unsuccessful. Married life has become a scourge for many. Disputes between couples, bickering between daughters-and-mothers-in-law, jealousy between sisters-in-law and couples failing to fulfil the rights of each other have become commonplace nowadays. The repercussions of this have adversely affected not only the married couple, but entire families and communities.

By the infinite grace of Allah Ta'ala and the direction of Mufti Ahmadur Rahman (May Allah be Merciful on him/her), I managed to diagnose the principle causes for divorce and friction between married couples while serving at the Ifta department of the Jamiatul Uloom Islamiyya. These are:

Problems with mothers-in-law and sisters-in-law (husband's sisters as well as husband's brothers' wives)

UNREASONABLE MOTHERS-IN-LAW

Ill-tempered husbands

Couples blaming each other for mishaps and constantly quarrelling.

Of course, wives are also to blame for such problems because of their immaturity, discourteous speech and inconsiderate behaviour. Fanning the flames of such squabbles are the insolent lessons that women learn from their mothers and other women coupled with the solidarity that mothers and sisters-in-law display in these situations. It has therefore been my aspiration for some time to compile for the Muslim wife a book containing advices that would ensure that such disputed never arise. If

(Allah forbid!) such a fire does catch on, these advices would serve to extinguish it without destroying the beautiful garden of marriage and without even uprooting a single flower from it.

By Allah Ta'ala's grace, I also managed to read the book of Shaykh Muhammad Ibraheem Saleem, titled "An Nisaa Howla Messenger of Allah (Peace be upon him)". It then occurred to me that based on this book and taking our present-day situation into consideration, I should compile a book dealing with the marital lives of six Sahabiya women so that their lives become role models for Muslim women to follow. In addition to this, the advices and experiences of our leading Muslim scholars will also be brought to the attention of our sisters, especially the gems from the lips of Moulana Ashraf Ali Thanwi (May Allah be Merciful on him/her)

Because this book has been compiled with people's current state of affairs in mind, the advices of various books have been randomly quoted in the best interests of today's woman. Therefore, the traditional arrangement and classification of subject matter has not been employed. Scholars of literature are therefore requested not to judge the book according to their standards. However, should they detect any errors or omissions; they will do me a great favour by bringing this to my notice.

Admitting my incompetence and many faults, I present this book for all readers. Should any reader find any literary or subjective errors, she/he will share in the rewards gained through this book by bringing the same to our notice. These will Insha Allah Ta'ala be corrected in future editions. Everyone who benefits from this book is requested to remember us in their du'as.

We sincerely pray to Allah Ta'ala to make this humble effort a means of salvation in both worlds for us and for every couple. May Allah Ta'ala also end all domestic disputes because this is the secret formula for success and for love to develop between couples. In this manner, future generations will be able to live peacefully under the graceful shadow of their parents, ensuring happiness for all.

An Offering of Thanks to Messenger of Allah (Peace be upon him) from all Muslim Women:

[Adapted from the "Kaarwaan Madinah by Moulana Sayyid Abul Hasan Nadwi (May Allah be Merciful on him]

We invoke the special mercies of Allah Ta'ala and peace on you, O Messenger of Allah (Peace be upon him). With the help of Allah Ta'ala, you removed us from the shackles of ignorance, from foolish customs and traditions. You have delivered us from the oppression of society and the tyranny of men. You stopped the burying of little girls alive and you warned against disobeying mothers. You even said that Jannah lies under the feet of mothers. You have given us a share in inheritance as mothers, sisters, daughters and wives. You did not even forget us when you delivered the momentous sermon at Arafah. You said, "Fear Allah Ta'ala with regard to your women because you acquired them with Allah Ta'ala's name." You also reminded men on numerous occasions to treat us kindly and to fulfil our rights.

On behalf of all women, may Allah Ta'ala grant you the best reward that He bestows on any of His Ambiya and on any of His chosen servants.

The Six Exemplary Women

1. **Ummul Mu'mineen Khadeeja bint Khuwaylid**
   (May Allah be pleased with him/her)
2. **Ummul Mu'mineen Sowda bint Zam'ah**
   (May Allah be pleased with him/her)
3. **Zaynab bint Muhammad bin Abdullah**
   (May Allah be pleased with him/her).
4. **Ruqayya bint Muhammad bin Abdullah**
   (May Allah be pleased with him/her)
5. **Ummul Hakeem bint Haarith**
   (May Allah be pleased with him/her)
6. **Khowla bint Maalik bin Tha'laba**
   (May Allah be pleased with him/her)

WHY WOMEN WERE CREATED?

Adam (Peace be upon him) lived in Jannah where he enjoyed every type of bounty and he was immersed in Allah Ta'ala's mercy at every step. However, he still yearned for something else. It was only when Allah Ta'ala created his spouse Hawwa (Peace be upon her) that Adam (Peace be upon him) experienced the joys of Jannah to their fullest and Jannah became a true paradise for him. The beautiful appearance of a delicate flower, the fragrance of a rose, the singing of a nightingale, the chirping of birds, the vivid colours of the setting sun and everything else that brings delight to the heart seem incomplete to the person who is without a spouse. With companion- ship, every bounty gives one true joy. Without a wife, man's life is empty and shapeless. A wife blows enthusiasm and colour into his life.

A wife is the true beauty of a man's life and his primary source of comfort and solace. She lights up his life and his life will be dull and dark without her. Women are the nucleus of society and the embellishment of mankind. She adds flavour to man's life. Without her, civilisations would be disorganised and stagnant. She blows the spirit into man's activities and her presence keeps him going. As a result, man is always progressing and exploring new ground.

Allah Ta'ala has given women beauty and the ability to calm the roughest waters. She is therefore a great source of comfort for the husband and dispels his loneliness. She instils zest in his life so that he continues doing what he has to do and never becomes bored with his daily routine. Without her, he would become frustrated with his mundane activities and may stop altogether.

The charm women add to life equates her to the petals of a rose, the delicate gems of a necklace, a sparkling dewdrop, the ripples of a stream and everything else that lends beauty to another. A wife cheers up her depressed husband and can turn hell into heaven. In fact, every king, minister, saint and even Allah Ta'ala's beloved Messenger of Allah (Peace be upon him) called woman a mother. He also declared that Jannah lies beneath the feet of mothers.

Just as the world would be deserted without people, a house without a pious woman would be deserted and fraught with problems. A good woman is the queen of her home and can command her husband to do anything within the ambit of the Shari'ah. However, before taking the reins of command into her hands, some sacrifices will have to be made. The crown of this queen is a crown of roses. Just as roses have thorns to contend with; a wife will have to be humble bonds-women before she becomes a queen. She will have to wear a crown of thorns before adorning the crown of roses. Such is the system of this world.

While a man was busy pounding kohl fine, the kohl asked him, "Why are you pounding me so fine?" The man replied, "So that you may become worthy of finding a place in the best organ of the best of creation (i.e. in man's eyes)."

Dear lady, because you are the ray of hope in every man's life, you have to make yourself pious. You have to ensure that you are particular about all your five Salahs that you don the Islamic Hijaab that you encourage the ladies in your locality to lead a religious life together with making an effort for this way of life to spread throughout the world. May Allah Ta'ala make you pious and the delight of your husband's eyes. *Aameen.*

THE TESTIMONY OF THE QURAN:

With concise words, the Quran has explained the purpose of woman's creation. If a wife fulfils this purpose, her husband will be the most fortunate man in the world. Otherwise, his life on earth will be reminiscent of Jahannam. According to the Ahadeeth, such a wife will make a person old before his time. Allah Ta'ala says in the opening verse of Surah Nisaa (Surah 4) that -

﴿ وَآتُواْ النَّسَاء صَدُقَاتِهِنَّ نِحْلَةً فَإِن طِبْنَ لَكُمْ عَن شَيْءٍ مِّنْهُ نَفْساً فَكُلُوهُ هَنِيئاً مَّرِيئاً ﴾ (النساء : ٤)

"He had created man's spouse from himself".

Allah Ta'ala says in Surah Roum,

﴿ وَمِنْ آيَاتِهِ أَنْ خَلَقَ لَكُم مِنْ أَنْفُسِكُمْ أَزْوَاجاً لِتَسْكُنُوا إِلَيْهَا وَجَعَلَ بَيْنَكُمْ مَوَدَّةً وَرَحْمَةً ﴾ (سورة الروم آيت ٢١)

"And from His signs is that He has created spouses for you from your own species so that you may find solace with her and He has placed love and mercy between you. There are certainly signs in this for people who contemplate."

[Surah 30, verse 21]

This solace and mutual love underpins the happiness and stability of a family and oils the wheels of civilisation. The woman is therefore the cradle of comfort for her husband. It is with her that he may satisfy his passions and stay away from sin so that his chastity may remain untainted.

A pious wife is the greatest bounty any man can have and nothing can be more valuable and special than her. She is there to love, to be loved and to care for her husband. When a man returns tired and frustrated after a hard day at work, he will forget all his fatigue and worries when he is welcomed home by a smiling and charming wife. A good wife gives a man vigour and enthusiasm and a few words from her are more revitalizing than glucose and vitamins.

The married couple ease the worries and concerns of each other by displaying mutual compassion. In this manner, they make life pleasant for each other. May Allah Ta'ala make every bride the source of comfort for her husband. *Aameen.*

THE DU'AA OF ALLAH'S TA'ALA SINCERE BONDSMEN

Describing the qualities of His chosen bondsmen, Allah Ta'ala says that they always make du'aa for good wives and children. Quoting their du'aa in Surah Furqaan,

﴿ وَالَّذِينَ يَقُولُونَ رَبَّنَا هَبْ لَنَا مِنْ أَزْوَاجِنَا وَذُرِّيَّاتِنَا قُرَّةَ أَعْيُنٍ وَاجْعَلْنَا لِلْمُتَّقِينَ إِمَاماً ﴾ (سورة الفرقان آيت ٧٤)

Allah Ta'ala says,

"Those who say, 'O our Rabb! Accord to us the coolness of our eyes from our spouses and children, and make us leaders of the pious.'"

This du'aa is a reminder to all Mu'mineen that they should also ask the same from Allah Ta'ala It is obvious that if a woman is not good-natured and pleasant, the couple cannot live happily together. A woman can be the coolness of a man's eyes only when she is good and pious. A man is therefore extremely fortunate if he finds a wife who is well-groomed, compassionate and intelligent. Insha Allah Ta'ala , if a bride or wife reads this book and sincerely practises the advices mentioned, the couple will quickly become the coolness of each other's eyes.

If a wife inculcates within herself the qualities which Islam teaches, she will soon conquer her husband's heart and he will attain the contentment of heart that a good wife should provide for him. He will then be prepared to make sacrifices for her and do whatever she asks. Nothing she asks will be too much for him.

NOTE: Every Muslim male and female should read the du'aa taught in the above verse of the Quran after every Fardh Salah. Especially boys and girls who have come of age should recite this du'aa.

The Pious Wife

خير متاع الدنيا المرأة الصالحة-

(الترغيب والترهيب ص ٢٧ ج٣)

When Messenger of Allah (Peace be upon him) received the first revelation, he was overcome with natural anxiety because it was the first time that he experienced something of that nature and it was the first time that he met an angel. During this troubled and difficult stage, it was his wife Khadeeja (May Allah be pleased with her) who provided the comfort and courage he needed.

Similarly, when Messenger of Allah (Peace be upon him) was leaving this world and experiencing what every dying person regards as Qiyamah, who was there to tend to him and comfort him? Although thousands of Companion of the Prophet (May Allah be pleased with him/her) were present in Madinah, the books of history and Ahadeeth make it clear that none of them were present with Messenger of Allah (Peace be upon him) then. At this time when Messenger of Allah (Peace be upon him) was departing to meet Allah Ta'ala, whose lap had the privilege to serve as a pillow for him? Neither was Abu Bakr (May Allah be pleased with him/her) nor Umar (May Allah be pleased with him/her) nor Uthmaan (May Allah be pleased with him/her) nor Ali (May Allah be pleased with him/her) nor any perform the other Companion of the Prophet present there. The good fortune belonged to none other than Messenger of Allah's beloved wife Aa'isha (May Allah be pleased with him/her).

Islam accords and exceptionally high esteem to women which one will not find in other cultures and nationalities regardless of the lip service they offer in support of women's rights. We will present to you the lives of some wives who reached tremendous heights and who engraved their undying love in the hearts of their husbands. We shall describe the excellent qualities of these women and discuss how they became the pride of their husband's lives and how they made their children worthy of entering Jannah.

If you inculcate these qualities in your life, you will also become the light of your husband's eyes and the most precious thing in the world for him. You will be the queen of your home, enjoy true love and respect and be his companion in public and in private.

ISLAM'S STANDARD OF JUDGING A GOOD WIFE

In Islam, the standard by which a good wife is judged is not her university degrees or college diplomas, all of which really do not matter to the husband. The most truthful Messenger of Allah (Peace be upon him) has mentioned,

لو كنت أمر أحداً أن يسجد لأحد لأمرتُ المرأة أنْ تسجد لِزوجها
(مشكوة ص ٢٨١)

"If I were to command anyone to prostrate to another (human), I would have certainly commanded a wife to prostrate to her husband."

A good wife would therefore be one who suppresses all her desires for her husband, prefer him above herself and sacrifice her own pleasures for him. She is one who would be prepared to lay down to sleep on the bed of thorns her husband provides, imagining it to be a bed of roses.

Dear wives! Regard the dry bread he gives you to be a delicious meal from Jannah and imagine the old clothes to be finery and jewellery. Turn a deaf ear to his scolding and imagine that the insults from your mother-and-sister-in-law are the kind words of your mother. Keep smiling though all the difficulties. Pass your life with tolerance and contentment. This will demonstrate that even in this fourteenth century after Hijrah women can be born who will not disgrace the names of their forebears, who were the true slaves of Allah Ta'ala and who would sacrifice themselves at the mere gestures of Khadeeja (May Allah be pleased with him/her) and Aa'isha R. It will be seen that obedience to Allah Ta'ala, fear for Allah Ta'ala can be rolled into one person together with obedience to the husband.

We make du'aa to Allah Ta'ala to allow us all the ability to practise what we will read in the ensuing narratives and the ability to do whatever pleases Him. May Allah Ta'ala make every Muslim wife the most precious thing in the world to her husband and may He make every Muslim husband the best of people who behaves excellently towards his wife. *Aameen*.

KHADEEJA (MAY ALLAH BE PLEASED WITH HIM/HER) HER LINEAGE

Her name was Khadeeja R, her family name was Ummu Hind and her title was Tahira. Her father was Khuwaylid, who was the son of Asad, who was the son of Abdul Uzza, who was the son of Qusay. It is from Qusay that her lineage meets that of Messenger of Allah (Peace be upon him).

When Messenger of Allah (Peace be upon him) was being harassed by the Quraysh, only two women supported him. They were Khadeeja (May Allah be pleased with him/her) bint Khuwaylid (May Allah be pleased with him/her) and Fatima bint Asad (May Allah be pleased with him/her). It is because of her loyal support that she is regarded as one of the world's best women. Recalling her loyalty and support, Messenger of Allah (Peace be upon him) mentioned,

آمنت بي إذ كفرني الناس

"She believed in me when the people falsified me",

وصدقتني إذ كذبني الناس

"She regarded me to be truthful when people called me a liar".

وواستني بمالها إذ حرمني الناس

"And she gave me financial assistance when people denied me wealth".

During the time when none were prepared to stand by the side of Messenger of Allah (Peace be upon him), it was Khadeeja (May Allah be pleased with him/her) who echoed his message whilst she was the first person to accept Islam.

KHADEEJA (MAY ALLAH BE PLEASED WITH HER) COMFORTS MESSENGER OF ALLAH (PEACE BE UPON HIM)

Khadeeja (May Allah be pleased with him/her) was always there to console Messenger of Allah (Peace be upon him) whenever the Mushrikeen harassed him. The comfort she provided would dispel his worries and relieve him of his burden. When Messenger of Allah (Peace be upon him) received the first revelation, he felt natural fear because it was the first experience of such a nature. He was visibly shaken when he arrived home. It was then that Khadeeja (May Allah be pleased with him/her) consoled him with words worth writing in gold. If every Muslim woman could console her husband so effectively, he will always refer to her when he experiences any anxiety, which is a prized certificate of merit for any woman.

Khadeeja (May Allah be pleased with him/her) said to Messenger of Allah (Peace be upon him).

كلا واللّه لا يخزيك اللّه أبداً أنك لتصل الرحم، وتحمل الكل وتكسب المعدوم،وتقرى الضيف وتعين على نوآءب الحق (مشكوة ص ٥٢٢)

"Allah Ta'ala shall never disgrace you and never forsake you because you maintain good family relations, assist people, provide for the needy and destitute, entertain guests and support all good causes." A person with qualities like these cannot be influenced by Shaytaan because Allah Ta'ala would never allow it to happen. She said this with such conviction that it consoled Messenger of Allah (Peace be upon him).

NOTE:

These words display true love and true loyalty that any husband would cherish. Only a person with true love can utter such comforting words. It is evident that his grief was her grief; his happiness, her happiness; his illness, her illness; his health, her health. A person like this recognises every good quality in her spouse and accommodates these in her heart. Therefore, when the occasion arose, she was able to express these to comfort him.

It is difficult to imagine that such wise, consoling and loving words could come from someone who grew up in the harsh desert of Arabia where there were neither schools, universities or finishing schools. In fact, a bit of thought would reveal that these words detail exactly how a person should lead her life.

All thanks are for Allah Ta'ala Who gave us the perfect example of a woman like Khadeeja (May Allah be pleased with him/her) to follow. Although a woman cannot be a Nabi, Allah Ta'ala has made the means for a woman's way of life to be emulated if she so desired it. The lives of all the wives of Messenger of Allah (Peace be upon him) provide women with perfect examples and lessons for leading their lives. Before doing something, Muslim women ought to first think about what the Sahabiyaat ladies (May Allah be pleased with her) would do in the same situation. They should think about the homes of these Sahabiyaat, their food, their clothing, their relationships with their husbands and every other aspect of their lives.

Reflect once again over her words. She said, "Allah Ta'ala shall never disgrace you and never forsake you because you maintain good family relations, assist people, provide for the needy and destitute, entertain guests and support all good causes."

It is actually possible for a woman to develop all these qualities in her husband. If a wife does not complain to her husband about his parents, his brothers, his sisters and other relatives and if she encourages him to associate with them cordially and to overlook their faults, she will be making him a person who maintains good family relations. Allah Ta'ala has also given the wife the ability to purge her husband's heart of any enmity and ill feelings he may have towards another family member. By eradicating any friction between him and his family members, she will be immensely rewarded in this world and in the Hereafter. In this manner, all will live in peace and harmony and Allah Ta'ala's mercy and blessings will continue to shower upon the entire family. When we talk about the family, it includes children also. Kids need entertainment, entertainment in line with Shariah is the best form of entertainment. For this purpose we recommend Zouq Shouq series (Urdu) and Story time Series (English) by Baitul Ilm Publishers for great stories, jokes, puzzles and fun facts. We must also be very particular about the guidelines Islam provides for upbringing of kids, for this purpose read 'Ideal Mother' and make your husband read 'Ideal Father' by Darul Huda Publishers.

With love and understanding, a wife may explain to her husband that if he does not maintain good relations with his family, it would be very difficult if not impossible for her and their children to foster good relations with them. If the husband is the eldest brother, she may tell him that because he enjoys the status of the father, it is unbecoming of him to get upset about trivial matters as women do. In fact, his father would be disappointed with such behaviour. If he is a younger brother, she should tell him to forgive and overlook because those who are younger ought to listen to and respect- their elders. She should explain to him that if he exercises tolerance and listens to his elders, his children will respect and obey him in future. In addition to this, Allah Ta'ala has promised tremendous rewards for the patient.

She should always encourage her husband to exercise patience irrespective of the difficulty that others give him. Even if (for example) his brothers have deprived him of his share of inheritance or if they have seized complete control of their shared property, the wife should stop him from severing relations with them by telling him that the commodities of this world are temporary. If the others want it for themselves, they may have it with pleasure. Everything a person receives in this world is predestined and Allah Ta'ala provides for all. If one door of sustenance seems to be closed, Allah Ta'ala will open another. Allah Ta'ala holds the treasures of the heavens and the earth in His hand and He grants what He wants to whom He wants. Allah Ta'ala will soon grant what is best in this world. Otherwise, He will surely give the full reward in the Hereafter - a reward that is everlasting.

It is not befitting of a Muslim to fight and to severe ties with others because of the perishable commodities of this world, especially if the others are his blood. In this manner, a wife can make her husband emulate the first Sunnah that Khadeeja (May Allah be pleased with him/her) mentioned, viz. maintaining good family relations.

A wife can also influence her husband to practise the second Sunnah mentioned above viz. assisting others. If a wife reduces her household expenses to a minimum, there will be enough money left over to assist others and to earn the everlasting rewards of the Hereafter. The needy and destitute will find a haven with such a family and guests will also have the best entertainment. A wife may also encourage her husband to employ the unemployed or to assist in finding them employment. In this way, she will share his rewards. Of course, if she earns her own money, she is at liberty to spend this also to assist the needy and support good causes.

Whenever a female guest visits, the wife should ensure that she does not leave without having something, even if it is a glass of plain water. The guest should be met with a smiling face, reminded about some aspect of Religion while talking and she should be encouraged to practice and propagate the Religion.

When the husband brings a guest home, the wife should prepare to the best of her ability, giving preference to the guest over herself. It is permissible and even encouraged that she prepares special meals that are normally not served at home. Of course, wastefulness is not encouraged. Although every guest attracts blessing to the home, pious people bring untold good and blessings to the home. The same attitude of selflessness should be displayed to all types of guests, irrespective of their standing. In fact, Messenger of Allah (Peace be upon him) even entertained Kuffaar guests.

One should never think that one is doing the guest a favour by entertaining him/her. It is in fact the guest doing one a favour by eating his own predestined sustenance at one's home and allowing one to share in the reward.

Guests should never be regarded as a burden. Although keeping the house clean, cooking and entertaining guests is no easy task, doing this solely for Allah Ta'ala's pleasure earn rewards that are too great to mention. In addition to this, the guests make heartfelt du'as for the host and hostess. Especially when the guest is a traveller, his du'as are most readily accepted.

If one's husband is not accustomed to bringing guests home, one should encourage him to do so. According to one's means, one should occasionally invite pious people home and feed them. One should also feed those in Allah Ta'ala's path. The food should not be extravagant, but something that the guests will enjoy even though it is simple and easy to prepare. Just as it is wrong for a guest to think that the host fed him something very simple, it is also wrong for the host to think that the guest will feel this. These notions should be removed from our minds. Everything should be done to please Allah Ta'ala. One should serve whatever one can afford and whatever can be easily prepared so that Allah Ta'ala should be pleased, irrespective of what people think.

We make du'aa to Allah Ta'ala makes every Muslim wife a splendid flower in the flourishing garden of the Religion of Muhammah (Peace be upon him) through the sterling example of Khadeeja (May Allah be pleased with him/her). *Aameen.*

SACRIFICING ONE'S WEALTH FOR ONE'S HUSBAND

Describing the qualities of Khadeeja (May Allah be pleased with him/her), Messenger of Allah (Peace be upon him) said,

وواستني بمالها إذ حرمني الناس

"She gave me financial assistance when people denied me wealth."

It is common knowledge that people love their wealth. It follows therefore that the person on whom one spends one's wealth is more beloved than the wealth. If one's husband requires one's financial assistance for any necessity of Religion or for some permissible worldly need, one should regard giving assistance as an honour. In fact, spending one's wealth or jewellery on one's husband when needed will win his heart and earn one tremendous rewards. Being generous with this is better than storing it in one's cupboard, looking at it occasionally and then losing it to someone else after one's death. The rewards of whatever one provides for one's husband to spend shall be made available on the Day of Qiyamah, when one will most need it.

If a woman's husband spends her wealth to spread Religion and to ensure that the orders of Allah Ta'ala and the teachings of Messenger of Allah (Peace be upon him) are practised throughout the globe, one will share a most elevated platform with Khadeeja q. Insha Allah when Allah Ta'ala will raise the wives of Ambiya (Peace be upon him)on the Day of Qiyamah and reward them for assisting their husbands in propagating the belief of Tauheed and for eradicating kufr and shirk, the Muslim wife who spent her wealth for her husband's Religion activities will also be rewarded with them. She will be rewarded with all these women who boosted the spirits of their husbands who in turn sacrificed their possessions and their faculties so that Allah Ta'ala's Religion reigns supreme on earth. Needless to say, it is also necessary for such a woman to lead a pious life reminiscent of the lives of all these women.

A wife has to be prepared to sacrifice everything for her husband, a quality which Khadeeja (May Allah be pleased with him/her) displayed on so many occasions. When she was to marry Messenger of Allah (Peace be upon him) , her father was unhappy that his daughter should marry the poor orphaned nephew of Abu Taalib. To win her father's approval, Khadeeja (May Allah be pleased with him/her) sent two Awqiya of silver or gold to Messenger of Allah (Peace be upon him) telling him to buy material, a sheep and certain other items with it. She told Messenger of Allah (Peace be upon him) that he should then give these things to her as a gift. When Messenger of Allah (Peace be upon him) sent these gifts, she showed them to her father, telling him that Messenger of Allah (Peace be upon him) had sent them. Seeing the expensive gifts, her father was pleased. This is an excellent example to all women, echoing the message that everything of this world pales into insignificance before the status of the husband.

It is necessary for every Muslim woman to display the same kind of selflessness for her husband and to spend whatever she can with love and affection. A poet says:

> "Dear friend! If you need my life, it is at
> your disposal And if you need anything
> that may be more valuable than my life,
> Do inform me of it so that I may offer it
> to you as well."
> *[This poem has been translated from Urdu]*

Learn to sacrifice for your husband, obey him, respect him, try to understand him and shower your love on him instead of making demands. Make him feel that he is most honoured, that he is more valuable to you than everything else and that everything has value because of his presence. When treated in this manner with love, together with du'as after every Fardh Salah, even the most ill tempered and ungrateful husband will be conquered. He will then appreciate everything that his wife does and will repent for his past behaviour. He will even remember his wife fondly long after her demise. His attitude will then resound the following words:

> "My dear candle of honour, light of my dreams!
> When you left, four hundred layers of darkness

arrived Now I can only wipe the tears that flow
Destiny has it that the ship is being thrust
towards the shores of patience
The children gather up the tears
flowing from my eyes
We think that we can turn and look away
But still lying there is the bed and the couch,
On which you would spend entire nights teaching the children
I now appreciate you now after you have left
Destiny has shattered with wasted tears
Come! Return to fill my home just one more time"
[This poem has been translated from Urdu]

ADVISING THE HUSBAND CORRECTLY

Another responsibility of the Muslim wife is to influence her husband to consult with her in all matters, whether religious or otherwise. In fact, when a Muslim carries out any worldly activity, it is also regarded as a Religion activity because he does everything for the pleasure of Allah Ta'ala. The husband should seek his wife's assistance in all matters and discuss these with her so that both of them can be happy about the outcome. A husband should never think that he may dictate matters because he is in a position of authority.

The Quran stipulates that a child should be breast-fed for two years. During this period, it is compulsory for the father to pay for the suckling mother. However, the couple have the prerogative to wean the child off milk before two years on condition that they have consulted with each other. Allah Ta'ala says about this in Surah Baqara

﴿ فَإِنْ أَرَادَا فِصَالاً عَنْ تَرَاضٍ مِنْهُمَا وَتَشَاوُرٍ فَلا جُنَاحَ عَلَيْهِمَا ﴾

(سورة بقرة آيت ٢٣٣)

"If the couple decide to wean the child by mutual consent and consultation, there shall be no sin upon either of them." This verse makes it clear that the couple should make domestic decisions after consultation.

The Quran also mentions that "Mashwara" (mutual consultation) is among the characteristics of the Mu'mineen.

﴿ وَأَقَامُوا الصَّلَاةَ وَأَمْرُهُمْ شُورَى بَيْنَهُمْ وَمِمَّا رَزَقْنَاهُمْ يُنفِقُونَ ﴾

(سورةالشورى آیت۳۸)

Allah Ta'ala says in Surah Shura that the Mu'mineen are people "who respond to (the commands of) their Rabb, who establish Salah, whose affairs (are decided) by mutual consultation between themselves, and who spend from what We have provided for them." The matter of consultation is given so much importance in the Shari'ah that the Quran mentions it together with Salah and zakaah.

أمرو النساء في بناتهن (رواه احمد وابو داؤد ص ٢٨٥)

Messenger of Allah (Peace be upon him) has mentioned, "Consult with your women concerning your daughters." This hadith enjoins fathers to consult with their wives concerning the marriage of their daughters.

The Seerah (biography) of Messenger of Allah (Peace be upon him) written by Ibn Hishaam (May Allah be pleased with him/her) describes Khadeeja (May Allah be pleased with him/her) as a woman.

وكانت له وزير صدق على الإسلام

"Who was a true advisor to Messenger of Allah (Peace be upon him) in the matters of Religion." Together with deep insight and excellent character, Khadeeja (May Allah be pleased with him/her) was endowed with sound intelligence. She had many years of experience with people and understood them well. Her opinions were therefore very sensible and valuable. She always gave Messenger of Allah (Peace be upon him) advice that lessened his grief and gave him all the support he needed.

This should be the behaviour of all Muslim women. Whenever her husband requires her advice, she should give the matter the attention it deserves, make du'aa to Allah Ta'ala and offer her best advice. If the matter is beyond her, she should ask advice from pious people in her family who are capable of providing some direction. If no one from her family is able to assist, advice should be sought from a pious person in the appropriate field. The husband should be referred to such a person or persons, just as Khadeeja (May Allah be pleased with him/her) referred Messenger of Allah (Peace be upon him) to her cousin Waraqa bin Naufal, who was learned in the previously revealed divine scriptures. Therefore, when Jibra'eel (Peace be upon him) came to the Messenger of Allah (Peace be upon him) with the first revelation, Khadeeja (May Allah be pleased with him/her) told Messenger of Allah (Peace be upon him) as much as she knew and then directed him to Waraqa bin Naufal, who knew much more than her.

After signing the Treaty of Hudaybiyyah, when Messenger of Allah (Peace be upon him) instructed the Companion of the Prophet to slaughter their animals and to shave their hair, no one responded. The Companion of the Prophet found it difficult to do this because they found it difficult to return without performing Umrah and they expected that the command might be reversed at any time. When Messenger of Allah (Peace be upon him) consulted his wife Ummu Salma (May Allah be pleased with her) about the issue, she advised Messenger of Allah (Peace be upon him) that he should do it first and that the Companion of the Prophet would soon follow his example. When Messenger of Allah (Peace be upon him) did as she had advised, the Companion of the Prophet followed suit. Her valuable advice therefore averted an extremely inconvenient and uncomfortable situation.

Today's women are also required to sometimes advise their husbands on Religious issues like their pious predecessors. In this way, they will also share the rewards of spreading Religion throughout the world. In fact, every Muslim wife should be concerned about how Religion should spread in her locality, her country and throughout the entire world. She should continue advising her husband in this regard. At the same time, she should also offer him sincere advice in matters of this world as well.

Some people are of the opinion that women should not be consulted when taking decisions. This opinion is incorrect because the advice of a pious, sensible and intelligent woman should be accepted. Besides the above two examples, the books of history are full of incidents in which the advice of Muslim women has tremendously benefited the Ummah and saved them from great difficulty. Of course, this does not mean that the wife should make the decisions in the house. Ultimately, it is the husband who takes the decisions. What his wife says shall be her opinion.

MAKING SACRIFICES FOR THE HUSBAND

When faced with any domestic crisis, the wife should bear with her husband and stand with him. She should not behave disloyally by forsaking him when times are tough. She should not fit the description of someone who said, "Gobble up the gifts and spit out the sacrifices." The wife should never remind the husband that something would not have happened if he acted on her advice. Let alone a Muslim wife, such behaviour is unbecoming of even a Kaafir wife. Everything happens by Allah Ta'ala's command. Neither a calamity nor a bounty that Allah Ta'ala ordains can be averted.

﴿ قُلْ لَنْ يُصِيبَنَا إِلَّا مَا كَتَبَ اللَّهُ لَنَا هُوَ مَوْلَانَا وَعَلَى اللَّهِ فَلْيَتَوَكَّلِ الْمُؤْمِنُونَ ﴾ (سورة التوبة: ٥١)

Allah Ta'ala says in the Surah Taubah, "Tell them, 'Only what Allah Ta'ala had ordained for us will affect us. He is our Protecting Friend and the believers should trust only in Him. Allah Ta'ala is All Knowing and will never abandon one in distress. When one pleads for his mercy, it is sure to come rushing to one's side.

The wife should be especially patient when her husband earns less because he is serving the Religion or engaged in some Halaal occupation. Patience must also be exercised when she experiences difficulty during his absence. She should never complain of these difficulties to others because speaking ill of the husband shall not alleviate the problem. In fact, the problem will be compounded and Allah Ta'ala will also be displeased with such a wife. She should perpetually make du'aa to Allah Ta'ala to alleviate the difficulty and also ask her children to make du'aa.

During the seventh year after Messenger of Allah announced his prophethood, the Quraysh decided to banish the family of Rasulullah (Peace be upon him) to a valley near Makkah and to completely ostracise them. This was done to stop Messenger of Allah (Peace be upon him) from propagating Islam. Consequently, Abu Taalib and all his family members joined Messenger of Allah (Peace be upon him) in what was referred to as the Valley of Abu Taalib. At his side was Khadeeja (May Allah be pleased with her).

وهي عند رسول اللّٰه ﷺ ومعه فى الشعب

(Serat-e-Ibn-e-Hasham143/2)

Although the condition was so harsh that the Muslims were forced to eat the leaves of trees, Khadeeja (May Allah be pleased with her) stayed with Messenger of Allah (Peace be upon him) and never deserted him. Because of Khadeeja (May Allah be pleased with her)'s influence on the people of Makkah, food was sometimes brought to the Muslims. However, this was scarce and the children were so starved that their cries could be heard from very far off.

Despite the hardship, Messenger of Allah (Peace be upon him) could not stop propagating Islam and the message continued. All this while, Messenger of Allah (Peace be upon him)'s family the Banu Haashim and Khadeeja (May Allah be pleased with her) patiently bore the hardship without once complaining and without blaming Messenger of Allah (Peace be upon him) for their predicament. This boycott lasted for three long years. Khadeeja (May Allah be pleased with her) displayed her loyalty to Messenger of Allah (Peace be upon him) for approximately thirty years, patiently enduring all the difficulties that came to them. May Allah Ta'ala reward Khadeeja (May Allah be pleased with her) abundantly on our behalf for the tremendous sacrifices she made for the spread of Islam.

It is therefore the duty of every Muslim wife to emulate the example of this Ummul Mu'mineen (Mother of the Mu'mineen). She should be her husband's deputy and aide in the propagation of Islam and should be prepared make every sacrifice in this cause. By doing this, they can also earn the great rewards that Khadeeja (May Allah be pleased with him/her) earned.

SERVING THE HUSBAND

Although Khadeeja (May Allah be pleased with him/her) was an influential, well-established and wealthy woman of the Quraysh, she personally served Messenger of Allah (Peace be upon him). A narration of Bukhari mentions that Khadeeja (May Allah be pleased with him/her) was once serving something to Messenger of Allah (Peace be upon him) in a dish when Jibra'eel (Peace be upon him) came and informed Messenger of Allah (Peace be upon him) that Allah Ta'ala had sent Salams (greetings of peace) to her. Messenger of Allah (Peace be upon him) said,

يا خديجة ، هذا جبريل يقرءك السلام من ربك

"O Khadeeja! Here is Jibra'eel (Peace be upon him) conveying the Salam of your Rabb to you." Khadeeja (May Allah be pleased with him/her) replied,

للّٰه السلام

ومنه السلام

وعلى جبرئيل السلام

"Allah Ta'ala is Himself the Giver of peace, all peace if from Him and peace be to Jibra'eel (Peace be upon him) as well."

This narration shows the elevated status of Khadeeja (May Allah be pleased with him/her) because Allah Ta'ala Himself send greetings to her. It can only be a chosen servant of Allah Ta'ala who can have this honour. According to another narration,

وبَشرَها ببيت فى الجنة من قصب لا صخب فيه ولا نصب

She was also given the glad tidings that she would have a palace in Jannah where there shall be neither noise nor fatigue.

Because of her devotion and dedication, Rasulullahs, said,

خير نسائها مريم بنت عمران وخير نسائها خديجة بنت خويلد

(مشكوة ص ٥٧٣)

"The best women (of this world) are Maryam bint Imraan and Khadeeja (May Allah be pleased with him/her) bint Khuwaylid."

The lives of the wives of Messenger of Allah (Peace be upon him) are recorded for Muslim women of every age to emulate. The manner in which they served Messenger of Allah (Peace be upon him) is a lesson for every Muslim wife so that every woman can earn the same rewards. Although we are presently discussing Khadeeja (May Allah be pleased with him/her), it is appropriate to mention a bit of the life of Aa'isha (May Allah be pleased with him/her) because the discussion revolves around serving one's husband.

In his biography of Aa'isha (May Allah be pleased with him/her),

Allaama Sayyid Sulaymaan Nadwi (May Allah be Merciful on him/her) states that although Aa'isha (May Allah be pleased with him/her) had a servant, she personally served Messenger of Allah (Peace be upon him). She personally crushed the wheat to make flour, cooked the food herself, made the beds and brought water for wudhu. She would also twine the garlands that were hung on Messenger of Allah (Peace be upon him)'s sacrificial animals. In addition to this, she used to comb his hair, perfume his body and wash his clothes all by herself. She used to keep his Miswaak and water ready at night and would always keep the Miswaak clean. Whenever Messenger of Allah (Peace be upon him) received any visitors, she would also attend to entertaining them.

Qais Ghifaari (May Allah be pleased with him/her), who was one of the Companion of the Prophet (Peace be upon him) of the Suffa narrates that Messenger of Allah (Peace be upon him) once told them all to accompany him to the room of Aa'isha (May Allah be pleased with him/her). When Messenger of Allah (Peace be upon him) asked Aa'isha (May Allah be pleased with him/her) to serve some food, she served something that she had already cooked. When Messenger of Allah (Peace be upon him) asked for something else, she served a dish made of dates. When Messenger of Allah (Peace be upon him) asked for something to drink, she brought a large container of milk and smaller container of water.

This was an example of a good wife. She considered it an honour to serve her husband and to do things herself. When a woman does this with the intention of fulfilling her husband's rights and pleasing Allah Ta'ala, her service will be regarded as Ibaadah. Of course, a wife should not be so engrossed in domestic work that she neglects her other acts of worship. It often occurs especially in Ramadhaan that women become so occupied with preparing several types of dishes, savouries, deserts and drinks that they find no time to engage in Ibaadah. As a result, they carry out no Nafl acts of Ibaadah and if they manage to perform their Fardh Salah, they perform it very late. Women should take heed not to invest all their energies in decorating their tablecloths because this will rob them of valuable time which could be invested in earning the rewards of the Hereafter; especially the valuable hours of Ramadhaan. Allah Ta'ala did not send women to this world only to tend to domestic chores. They also need to prepare for their lives in the Hereafter. A single moment wasted in this world will be a source of regret in the Aakhirah (Hereafter), even if a person enters Jannah. A Hadith mentions that the only regret of a person entering Jannah will be the moments that he spends without Dhikr.

It is therefore important for every Muslim wife to spend as little time as possible in cooking and to devote the majority of her time to Ibaadah, Dhikr, learning and teaching Religion and propagating Religion for Allah Ta'ala's pleasure.

OBEYING THE HUSBAND COMPLETELY

Khadeeja (May Allah be pleased with him/her) was such an obedient wife that even before the five daily Salah were made obligatory, she used to perform optional Salah with Messenger of Allah (Peace be upon him) . The historian Ibn SA'd (May Allah be pleased with him/her) writes, "Messenger of Allah (Peace be upon him) and Khadeeja (May Allah be pleased with him/her) secretly performed Salah as long as Allah wished."

مَكَثَ رَسول اللّه ﷺ وخديجة يصليان سراً ماشاء اللّه

Khadeeja (May Allah be pleased with him/her) had cast herself into the mould of her husband. According to a narration of Imaam Ahmad I's "Musnad", Khadeeja (May Allah be pleased with him/her) stopped worshipping idols long before Messenger of Allah (Peace be upon him) even declared his prophethood. It is the trait of a good wife that when her husband is practising the truth, she should do as he does and think as he thinks. Her husband should view her as he wants her to be. This is advice to all Muslim women from the first Muslim of this Ummah, the first Mother of the Mu'mineen, the first wife of Messenger of Allah (Peace be upon him).

Dear sister! If you also cast yourselves in the mould of Khadeeja (May Allah be pleased with him/her) and obey every instruction of your husband when his instructions conform to the Shari'ah, Allah Ta'ala will be extremely pleased with you. When Allah Ta'ala is pleased with one, difficulties will disappear and one's affairs will be manageable.

One should always bear in mind that after marriage, nothing is done for oneself. One then eats for one's husband, dresses for him and does everything else to please him because he is one's lifelong companion and the crown on one's head. When one does this, one will find that just as Allah Ta'ala sent greetings of peace to Khadeeja (May Allah be pleased with him/her), Allah Ta'ala bless one's home with peace and comfort. As a result of this peace, the children will live in harmony and an atmosphere of love will exude from the home. Such a home will then be reminiscent of Jannah.

If one's husband performs Tahajjud and other Nafl Salahs, one should make an effort to do so as well. One should recite Quran with him and join in him in his acts of Ibaadah. One should never think that one's responsibilities are restricted to managing the home and rearing the children. Fix a time to engage in Dhikr and teach the children how to make Dhikr. Teach them Allah Ta'ala 's names, make them recite Quran daily and fix a time for making du'aa daily.

If one's husband is not inclined towards Ibaadah, one should make du'aa to Allah Ta'ala to make him pious and also consult with one's seniors so that they may advise one how to influence him. Encourage him first to be regular with his Fardh Salah and the Waajibaat and Nawaafil. Encourage him to spend time in Allah Ta'ala's path and Insha Allah Ta'ala he will soon change for the better.

Some Ahadeeth Concerning Obeying the Husband and Fulfilling his Rights

The following Ahadeeth make it clear that it is extremely important for a wife to obey the instructions of her husband. Ponder over these Ahadeeth and make the intention to practise. Also make du'aa to Allah Ta'ala to assist one in practising.

Messenger of Allah (Peace be upon him) said, "The woman who performs her five daily Salah, who fasts during Ramadhaan, who protects her chastity and who obeys her husband has the choice of entering Jannah from whichever door she pleases."
["Mishkaat" Pg. 281]

Here are so many ways of entering Jannah. By obeying the lawful commands of one's husband, one will live harmoniously in this world and be able to enjoy the bliss of Jannah eternally in the Hereafter. Irrespective of what a woman looks like in this world, if she performs her Salah, fasts during Ramadhaan, safeguards her chastity and obeys her husband, she will be more beautiful and honoured than the damsels of Jannah.

In his Tafseer "Ruhul Ma'aani", Allaama Aalusi (May Allah be Merciful on him/her) has quoted a narration in which Ummu Salma (May Allah be pleased with him/her) asked Messenger of Allah (Peace be upon him) whether the "Hoor Een" (damsels of Jannah) or the Mu'min wives of this world will be more beautiful. Messenger of Allah (Peace be upon him) told her that the Mu'min wives of this world will be made more beautiful than the "Hoor Een". When she asked the reason for this, Messenger of Allah (Peace be upon him) replied,

بصلاتهنَ وَصِيَامهنَ وعبادتهن ألبس اللّه وجوههن النُّورْ
(روح المعانى ص ١٢۶، ج٢٧)

"Because of their Salah, their fasting and their Ibaad- ah, Allah Ta'ala shall cover their faces with Noor (celestial light)."

The beauty of a person whose face exudes Noor cannot be imagined. While the "Hoor Een" will not have this privilege, it will be exclusive to the believing women of this world.

Tabraani has narrated that some women during the time of Messenger of Allah (Peace be upon him) sent one of them to pose a question to Messenger of Allah (Peace be upon him). When the lady arrived, she said, "O Messenger of Allah (Peace be upon him)! I have been sent on behalf of the other women. Jihad has been made Fardh on men. They are rewarded when they are victorious of if they are injured. If they are martyred, they attain a great status and their Rabb feeds them and allows them to live peacefully in the next life. We wish to know what will be our reward for serving these men. "Messenger of Allah (Peace be upon him) replied,

أبْلِغِيْ مَنْ لَقِيتَ مِنْ النسآء أنَّ طَاعَةُ الزَوجُ وإعْتِرَافاً بِحَقِّه يعدِّل ذَلِكَ وَقَلِيلٌ مِنْكُنَّ مَنْ يَفْعَلُه

(الجامع الكبير ج٢، ص۴۶۴، الترغيب، والترهيب للمنذرى ٤/١٢١)

"Tell every woman you meet that when a woman obeys her husband and acknowledges the rights of her husband, her reward will equal that of her husband. However, few of you do this."

If a woman learns to obey all her husband's lawful instructions, she will attain the reward of enduring hunger, thirst, injuries, illness and even martyrdom although she has not left her home. If her soul leaves her while she is lying on her comfortable bed, she can attain the status of a Shaheed (martyr) who has laid down his life for the Religion of Allah Ta'ala.

When a woman obeys her husband, she will be saving the family from ruination and her husband will have true love for her in his heart. The family will then be saved from the endless quarrels and bitterness that destroy even the most respectable homes.

Messenger of Allah (Peace be upon him) has mentioned that a woman will enter Jannah if she passes away when her husband is pleased with her. *[Tirmidhi Vol. 1 Pg. 219]*

Messenger of Allah (Peace be upon him) said, "If I were to command anyone to prostrate to another, I would have commanded wives to prostrate to their husbands. If a husband commands his wife to move a rock from one mountain to another mountain and then back to the first mountain, she should do as he says."
["Mishkaat" Pg. 281 from Ibn Majah]

Tirmidhi (Vol. 1 Pg. 219) reports that Messenger of Allah (Peace be upon him) said, "If a husband calls his wife to bed, she should respond even if she is busy at the stove." This means that she is obliged to respond to his call even if she is tending to something important.

According to another Hadith, the angels curse the wife who does not respond when her husband calls her to bed and he spends the night angry with her.
[Muslim Vol. 2 Pg. 1059]

Messenger of Allah (Peace be upon him) said that when a woman troubles her husband, his wife in the Hereafter says to her, "Woe to you! Do not bother him so! He is only your guest. After a few days he shall leave you to return to us." *[Ibn Majah Vol. 1 Pg. 649; Ahmad Vol. 5 Pg. 242; Jaami'ul Usool Vol. 6 Pg. 497]*

Messenger of Allah (Peace be upon him) said that there are three categories of people whose Salah and every good act is not accepted. The three are: (1) The slave who escapes from his/her master, (2) the woman whose husband is displeased with her and (3) the person who is drunk until he becomes sober. *["At Targheeb wat Tarheeb" Vol. 4 Pg. 128; Fat'hul Baari Vol. 9 Pg.294]*

Someone asked, "O Messenger of Allah (Peace be upon him)! Who is the best woman?" Messenger of Allah (Peace be upon him) replied, "The woman who pleases her husband when he sees her, who obeys him when he speaks to her and who does not betray him with regard to her chastity and his wealth."

The Advice of a Pious Father to his Daughter to be married

The above Ahadeeth outline the characteristics of a good wife. They may be translated in the following:

"A good wife gives her all for her husband. Her happiness is when her husband is happy. She is prepared to sacrifice her spirit, her ambitions, her desires and her comfort for her husband. She regards herself as a wife and a slave. For the sake of her husband, she regards disgrace as honour and a bed of thorns as a bed of flowers. Listen well O my innocent daughter! You will soon be a new bride and a daughter-in-law. You are entering a new phase in your life. Until now, you have been playing and eating and sleeping without a worry. You were happy and laughing all the time. Things will be changing now. You will now have responsibilities and you will be living under a new rule. Until now you have been living for yourself. From tomorrow, you will be serving others. The one who was the charm people's eyes and who grew up in a cradle of hopes will now be handed over in the service of others."

"Remember that whatever good or bad happens will be for that day. Take things a step at a time. You will need to restrain yourself because the journey ahead is not going to be an easy one. The responsibilities will be difficult but, O Muslim, remember that the rewards and glad tidings are also tremendous."

"Ummu Salma (May Allah be pleased with him/her) narrates from the one who was sent as a mercy to the universe, 'The woman who passes every stage of her life and finally reaches the final stage while her husband is pleased with her, she will surely enter Jannah. It is as if there is no barrier between Jannah and her.' Dear daughter! Even the worst difficulties of life are temporary. Keep the final stage of life in front of you and Allah Ta'ala will turn every thorn into a flower and every stone into water."

An Obedient Wife

The personality of Umar bin Abdul Azeez (May Allah be Merciful on him/her) needs no introduction. He is regarded by many as the fifth after the four Khulafa Raashideen. His wife Fatima bint Abdil Malik has mentioned that although there may be others who performed more Salah and wudhu than Umar bin Abdul Azeez (May Allah be Merciful to him), she has never seen anyone who feared Allah Ta'ala more than him. He used to remain on the Musalla after the Isha Salah and continue making du'aa and weeping until sleep overcame him. When he awoke, he used to continue in this manner the entire night.

His wife was the daughter of the famous king Abdul Malik. Among the fortune of jewellery that her father had given was a necklace that no other woman possessed. When Umar bin Abdul Azeez (May Allah be Merciful on him/her) became the Khalifa, he gave his wife the choice of either separating from him or depositing all her jewellery in the public treasury because he disliked living in a house with so much wealth. She replied, "What is the worth of all these treasures? I shall never part from you in exchange for even more than this." All her jewellery was then deposited in the state treasury for the benefit of the masses.

Here was a woman whose father, grandfather; brother and husband were all kings. Despite growing up in the lap of luxury, she was prepared to forsake everything to please her husband. Her sacrifices were so great that the pages of history still mention her name and she will always remain a role model for all women.

After the demise of her husband, her brother Yazeed became king. He told his sister that he could return her jewellery to her if she pleased. She said, "I was not happy with it during my husband's lifetime, how can it bring me any pleasure now?" With this sentence she expressed her sincere loyalty by not doing anything that would displease him even after his demise. May Allah Ta'ala make all Muslim wives loyal and obedient to the husbands. *Aameen.*

The Demise of Khadeeja (May Allah be pleased with him/her)

Khadeeja (May Allah be pleased with him/her) remained in Messenger of Allah's (Peace be upon him) wedlock for twenty-five years. She passed away in Ramadan ten years after Messenger of Allah (Peace be upon him) announced his prophet hood, which was three years before the Hijrah. She was then 64 years old. Because the Janaazah Salah was not ordained at that time, no Janaazah Salah took place and Messenger of Allah (Peace be upon him) himself lowered the body of his companion, advisor and aide into the grave. The moment was so heart-rending that no pen can describe. In carrying out his tremendous task of propagating Islam, Khadeeja (May Allah be pleased with him/her) had always been invaluable to him. She would console him in his distress, advise him when he needed advice and sacrifice everything she had for him.

An innumerable amount of stones and pebbles break off from mountains and hills. Without any regard for them, people and animals merely trample on them. If one of these stones has to become a ruby or a diamond more precious than the kingdoms of the world, how distressed will one become if it has to be destroyed?

The number of raindrops falling on the ocean every year is also countless. From all of these, one enters an open oyster and is transformed into a priceless pearl which is worthy of being set in the crown of a king. If someone casts this pearl back into the ocean, one cannot imagine the grief it will cause to those who realise its value.

The leaves, roots and plants of the wild are also plenty for animals to feed on. If among these there is an extremely rare and delicate rose that can produce a most exquisite perfume, one cannot imagine the loss to mankind if this rose falls prey to harsh weather and wilts away.

Spiritually, time is neither measured by man's calendar nor by the earth's orbit around the sun. The appointed time for a soul to return to Allah Ta'ala is when it has perfected itself. There is therefore no necessity to grieve excessively when a person leaves this world. To Allah Ta'ala do we belong and to Him shall we all return.

Messenger of Allah (Peace be upon him) himself declared the year in which Khadeeja (May Allah be pleased with him/her) passed away as the year of grief. Although Allaama Sayyid Sulaymaan Nadwi was not a poet, he wrote the following couplet in memory of his wife to whom he was much attached:

"Upon your departure, it appeared as if
time would be thrown into chaos
It is strange that the Last Day did not
end time when you left."
[This poem has been translated from Urdu]

Du'aa

O"Allah Ta'ala! Make our girls and women like Khadeeja (May Allah be pleased with him/her) grant them her pure habits, her character, her chastity, her love, her obedience, her concern for the Aakhirah, her Taqwa and her loyalty. O Allah Ta'ala! Make the pure personality of Khadeeja (May Allah be pleased with him/her) common among the new generation of Muslims. Grant us all the ability to do as she did. O Allah Ta'ala! Fill her grave with peace and tranquillity and elevate her stages abundantly. Grant her the best of rewards on our behalf. *Aameen.*"

SALUTATIONS OF PEACE FROM US ALL

Every Muslim sends salutations of peace to Khadeeja (May Allah be pleased with him/her), the first believer of this Ummah, the first "Mother of the Mu'mineen" and the honoured lady who received greetings of peace from none other than the Rabb of the universe.

There is a lesson for Muslims in every detail of her pure life. By following her noble example خيرمتاع الدنيا every wife can become the delight of her husband's eyes and the most precious thing for him in this world. ليسكن إليها She will then become a source of solace and comfort for him and thus fulfil the purpose of her creation.

Therefore, every wife should sincerely try to follow her example and make the following du'aa after every Salah: "O Allah Ta'ala! Grant me the same character, understanding, obedience and self-sacrifice that you blessed Khadeeja (May Allah be pleased with him/her) with. Also bless my daughters, sisters and all Muslim women with the same sterling qualities. *Aameen.*"

This du'aa should be made as often as possible. If Allah Ta'ala accepts this du'aa, one will be the most fortunate person both in terms of this world and in terms of the Hereafter. Ummu Salma (May Allah be pleased with him/her) has narrated that she heard Messenger of Allah (Peace be upon him) say that

عن أم سلمة رضي الله عنها تقول سمعت رسول الله ﷺ يقول أيما إمرأة ماتت وزوجها عنها راض دخلت الجنة

(ترمذي ص٢١٩ ج ١ كتاب الرضاع)

"A woman will enter Jannah if she passes away when her husband is pleased with her." [Tirmidhi Vol. 1 Pg. 219]

Can a woman have any desire greater than that she should be Allah Ta'ala's guest in Jannah? This is the ultimate aspiration. Allah Ta'ala declares in His Quran,

﴿ فَمَنْ زُحْزِحَ عَنِ النَّارِ وَأُدْخِلَ الْجَنَّةَ فَقَدْ فَازَ ﴾ (آل عمران: من الآية١٨٥)

"Whoever is saved from the fire and entered into Jannah shall truly be successful."

One should constantly ponder over this Hadith and Quranic verse. By doing so, it will become easy for one to carry out the responsibilities of being a good wife and a good daughter-in-law. Allah Ta'ala will then assist one every step of the way.

You may say that everything being said seems biased. Everything said thus far is definitely directed at women because they are being addressed in this book. Men have a separate set of responsibilities. When a woman fulfils her responsibilities, her husband will automatically discharge his. The advices to men have been published in a separate book titled "Gift to a Husband".

Life with one's in-laws can really be difficult. While the insults of a mother-in-law cut the heart more effectively than a knife through butter, the presence of the husband's elder and younger sisters can be a terrible nuisance. The husband's affection towards his wife often seems to cause hurt to his sisters for no good reason whatsoever. What makes all of this unbearable is when the husband is ill-tempered. However, patience will soon win the day.

The Ummah has been shown the examples of exemplary wives like Khadeeja (May Allah be pleased with him/her) and Aa'isha (May Allah be pleased with him/her). Keeping their lives in mind, every Muslim wife should also not forget the words of Messenger of Allah (Peace be upon him) when he said that nothing can stop her from Jannah if she passes away when her husband is pleased with her. Keep this Hadith in mind at all times and every bitterness will be sweet. The thorns that people throw at you will then seem like rose petals and Allah Ta'ala will be your Protector and Assistant. May Allah Ta'ala save every Muslim woman from the bane of a temperamental husband and inconsiderate mothers-and-sisters-in-law. *Aameen.*

We will now discuss the exemplary life of Messenger of Allah's (Peace be upon him) second wife Sauda bint Zam'ah (May Allah be pleased with him/her). Before reading, one should make du'aa to Allah Ta'ala to make one like her. *Aameen.*

Sauda bint Zam'ah (May Allah be pleased with him/her)

CONVERSION TO ISLAM

Sauda bint Zam'ah (May Allah be pleased with him/her) accepted Islam during the very early stages and therefore had the honour of being included among the earliest Muslims. She was also among the early immigrants to Abyssinia. After Khadeeja (May Allah be pleased with him/her) passed away, Khowla bint Hakeem (May Allah be pleased with him/her) the wife of Uthmaan bin Madh'oon t asked Messenger of Allah (Peace be upon him) whether he needed another wife. Messenger of Allah (Peace be upon him) told her that Khadeeja (May Allah be pleased with him/her) always tended to the children and the house. Khowla (May Allah be pleased with him/her) bint Hakeem (May Allah be pleased with him/her) realised from this that Messenger of Allah (Peace be upon him) certainly needed a wife to tend to these matters. She therefore set out to find a lady who was experienced enough to care for Messenger of Allah's (Peace be upon him) daughters and to manage domestic affairs. The lady she found was Sauda bint Zam'ah (May Allah be pleased with him/her).

Sauda (May Allah be pleased with him/her) bint Zam'ah (May Allah be pleased with him/her) belonged to the Banu Najjaar tribe of Madinah and was married to Messenger of Allah (Peace be upon him) in Ramadan, ten years after Messenger of Allah (Peace be upon him) announced his prophethood. When Messenger of Allah (Peace be upon him) performed Hajj during the 10th year after Hijrah, he sent Sauda (May Allah be pleased with him/her) bint Zam'ah (May Allah be pleased with him/her) ahead of the others from Muzdalifa because she had difficulty manoeuvring through the crowds on account of her size.

Forfeiting her Turn for the pleasure of her Husband A person may take his own right and simultaneously fulfil the rights of others without infringing on theirs. On the other hand, a person may also surrender all or part of his right to others. This is referred to as preferring others above oneself, an act which Sauda (May Allah be pleased with him/her) bint Zam'ah (May Allah be pleased with him/her) displayed when she gave over her turn to be with Messenger of Allah (Peace be upon him) to Aa'isha (May Allah be pleased with him/her).

> **NOTE:** Every woman who is a co-wife should bear in mind that she will receive from her husband only that which is predestined for her. Similarly, what was not destined for her shall never reach her irrespective of the number of co-wives she shares her husband with. She will receive whatever she is receiving even if she were the only wife. Of course, if the husband behaves unjustly towards the wife, he will be answerable to Allah Ta'ala. The Ahadeeth have mentioned severe warnings against displaying partiality towards one's wives.

Sauda (May Allah be pleased with him/her) bint Zam'ah (May Allah be pleased with him/her) awarded her turn to Aa'isha (May Allah be pleased with him/her) because she understood that Messenger of Allah (Peace be upon him) had great love for Aa'isha (May Allah be pleased with him/her). She therefore pleased her husband and became worthy of the glad tidings of Jannah that are promised for the woman whose husband is pleased with her.

Sincerely Obeying the Husband

After performing the Farewell Hajj, Messenger of Allah (Peace be upon him) instructed his wives saying, "Stay within your homes after my demise." Sauda (May Allah be pleased with him/her) bint Zam'ah (May Allah be pleased with him/her) took this instruction to heart and never performed Hajj again even though she had the means. She said, "I have performed both Hajj and Umrah. I am now staying at home in conformance with the instruction of Messenger of Allah (Peace be upon him)." *[Tabaqaat Ibn Sa'd Vol. 8 Pg. 37]*

Although Hajj and Umrah are great acts of Ibaadah; Sauda (May Allah be pleased with him/her) bint Zam'ah (May Allah be pleased with him/her), opted not to perform them because they entailed leaving the home. The condition of women today is indeed a far cry from that of the women during the time of Messenger of Allah (Peace be upon him). Nowadays, let alone not obeying the husband who prevents his wife from something virtuous (like Hajj or Umrah), many women do not even obey their husbands who tell them not to carry out acts that are sinful.

When the husband issues and instruction to his wife, she will earn the reward of Ibaadah by obeying his instruction. By obeying his instructions she will therefore earn the rewards earned for Sadaqah or for Tahajjud Salah. In fact, her reward will be even greater because avoiding a Haraam act (such as disobedience) is a sign that one's Imaan is sincere (and this earns one the reward of carrying out a Fardh act). When a woman keeps this in mind, it will be easy for her to obey any instruction that her husband issues.

If one's husband prevents one from carrying out any of one's permissible desires, one should make du'aa to Allah Ta'ala saying, "O Allah Ta'ala You are the only One Who fulfils needs. Fulfil this desire of mine and make my husband the means of fulfilling it. Change his 'No' into 'Yes'. O the One in Whose control is the hearts of man! Nothing is difficult for you." When the subject arises and he is adamant about not allowing one, the matter should not be debated. It should be left to be until another time when he is in a good mood. The matter should then be discussed amicably. Insha Allah Ta'ala, Allah Ta'ala will certainly soften his heart and if your desire cannot be adequately realised, he will ensure that he pleases you in some other way.

The wife who adorns herself with the robe of obedience and who learns to obey every lawful instruction of her husband shall convert this mundane existence into a Garden of Eden. Such a wife makes her pauper husband a king without a throne or crown. Whether one believes this or not, experience will prove it beyond doubt.

If only women will understand this. When a man enters his shack on a sweltering day and finds his obedient wife smiling with him, he will feel such delight in his heart which even air-conditioning and ice-cream cannot provide. In fact, even all the riches of a monarch cannot provide such inner delight. Every difficulty will be considerably eased for such a husband and nothing will be too much for him to handle. Everything will have flavour for the husband as well as for the children. Their simple food will be delicious, their simple home will provide the comforts of a palace and they will enjoy contentment without possessing the visible means.

The first quality of a good wife that Messenger of Allah (Peace be upon him) mentioned is إن أمرها إطاعته she is obedient to her husband when he instructs her to do something. May Allah Ta'ala make all women obedient to their husbands so that these men can have Jannah in both worlds. *Aameen.*

Generosity

It was not the general habit of women during the early days of Islam to collect money because they were always conscious of the fact that the things of this world are temporary. Umar (May Allah be pleased with him/her) once sent a bag to Sauda (May Allah be pleased with him/her) bint Zam'ah (May Allah be pleased with him/her). When it was brought to her, she asked the carrier what was in it. When he told her that the bag was full of Dirhams, she remarked, "Are Dirhams sent in bags like dates?" She then distributed all the money to the needy. Sauda (May Allah be pleased with him/her) bint Zam'ah (May Allah be pleased with him/her) used to treat skins from Taa'if, sell them and use the profits generously in good cause. *[Isaabah Vol. 8 Pg. 918]*

When one has great concern for the Aakhirah, one will find it easy to spend in good causes because one realises that what is amassed and remains in the cupboard will be of no benefit to one and will be left behind for someone else. One then knows that whatever is being spent in Allah Ta'ala's way shall certainly be rewarded in the Hereafter and will please Allah Ta'ala tremendously.

AN EASY WAY OF BECOMING GENEROUS

At the outset, it is necessary for a woman to identify which items in the house belong to her and which items belong to her husband. Even the smallest and largest items in the house should be accounted for. The Shari'ah requires this specification of ownership for every item to avoid disputes. Even if the husband brings four cups into the house, it should be made clear whether they are a gift to his wife or whether they belong to him.

Once this is done, the mate should clean her cupboards every month and single out all items that she does not need or which she uses very scarcely. Such items should immediately be given away to deserving people, especially deserving Muslims. One should also have the conviction that if one ever needs such an item in future, Allah Ta'ala will provide it after one performs two Rakaahs of Salah.

The Testimony of a Co-Wife

Referring to her magnanimity, Aa'isha (May Allah be pleased with him/her) mentioned,

مَا من النَاس إمرأة أحب إلى أنْ أكون في مِسلاَخها مِنْ سَوْدَة

"Besides Sauda (May Allah be pleased with him/her), there is no person (woman) in whose body I would prefer my soul to be instilled."

It is a tremendous accolade to a woman when her co-wife praises her. May Allah Ta'ala instil the qualities of Sauda (May Allah be pleased with him/her) bint Zam'ah (May Allah be pleased with him/her) in every Muslim woman. *Aameen.*

HER DEMISE

Sauda (May Allah be pleased with him/her) bint Zam'ah (May Allah be pleased with him/her) passed away during the last years of Umar's (May Allah be pleased with him/her) Khilaafah. This was in the 32nd year after Hijrah. The wives of Messenger of Allah (Peace be upon him) once asked him which of them would pass away first. Messenger of Allah (Peace be upon him) replied,

أسرعكن لحوقابي أطوالكن يَدَا (مشكوة ص ١٦٥)

"The first of you to meet me shall be the one with the longest arms."

Taking the literal meaning of the statement, they started measuring the length of their arms and found that the arms of Sauda (May Allah be pleased with him/her) bint Zam'ah (May Allah be pleased with him/her) were the longest. However, when Zaynab (May Allah be pleased with him/her) bint Jahash (May Allah be pleased with him/her) was the first to pass away after Messenger of Allah (Peace be upon him), they realised that Messenger of Allah (Peace be upon him) was referring to the wife who was the most generous.

Zaynab (May Allah be pleased with him/her) bint Muhammad (Peace be upon him)

A LOYAL WIFE

Fifteen centuries have passed since the personality of Zaynab (May Allah be pleased with him/her) bint Muhammad (Peace be upon him) graced the earth with her presence. However, her name is echoed even today because of her sincere Imaan and her loyalty and love for her husband. She is an example of self-sacrifice to every Muslim woman until Qiyamah.

Zaynab (May Allah be pleased with him/her) was the eldest daughter of Messenger of Allah (Peace be upon him). She was born ten years before Messenger of Allah (Peace be upon him) announced his prophet hood when he was thirty years old. When she was married to her cousin (mother's sister's son) Abul Aas, her mother gave her a valuable necklace to take with her.

The couple lived happily together. When the light of Islam lit the earth darkened by kufr (Disbelief), she accepted the Religion brought by her father. However, her husband did not accept Islam then. She exhorted him to accept, but he refused to do so. She then told him that despite her profound love for him, she could not live with him if he did not accept Islam. She made it clear to him that although it would be a painful separation, she would tolerate this rather than live with him when he would not accept the oneness of Allah Ta'ala.

SEPARATION FROM HER HUSBAND

Addressing her husband, Zaynab (May Allah be pleased with him/her) said,

قَلِيْلًا يَاصَاحِبِي، لَسْتُ حَلالِكَ، فَأَسْلِمْنِي إِلَى أَبِي، أَوْأَسْلِم مَعِي، لَنْ
تَكُونَ زَيْنَبُ لَكَ بَعْدَ اليَوم إلا أَنْ تؤمِن بِمَا آمَنْتَ

"*Think awhile. I am not lawful for you. Either hand me over to my father or accept Islam with me. Zaynab (May Allah be pleased with him/her) is not yours after this day unless you believe in what Zaynab (May Allah be pleased with him/her) believes.*"

Although the Sahabiyaat had great love for the husbands, they did not compromise on their Islamic beliefs. Remaining staunch Muslims, their love for their husbands made them try their best to make their husbands Muslims. It was because of this love and concern that Allah Ta'ala reunited these couples once again.

When Zaynab's (May Allah be pleased with him/her) husband Abul Aas was captured by the Muslims during the Battle of Badr and a delegation left for Madinah to ransom the captives, Zaynab (May Allah be pleased with him/her) sent her cherished necklace with them to free her husband. Not only was she fulfilling the rights of the love she had for her husband, but she also realised that a man becomes the slave of someone who does him a favour. الإنسان عبدالإحسان This favour was to become the means of her migrating to Madinah and meeting her beloved father (Peace be upon him). When Messenger of Allah (Peace be upon him) saw the necklace that once belonged to Khadeeja (May Allah be pleased with him/her), he consulted the Companion of the Prophet (May Allah be pleased with him/her) and they decided that the necklace should be sent back to Zaynab (May Allah be pleased with him/her) and that Abul Aas (May Allah be pleased with him/her) should be set free on condition that he sent Zaynab (May Allah be pleased with him/her) to Madinah.

Upon his return to Makkah, Abul Aas (May Allah be pleased with him/her) told Zaynab (May Allah be pleased with him/her) that she was to return to her father.

عُودِي إِلى أَبِيكِ يَا زَيْنَبْ

Although Abul Aas (May Allah be pleased with him/her) had not accepted Islam by then, Zaynab (May Allah be pleased with him/her) had already instilled the love of Islam in his heart. Consequently, Abul Aas (May Allah be pleased with him/her) told his brother Kinaana to accompany Zaynab (May Allah be pleased with him/her) out of Makkah where Zaid bin Haaritha (May Allah be pleased with him/her) and a few other Muslims were waiting to escort her to Madinah. He could not accompany her personally because he was unable to bear the separation. He said to his brother, "I do not wish any other woman of the Quraysh to be in exchange for Zaynab (May Allah be pleased with him/her). I cannot bear to be parted from her." He also instructed his brother not to allow anyone to approach her even if he had to use all his arrows in her defence. However, because of resistance from the Quraysh, Zaynab (May Allah be pleased with him/her) was unable to leave Makkah that day. It was only at night that she was handed over to the Muslim escort and preceded with them to Madinah.

LOYALTY TO HER HUSBAND

While Zaynab (May Allah be pleased with him/her) was living in Madinah, a Muslim contingent under the leadership of Zaid (May Allah be pleased with him/her) bin Haaritha (May Allah be pleased with him/her) attacked a Makkan caravan at a place called Ees and captured the *Mushrikeen* (Polytheists) manning the caravan. Among these captives was Abul Aasr. Upon reaching Madinah, Abul Aasr requested Zaynab (May Allah be pleased with him/her) to grant him amnesty. Still loyal to him, she acceded to his request and announced to all the Muslims that they could not harm Abul Aas (May Allah be pleased with him/her) because he was now under her protection. Messenger of Allah (Peace be upon him) sanctioned her amnesty and advised her saying,

يَأيها النَّاسْ أنِّي قَدْ أَجَّرْتُ العَاصَ بِنْ الرَّبيع فهُو فِي حِمَايَتِي وَأمْنِي

"*Beloved daughter! Look after your guest but do not have any relations with him because you are not lawful for him as long as he is still a Mushrik (polytheist)."*

أي بنية أكرمي مثواه، ولا تخلص اليه،فإنك لاتحلين له ما دام مشركا.

Out of respect for Messenger of Allah (Peace be upon him) and Zaynab R, the Companion of the Prophet (May Allah be pleased with him/her) returned the captured wealth to Abul Aas (May Allah be pleased with him/her) and prepared to send him back to Makkah. During this time, someone told him that if he accepted Islam, he could remain in Makkah and keep all the wealth of the caravan which belonged to the Makkans. In response to this, Abul Aas (May Allah be pleased with him/her) replied, "It would be a bad start to my Islam if I were to betray a trust."

بئس ما أبدا به إسلامي أن أخون أمانتي

He then left for Makkah and after returning all the goods of the caravan to their respective owners, he announced,

يا معشر قريش ، هل بقي لأحد منكم مَال؟ قالوا لَا فجزاك اللّه خيرا، وقد وجدناك وفيا كريما قال : فأنا أشهد أن لا إله إلا اللّه وأن محمدا عبده ورسوله .

"O gathering of the Quraysh! Is the wealth of any person still with me?" "No," they responded, "may Alluh Ta'ala reward you abundantly. We have found you to be one who delivers the trusts given to him and one who is honourable." He then declared, "I testify that there is none worthy of worship but Allah Ta'ala and I testify that Muhammad (Peace be upon him) is Allah Ta'ala's bondsman and messenger. The only factor that prevented me from accepting Islam in Madinah was the thought that you would say that I accepted Islam so that I could usurp your wealth. I now declare my Imaan after Allah Ta'ala has allowed me to return your trusts."

He then returned to Madinah where his marriage to Zaynab (May Allah be pleased with him/her) was renewed and the couple were reunited. However, Zaynab (May Allah be pleased with him/her) was preparing to leave this world by then and she passed away a short while after being reunited. Nevertheless, Allah Ta'ala made her realise her dream of seeing her husband accept Islam and thus being rescued from eternal damnation in *Jahannam* (Hell).

When she passed away in the 8th year after Hijrah, Ummu Ayman (May Allah be pleased with him/her), Sauda (May Allah be pleased with him/her), Ummu Salma (May Allah be pleased with him/her) and Ummu Atiyya (May Allah be pleased with him/her) bathed her body under direction from Messenger of Allah (Peace be upon him). Messenger of Allah (Peace be upon him) performed the Janaazah Salah and placed the body in the grave. Messenger of Allah (Peace be upon him) was extremely grieved upon her demise. *["Tabaqaat Ibn Sa'd" Vol. 8 Pg. 24, Bukhari Vol. 1 Pg. 167, Muslims Vol. 1 Pg. 324 and "Asadul Ghaaba" Vol. 5 Pg. 468]*

NOTE: If women inculcate certain important qualities in their lives, they will be able to convert their homes to gardens of Bliss. These qualities are clearly displayed in the life of Zaynab (May Allah be pleased with him/her). The first is that the wife should be deeply in love with her husband. It is obvious that Zaynab (May Allah be pleased with him/her) possessed such love because, to free her husband, she was prepared to part with her expensive necklace which her mother had given her as a legacy, and which was handed down from generation to generation. After undergoing hardships and separation because of her husband's refusal to accept Islam, she immediately accepted his request for amnesty.

It was because of her excellent qualities that Abul Aas (May Allah be pleased with him/her) said to his brother Kinaana,

فما أحب أن لي بها إمرأة من قريش ، وأنك تعلم أن لا طاقة لي بأن أفارقها .

"I do not wish any other woman of the Quraysh to be in exchange for Zaynab (May Allah be pleased with him/her). I cannot bear to be parted from her."

However, Abul Aas (May Allah be pleased with him/her) had to send Zaynab (May Allah be pleased with him/her) to Madinah because he had promised Messenger of Allah (Peace be upon him) that he would and the Arabs (though Mushrikeen) always honoured their word. May Allah Ta'ala grant every Muslim the quality of keeping promises. *Aameen.*

Testimony of the Husband

The status of a loving wife is at its height when her husband testifies that there is none as good as she and if he has to search for a wife with her sterling qualities, he will be unable to find someone. The life of Zaynab (May Allah be pleased with him/her) is an example for all women to follow. Her excellent behaviour towards her Mushrik husband is exemplary and won him over to Islam.

Many Muslim women swayed the sword of love on their husbands to convert them to Islam. This sword proved effective even against men who had sworn that were prepared to commit suicide rather than accept Islam. This incident of Zaynab (May Allah be pleased with him/her) teaches the wives of the world how to love their husbands and to sacrifice everything for them. A wife should be content with what her husband provides and she should not complain when she does not have something. At the same time, every wife needs to be concerned that her husband should be saved from Jahannam. She should therefore encourage him to carry out good deeds and to refrain from sin. At the same time, she should ensure that she does not become the cause for her husband or her children suffering any loss in the Hereafter.

أفضله لسان ذاكر وقلب شاكر وزوجة مؤمنة تعينه مؤمنة تعينه على إيمانه

(الترغيب والترهيب ص ٢٨، ج٣)

The Companion of the Prophet (May Allah be pleased with him/her) once expressed the desire to know which type of wealth was best. Messenger of Allah (Peace be upon him) told them that the best wealth was a tongue that engages in Allah Ta'ala 's Dhikr, a heart that is grateful and a Muslim wife who assists her husband in his faith. This Hadith makes it clear that money, property and businesses are not the real wealth of this world. True wealth is a tongue that engages in Allah Ta'ala's Dhikr, a heart that is grateful and a Muslim wife who assists her husband in his faith.

Therefore, together with making an effort to reform herself inwardly and outwardly, a Muslim wife also has the responsibility of rejuvenating her husband's Imaan. Her daily effort should be to deepen the roots of his conviction in Allah Ta'ala so that he becomes totally convinced that Allah Ta'ala is All Knowing and Capable of doing whatever He pleases. She should also send him to gatherings where his Imaan is refreshed and where he is reminded about death and the Hereafter. Where possible, she should also attend such gatherings when attendance does not violate any laws of the Shari'ah. She should consolidate the conviction that everything happens by the will of Allah Ta'ala. Even if a glass breaks or some other greater disaster takes place, she should immediately say:

إِنَّا لِلَّهِ وَإِنَّا إِلَيْهِ رَاجِعُونَ اللَّهُمَّ أجِرْنِيْ فى مُصِيبَتِي وأَخْلِفْ لِي خيرًا مِنها

(الترغيب والترهيب ص ١٧٣، ج٣)

"To Allah Ta'ala do we belong and to Him shall we return. O Allah Ta'ala ! Reward me in my calamity and grant me something better."

One should reflect on the meaning of this du'aa and explain it to one's husband and children to console them.

A good wife should remind her husband about his five daily Salahs, fasting and reciting the Quran daily. She should explain the virtues of these and other acts of Ibaadah and encourage him with wisdom and love. By encouraging her husband and children to fulfil their duties to the Religion and to practise the Sunnahs of Messenger of Allah (Peace be upon him), she will be doing them all a great favour.

She should also stipulate a time during the day to gather and recite Religion i books to them. Excellent books for this purpose are "Fadhaa'ile A'maal", "Fadhaa'ile Sadaqaat" and "Behisti Zewar". Such a woman receives the du'as of Messenger of Allah (Peace be upon him) People usually request pious people and saints for their du'as whenever they have the opportunity and regard this to be a source of great fortune. One cannot imagine the fortune of a person who receives the du'as of the greatest of all saints and pious people, Messenger of Allah (Peace be upon him). Messenger of Allah (Peace be upon him) made the following du'aa, "May Allah Ta'ala shower His mercy on the woman who wakes up for Tahajjud, performs her Salah and wakes her husband up as well. If he does not wake up, she lovingly sprinkles some water on his face." A man who marries someone who performs Tahajjud and wakes him up as well should certainly regard himself as a king even though he has no throne or crown.

Love for the Husband

A couple can truly enjoy happiness in their marriage when they are compatible. Without this, their lives would become miserable and bland. Irrespective of a woman's education and beauty, she will never really be the true beloved of her husband if she is not obedient to him. The most effective manner of harnessing the husband's sincere love is to obey him and serve him with love and devotion.

Homes in which the wives sincerely love their husbands and obey them are not tainted by quarrels and friction. On the other hand, life becomes hell in the homes of women who disobey their husbands and who have a terse reply for everything he says. Such homes are speedily deprived of blessings and good. One should always remember that love for his wife is the elixir which adds happiness to a husband's life. It ensures that his health remains sound, that his youth is perpetuated and that his Imaan is fortified. Even though Adam (Peace be upon him) had every bounty he could imagine in Jannah, his heart was still not content until Allah Ta'ala created Hawwa (Peace be upon him) to be Adam's (Peace be upon him) wife.

When the Quran states that

خَلَقَ مِنْهَا زَوْجَهَا

"Women have been created so that man"

It refers to every conceivable thing that provides comfort such as peace, contentment, and cure from anxiety, cure from physical illnesses and a boost to one's Imaan. It is only with a good wife that a person experiences true pleasure in everything he does. Therefore, Messenger of Allah (Peace be upon him) said, "There is nothing better for two lovers than marriage."

لم یر للمتحابین مثل النکاح (إبن ماجه ص ۱۳۳ مطبوعه قدیمی کتب خانه)

Every husband looks for love in the heart of his wife and searches every act and gesture of hers to detect the love she has for him. When he finds this, he will be comforted. A wife should therefore put on a smiling face whenever she meets her husband. If he upsets her in any way, she should exercise patience and continue speaking sweetly because he finds comfort in her words. When deprived of this, he will wilt away and fade.

Every wife should understand that her affection is sufficient to dissolve her husband's fatigue and dispel his every difficulty. This is what her husband wants from her. When the wife is a devout Muslim, the husband becomes pleased. He wants her to display excellent character so that his children can have a good upbringing. He wants her to have a friendly disposition so that the couple can earn the du'as of his parents and family. He wants her to treat the wives of his friends and neighbours well so that he can enjoy a respectable position among them. He wants her to be content with what he provides for her so that he does not have to tire himself earning more and more. He wants her to maintain a high standard of personal hygiene and to dress smartly so that he may protect his eyes from gazing at other women. He wants her to keep herself beautiful to safeguard his chastity. He wants her to conceal herself from strange men so that he can have faith in her. He wants her to wear the earrings of obedience. He wants her to apply the henna of thriftiness to her hands so that his wealth is not wasted. He wants her to wear the necklace of trustworthiness so that he can trust her in his absence.

The wife who inculcates all these good qualities in her life will be everything to her husband. All she as to do besides this is to be concerned about how she will face Allah Ta'ala on the Day of Qiyamah and make an effort to spread Religion among her family and among other women.

Wise men always maintain that the most unfortunate person is he who feels unfortunate with his wife and children. On the other hand, the most fortunate man is he who feels fortunate and happy with his wife and children. May Allah Ta'ala make every person as fortunate as this.

Women who make Men Old Before their Time

اللّٰهم إني أعوذ بك من إمرأة تشيبني قبل المشيب . صحبهما اللّٰه

Messenger of Allah (Peace be upon him) used to make the following du'aa,

"O Allah Ta'ala! I seek Your protection from a wife who makes me old before my time."

May Allah Ta'ala safeguard every woman from qualities that make her destroy the youth of her husband, and may Allah Ta'ala save every man from such a wife. My grandfather Haaji Ayyoob used to say that when the lunch and supper of a family burns, it causes instant difficulty and hunger for the entire family for that day. However, when a wife is ill tempered and disobedient, the family is put through a lifetime of difficulty, bordering on the brink of destruction.

Haafidh Yusuf who is a friend of mine often speaks about his friend Habeeb who used to tell his wife to get married after his death. When asked why he told her this, he would say, "So that the other husband should know why Habeeb died so soon."

A humorous tale is related about a person whose lips were black. When asked the reason for this, he said, "My wife left for Lahore today. I was so happy when she left that I kissed the coaches of the train that carried her."

Her son and daughter-in-law were having an argument when an old lady heard the sound of breaking glass. Hurrying downstairs to see what had happened, the old lady saw that the pieces of an expensive vase were scattered about. "Who broke this antique?" she said in disbelief. "Your daughter-in-law," replied her son. "Nonsense!" blurted his wife. "It hit the wall and broke only because he moved when I threw it at him."

After divorcing his wife, a poet wrote:

طعنت امامة بالطلاق ونجوت من غل الوثاق

بانت فلم يـــــالم لهـــا قلبى ولم تدمع مافي

ودواء مـــالا تشتهيه النفس تعجيـل الفـراق

والعيش ليس بطيب بين إثنين فى غير إتفاق

لو لم أرح بفراقهمـــا لأرحت نفسى بالإباق

(رواه الأصمعي رحمه الله ، المرأة المثالية ص ٧٣)

"Umamah left with a divorce and I have been delivered
from a suffocating yoke
Neither does my heart grieve with her parting, nor do my eyes tear
It (divorce) was the only cure (for her insolence), a cure that no one really wants
to use because of its instant results
Life is not life for a couple with incompatibility on the prowl
Were she not separated like this, I would have had relief only by running off
somewhere."

A poor Arab poet was distraught because his wife constantly nagged, insulted him, quarrelled with him and never behaved cordially with him. Neither did she bother to keep herself tidy, nor was she particular about her Salah. In fact, she did everything that displeased Allah Ta'ala. This led him to write:

تنحى ، فاجلسي مني بعيدا ، أراح اللّٰه منك العالمينا

حياتك ما علمت حياة سوء وموتك قد يسر الصالحين

"Get away! Stay far away from me! May Allah Ta'ala save the men of the
universe from you!
In my knowledge, your life has been an evil life (because you have displeased
Allah Ta'ala and people)
Your death shall certainly give joy to every good person."

A person approached a renowned poet in Delhi and requested that the poet teach him the art of poetry. The poet said, "Poetry cannot be taught. A person says poetry when in ecstasy. When he is afflicted by a calamity or overcome by intense love, poetical words flow from his lips and he becomes a poet."

It is perhaps the calamity of a terrible wife that prompts many men to become poets. An Arab poet whose wife was causing him untold grief once wrote:

لقد كنت محتاجاً إلى موت زوجتي ولكن قرين السوء باقي معمر

فيا ليتها صارت إلى القبر عاجلاً وعذبها فيه نكير ومنكر

"I am desperately awaiting her death but I fear that an evil companion lives very long.

How I wish that she leaves soon for her grave where she should be punished by Munkar and Nakeer."

المرأة السوء غل يلقيه اللّٰه تعالى في عنق من يشاء من عباده

A bad wife has often been described in classical works as a yoke which Allah Ta'ala casts on the necks of who- ever He pleases.

THE GOOD INFLUENCE THAT A PIOUS MOTHER HAS ON HER DAUGHTER

It is hardly surprising that Zaynab (May Allah be pleased with him/her) was so loyal and compassionate towards her husband because her mother Khadeeja (May Allah be pleased with him/her) was the same. Because daughters learn from their mothers, our saintly predecessors always advise people that when they are looking for a girl for the son, they should investigate the relationship between the girl's parents. They should enquire about the conduct of the girl's mother from her relatives because behaviour of the mother almost always rubs off on the daughter.

Our pious predecessors have emphasised that girls should always be taught to speak softly, even when they are young. Whenever a young girl speaks loudly, the mother should affectionately place her hand on the child's head and explain to her that girls ought to speak softly.

The result of being raised by a pious mother we see in Umamah the daughter of Zaynab (May Allah be pleased with him/her) who grew up with the excellent qualities of her mother and grandmother. By being a good wife, a woman not only teaches her daughters to be good wives, but she also upbrings many generations of good wives in her granddaughters and great granddaughters. Not only will her husband and sons-in-law remember her fondly in their du'as, but so too will men of many generations who marry her descendants. Even as a Mushrik, Abul Aas (May Allah be pleased with him/her) used to say on his journeys to Shaam,

بنت الأمين جزاها اللّه صالحة كل بعل سيثنى بالذى عِلْمًا

"*May Allah Ta'ala abundantly reward the daughter of Ameen on behalf of every husband who comes to know of her.*"

If a woman does not take heed, the opposite will take place. If a woman behaves insolently with her husband, is ungrateful and does not honour him as she should, the ill effects of her behaviour will certainly rub off onto her daughters, granddaughters and great granddaughters. She can then expect no good du'as to reach her.

We make du'aa to Allah Ta'ala to cast the graceful shadow of Zaynab (May Allah be pleased with him/her) on all our daughters and that Allah Ta'ala shower her with His mercy. May Allah Ta'ala also fill our hearts with sincere love for our husbands.

We shall now discuss the life of Messenger of Allah's (Peace be upon him) second daughter Ruqayya (May Allah be pleased with him/her).

Ruqayyah bint Muhammad (Peace be upon him)

The Wife of Usman daughter of Messenger of Allah (Peace be upon him) and the third daughter of Khadeeja (May Allah be pleased with him/her).She had an only son by the name of Abdullah and made Hijrah with Usman (May Allah be pleased with him/her) to the distant land of Abyssinia, leaving behind her hearth and home for the protection of her Religion. She set a sterling example to the women of the world, teaching them love for their Religion and devotion to their husbands.

Ruqayya (May Allah be pleased with him/her) was first married to Utba who was the son of Abu Lahab. However, she had not yet started living with her husband when Abu Lahab instructed his son to divorce her because Messenger of Allah (Peace be upon him) had announced his prophethood. She was then married to Usman (May Allah be pleased with him/her) five years after Nabuwwah (i.e. after Messenger of Allah (Peace be upon him) announced his prophethood), Usman (May Allah be pleased with him/her) and Ruqayya (May Allah be pleased with him/her) migrated to Abyssinia. For a long while afterwards, Messenger of Allah (Peace be upon him) received no news from his daughter until a woman of the Quraysh informed him that the couple were well. Messenger of Allah (Peace be upon him) said:

صحبهما الله

"*May Allah Ta'ala be their companion.*"

This is a du'aa that every parent should make for their children, especially for those children who are travelling. Messenger of Allah (Peace be upon him) then remarked,

أن عثمان لأول من هاجر إلى اللّٰه بأهله بعد لوط

"*Usman (May Allah be pleased with him/her) is the first person since Loot (Peace be upon him) to migrate with his family.*"

When Ruqayya (May Allah be pleased with him/her) returned to Makkah, her beloved mother had already left this world, a shock that she had to endure with patience.

THE SECOND MIGRATION

The time soon arrived when all the Muslims were commanded to migrate to Madinah because the Muslims now had a place of their own where they could consolidate and use as a base to spread Islam. From here they were able to send people throughout the world to carry the message of Islam to mankind so that they could be saved from the fire of Jahannam. Here they could practise Islam in peace and extend invitations to Islam to people near and far. As for those *Kuffaar* (Disbelievers) who refused to accept Islam, they were not forced to do so and merely had to pay a small tax called "*Jizya*" so that they could continue living in the Muslim state. By living with the Muslims, they were given the opportunity to be first-hand witnesses to the lives and practices of the Muslims. This attracted them to Islam and encouraged them to become Muslims.

Madinah had become a centre for the propagation of Islam and a place where new Muslims could learn Islam and have the opportunity to practise it before transmitting the message to others. The *Hijrah* (migration) to Madinah was extremely difficult for the Muslims because it meant leaving their homes, their properties, their kith and kin and everything that had sentimental value. The trial was immense. Notwithstanding all of this, Ruqayya (May Allah be pleased with him/her) had made Hijrah to Abyssinia and then again to Madinah so that this Religion of Islam could be preserved and become a means of saving mankind from Jahannam. Every Muslim during those times had the burning desire in their hearts that every Arab, every non-Arab, every Jew, every Christian, every Hindu, every fire-worshipper, every black and every white should be saved from Jahannam.

When Usman (May Allah be pleased with him/her) and Ruqayya (May Allah be pleased with him/her) reached Madinah, they stayed at the home of Aws bin Thaabit (May Allah be pleased with him/her) they now had the opportunity to recover from the fatigue of long travels and to settle down. The duty of Messenger of Allah (Peace be upon him) was close to realisation. However, Allah Ta'ala had decided that it was time to call Ruqayya (May Allah be pleased with him/her) back from this world so that He may confer on her the great rewards she deserved after the sufferings she endured for Islam, for living in a foreign land for the sake of Islam, for separating from her beloved mother, for suffering the pain of divorce for Islam and for everything she did to please Allah Ta'ala.

THE DEMISE OF RUQAYYA (MAY ALLAH BE PLEASED WITH HIM/HER)

Ruqayya (May Allah be pleased with him/her) left to meet Allah Ta'ala during the 2nd year after Hijrah when Messenger of Allah (Peace be upon him) had left for the Battle of Badr. She fell seriously ill before the Battle and Messenger of Allah (Peace be upon him) instructed Usman (May Allah be pleased with him/her) to stay behind to tend to her. At the precise moment when Zaid (May Allah be pleased with him/her) bin Haaritha (May Allah be pleased with him/her) announced in Madinah that the Muslims were victorious at Badr, this jewel of Messenger of Allah's eye left the world. This was not a journey like the one to Abyssinia from where she returned. She left on the journey from which none has ever returned.

Because Messenger of Allah (Peace be upon him) had been at Badr, he was not present for the burial, but when he returned to Madinah, he visited her grave. No pen can express the grief of a father who lost his daughter. Her two sisters wept at her departure and her little son Abdullah was without his mother. She may have dreamt of seeing her little son grow up into a young boy full of life and then into a strong man like his grandfather (Peace be upon him). However, these dreams ended when she had to respond to the call of death. She had left this world just when the time had arrived to settle and find happiness in Madinah, when the Muslims were gaining a strong foothold and were getting poised to conquer not only Makkah, but the entire Arabian Peninsula and territories beyond.

May Allah Ta'ala bless her with peace and His mercy on behalf of every Muslim present today and every Muslim to come until the Day of Qiyamah. May Allah Ta'ala bless our women with her noble and pure qualities. *Aameen.*

Ummu Hakeem (May Allah be pleased with him/her) Bint Haarith (May Allah be pleased with him/her) Sacrifice

Together with being a woman of great courage and making tremendous sacrifices for Deen, Ummu Hakeem (May Allah be pleased with him/her) had great love for her husband. Before accepting Islam, she fought along side her husband in the Battle of Uhud against the Muslims. When the Muslims conquered Makkah, the understanding of Islam that she had by then developed made her accept Islam very quickly. However, her husband, who was the son of the notorious Abu Jahal, refused to accept Islam and fled to Yemen.

CONCERN FOR HER HUSBAND

Like a true loyal and loving wife, she sought amnesty from Messenger of Allah (Peace be upon him) on behalf of her husband. The magnanimous Messenger of Allah (Peace be upon him) accepted her request and like he had given amnesty to people who were his sworn enemies, he did the same for her husband. Armed with love for her husband and the intense determination to save him from Jahannam, Umm-e-Hakeem (May Allah be pleased with him/her) searched for him until she found him in Yemen. She called for him just as he was about to board a ship and leave the Arabian shores. Addressing him with great love and compassion, she called out, "O my uncle's son!" This address was sufficient to harness his attention because people readily respond to family members.

جئتك من أوصل الناس وأبر الناس وخير الناس!

She said to him,
"I have come to you from one who is most particular about maintaining good family ties, one who treats people most kindly and one who is the best of people. Do not destroy yourself. Accept Islam and come with me. I have sought amnesty from Messenger of Allah (Peace be upon him) on your behalf and he has granted it."

"Did you really do this?" he asked. When she confirmed that she had, he accepted Islam and returned to Makkah. Thereafter, he proved to be a great warrior of Islam and fought fiercely in all the consequent battles, laying his life down for the Religion of all time. During the Khilaafah of Abu Bakr (May Allah be pleased with him/her) Umm-e-Hakeem (May Allah be pleased with him/her) and her husband Ikrama (May Allah be pleased with him/her) left to fight at Yarmook, a place bordering Syria. It was there that her husband was martyred and entered into the mercy of Allah Ta'ala.

HER SECOND MARRIAGE

After completing her Iddah (waiting period after her husband's death), Umm-e-Hakeem (May Allah be pleased with him/her) married Khaalid (May Allah be pleased with him/her) bin Sa'eed (May Allah be pleased with him/her) in an area of Damascus called Marjus Safar. As her husband prepared to make the customary marriage arrangements, she said to him, "The Romans may attack at any time so why don't we spend some time together." Khaalid (May Allah be pleased with him/her) bin Sa'eed (May Allah be pleased with him/her) agreed and told her that he was sure that he was going to be martyred in the battle against the Romans. The couple therefore met in a tent near a bridge, which is still referred to as the bridge of Ummu Hakeem r.

As he had anticipated, her husband was martyred in the battle. Being the niece of Islam's great warrior Khaalid (May Allah be pleased with him/her) bin Waleed (May Allah be pleased with him/her) (her mother was his sister), she stood up to fight against the Kuffaar. She took a tent peg in her hand and single-handedly killed seven Kuffaar soldiers.

Sheikh Zakariyya (May Allah be Merciful on him/her) writes: "Let alone the women of our times, even the men would not be prepared to get married under such circumstances. Even if a woman married at such a time, she would have mourned for a very long time after her husband's death. Notwithstanding the loss of her husband, this pious servant of Allah Ta'ala participated in the Jihaad herself and even killed seven enemy soldiers."

IT IS THE RESPONSIBILITY OF THE WIFE TO MAKE HER HUSBAND LEAD A PIOUS LIFE

Moulana Ashraf Ali Thanwi (May Allah be Merciful on him/her) has mentioned that one of the greatest failings of women in respect of the rights they owe to their husbands is that they make no effort to save them from Jahannam. They do not care whether their husbands are earning Halaal or Haraam wealth to sustain their lavish lifestyles. If the husband is engaged in earning Haraam, the wife should advise him to desist and to fulfil all the obligations due from him to others. In the same way, she should advise him to fulfil all his obligations to Allah Ta'ala if he is negligent of this. It is regrettable that a woman will do everything to convince her husband to do something when there is benefit in it for her. However, she is negligent of convincing him to fulfil his obligations towards Islam, which is her Religion as well.

It is not at all difficult for a woman to make her husband religious. However, it is necessary for her to be religious as well. When she is a practical Muslim who is particular about her religious obligations, Insha Allah Ta'ala her words will soon take effect. A good wife and mother should not send her husband and sons out to work without explaining that earning a living is not the reason and objective of their creation. She should therefore encourage them to give some time for Religion and to spend some time in the Masjid. She should also encourage them to assist those serving the Deen, to visit their relatives, to visit the sick, to recite Surah Yaaseen daily and to engage in efforts to ensure that every person in the community becomes a good Muslim who practises the Sunnah.

She should emphasise that it is not befitting of a Muslim to spend all his valuable time in mundane pursuits. She should tell them that no prophet will come after Messenger of Allah, so it is the responsibility of every Muslim male and female to save mankind from Jahannam as the Ambiya h did. The effort of a Muslim should be directed at eliminating Kufr from the world and making every person someone who does everything to please Allah Ta'ala only. Of course, some time will have to be spent for this. One should also say these things to one's visitors so that they may also be encouraged to practise and propagate Deen.

Just as the men and women made sacrifices for this Religion to be elevated, every male and female Muslim living today should also make some sacrifices. Every Muslim wife should apply herself to the task of reviving the spirit of Islam within her home and within her community and she should continue making du'aa to Allah Ta'ala for this objective to be realised. She should also make du'aa to Allah Ta'ala to grant her the ability to sustain such efforts and to forgive her for her shortcomings in this regard.

MAKING HER HUSBAND A MUSLIM THROUGH MARRIAGE

Anas (May Allah be pleased with him/her) narrates that his mother Umm-e-Sulaym (May Allah be pleased with him/her) had received a marriage proposal from Abu Talha (May Allah be pleased with him/her) before he accepted Islam. She said to him, "Abu Talha, do you realise that you are worshipping a tree that grows from the ground?" When he admitted that he did realise this, she said, "Are you not ashamed at worshipping a tree. If you accept Islam, I shall not ask you for a dowry to marry me." He then took leave to think about the matter. He returned later and declared,

أشهد أن لا إله إلا اللّه وأشهد أن محمدًا رسول اللّه

"I testify that there is none worthy of worship but Allah Ta'alaand I testify that Muhammad (Peace be upon him)is Allah Ta'ala's messenger."

Umm-e-Sulaym (May Allah be pleased with him/her) then asked her son Anas (May Allah be pleased with him/her) to perform the Nikaah (marriage) and the two were married.

AN EXAMPLE OF A WOMAN CHANGINGHER HUSBAND FOR THE BETTER

An important lesson that we learnt from the story of Umm-e-Hakeem (May Allah be pleased with him/her) is that after she converted to Islam she greatly exerted herself to convince her husband to accept Islam as well. She was therefore responsible for saving him from Jahannam and allowing him to enter Jannah. Being a courageous woman herself, she encouraged him to fight in Jihaad until he met with martyrdom and earned the highest positions in the Hereafter. The same occurred with her second husband. Allah Ta'ala therefore granted Umm-e-Hakeem (May Allah be pleased with him/her) the honour of being the wife of two martyrs. Her life was a great lesson to all Muslim women until Qiyamah.

There are many women whose husbands may be Muslims but are neglecting their duties to Islam or may be committing sins. Because of this behaviour they may be taking themselves to Jahannam. It is therefore the duty of the wife to guide him towards righteousness. For achieving this aim, she should first win his love and confidence by obeying his instructions and not backchatting. She should then make du'aa to Allah Ta'ala saying, "O Allah Ta'ala! Make my husband/son/brother pious men who are particular about their salah and who stay away from sin. Give them the love for good deeds and make them warriors and preachers of Religion who will water the flourishing garden of Messenger of Allah. Grace them with martyrdom as they strive to propagate Your Religion to the far corners of the world. Remove the handcuffs of cowardice from their hands and the yoke of fear from their necks. Extract from their hearts the notion of living eternally in this world. Make their hearts and minds evergreen with love for You and Your Prophet (Peace be upon him). Make it easy for them to sacrifice for Your Religion and give their lives for it. *Aameen*."

After adopting piety yourself, winning his love and making sincere du'aa to Allah Ta'ala, start encouraging him towards righteousness with love and respect. Turn him away from evils such as interest, cheating and lying in business, selling stolen goods, denying creditors their money and giving and accepting bribes. Keep reminding him in an appropriate manner, keep sending him to good environments and cry to Allah Ta'ala in du'aa at night so that AllahTa'ala may guide him.

If the son of Abu Jahal could be convinced by his wife to accept Islam, there is no reason why the heart of a Muslim husband, brother or son cannot be changed to practise the injunctions of the Shari'ah. If a woman sincerely cries to Allah Ta'ala for guidance, lovingly gives encouragement and despite being treated shabbily, she treats kindly, she will Insha Allah Ta'ala be able to effect a positive change.

At a time when there were no cars or trains, Umm-e-Hakeem (May Allah be pleased with him/her) crossed the mountains of Makkah and travelled hundreds of miles over rocky terrain in the scorching desert heat to reach her husband in Yemen. From there she still travelled with him all the way back to Makkah.

In addition to fulfilling the rights of her husband, Umm-e-Hakeem (May Allah be pleased with him/her) also fulfilled the rights of Islam by assisting in Jihaad so that Islam could spread throughout the world. She understood that the responsibility of Muslim women is not confined to her home. When the need arose for her to leave hearth and home to make Hijrah (migrate) to Shaam for the sake of Islam, she did not hesitate to accompany her husband. In the same way, Ruqayya (May Allah be pleased with him/her) made Hijrah to Abyssinia, Khansa (May Allah be pleased with him/her) made Hijrah to Iraq with her sons and Umm-e-Haraam (May Allah be pleased with him/her) made Hijrah to Cyprus where she passed away and was buried. Like these, there were many other Sahabiyaat who made Hijrah with their husbands or with other family members to distant parts of the world, where they passed away.

Their graves in these foreign lands address women to come until Qiyamah, telling them that they made Hijrah for Allah Ta'ala's pleasure to these lands, enduring the hardships of journey and resettling. Eventually, when Allah Ta'ala called for them to surrender their souls, they did so while still striving to elevate the Kalimah of Islam. Muslim women of today are also encouraged to create the spirit of Islam within their hearts and to apply themselves to the propagation of Islam. They should apply their minds, bodies, wealth and zest to the propagation of Islam so that it reaches every home in the world. This enthusiasm should be passed on to the entire family and imbued in the hearts of every mother and daughter.

THERE IS NO HARM FOR A WIDOW TO REMARRY

An important lesson that we glean from the story of Umm-e-Hakeem (May Allah be pleased with him/her) is that instead of mourning for years after her husband's death, a woman should continue serving the Religion as soon as her Iddah expires. Because Nikaah is a command of Allah Ta'ala, she should not be ashamed of remarrying if the opportunity arises. Messenger of Allah (Peace be upon him) has mentioned that when a suitable person of good character and piety proposes for a woman, her family should get her married. If they do not, there will be a calamity and widespread anarchy on earth.

The books of history cite the incidents of many Sahabiyaat (May Allah be pleased with him/her) who married after being widowed, thereby setting an example for all women until Qiyamah. Aatika (May Allah be pleased with him/her) bint Amar bin Nufayl AdawiyyaR was first married to Abdullah, the son of Abu Bakr. When he was martyred at Taa'if, she was extremely grieved and said,

فأليت لاتنفك عيني حزينة

عليك ولاينفك جسدي أغبرا

"I swear that grief shall never part from my eyes nor will dust leave my body."

Later on, she married Zaid bin Khattaabr, who was martyred at Yamaamah. She then married Umar (May Allah be pleased with him/her), who was also martyred as he led the Fajr Salah. She recited the following words of poetry when Umar (May Allah be pleased with him/her) passed away:

عين جودي بعبرة ونجيب

لاتملي على الامام النجيب

فجعتنى المؤمن بالفارس المعلم

يوم الهياج والتثويب

قل لأهل الضرآء والبؤس موتوا

قد سقته المنون كأس شعوب

"Generously pour your tears forth, O eyes And do not tire from weeping over the chosen leader The sudden death of the skilled horseman has shocked me On a day of war and revenge Announce to the poor and dejected

'You all may as well die' because death has claimed the soul of he who assisted the poor and who was a friend to the dejected."

After the demise of Umar (May Allah be pleased with him/her), she was married to Zubayr bin Awaam (May Allah be pleased with him/her) When he was also martyred, Ali (May Allah be pleased with him/

her) proposed for her hand in marriage. However, she declined the offer saying, "I cannot be so generous with your life (i.e., it should not be that you are also martyred)." It has been narrated that her first husband gave her some wealth on condition that she does not remarry. However, Umar (May Allah be pleased with him/her) told her that such a bequest was not permissible because nobody can forbid something that is Halaal. He advised her to give the money to her late husband's heirs and then to get married. *["Al Isaabah" Vol. 4 Pg. 357]*

This incident makes it clear that a husband's bequest for his wife not to remarry is not permissible. In fact, if she fears falling into sin by remaining single, it is compulsory for her not to abide by the bequest.

Besides Aatika (May Allah be pleased with him/her), there were many other Sahabiyaat who remarried after their husbands passed away or after being divorced from their husbands. Asma bint Umays (May Allah be pleased with him/her) was first married to Ja'far (May Allah be pleased with him/her) When he was martyred in the Battle of Mauta, she married Abu Bakr (May Allah be pleased with him/her) and then Ali (May Allah be pleased with him/her) when Abu Bakr (May Allah be pleased with him/her) passed away. *["Al Isaabah" Vol. 4 Pg. 231]*

Umm-e-Kulthoom (May Allah be pleased with him/her) was first married to Zaid bin Haaritha (May Allah be pleased with him/her) When he was martyred in the Battle of Mauta, she married Zubayr bin Awaam (May Allah be pleased with him/her) and then Abdur Rahmaan bin Awf (May Allah be pleased with him/her) after Zubayr (May Allah be pleased with him/her) divorced her. When Abdur Rahmaan bin Awf (May Allah be pleased with him/her) passed away, she married Amar bin Al Aas (May Allah be pleased with him/her) *["Al Isaabah" Vol. 4 Pg. 491]*

Marrying widows and divorcees was not looked down upon during the time of Messenger of Allah. Neither did the widowed or divorced women look down on remarrying, nor did the men who married them. It is common knowledge that besides Aa'isha (May Allah be pleased with him/her), all Messenger of Allah's wives were widows. If this practice were common today, there would be no brothels and such dens of vice. Women would have someone to take care of them and their children if they ever lost their husbands. At the same time, if a wife is unable to satisfy her husband on reasonable grounds, he will not have to resort to illicit means of satisfying himself because his other wife/wives will surely be able to satisfy him. In this manner the chastity of men and women will be safeguarded and there would not be the flood of illegitimate children we see today. This will effectively purge our communities of the many physical and spiritual diseases that are so common. Men and women alike will be saved from sin and immoral behaviour and widows and orphans will not be left destitute. According to Allah Ta'ala's promise, there will then be abundant blessings in sustenance.

When such an environment is created, women will not even find it difficult to allow their husbands to take other wives. There will bring great joy in everyone's lives when men fulfil the rights of all their wives and provide equally for all. The situation will be even more blessed when men do this with the intention of assisting widows, divorcees and orphans. Such are the teachings of the Shari'ah and the practice of Allah Ta'ala I's chosen servants. It is a cure for social ills, a shield against sin and a guarantee for success in both worlds. Likewise, it will also eliminate poverty and open the doors to prosperity.

A woman without a husband is a pauper

Men and women should always bear in mind that Messenger of Allah (Peace be upon him) said, "A man without a wife is a pauper." "Even if he is wealthy?" asked the Companion of the Prophet. Rasululla (Peace be upon him) replied, "He is a pauper even though he is wealthy." Messenger of Allah (Peace be upon him) then added, "A woman without a husband is a pauper." "Even if she is wealthy?" asked the Companion of the Prophet. Messenger of Allah (Peace be upon him) replied, "She is a pauper even though she is wealthy." *[Jam'ul Fawaa'id Vol. 1 Pg. 216]*

Messenger of Allah (Peace be upon him) once asked Ukaaf bin Bishr Tameemi (May Allah be pleased with him/her). whether he was married. When he replied in the negative, Messenger of Allah (Peace be upon him) asked him whether he owned a slave woman. When he again replied in the negative, Messenger of Allah (Peace be upon him) said to him, "If you have not married despite having the ability and the wealth to marry, you must be one of Shaytan's brothers." *[Jam'ul Fawaa'id]*

When a man or woman is ready for marriage, the Shari'ah of Islam does not approve of their decision to remain single. The Shari'ah has laid tremendous emphasis on marriage so that many evils and sin should not take place at all. Marriage seals the avenues to immorality, fornication and a range of other evils that have devastating consequences. Messenger of Allah (Peace be upon him) once mentioned, "I also marry. Whoever is averse to my practices is not from me." In saying this, Messenger of Allah (Peace be upon him) has warned Muslims that they should not regard themselves as one of his followers if they choose to remain single. Messenger of Allah (Peace be upon him) has also described such people as Shaytaan's brothers i.e. Shaytaan's assistants in spreading evil and corruption.

Together with emphasising the importance of marriage to safeguard people's chastity, Allah Ta'ala has also promised poor people that He shall grant them wealth if they marry. Allah Ta'ala says, "Marry those from you who are unmarried and those slave men and women who are righteous. If they are poor then Allah Ta'ala will make each of them wealthy by His grace. Allah Ta'ala is of ample means, All Knowing."

It is therefore incorrect to stay single because even if one does not possess enough wealth, Allah Ta'ala shall grant one the wealth when one marries. Abdullah bin Mas'ood (May Allah be pleased with him/her) has mentioned, "Even if I had only ten days of life left, I would prefer getting married instead of being single."

Both wives of Maaz bin Jabal (May Allah be pleased with him/her) passed away in a plague and he was also afflicted by it. Despite this, he told his friends to get him married because he did not want to meet Allah Ta'ala as an unmarried person. *[Sharh Ihyaa]*

After his first wife passed away, Moulana Fadhlul Rahman (May Allah be pleased with him/her) remarried when he was over a hundred years old. He was then suffering from fistulas because of a disease that had afflicted him. The diligent wife used to tend to him and regularly clean his wounds as no other person would. Haji Imdadullah (May Allah be pleased with him/her) also married a second wife towards the end of his life. This conscientious wife served him as well as his first wife who had become blind.

MARRIAGE BRINGS WEALTH AND AVERTS POVERTY

Abdullah bin Mas'ood (May Allah be pleased with him/her) reports that Messenger of Allah (Peace be upon him) said, "Seek wealth through marriage."

Aa'isha (May Allah be pleased with him/her) narrated that Rasulullaah (Peace be upon him) said, "Get married because women will be a source of wealth for you." This means that a wife will bring blessings in one's earnings. There were many incidents during the time of Messenger of Allah (Peace be upon him) when poor people were blessed with wealth after marrying. In fact, Messenger of Allah (Peace be upon him) would encourage poor people to marry so that they could be self-sufficient. Messenger of Allah (Peace be upon him) told a Sahabi to to get married when all he possessed was an iron ring. Messenger of Allah (Peace be upon him) married another Sahabi t who had no possessions and stipulated that the dowry should be that he teaches his wife what portion of the Quran he knew. Messenger of Allah (Peace be upon him) permitted another person to get married when all he possessed was the upper and lower garments that he wore. All another Sahabi t could afford to give his wife when they married was a pair shoes. In fact, Messenger of Allah (Peace be upon him) also permitted another person to get married when all he had to give his wife was some dates and a barley drink. Refer to the chapters of dowry in Ahadeeth books like "Mishkaat", "Bukhari" and "Muslim" for more details. These are being omitted in the interests of brevity. One may also refer to the Urdu booklet titled "Islam ka Nizaame Ismat aw Iffat" written by Moulana BurhaanuddinSambali.

The purpose of stating the above is to inform all Muslim widows and divorcees that they should try to get married as soon as their Iddah expires. Other women should assist them in this and none should prevent their husbands from marrying other women especially when they intend marrying widows, divorcees or women who were unable to get married for valid reasons. When a man is capable of marrying other wives in strict conformance with the Shari'ah and with the intention of assisting them, his wife becomes an obstacle instead of assisting him. This indicates that his wife has no compassion for other distressed women.

Islam lays emphasis on marriage so that the chastity of Muslim societies may be protected, so that modesty may prevail and so that children are conceived legitimately. In this manner, the world would be free from immorality and promiscuity.

Why is it Necessary for a Widow to Remarry?

In his book "Mukhzin Akhlaaq", Moulana Subhaani (May Allah be Merciful on him/her) recounts the incident of a women from Azeemabaad who was widowed at an early age. She spend her entire days and nights reciting the Quran and also fasted every day. She used to break her fast every day with dry bread or leftover wheat grains. She continued this practice until her old age. Because of her extreme piety, hundreds of women became her devotees. Before she passed away, she called for her devotees and asked them, "How do you think I lived a life of chastity and abstinence?" The women expressed their surprise that anyone could have led such a morally upright life without even seeing the face of a man and subsisting on dry bread and some wheat or barley. She then said to them, "Listen to the condition of me heart. From my young days until I became old, I often heard the voice of the night watchman as I recited Quran and I always thought of how I may reach him. However, fear for Allah Ta'ala and fear for being disgraced always stopped me. I implore you to never allow a young widow to remain single."

This incident makes it clear that regardless of a woman's piety and abstinent lifestyle, instinctive passions will always prey on her. The same applies to men. When such instincts seize hold of a person, even the animals are not safe from him/her. When their sons or daughters grow up, people usually busy themselves saving money for extravagant trousseaus and weddings receptions. Together with this, they also make elaborate preparations for useless customary practices like "Mendhi" nights etc. These are all futile and wasteful and not required by the Shari'ah. All the Shari'ah requires for marriage is that the man pays dowry to his wife. This dowry is a small amount which any man can afford and which does not necessarily have to paid immediately on marriage. If the bride agrees, payment can be deferred to a later time. It is therefore imperative that a woman should be married as soon as she finds a suitable partner. If a man can fulfil the rights of multiple wives, his first wife should not be an obstacle.

AN INCIDENT OF A SAINT

It has been related that a saint lost his wife. While someone was assisting him to make wudhu towards the end of his life, he cried out in a pain-filled voice, "O Allah Ta'ala! Only You are excellent Alone." Despite being a great poet, Aalim and philosopher, he also felt that his life was empty without his wife. One's husband or wife is the valuable factor that gives substance and worth to one's life, without whom life will be lustreless and without spirit. The person who lives without a spouse opposes man's nature and this nature shall soon exact revenge from him.

Khowla bint Maalik bin Tha'laba (My Allah be pleased with her)

Khowla bint Maalik (May Allah be pleased with him/her) was an extremely eloquent and well-spoken person. Her story is being related to teach all Muslim women what to do when they have problems with their husbands. She has mentioned, "By Allah Ta'ala! The opening verses of Surah Mujaadala (Surah 58) were revealed concerning myself and my husband Aws bin Saamit r."When he grew old, he became irritable. One day, when he became angry with her, he blurted out the words, "You are like the back of my mother to me." When he made advances to her, she exclaimed,

كلا والذي نفسي بيده لا تخلص إلي

"Never! By the Being in whose control is my life, you shall never approach me!"

She therefore forbade him from engaging in any relationship with her until they clarified the matter with Messenger of Allah (Peace be upon him) As hard as he tried to get her to submit to his advances, she fought him off and he was left helpless.

She then went to Messenger of Allah (Peace be upon him) and presented her case thus.

يا رسول اللّه، أكل شبابي ونثرت له بطني، حتى إذا كبر سني، وانقطع ولدي، ظاهر مني! اللّهم إني أشكوا إليك

"O Messenger of Allah! My husband has consumed my youth and I have given birth to his children. I have served him all my life and now that I am an old woman

and my children have left me, he has carried out Zihaar with me. If my small children are left with me, they would probably die of starvation and if they are left with my husband, they would be destroyed."

As she was saying this, she raised her eyes to the heavens saying, "O Allah Ta'ala plead my case before You. Reveal a command to Your Nabi (Peace be upon him)so that my difficulty is alleviated."

Allah Ta'ala then revealed the opening verses of Surah Mujaadalah saying,

﴿ قَدْ سَمِعَ اللَّهُ قَوْلَ الَّتِي تُجَادِلُكَ فِي زَوْجِهَا وَتَشْتَكِي إِلَى اللَّهِ وَاللَّهُ يَسْمَعُ تَحَاوُرَكُمَا إِنَّ اللَّهَ سَمِيعٌ بَصِيرٌ ﴾ (سورة المجادلة آيت ١).

"Allah Ta'ala had certainly heard the speech of the lady who debated with you concerning her husband and who complained to Allah Ta'ala. Allah Ta'ala was listening to your discussion. Verily Allah Ta'ala is All Hearing, All Seeing."

[Ma'aariful Quran Vol. 8 Pg. 331]

يا خوله، إبن عمك شيخ كبير فاتقي اللّٰه

Messenger of Allah (Peace be upon him) then addressed Khowla (May Allah be pleased with him/her) saying, "O Khowla! Your cousin (husband) has grown old, so fear Allah Ta'ala with regard to him (i.e. exercise patience with him)." When the verses pertaining to Dhihaar were revealed, Messenger of Allah (Peace be upon him) told Khowla (May Allah be pleased with him/her) to inform her husband that he would have to free a slave in expiation of his act (of Dhihaar). When she told Messenger of Allah (Peace be upon him) that he was unable to do this, Messenger of Allah (Peace be upon him) said that he will then have to fast for two consecutive months. When she submitted that he was unable to do this also, Messenger of Allah (Peace be upon him) mentioned that he should then feed two meals to sixty poor people. When she informed Messenger of Allah (Peace be upon him) that her husband would not be able to afford this either, Messenger of Allah (Peace be upon him) offered to assist by supplying some dates. Khowla (May Allah be pleased with him/her) then said that she would also supply some dates to assist her husband.

Thereupon, Messenger of Allah (Peace be upon him) said, "You have done well. Go and act charitably towards him and treat him kindly."

قد أصبت وأحسنت فاذهبي فتصدقي به عنه، ثم أستوصي بإبن عمك خيرًا.

Khowla (May Allah be pleased with him/her) was such a distinguished woman in Islamic history that Allah Ta'ala responded to her plea and the Ummah will remember her as long as the Quran is recited. Umar (May Allah be pleased with him/her) was once riding his donkey when an old lady stopped him to say something. When Umar (May Allah be pleased with him/her) stopped, the people asked him why he stopped for a frail old woman. Umar (May Allah be pleased with him/her) said to them,

أتدرون من هذه العجوز؟ هي خولة بنت ثعلبة، سمع اللّٰه قولها فوق سبع سموت، أيسمع رب العالمين قولها ، ولا يسمعه عمر .

"Don't you know who this old lady is? She is Khowla bint Tha'laba R. Allah Ta'ala listened to her from above the seven heavens. How can Umar not listen to her when Allah Ta'ala did."

The story of Khowla (May Allah be pleased with him/her) displays the perfect confidence that a Muslim should have in Allah Ta'ala. Allah Ta'ala will always provide the solution for every problem because He brings ease after every difficulty. Everything comes from Him. Allah Ta'ala says in the Quran,

﴿ وَأَنَّهُ هُوَ أَضْحَكَ وَأَبْكَى ﴾ (سورة النجم آية٤٣)

"It is certainly Him Allah Ta'ala Who makes (people) laugh and cry."

﴿ وَأَنَّهُ هُوَ أَمَاتَ وَأَحْيَا ﴾ (سورة النجم:٤٤)

"It is only He Who gives death and life…Verily He grants affluence and poverty."

Allah Ta'ala creates every favourable condition just as he creates every unfavourable condition. He makes people happy just as He can make them sad."

﴿ وَأَنَّهُ هُوَ أَغْنَى وَأَقْنَى ﴾ (سورة النجم آية: ٤٦)

"He gives wealth to whoever He pleases and takes wealth from whoever He pleases."

There is therefore no need for anyone to be despondent. When faced by any difficulty, all that one needs to do is to perform wudhu, perform two Rakaahs salah with concentration and then plead to Allah Ta'ala. One should supplicate to Allah Ta'ala by saying what Khowla (May Allah be pleased with him/her) said. She said,

اللّهم إني أشكو إليك

"O Allah Ta'ala! I complain to You. O Allah Ta'ala! I plead my case to you. O Allah Ta'ala! My home is deserted and my children are distressed. Reveal a command to Your Nabi (Peace be upon him)so that my difficulty is alleviated."

﴿ يَا أَيُّهَا الَّذِينَ آمَنُوا اسْتَعِينُوا بِالصَّبْرِ وَالصَّلاةِ إِنَّ اللَّهَ مَعَ الصَّابِرِينَ ﴾
(البقرة:١٥٣)

Allah Ta'ala says in the Quran,

"O you who believe! Seek help by means of patience and salah. Verily Allah Ta'ala is with the patient ones."

It is therefore necessary for every woman to plead to Allah Ta'ala for the solutions to all her domestic problems. Allah Ta'ala is the Only One who can solve one's problems. Whenever a woman is faced with a serious problem, she should seek counsel from a reliable person so that it may be addressed. This is necessary because when certain problems are pent up, they cause one's mental and physical health to deteriorate. Although Allah Ta'ala is the One who solves all problems, Allah Ta'ala has instructed us to consult with others. Even Messenger of Allah (Peace be upon him) consulted with the Companion of the Prophet When Messenger of Allah (Peace be upon him) received the first revelation, he did not keep the anxiety to himself and bottle it up within himself. Instead, he told Khadeeja (May Allah be pleased with him/her) about it and together with consoling him, she took him to her cousin Waraqa bin Naufal who was learned in the previous scriptures. In this manner, Messenger of Allah's found comfort and reassurance.

BEING PATIENT WITH AN AGED HUSBAND

The incident of Khowla (May Allah be pleased with him/her) also teaches us that when one's husband becomes irritable and difficult as he becomes old, one should exercise patience even though he may sometimes become intolerable. When Khowla (May Allah be pleased with him/her) complained of this to Messenger of Allah, he advised her saying,"O Khowla! You cousin (husband) has grown old, so fear Allah Ta'ala with regard to him (i.e. exercise patience with him)." This means that a woman should be even more patient when her husband ages and will therefore receive greater rewards.

When a person is young and healthy, everyone is prepared to be with him. However, when he grows old and becomes sickly and temperamental, people stay far from him because they will have to offer some services. At this stage, it will be only a good wife who will stay loyal to her husband. Only a good wife will agree with everything her husband says at this stage and who will fulfil his every wish before he expresses it. It is only such a dedicated wife who will refrain from anything he dislikes and who will take the blame for anything that he finds unpleasant.

If she becomes frustrated with his behaviour, she should think that Allah Ta'ala readily forgives when people fail to fulfil the rights they owe to Him. Similarly, she should also forgive him. If she does this, the spiritual benefit she will receive shall be tremendous and so too will be the rewards she will receive.

WHAT SHOULD THE WIFE DO WHEN HER HUSBAND IS AT FAULT?

Moulana Ashraf Ali Thanwi (May Allah be Merciful on him/her) tells women that if they also become angry when their husbands do, it means that they regard themselves equal to or better than men. This is so because a person usually gets angry with someone lower in status. One never gets angry with someone higher in rank. A woman should therefore not backchat when her husband is angry. If the husband is angry for no good reason, she should remain silent and explain his folly to him when he has calmed down. She should then kindly tell him that he ought to listen to her side to the story before drawing conclusions. This approach will prompt the man to show regard for his wife because he will realise that she is sensible and intelligent. He will then appreciate her much more and respect her. *["Wa'z Huqooqul Bayt" Pg. 51]*

THE FAILING OF HUSBAND AND WIFE AND A WORD OF CAUTION TO BOTH

When Khowla (May Allah be pleased with him/her) became angry just as her husband had become, he uttered the words of Dhihaar, which they both regretted. Fortunately, all he had to do to have her back as his wife was to pay the Kaffaara (expiation), after which their marriage was restored to normal. However, there are many instances when a woman does not keep quiet and is not prepared to admit her mistake. She rants and raves incessantly until the husband resorts to violence or he divorces her. This tragedy can be easily averted if the wife says that the mistake was hers and that she will not repeat it (even if the mistake is his). However, many women tend to prolong the argument to prove their point until the husband does something regrettable.

The consequences of the husband's reaction are not confined to the couple, but affect the families of both. The ill effects of this permeate the fabric of both families and are even felt by the children and grandchildren of the couple. People then have the opportunity to fabricate tales and publicise them, thereby bringing disgrace to the families involved. People will then be heard saying that a certain person's daughter could not run a home or that someone's mother is a divorcee, causing hurt to the person.

Therefore, Moulana Thanwi (May Allah be Merciful on him/her) has written that it is unfortunate that many women fail to understand the temperament of their husbands and speak out of turn when his mood is not at its best. If one party keeps silent, the argument will end. However, instead of stifling the argument, they give it more impetus by prolonging it, eventually leading to a divorce. Both end up regretting the consequences, which affects not only the couple, but their entire families. *["Aadaab Insaaniyat" Pg. 213 and "Tuhfa Zowjayn" Pg. 181]*

There are also many foolish women who become widows by daring their husbands to divorce them. Divorce should never be mentioned. It should be borne in mind that divorce will be effective whether it is said in jest or in anger. It is like pulling the trigger of a loaded gun. When the bullet kills someone, claiming that the gun was fired in jest or in anger will not bring the person back to life. Losing one's temper is not a valid excuse. Every person should learn to control his temper using the methods that the Shari'ah has prescribed.

We will now quote two cases where matters would have not reached where they did if the husband and wife had exercised more caution. Correspondence of this nature reaches the Daarul Ifta daily. May Allah Ta'ala save us and all Muslims from the evils of Shaytaan and the Nafs, which plague family life with bitterness, enmity, animosity, ridicule and disgrace. We will present these cases in the form of a dialogue for easier understanding. A common fault of women is highlighted in these cases, which seems insignificant but which brings destruction to everyone belonging to their families. A plea is made to all women to avoid the behaviour displayed in these incidents. Among these are the evil traits of justifying a wrong, using fire to fight fire and refusing to admit one's mistake.

THE FIRST INCIDENT

Tired after returning from working long in the sun, the husband rings the bell of his home. Still busy in the bathroom, the wife takes some time before opening. When she eventually, lets him in, he is irritated and bangs the door closed. The ensuing argument is as follows:

HUSBAND: I've been ringing the bell for the past half hour. Don't you care that I have been standing in the heat for so long?

WIFE: Couldn't you wait for two minutes? I was in the bathroom and heard the doorbell only now. Besides, you don't even know how to close a door quietly!

HUSBAND: You know very well that I return at this time yet you decide that it's necessary to have a bath now!

WIFE: You have no idea how much work I have! The children have not given me a moment's rest the entire day. Now you return to make my life a bigger misery. Do my work for a day and you will know what it's like?

HUSBAND: I cannot live with you! Go to your mother's!

THE SECOND INCIDENT

The husband asks for some tea. The wife serves the tea, unmindful of the many tea leaves that have remained behind after straining.

HUSBAND: Don't you know how to make tea, or do I have to teach you?

WIFE: What's the matter?

HUSBAND: Look at how many tea leaves have remained behind in the cup!

WIFE: Can't you even take this much? Make the tea yourself and you will come to know! It is very easy for you to give orders. I have to look after you, care for the children, cook the food and do everything in this house!

HUSBAND: Is that how you speak to me? Get out of my house!

Hearing the commotion, the neighbours gathered and in their presence, the husband said things that he wished he had never spoken. The couple were then separated never to be reunited.

You decide. If either the husband or the wife in either situation had remained silent at the outburst of the other, they would have remained husband and wife. If you are a husband, you should take heed not to behave as the men in the above incidents did. If you are a wife, you should beware not to do what the wives in these incidents did. May Allah Ta'ala save all couples from kindling the fires of disunity. The flames of discord in a home destroy one's devotion to Religion as well as one's performance in one's worldly affairs.

Ruling: Ulama have mentioned that after ringing the bell or knocking at the door, the husband should wait for as long as it takes his wife to perform four Rakaahs of salah and come to the door. Thereafter, he should ring the second and the third time. The etiquette of seeking permission to enter a room or a house have been discussed in my book "Islam awr Tarbiyyate Awlad", which examines the upbringing of children in Islam. It was thought appropriate to quote the excerpt from that book here for the benefit of our readers.

The Etiquette of Entering a Home

FIRST GREET WITH SALAM AND THEN ASK PERMISSION TO ENTER

Imaam Abu Dawood (May Allah be Merciful on him/her) has narrated that a person from the Banu Aamir tribe came to meet Messenger of Allah (Peace be upon him) while Messenger of Allahwas at home. When he arrived at the door, he called out, "May I enter?" Messenger of Allah (Peace be upon him) said to his attendant, "Go and teach him the method of seeking permission for entry and tell him to say, 'As Salamu Alaykum. May I enter?'" The person heard this and immediately said, "As Salamu Alaykum. May I enter?" Messenger of Allah (Peace be upon him) then permitted him to enter.

IDENTIFY YOURSELF WHEN REQUESTING PERMISSION TO ENTER

In the famous hadith of Bukhari and Muslim concerning the Mi'raaj, Messenger of Allah (Peace be upon him) had mentioned that when he and Jibra'eel (Peace be upon him) approached the gates of the first heaven and requested permission to enter, the gatekeeper asked who it was. When Jibra'eel eidentified himself, the gatekeeper asked who was with him. Jibra'eel (Peace be upon him) replied that Muhammad (Peace be upon him) was with him. The gates were then opened for them. The same procedure took place at the gates of every heaven.

Another hadith of Bukhari and Muslim is related from Abu Moosa Ash'ari r. He says that he once accompanied Messenger of Allah (Peace be upon him) to an orchard and acted as gatekeeper of the orchard. When Abu Bakr (May Allah be pleased with him/her) arrived and knocked, Abu Moosa (May Allah be pleased with him/her) asked who it was. He let Abu Bakr (May Allah be pleased with him/her) in after he had identified himself. The same happened when Umar (May Allah be pleased with him/her) and usman (May Allah be pleased with him/her) arrived shortly afterwards. They were all required to identify themselves before being allowed to enter.

Bukhari and Muslim have reported another hadith in this regard from Jaabir r. He narrates that he once knocked on Messenger of Allah's door. When Rasulullah (Peace be upon him) asked who it was, he replied,"It is me."Rasulullah (Peace be upon him) said,"What is' It is me','It is me'?"Messenger of Allah (Peace be upon him) disliked this ambiguous reply. It is therefore necessary for a person to state who he is and who he wishes to meet.

ONE SHOULD THRICE SEEK PERMISSION TO ENTER

Abu Moosa (May Allah be pleased with him/her) narrates that Messenger of Allah (Peace be upon him) said, "Permission to enter should be sought thrice. If permission is granted then all is fine. Otherwise, one should leave." It is preferable that the duration between each of the three knocks should be equal to the time that it takes a person to perform four Rakaahs of salah because the person in the house could be performing salah or answering the call of nature.

NEVER KNOCK THE DOOR TOO LOUDLY

One should be especially cautious about this when the person in the house is one's father, one's teacher or some other person to whom great respect ought to be shown. In his book "Adabul Mufrid", Imaam Bukharikl narrates from Anas (May Allah be pleased with him/her) that whenever he wished to enter the residence of Messenger of Allah (Peace be upon him) he would knock with his fingers. It has also been reported that our pious predecessors used to knock on the doors of their elders using only the nails of their fingers. This displays the immense respect that they showed towards their seniors.

The above applies when the person in the house is near to the door.

However, when he is far from the door, one should knock as loud as it is necessary for him to hear the knocking. When there is a doorbell to be rung, the visitor should ring it gently so that the people of the house may sense that the visitor is a gentle and cultured person.

Reducing Anger

In her best interests and in the best interests of her children and family, the wife should immediately ask for forgiveness as soon as she notices her husband lose his temper even though she is not at fault. When he scolds her, she should neither reply to him nor remain absolutely silent because either option would make matters worse. She should rather admit that the fault was hers (even it was not) and then ask for forgiveness. Besides this, the following guidelines are valuable for reducing anger.

1. Teach the du'as for entering the home to your husband and children and ensure that they recite these du'as every time they enter. When entering they should recite,"

أَعُوذُ بِاللَّهِ مِنَ الشَّيطَانِ الرَجِيم بِسْمِ اللَّهِ الرَّحْمَنِ الرَّحِيمِ ",

Surah Ikhlaas, Durood Shareef and the following du'aa:

اللَّهم إني أسئلك خيرالمولج وخيرا المخرج بسم اللَّه ولجنا وبسم اللَّه خرجنا وعلى اللَّه ربنا توكلنا (ابوداؤد ص ٣٣٩ ج٢)

"O Allah Ta'ala! I ask you for the good of entering and the good of leaving. We enter with the name of Allah Ta'ala and we leave with the name of Allah Ta'alaand in Allah Ta'ala Alone do we trust."

[Abu Dawood Vol. 2 Pg. 339]

The family should also learn the meaning of this du'aa so that they may consciously ask Allah Ta'ala for what the du'aa entails. When the family enters the home after reciting "A'oozhu Billahi Minash Shaytanir Rajeem", no Shaytan can enter the house to cause disputes and problems in the household.

Jaabir (May Allah be pleased with him/her) has narrated from Messenger of Allah (Peace be upon him) that when a person takes Allah Ta'ala's name at the time of entering his home and at the time of eating, Shaytaan says to his companions, "There is neither accommodation nor food for us here." On the other hand, when a person does not take Allah Ta'ala's name when entering his house, Shaytaan tells his companions,

"You have found accommodation for the night." Thereafter, when he fails to take Allah Ta'ala's name before eating, Shaytaan tells his companions, "You have food for the night." [Muslim, Abu Dawood and Ibn Majah]

NOTE: To be able to remember Allah Ta'ala at all times and using the correct words, one should keep the following two books handy:

a. "Masnoon du'as" by Mufti Aashiq Ilaahi (Rahmatullah Alayh)
b. Translation and commentary of "Hisn-e-Haseen", also by Mufti Aashiq Ilaahi (Rahima hullahu Taala)

One should learn the du'as mentioned in these books and teach them to one's children. One should also keep with one a book with a collection of things to recite (referred to as Wazaa'if).

2. Another course of action to follow is that when one becomes extremely angry, one should recite,

أعوذ بالله من الشيطن الرجيم

And immediately drink water. If one's husband is also angry, he should also be given water to drink.

THE FIRST CURE FOR ANGER: WUDHU

The Ahadeeth mention that when one becomes angry while standing, one should sit down. If one is sitting, one should then lie down. When the couple are having an argument, each one should try to remind the other to sit down, lie down, drink water or make wudhu.

Anger is extremely destructive and can cause many physical ailments.

In addition to this, it also causes enmity and hatred between people. One is tremendously rewarded for swallowing one's anger. On the other hand, if one's does not control one's anger, one will become a criminal instead of a reformer. It is therefore imperative that one maintains a balance of mind when anger begins to set in. This is important for every husband, mother and teacher.

The Quran teaches us that instead of doing something hastily without thought, one should ponder over one's course of action and plan a strategy that will be in the best interests of all involved. Therefore, the solution to a problem should be such that the wife/employee/student realises his/her mistake while the husband emplo- yer/teacher is still filled with love and concern for them instead of resorting to anger and violence. In this manner, the problem will be solved without and ill feelings being created. In fact, after the problem is solved in this amicable manner, one's spouse and children will have even more love and respect for one than they had previously. This principle should always be kept in mind.

Any evil should always be repelled with something good and not with something equally evil. If this is done, the result will be that even an archenemy will become a bosom friend. This is the teaching of the Quran.

THE SECOND CURE

Messenger of Allah (Peace be upon him) said,

من كظم غيظا وهو يستطيع ان ينفذه دعاه اللّٰه يوم القيامة على رؤوس

الخلائق حتى يخيره فى أي الحور العين شاء

"*Whoever swallows his anger while in the position to vent it, Allah Ta'ala shall call him before the entire creation on the Day of Qiyamah and permit him to choose whichever damsel of Jannah he pleases.*" *[Tirmidhi Vol. 2 Pg. 22; Abu Dawood Vol. 2 Pg. 33]*

﴿ وَإِذَا مَا غَضِبُوا هُمْ يَغْفِرُونَ ﴾ (سورة الشورى آيت ٣٧)

Describing the true Mu'min in the Quran, Allah Ta'ala says that they are people "who pardon when they are angry."

[Surah Shura (Surah 42), verse 37]

﴿ الَّذِينَ يُنْفِقُونَ فِي السَّرَّاءِ وَالضَّرَّاءِ وَالْكَاظِمِينَ الْغَيْظَ وَالْعَافِينَ عَنِ النَّاسِ وَاللَّهُ يُحِبُّ الْمُحْسِنِينَ ﴾ (سورة آل عمران آيت ١٣٤)

In Surah Aal Imraan, Allah Ta'ala describes the pious and abstinent Mu'mineen when He says that they are "Those who spend in ease and adversity, swallow their anger and forgive people. Allah Ta'ala loves those who do good..." Discussing this verse in his book Fadhaa'il Sadaqaat, Sheik Muhammad Zakariyya (May Allah be Merciful on him/her) writes that swallowing one's anger and forgiving people are exceptionally noble qualities which are used to praise the Mu'mineen.

Ulama have mentioned that whenever a Mu'min errs, one should make excuses for the error and then explain to one's heart that it should not harbour ill feelings towards the person because s/he had so many excuses for the error. If one's heart still refuses to accept, one should censure one's heart for being so hard and unrelenting. One should tell oneself that a Mu'min ought to accept the excuse of another. Messenger of Allah (Peace be upon him) has mentioned that the person who does not accept his brother's excuse shall be very sinful.

According to another hadith, the sip that Allah Ta'ala most loves is the sip that a person takes as he swallows his anger.

THE THIRD CURE

Imaam Ahmad (May Allah be Merciful on him/her) has reported a hadith in which Messenger of Allah (Peace be upon him) said,

إذا غضب أحدكم فليسكت

"*When any of you becomes angry, he should remain silent.*"

Therefore, when husband and wife start getting angry, the wife should remind her husband about this instruction of Messenger of Allah (Peace be upon him) and encourage him to abide by this instruction because one's success in this world and in the Hereafter shall be guaranteed when one follows the commands of Messenger of Allah. She should admit her fault and tell him that it will not happen again. The couple should then engage in some other activity so that the matter is forgotten.

THE FOURTH CURE

When the couple are about to start an argument, they should leave the place immediately. The wife may step awhile outdoors and the husband may go to the Masjid. They may then perform salah or recite a bit of the Quran until their anger subsides.

Messenger of Allah (Peace be upon him) said,

ألا وإن الغضب جمرة تتوقد فى قلب إبن آدم ألا ترون إلى إنتفاخ أوداجه

وأحمرا عينيه، ومن أحس من ذلك شيء فالأرض الأرض

"Behold! Anger is a burning coal that ignites the heart of a person. Do you not see the dilation of the angry person's veins and the redness of his eyes? Whoever senses this happening to him should resort to the earth. He should resort to the earth i.e. he should lie down and think about his final abode in the grave."

THE FIFTH CURE

A person who frequently gets angry should write the following sentence on a paper and hang it on where he will see it often. The sentence is:

"Allah Ta'ala has more power over you than you have over others."

This will remind one that Allah Ta'ala has more power over one than one has over one's wife, children, employees, students and everyone who is one's subordinates. Despite this, Allah Ta'ala does not punish anyone more than the person deserves. A person shall be accountable for any injustice that he perpetrates in this world. Allah Ta'ala is at liberty to punish a person for this in this world as well as in the Hereafter.

Cowardly indeed is the person who becomes angry with someone weaker than himself, but when confronted by someone stronger than himself he manages to control his anger. By writing down the above sentence and keeping it in mind, one will be able to keep one's temper well under control.

THE SIXTH CURE

Messenger of Allah (Peace be upon him) said,

"When any of you becomes angry, he should sit and if his anger still persists, he should lie down."
[Abu Dawood Vol. 2 Pg. 303]

After this prescription to brings one's anger under control, there is no need for another prescription. When standing, one is far from the ground. When sitting, one will be closer to the ground and when lying down, one will be closest to the ground. This proximity to the ground is effective in reducing anger because Allah Ta'ala has imbued the ground with the quality of humility. When sitting and lying down, this quality will rub off onto the angry person and reduce anger because humility is the converse of anger and pride.

Experience shows that when a person becomes angry, he is inclined to get himself into a position to grab or hit the object of anger. Therefore, if he is lying down, he will instinctively sit up or stand up. It follows therefore that by reversing the instinctive position of anger, it will be considerably reduced.
["Tuhfa Zowjayn" Pg. 162]

By employing these methods, one will be able to control one's anger. When this is achieved, one will no longer darken the happiness of others and one will no longer deprive oneself of the friendship of good friends. Families will not be wrecked and one will neither be responsible for extinguishing the candles of joy blazing in the hearts of others nor for silencing the nightingales singing songs of mirth in their bosoms.

Besides employing the above methods of reducing one's anger, one should also consult pious people. At the end of this book we will include the names, addresses and contact numbers of some eminent Ulama and Muftees whom one may consult. Insha Allah Ta'ala, one will receive the necessary guidance from them.

The Deadly Poison of Backchat

Moulana Ashraf Ali Thanwi (May Allah be Merciful on him/her) writes that if women learn to control their tongues, they would be damsels of Jannah walking on earth. The tongue holds a sting more harmful than a scorpion. Even when her husband is holding a sensible discussion with her, she continues saying whatever pleases her just so that she may have her say. If merely speaking without relevance entailed constructive debate, the donkey would be the best debater. *["Islaah Khawateen" Pg. 183]*

If women exercise patience and keep silent when their husbands scold them in anger, they will soon become like the pure damsels of Jannah. When their husbands gain control over themselves, they will feel ashamed of their behaviour and they will stop getting angry so often. If the wife backchats, the situation can get out of control and her husband may say or do something that both will regret. *["Behisti Zewar" Pg. 41]*

Moulana Ashraf Ali Thanwi l; is quoted as saying that a woman's acid tongue is the root of rot setting into marriages. He adds that if this evil trait can be removed from women, they will become damsels of Jannah. This is the advice of Moulana Ashraf Ali Thanwi (May Allah be Merciful on him/her) has written hundreds of books and who is regarded as the reformer of his century and a great Imaam. He possessed a thorough understanding of the Quran and the Ahadeeth and understood the psychology of women. If women practise what he advised, they will convert their homes into gardens of Jannah.

All women achieve by backchat is to make their husbands lose their feelings of sympathy and compassion. When a woman relentlessly harps on an issue and nags, her husband's heart becomes detached from her even though he is a good and caring person. No man can tolerate his wife's backchat. Therefore, she should never entertain the hope that he will swallow her insolence thinking it to be a drink of honey.

One of the best attributes that women possess is their ability to talk sweetly. Talking sweetly is a charm that can win over the hardest hearts. An adage is common in Urdu which states that a sweet tongue captures nations and can tie an elephant by a strand of hair. By speaking sweetly to her husband, a woman can make him forget all her faults. On the contrary, the husband of a woman who has every virtue will quickly forget all her virtues if she speaks insolently.

Be Concerned about Your Husband's Comfort

A wife should always be conscious about her husband's food, clothing, health, rest and amenities. His happiness should be hers and his grief should also be hers. It is therefore imperative that every wife acquaints herself with her husband's likes and dislikes. She should know exactly what pleases him and what does not. Her most vital task is fulfilling his instructions and seeing to his every need. Intelligent women win over their husbands by diligently serving their husbands. The husband will then be cognisant of her every desire and will do anything to please her. Life then becomes pleasurable for both.

Women who think that they can rule their husbands with their beauty are grossly mistaken. A man is slave to the wife who serves him and not to the wife who is only beautiful. After a tiring day at work, the sight of a dutiful wife is enough to make any man forget his fatigue.

MAKE YOUR HUSBAND YOUR FRIEND

To lead a happy life, a woman has to make her husband her friend. Only one's spouse can be one's true friend. The couple's hearts cannot be united if the wife does not regard her husband as her friend. Once their hearts are united, love will grow between the couple and they will be comforted by each other.

HOW TO MAKE YOUR HUSBAND YOUR FRIEND

1. By convincing yourself that you have no friend truer than your husband.

2. Have complete trust in him.
3. Never lie to him and never hide anything from him.
4. Never interfere in his matters especially when he is away.
5. Make every effort to increase your respect for him. One of the methods of doing this is to praise him in front of others.
6. Assist him with mind, money and matter when he is in difficulty. Forget your personal needs during such times and do everything possible to give him relief. These are the occasions to win his love and trust.
7. Express happiness when he is happy and sadness when he is sad.
8. When he is worried about something, do everything in your power to relieve his worry and tell him things to make him happy.
9. Always be conscious of things that please him and things that upset him.
10. Be thrifty with the money he gives you and be content with it.
11. Never make unreasonable demands on him for things that are not necessary. Make do with whatever he gives.

FACTORS THAT ATTRACT THE HUSBAND

Women should inculcate the following qualities in their lives to win their husbands over:

1. Refrain from all major and minor sins. If a sin is committed, repent immediately.
2. Treat him according to his disposition.
3. Keeping within the bounds of the Shari'ah, be the woman he wants you to be.
4. Always be patient and tolerant.
5. Speak sweetly and always wear a smiling face.
6. Beautify yourself for him without disregarding the constraints of the Shari'ah.

A WIFE SHOULD NEVER LOOK DOWN ON HER HUSBAND

Irrespective of the husband's status in society, it is compulsory for his wife to obey his instructions. Just as a nation is constrained to obey its leader, a wife must also do the same. When good Muslims like the Companion of the Prophet had to obey a tyrannical governor like Hajjaaj bin Yusuf, why should a woman not obey her husband? There is no doubt in the fact that husbands can neither be worse than Hajjaaj nor can wives be better than the Companion of the Prophet.

The fact that the Shari'ah regards men to be senior in status than women is explicitly mentioned in the Quran and the Ahadeeth. When every woman has witnesses to attest to her marriage, why then should she not obey her husband? Of course, the husband cannot stop his wife from her Fardh obligations and she may not obey him if he stops her from these. However, she is obliged to obey him if he orders her not to carry out any Nafl act of worship. The Shari'ah has attached so much importance to obeying the husband that if he instructs her to delay her salah when there is ample time to perform it in its proper time, she should obey him. If a woman's husband instructs her to commit a sin, she is obliged not to obey him. If (Allah Ta'ala forbid!) he carries out an act of kufr or says words of kufr, she needs no Fatwa to decide that she should be immediately separated from him.

When a woman's husband tells her to leave aside her Wazeefas (optional daily recitation of the Quran or du'as) to render him some service, she should do as he says. She should never think that her piety will be reduced if she forsakes these Wazeefas. On the contrary, her piety will be increased by serving him. Piety is acquired by fulfilling the injunctions of the Shari'ah and not by doing what one merely thinks is good. Obeying one's husband is a command of the Shari'ah and therefore putting aside one's optional acts of worship for the explicit command of the Shari'ah will definitely earn Allah Ta'ala's pleasure and augment one's piety. *["Islaah Khawateen"]*

NOTE: It often occurs that women are more academically educated than their husbands, either in religious education or in secular education. This is gives her no reason to look down on him because she still owes him the high level of honour and respect that a husband deserves.

Diagnosis and Treatment of Two Evil Traits in Many Women - The First Evil Trait

An exceptionally evil trait that is common among women is that they never seem to forget the smallest excuses to refresh an argument. When the opportunity arises, they will recall little details and carry out laborious nitpicking exercises to prove their point. Although their argument may not be strong, they tend to prolong the matter indefinitely. There is scarcely a home that is free from this malady.

Almost every quarrel between mother and daughter, between mother-in-law and daughter-in- law and between sisters-in-law are a result of suspicion and unverified information. They hear stories about their in-laws from other women who spice up the details by adding hundreds of lies, misleading adjectives, adverbs and expressions. In her foolishness, the woman records all of this in her memory bank and, adding a host of other details to it, she concludes that the information is correct and that she well understands the intentions of every speaker mentioned in the stories.

A typical scenario is as follows: The housekeeper approaches the elder daughter-in-law living with her in-laws and says, "Dear, I must tell you about the rice you cooked today. Well, your sister-in-law (your husband's younger brother's wife) said that her husband was outraged about the food and said, 'Doesn't my brother's wife know how to make rice after all these years? She disgraced us in front of all the guests.' And that's not all..." She then proceeds to convey a series of other tales about the younger daughter-in-law, which the elder daughter-in-law believes without question.

Thereafter, adding some spice to the incident, the elder daughter-in-law relates the incident to the mother-in-law. With a few tears added to it, the mother-in-law is convinced about the story. The mother-in-law then begins formulating schemes to "fix" the younger daughter-in-law because her mind has already called for witnesses from her past memories and it has already acted as judge to condemn the innocent lady. The housekeeper was sufficient as a prosecutor and the elder daughter-in-law was the plaintiff lodging the case. The case is then lodged before the younger sister-in-law who represents the High Court. The final judgement is then given by the elder sister-in-law.

When it is the younger daughter-in-law's turn to cook, fate has it that a little extra water fell into the rice or a little extra salt fell into the gravy. According to plan, the other women in the house launch their attack at the table.

"Look at how you cook!" someone calls out.
"You think that we are little girls!" another shouts.
"And you dare to insult us!" commented a third.

Surprised at the outburst, the younger daughter- in-law denies that she said anything, adding that even her two recording angels knew nothing about it. When she asks to be informed about the source of the information, the others say, "We will not betray our informant. She is an extremely honest and pious woman who will never say anything she never heard." The fact that the housekeeper has worked for the family for many years is now suddenly used a mark of her piety whereas it has nothing to do with this. After this, insults and accusation are freely exchanged and the house becomes a battlefield where even parties remotely related have their names smeared.

The entire scene described above and so many other similar incidents are based entirely on hearsay and unconfirmed reports. It is best not to listen to gossip and if one does hear about a complaint about oneself, the truth of the matter has to be confirmed directly from the source. This is the prescribed method of handling such matters according to the Shari'ah. Whenever one has a complaint against another, the matter should be addressed to the person himself without revealing it to others. Once the sprouts of ill-feelings are allowed to take root in the heart, they swiftly develop into deep-rooted trees that cannot be uprooted without much difficulty and damage to the heart.

Therefore, if any one has a complaint against another someone, the matter should be resolved as quickly as possible and there should be no ill-feelings between the two. If the cause of the complaint is found to be unauthentic, then this will be clarified for life and unnecessary rancour will be eliminated. By clarifying matters, tale carriers will be exposed and they will stop their evil practice.

An Interesting Incident

It has been narrated that a wolf was on the prowl one morning, searching for food to feed himself and his family. He happened to overhear a woman saying to her son, "If you do not learn your lessons, I shall feed your goats to a wolf." The wolf was ecstatic and waited there so that the goats could be fed to him. However, he waited until the evening without getting anything. That evening, he heard the mother saying, "Son, Mashaa Allah Ta'ala, you are a very good child. You must have learnt your lessons. Now if a wolf comes to eat your goats, we shall kill it." Hearing this, the wolf wasted no time to run away. When he returned to his family without food, his wife asked him what had happened. After relating the incident to her, he added,

حدث هذالي، لأني صدقت إمراة

"This happened to me because I took the word of a woman."

["Zahraat min Rowdhil Mar'atil Muslima" Pg. 126]

This incident tells every Muslim male and female not to trust the word of any woman without verification. It is best to disregard what they say.

A DU'AA THAT EVERY WOMAN SHOULD MAKE

One should always bear in mind that malice is not merely a sin but it opens the doors to many other sin as well. It is form of sweetened anger. It gradually contaminates the entire heart as it fills every part of the heart with grief and unrest. Because it more commonly affects women, every woman should make the following du'aa after every salah:

"O our Rabb! Do not place in my heart any malice for the Mu'mineen. O our Rabb! Indeed You are the Most Forgiving, Most Merciful."

If Allah Ta'ala purges one's heart from malice, it is an extremely great favour from Him. One should always wish the best for others and never wish evil to befall anyone. One should endeavour to conceal the faults of everyone else and to look for only their good qualities. The bounty of cleansing the heart from malice and animosity is such a great favour that it is counted as being among the bounties of Jannah. In Surah Hijr,

﴿ وَنَزَعْنَا مَا فِي صُدُورِهِمْ مِنْ غِلٍّ إِخْوَاناً عَلَى سُرُرٍ مُتَقَابِلِين ﴾

(سورة الحجر آيت ٤٧)

Allah Ta'ala says about the people of Jannah, "We shall remove any animosity that may be in their breasts (before they enter Jannah). As brothers they will be seated on couches, facing each other."

THE SECOND EVIL TRAIT

Although this trait is also found in some men, it is especially common among women. The trait is that when an argument arises, they dig out past incidents which have already been resolved and forgiven. As a result, even though the incident at hand is trivial, the reminder of a past incident generates a fresh argument leading, to an extremely combustible situation. The situation becomes graver when the reminder is phrased insensitively a skill of expression that many women have perfected to an art.

Therefore, women should try to forget such matters as soon as possible. Whenever someone brings any gossip to you, rebuke them and refuse to listen. Tell them that he are causing friction between Muslims and should stop visiting your home if they persist in carrying tales. At the same time, you should warn other women about such a tale-carrier so that they do not fall prey to her deception.

Moulana Ashraf Ali Thanwi (May Allah be Merciful on him/her) has mentioned that it is tragic that women nowadays actually wait for women to come from other towns so that they may ask them what other women are speaking. The embellished information that these women carry lay the foundation to suspicion and very soon, an entire building of malice and ill-feelings is constructed. The finishing touches to the building are added when the women begin using the telephone to spread the word around.

The entire network of women then spices up the stories even further so that the house of mistrust and malice becomes properly furnished. Eventually, two Muslim homes are irreconcilably divided and Allah Ta'ala's wrath is directed against everyone concerned.

Remember! Causing disunity between two Muslims is a grave sin. When Messenger of Allah (Peace be upon him) was about to inform the Companion of the Prophet about the date of "Laylatul Qadr", the ill effect of a dispute between two Muslims caused this knowledge to be lifted from the heart of Messenger of Allah (Peace be upon him) Messenger of Allah (Peace be upon him) said on hat occasion, "I came to inform you about the exact night on which "Laylatul Qadr" will take place but the argument between such and such persons caused this information to be lifted from me. Perhaps this is better in Allah Ta'ala's knowledge." *[Bukhari]*

Messenger of Allah (Peace be upon him) once said to the Companion of the Prophet, "Should I not show you an act better than salah, fasting and Sadaqa?" When the Companion of the Prophet begged to be informed, Messenger of Allah (Peace be upon him) said, "Maintaining good relations between yourselves is the best deed. Fighting between yourselves shaves off your Religion i.e., just as a razor instantly removes hair, in-fighting instantly removes Religion from people's lives."

Every woman should therefore take heed not to engage in gossip and not to listen to gossip. Nothing should be spoken about which is not necessary because one will suffer the penalty for gossiping in this world as well as in the Hereafter. The Quran explicitly condemns backbiting and entertaining evil thoughts of others. *["Huququz Zowjayn" Pg. 324; "Islaah Khawateen" Pg. 219]*

ANIMOSITY BETWEEN WOMEN CAUSES ANIMOSITY BETWEEN MEN

It often occurs that a woman complains to her husband about everything that his mother and sisters tell her in addition to the fights that the children of the family had with her children. She dramatises the situation and tells him that he should do something about it. Although the husband is tired and weary after a hard day at work, he suddenly becomes rejuvenated when hearing this because of the shallowness of his perception. In his rage, he may even hurt someone and cases have been reported where people were killed because of such insensitiveness. Eventually, the relationship between blood brothers is eternally severed all because of one woman.

Every woman should bear in mind that if she does not desist from causing dissention between two brothers and between mother and son, the time is not far off when someone like her may cause the same disunity between herself and her sons or between her sons. The adage is famous that states that one will be treated as one treats others. A famous Arabic saying goes:

كما تدين تدان

"You will receive what you dish out. If you do not believe this, try it and find out. Jannah is a reality and Jahannam is also a reality. If you do not believe this, then die and find out."

AN APPEAL TO MEN

Husbands are urged not to listen to such complaints of their wives. Affectionately place your hand on her mouth when she starts speaking about such things. When a woman can lie about something she sees, she can certainly do so concerning the things she hears from others. History testifies to the fact that women have deceived countless men who were reputed to be great intellectuals, professors and philosophers. A poet says:

"Akbar was not killed by any army of the enemy
Akbar was martyred by the pinch of a woman."

It is therefore imperative that men do not listen to the complaints and charges that women level against other. If something of this sort is overheard, one should pay no heed to it. Instead, one should encourage one's wife to forgive by explaining the virtues of forgiveness. Explain to her that if she will exercise patience and tolerate the difficulties, Insha Allah Ta'ala her progeny will also be tolerant towards her. Make her understand that all the arguments boil down to petty squabbles that are not worth the fuss being made about them. Tell her that this world is a place of trials and difficulties which will all pass by. True peace and contentment is reserved for the Aakhirah, where the fruits of one's patience will be realised. The sign of a courageous person is that s/he tolerates the difficulties that others present without fussing about them.

If there have been problems among the children, explain to her that the family's children are all like your own. If any of your children are involved in a fight, it will be cruel for someone else to exact revenge from the child. The same should apply to all the children of the family. Just as one would explain to one's own children what is right, so too should one explain the right to one's nephews, nieces and other children of the family. Give them some sweets or chocolates and tell them what to do and what not to do. Recite "Bismillaahir Rahmaan nir Raheem" seven times and blow on their food or drink as explained earlier in this book. This is an extremely effective prescription to calm children who are aggressive and who frequently throw tantrums. One may also recite "Yaa Lateef" seven times, blow on some water and give the child to drink. When children misbehave, adults should not imitate their behaviour by becoming abusive and violent. Instead, one should adopt an attitude of understanding and ingenuity.

It is also necessary to explain to one's wife that if she is the eldest sister-in-law, she should show more concern and behave like a mother towards the other sisters-in-law. Just as a mother does not abandon her child for misbehaviour, she should also not severe ties with the others when they do something wrong. If your wife is a younger sister-in-law, tell her that she should regard the other sisters-in-law as her real sisters. Just as she would not consider the scolding of her real sister to be a sign of enmity, she should believe the same to be true in the case of her elder sisters-in law. Not only Islam, but all Religion (Peace be upon him) teach their followers to respect elders. Therefore, when one's elders treat one shabbily, the best recourse is to exercise patience and continue living together with love. In this manner, Allah Ta'ala will give respect to one and grant one obedient children.

A husband should advise his wife in this manner instead of becoming angry with everyone else. Moulana Ashraf Ali Thanwi (May Allah be Merciful on him/her) said, "In my opinion, husbands should tell their wives that even though they may be truthful in their reports about others, they (the husbands) will not believe them. Of course, I am not saying that all husbands are like this (i.e. spineless and affected by whatever their wives tell them). There are many husbands who behave like real men by using their intelligence when such situations arise." *["Tuhfa Zowjayn" Pg. 82]*

A husband should not start fighting with one's little brothers (especially if they are without a father or mother) or with one's parents and sisters merely because one's wife complained about them. If you are unable to explain matters to your wife, never scold your mother even though it may be her fault. Rather arrange separate quarters for your wife or if this is not possible, arrange a separate kitchen for her. Never rebuke your mother for anything because she is your mother and deserves the highest respect. Of course, you should never oppress your wife because of your mother. To fulfil the rights of both mother and wife, the best course of action is to arrange for them to live or cook separately.

When there is friction between mother-in-law and daughter-in-law, it is senseless to force them to live together, thereby destroying the lives of the innocent children who will have to see their mother and grandmother always at loggerheads. When living separately, each of the two will be at ease and the friction will disappear. This is the instruction of the Shari'ah and it holds immense benefit for one's well being in this world as well as in the hereafter.

CARING FOR ORPHANED BROTHERS AND SISTERS-IN-LAW

When one is charged with caring for one's orphaned brothers and sisters, one should deal with them kindly when one's wife complains about them. This is because orphaned children are really not among the living since their spirit died with their parents. It is therefore inappropriate to hit a dead spirit. In fact, even showering excessive love on an orphan cannot revive his/her spirit. There is always a sense of gloominess about them and they can always sense death. In fact, Moulana Ashraf Ali Thanwi (May Allah be Merciful on him/her) has mentioned that when an orphan and another child are seated together and something is placed before them with the instruction that the one who grabs it first shall keep it, the orphan will not even attempt to take it. This is because the orphan's heart is dead. *["Islaah Khawateen" Pg. 224]*

It is therefore necessary that women caring for their orphaned brothers-or-sisters-in-law should give them extra attention and be gentle with them. Men who are charged with this duty should also be gentle and loving and should take care never to overreact to their wives exaggerated complaints. May Allah Ta'ala grant everyone the ability to practise accordingly.

TWO PRINCIPLES FOR AVOIDING DOMESTIC DISPUTES

If women adhere to the two principles mentioned hereunder, I am certain that all her disputes with her husband will be effectively terminated. Failure to implement these two principles has led to many unnecessary arguments and divorces as well as unnecessary scolding and abuse of children because of the great tension within the household. Insha Allah Ta'ala, when these two principles are implemented, the qualities of love, understanding, self-sacrifice, gentleness and service-above-self will be created and consolidated.

THE FIRST PRINCIPLE

This principle entails learning to frequently use the word "Alright". To avoid arguments, one should agree and say "Alright" even if one's husband says that day is night. If he says that you should cook something, say "Alright" and if he says that you need to go somewhere today, say, "Alright". In other words, agree to whatever he says. Even if he does not want you to mix with certain people, do not argue with him. For example, if he tells you not to attend a wedding hosted by your brother, tell him that you accept what he says and will not attend because he is more important to you than your brother. Thereafter, make du'aa to Allah Ta'ala saying, "O Allah Ta'ala! The hearts of men are in Your control. O Allah Ta'ala! Fulfil my desire if it is good for me because none can repeal Your decision. However, if there is harm for me in what I desire, remove the desire from my heart."

When your husband is in a good mood, tell him sweetly that the occasion your brother's house is one of happiness and joy and their happiness will be incomplete without your presence. Explain to him why you should attend without offending him in any way. Also tell him that you would appreciate his generous gesture if he permitted you to attend. If you are a good wife, there is scarcely a man in this world who would still refuse permission. This approach should be adopted for any other purpose as well. If after this he still refuses, exercise patience and accept what he says. It will not be long thereafter that he will have perfect reliance and confidence in you. He will then accede to all your requests and will even consult you in all matters.

Because Allah Ta'ala has made men leaders of women, every man expects his wife to listen to him. A wife should therefore abide by whatever her husband decides. Of course, she may present her opinion on any matter and he will certainly consider it. However, the final decision is his. If a woman wants her word to be binding on her husband and effuses to acknowledge that he is her leader, she is opposing Allah Ta'ala's natural system as well as the Shari'ah. In fact, she is also opposing logic and will therefore be the cause of dissention in the home. A husband will never be able to point a finger at his wife if she accepts him as her leader and does everything that pleases him.

Whenever a woman is leaving her father's home as a bride, she should always remember that following advice that a father gave to his daughter. He said:

> "O my beloved daughter, the light of my eyes
> O the radiance of my home, the delight of my life
> Remember this advice of your father,
> but my daughter
> Bear in mind that since time began, the nature
> of every daughter
> has been one of patience and contentment
> Never let every little thing cause tears of bloodto flow
> Tolerate everything that life presents
> Keep the pleasure of your lifelong companion
> ahead of everything and everyone for as
> long as you live, and please
> Never allow a blemish to taint your father's name
> The du'as of your parents are ever with you, so
> May this journey of your life be ever so blessed."
> *[Translated from an Urdu poem]*

THE SECOND PRINCIPLE

Acquaint yourself with asking forgiveness. Accept responsibility for your actions, admit your faults and add that you will do your best never to repeat what you did wrong. Remember that a couple are both mature and sane adults who will be living with each other for 365 days a year, 24 hours a day. Disputes and disagreements are therefore bound to happen.

Many stages of life will pass when there will be happiness as well as joy, illness as well as good health, hope as well as despondency. There may be times when the couple will have to contend with their children having problems at school or coming home with pains and injuries due to either their own negligence or negligence on the part of the school staff. There may be times when the husband may become unemployed or his business may suffer a loss. There may also be times when the food may burn or may not be according to taste. In addition to all of this, there may be problems with in-laws or with one's temperamental husband. The solution to all of these problems is fear for Allah Ta'ala, commonly referred to as Taqwa.

When a couple are imbued with the quality of Taqwa, they will be cautious not to hurt each other's feelings. They will be apprehensive of standing before Allah Ta'ala on the Day of Judgement because they will have to answer for every deed they carried out and for every word they spoke. If the couple are pious and imbued with Taqwa, they will be united and will brave rough waters side-by-side. However, if any disputes arise, the wife should always remember that she should seek pardon and assure her husband that she would not repeat herself. Instead of proving her innocence during the heat of the moment and prolonging the argument, she should concede that the fault was hers and that she will not repeat what she had done or said.

The act of seeking forgiveness is so effective that it even melted the heart of the notorious Hajjaj bin Yusuf. While on a journey, Hajjaj once passed by a villager and asked him what he thought about his governor. The villager complained about the governor and said that he was a tyrant. Hajjaj then asked him, "Do you know who I am?" When the villager declared that he did not know, Hajjaaj said that he was the governor Hajjaj. The villager the asked, "Do you know who I am?" When Hajjaj declared that he did not know, the villager said,"I am a slave and I become insane for three days every month. Today happens to be the first of the three days so please forgive me." Hajjaj laughed and let the man go free.

There are so many little squabbles between husband and wife which eventually lead to grave consequences. All of these can be avoided if the wife takes the initiative to apologise and seek forgiveness. If every woman takes a lesson from the villager in the above story, many problems will be solved. By calling himself a madman and seeking pardon, he managed to save himself from grievous harm. Similarly, if the wife has to admit that the fault is hers and that she would never repeat her mistake, she would also be saving herself from great harm. Every person is prone to err. However, the punishment of the criminal who confesses is lighter than that of the criminal who is found guilty after insisting that he is innocent.

"Why did you do that!" "How did it happen while you were standing there watching?" "You and your family are all the same!" "How did the food burn? Were you not checking on it?" "How could you speak to my mother like that!" "My sister came here and you could not even greet her properly!" "I did you a favour by marrying you. Otherwise no one would have taken you!"

These are but a few examples of what many uncaring men tell their wives. However, the reply of an intelligent wife to all of these and thousands of other allegations is simply to say, "Sorry, I made a mistake. Please forgive me. I shall not do it again." Once she says this, a threatening inferno will be reduced to nothing. This is the standard answer to every situation and it will disarm Shaytaan completely. Only a foolish wife will contest what her husband says by counter questioning him and denying everything she did. Instead of excusing herself by saying "Sorry, I made a mistake. Please forgive me", she will tell him that he raves on about nothing or that he should do the work himself. The argument then develops into a raging war, often ending in divorce. May Allah Ta'ala save all Muslim couples from such disputes. *Aameen.*

An Excellent Method of Softening One's Husband

Here is an excellent elixir that will save women from many a difficulty. It will turn a tyrannical husband into a lamb, a foolish husband into a sensible human being and an irreligious husband into a pious man. The formula for this is that whenever there is an altercation between your husband and yourself, never immediately try to justify what has happened. Even if the fault is his, admit that it was yours and ask for forgiveness. This will save you from the consequences of his anger and will allow him to cool down. When his temper has subsided, speak to him nicely and explain to him that it is wrong for him to continuously scold you without verifying the matter. Then clarify the contentious matter with him. He will then feel ashamed of himself and will always think before doing or saying anything in future.

Admitting one's fault and seeking forgiveness can soften the hardest hearts and extinguish the severest flames of wrath and fury. It can also turn an arch enemy into a bosom friend. In the words of the Creator of man,

﴿ وَلَا تَسْتَوِي الْحَسَنَةُ وَلَا السَّيِّئَةُ ادْفَعْ بِالَّتِي هِيَ أَحْسَنُ فَإِذَا الَّذِي بَيْنَكَ وَبَيْنَهُ عَدَاوَةٌ كَأَنَّهُ وَلِيٌّ حَمِيمٌ ﴾ (فصلت: ٣٤)

"Good and evil cannot be equal. Resist with that which is best, and the one between yourself and whom there was enmity will instantly become like your bosom friend." [Surah HaaMeem Sajdah (Surah 41), verse 34]

When one fights evil with good such as replying to someone's swearing by using sweet words, the person will soften. In fact, a wise man once claimed that if one eats something sweet when in anger, one will begin saying sweet words. Try this for yourself and see the results. When a woman regards her husband to be her pride and honour, her leader, her means of entering Jannah and her true friend, his little hut will be like a palace for her. Even though she may not be able to have the best of foods, clothing and furniture, she will count her home as being among the dwellings of Jannah. In the words of Sheikh Saadi, "A good and obedient wife can turn a pauper into a prince." If a man gets a good wife who is also pretty, he will be extremely fortunate. However, if she is only beautiful without a good character and without piety, she will be a bane for him instead. May Allah Ta'ala save all Muslim men fom such women. *Aameen*.

A MIRACLE CURE

Moulana Ashraf Ali Thanwi (May Allah be Merciful on him/her) has reported the incident of a woman whose tongue was extremely malicious. Because of her insolence, her husband often hit her. However, her tongue could not be silenced even while hitting her. Annoyed and frustrated with all the hiding, she eventually approached a saint for advice. She requested him to give her a Ta'weez (an amulet) that would tame her husband and make him subservient to her and to make him love her. The saint somehow realised that she was being beaten because of her malicious tongue. He therefore asked her to bring him some water so that he could recite something and blow into the water. When she did this, he told her that whenever her husband was angry, she should take a handful of the water into her mouth and sit down. If she did this, he said, her husband would stop hitting her.

When she started doing this every time her husband became angry, she was too occupied to tell him anything and he gradually became angry less often until he finally stopped getting angry with her. Allah Ta'ala has granted women the ability to do get away with many things by merely speaking sweetly with their husbands. When a woman kindly asks her husband to forgive her, he has no option but to forgive. It is probably for this reason that the evidence of only women in many court proceedings is not accepted. By shedding a few tears, a woman can turn the heart of a judge into wax and easily have judgement passed in her favour. Even the brothers of Yusuf (May Allah be Merciful on him/her) used their tears to convince their father of their innocence.

A malicious tongue is a common disease among women and stems from pride. They continue arguing their case so that they never have to bow their head in submission. May Allah Ta'ala grant all women the ability to admit their faults and ask for forgiveness. May Allah Ta'alaalso grant all men the ability to run their homes efficiently and the ability to resolve disputes amicably after hearing all sides. *Aameen.*

A WOMAN'S ABILITY TO TAME A MAN

A story is narrated about a woman who was constantly at loggerheads with her husband. She was concerned about the fact that not a day would pass without an argument between the two. A friend of hers advised her to consult a certain renowned *Hakeem* (practitioner in alternative medicine) in the area. When she consulted the learned man, she expressed her concern that the problem between her and her husband may be the result of black magic or an evil spirit. She said to him that her husband constantly became angry with her at the slightest provocation, after which she would also fly into a towering rage, making the situation worse. The Hakeem told her that he would be able to cure her quite easily on condition that she brought him three hairs from a lion's nape.

Leaving his premises, she immediately started formulating a plan to acquire the hairs from a lion. Taking a piece of meat, she proceeded to the local zoo. She threw the meat to the lion that readily ate it up. She then made it a ritual to take a piece of meat to the lion each day at the same time so that the lion would become familiar with her. Each day she threw the meat closer to the bars of the cage so the lion came closer to her. Eventually, the lion became so comfortable with her that was able to stroke it on its neck as it ate the meat. When this situation prevailed, she seized the opportunity to quickly pluck three hairs from its nape.

When the Hakeem learned how she was able to get the hairs from the lion, he smote his forehead and said, "Alas! You managed to tame a lion and get it eating from your hand. You can then very well win your husband over because he is definitely not as wild as a lion. Just as you were able to tame the lion by feeding it regularly, you can certainly win your husband's confidence in some way. Take care of him and you will soon have him eating from your hand. This will solve all your problems."

The woman happily left the Hakeem with a resolution that she would do her utmost to please her husband.

If every Muslim wife abstains from backchat and admits her mistakes without trying to justify them, she will soon win the confidence of her husband and her in-laws. This approach will be even more effective if she accepts responsibility for wrongs that she did not do.

WOMEN CANNOT BE EQUAL TO MEN

Moulana Ashraf Ali Thanwi (May Allah be Merciful on him/her) explains that distinction between man and woman is so irreconcilable that Messenger of Allah (Peace be upon him) said, "If I were to command anyone to prostrate before a being besides Allah, Ta'ala would have commanded women to prostrate before their husbands." *[Tirmidhi Vol. 1 Pg. 219]*

This hadith makes it clear that the position of a husband in the Shari'ah is so great that his wife ought to prostrate before him if this were permissible. Women should bear in mind that they should never become angry with their husbands because one may become angry only with those people who are inferior than or equal to oneself. Becoming angry with one's husband and justifying one's wrongs are wrongs themselves. There is a common adage in Urdu which states that making excuses for one's wrongs is worse than the wrong itself. If a woman truly believes that she is subservient to her husband, she will find it impossible to become angry with him irrespective of how angry he makes her.

Every wife should therefore accept her status and realise that Allah Ta'ala has made men the leaders of women and they should therefore remain silent when their husbands are angry. Women should purge their minds of the misconception that they are superior to or equal to men. It is only when the husband's anger has subsided that she may tell him, "I had admitted that I was wrong that time. I now wish to explain why you were wrong on that account. Because you did not give me the chance to clarify the situation and because you did not enquire about the facts, you unnecessarily became angry with me." When the affair is clarified in an amicable manner like this, it will be easily resolved and the husband's confidence in his wife will keep growing. *["Tuhfa Zowjayn" Pg. 51]*

AN EFFECTIVE MANNER OF CREATING LOVE IN YOUR HUSBAND'S HEART

When your husband returns home in the evenings or when he returns from a journey, spare some time to welcome him and to be with him irrespective of the work you still have pending. It should never occur that you are so indifferent towards him that you have no idea when he arrives and when he leaves. Remember that a friendly greeting, a smiling face and a caring attitude are more effective in sweetening the mouth and heart of a husband than all the sweets, chocolates and sweetmeats of the world. It is therefore noticed that sweets and chocolates are used more in homes that are without the sweet tongue of a good wife and without her sweet attitude to alter the bitterness of worries and grief.

WHEN ALLAH TA'ALA LOOKS AT A COUPLE WITH LOVE AND MERCY

In his book "Showhar ke Huqooq", Mufti Taqi usmani (May Allah be Merciful on him/her) quotes a hadith that he has not personally read in any compilation of Ahadeeth, but which he read in the advices of Moulana Ashraf Ali Thanwi (May Allah be Merciful on him/her) and which Moulana Ashraf Ali Thanwi (May Allah be Merciful on him/her) has quoted in several books. The hadith states that when a man arrives home and looks at his wife with love and she in turn looks at him with love, Allah Ta'ala looks at the two of them with mercy. A loving relationship between husband and wife therefore benefits the couple in the Aakhirah just as it does in this world.

Every wife should therefore do everything to please her husband and should realise that the success of her life in this world as well as in the Hereafter depends on how she treats her husband. Unfortunate indeed is the wife who does not care to meet her tired husband at the door. In fact, a wife ought to do everything that pleases her husband before he can even ask her for it. Even if it means giving him a glass of plain water, when this is done with love and concern, the gesture would even melt a heart of stone. Although the glass of water may not have any vitamin supplement or tonic, it will provide every type of vitamin to his exhausted body. Try it and see.

If a wife realises her value in society, she will come to know that she performs the vital function of injecting life and vigour into her husband, thereby adding vitality to the entire society. When your husband returns home, do not immediately begin relating the problems of the day. Allow him time to first rest, to regain his composure and to complete any necessities he may need to attend to first. Thereafter, you may tell him whatever is necessary without adding the things that are not absolutely necessary. Present a rose to him when greeting him because the scent will raise his spirits. Get he children washed and dressed before he arrives and teach them the proper etiquette of greeting. When your husband returns, he will find their sweet voices more relieving than any pain-killing medication on the market.

If only women would learn all of this, dress presentably when their husbands arrive home and wash off their fatigue with the soap of a gleaming smile. By recalling the immense rewards that a mother will receive when tolerating the crying and disturbances of the children and the irritation presented by others, one will be able to overcome every difficulty. In addition to this, one's husband will behave more compassionately towards one and will sympathise with your pains and problems. Decorate your tablecloth with the best of whatever your husband can afford and have the food ready on time. When this is done diligently, even the most ordinary food will be a sumptuous meal for him. If the food is delayed for some reason, request him to excuse you for the inconvenience.

A SMILE REVIVES THE HEART

A smile opens the doors of the soul. Because the soul affects the mind and the mind affects the heart, a mere smile will instantly rejuvenate a strained heart. A beautiful wife is not necessarily one who has attractive physical features. A beautiful wife is one who brings happiness to her husband's heart. Seeing a smiling face automatically prompts one to smile. A person who is always smiling attracts others and they enjoy being with such a person. On the contrary, no one enjoys being with a person whose face is always sour and whose constant frowning has caused deep creases on his/her forehead. People avoid such persons and they tend to dampen the spirits of others as well.

A French writer has mentioned that the heart is made most happy when a happy and smiling person is with one. The saying has been quoted from a book dating more than 1800 years. It reads: "Hapiness in the heart is as beneficial as any excellent medicine." A certain Doctor Hugh Lang has written that smiling and laughing is an excellent exercise which also aids in digestion. A Doctor Marshall said, "If you are an intelligent person, you will smile often." Another prominent doctor has mentioned that the most destructive day of one's life is the day in which one did not smile.

It is therefore extremely necessary for every wife to do her best wear a smiling face whenever she meets her husband. She should also teach her children the importance of this. The husband and children should also ensure that they wear a smiling face when entering the home. Every member of the family should bear in mind that a smiling face places smiles on others. An effective manner of creating love between husband and wife is to keep smiling to each other and to refrain from speaking about things that make one unhappy. A smiling face is truly a great bounty of Allah Ta'ala.

A Pious Lady called Umm-e-Sulaym (May Allah be pleased with him/her)

Umm-e-Sulaym (May Allah be pleased with him/her) was one of those fortunate women of the Sahabiyaat about whom Messenger of Allah (Peace be upon him) said that they would enter Jannah. Her real name was Rumaysa. Jaabir rnarrates that Rasulullahssaid, "I saw myself walking in the gardens of Jannah when I suddenly beheld Abu Talha's wife Rumaysa." There are several incidents in her life that make her one of the most distinguished Sahabiyaat (May Allah be pleased with him/her). Haafidh Abu Nu'aym Isfahaani (A.R) has narrated several incidents about her in his book "Hilyatul Awliya" (Vol. 2 Pgs. 57-61). The following are a few of these incidents with some explanatory notes.

AS A PREACHER

Umm-e-Sulaym (May Allah be pleased with him/her) had received a marriage proposal from Abu Talha (May Allah be pleased with him/her) before he accepted Islam. She said to him, "Abu Talha, do you realise that you are worshipping a tree that grows from the ground and that an Abyssinian man from a certain tribe had placed it where it is?" When he admitted that he did realise this, she said, "Are you not ashamed at worshipping a tree. I would not have declined your proposal if I had not already accepted Islam. However, if you accept Islam, I shall not ask you for a dowry to marry me." Abu Talha t said, "But my accepting Islam is not sufficient dowry for a woman like yourself." "What do you consider as sufficient dowry?" "Gold and silver," he replied. She said, "I have no need for gold and silver. All I need is for you to accept Islam."

Abu Talha (May Allah be pleased with him/her) then left to meet Messenger of Allah. Messenger of Allah (Peace be upon him) was in the company of some other Companion of the Prophet when he noticed Abu Talha (May Allah be pleased with him/her) approach. Messenger of Allah (Peace be upon him) said to them, "I see the light of Islam shining between the eyes of Abu Talha." Abu Talha (May Allah be pleased with him/her) accepted Islam and married Umm-e-Sulaym (May Allah be pleased with him/her).

AS A WARRIOR

Anas (May Allah be pleased with him/her) narrates that during the Battle of Uhud he saw Aa'isha (May Allah be pleased with him/her) and Umm-e-Sulaym (May Allah be pleased with him/her) carrying filled water bags on their backs to the MujaahiReligion on the battlefield. Whenever the water finished, they would return to refill it. The laws of Hijaab were not yet revealed at that time.

During the Battle of Hunayn, Abu Talha (May Allah be pleased with him/her) saw Umm-e-Sulaym (May Allah be pleased with him/her) standing with a dagger in her hand. When he asked her what the matter was, she replied, "I am holding this dagger because I intend to plunge it into the belly of any Kaafir who comes close to me." When Abu Talha (May Allah be pleased with him/her) related this to Messenger of Allah, Messenger of Allah (Peace be upon him) appreciated her spirit and he told Umm-e-Sulaym (May Allah be pleased with him/her) that she would not need the dagger because Allah Ta'ala was sufficient for her.

AS A PILLAR OF FORTITUDE AND WISDOM

A child of Abu Talha (May Allah be pleased with him/her) was very ill when he left home to tend to his affairs. While he was away, the child passed away. Ummu Sulaym (May Allah be pleased with him/her) wrapped the child in a sheet, left him in the room where he passed away and began preparing food for her husband. Because Abu Talha (May Allah be pleased with him/her) was fasting that day, she did not want to upset him by revealing the news to him immediately. When he arrived, he asked about the child and proceeded to the room to see him. Ummu Sulaym

(May Allah be pleased with him/her) told him that the child was at peace and that there was no need to see him. Satisfied that his child was well, Abu Talha (May Allah be pleased with him/her) did not enter the room.

He then ate comfortably and Ummu Sulaym (May Allah be pleased with him/her) gave no hint to darken his spirits. The couple spent the night as any happy couple would. When the two awoke for the Tahajjud salah, she said to him, "The people of a certain tribe are strange. Another tribe lent them something but they refuse to part with it, thinking that it belongs to them. When asked to return the thing they borrowed, they now become angry instead of returning it." Abu Talha (May Allah be pleased with him/her) said, "Their behaviour is very bad and extremely unjust." Ummu Sulaym (May Allah be pleased with him/her) then told her husband, "Allah Ta'ala has loaned you your child and has now asked for him back. Allah Ta'ala is his Master and all we can do is to exercise patience."

يا أبا طلحة بارك اللّه لكما في ليلتكما

Shocked at his wife's behaviour, Abu Talha (May Allah be pleased with him/her) complained to Messenger of Allah. Commending the behaviour of Ummu Sulaym (May Allah be pleased with him/her), Messenger of Allah (Peace be upon him) prayed, "O Abu Talha! May Allah Ta'ala bless your night." As a result of this du'aa, a son called Abdullah was born to the couple as a result of their night's relationship. This son Abdullah had nine sons all of whom were learned scholars of the Quran.

MESSENGER OF ALLAH'S CONCERN FOR HER

Anas (May Allah be pleased with him/her) [who was the son of Ummu Sulaym (May Allah be pleased with him/her)] narrates that besides the homes of his wives, the only home in Madinah that Messenger of Allah (Peace be upon him) frequented was the home of Ummu Sulaym (May Allah be pleased with him/her). When someone asked Messenger of Allah (Peace be upon him) for the reason, he replied, "I feel sorry for her because her brother was killed before my eyes."

Anas (May Allah be pleased with him/her) also narrates that Messenger of Allah (Peace be upon him) was sleeping at their house one afternoon. Because of the heat, his body began to perspire excessively. Being a Mahram to Messenger of Allah, Ummu Sulaym (May Allah be pleased with him/her) began collecting the perspiration in a piece of glass. Messenger of Allah (Peace be upon him) awoke when he felt her doing this. When he asked her what she was doing, she replied that she was collecting his perspiration to add to her perfumes because his perspiration was more fragrant than perfumes.

HER SACRIFICES FOR THE PROPAGATION OF RELIGION AND THE GLAD TIDINGS OF MESSENGER OF ALLAH

When Ummu Sulaym (May Allah be pleased with him/her) fell pregnant after the du'aa of Messenger of Allah (Peace be upon him) and was in the final stages of pregnancy,

بارك اللّٰه لكما في ليلتكما

Her husband Abu Talha (May Allah be pleased with him/her) was preparing to leave on a Jihaad expedition. She insisted that she would accompany the expedition so that she should not be deprived of the honour of accompanying a Jihaad expedition led by Messenger of Allah (Peace be upon him) Because the journey was going to be a tedious one, which would prove difficult for a pregnant woman Abu Talha (May Allah be pleased with him/her) sought permission from Messenger of Allah (Peace be upon him) for her to accompany them. She therefore accompanied the expedition.

She was also with the Muslim army when the Muslims conquered Makkah as well as when the marched to Hunayn. Here were occasions when even healthy men would be reluctant to participate. However, Ummu Sulaym's (May Allah be pleased with him/her) fervour to serve Religion was so great that she even participated when she was in a weakened condition of the final stages of her pregnancy. Determined to purify Allah Ta'ala's earth from the filth of kufr, she marched with the Muslim army. Allah Ta'ala made the Muslims victorious and she returned with them to Madinah. On the last leg of the journey, before entering Madinah, she began experiencing labour pains.

Anxious that they should not lag behind the rest and not enter Madinah with Messenger of Allah, Abu Talha (May Allah be pleased with him/her) made the following du'aa:

أنك تعلم يا رب أنه يعجبنى أن أخرج مع رسولك إذا خرج وأدخل معه

إذا دخل، وقد أحتبست بما ترى

"O my Rabb! You know well that I love to leave Mad- inah with Messenger of Allah (Peace be upon him) and that I love to enter Madinah with Messenger of Allah. I am now delayed by that matter that You see."Allah Ta'ala always responds to the du'as of His beloved who are prepared to sacrifice everything for Him."

As soon as he completed his du'aa, Ummu Sulaym (May Allah be pleased with him/her) told

يا أبا طلحة، ما أجد الذي كنت أجد أنطلق

Him that the labour pains had vanished and that they may proceed with the rest. The pains returned once they reached Madinah and she delivered a bouncing baby boy.

يا أنس! لا يرضعه أحد حتى تغدو به على رسول الله

As soon as the child was born, she called for her son Anas (May Allah be pleased with him/her) and sent the baby with him to Messenger of Allah (Peace be upon him) saying that none should feed the child until the child was taken to Messenger of Allah.

When Anas (May Allah be pleased with him/her) brought the child, Messenger of Allah (Peace be upon him) said,

لعل أم سليم ولدت

"It seems as if Umm-e-Sulaym (May Allah be pleased with him/her) has delivered."

When Anas (May Allah be pleased with him/her) confirmed this, Messenger of Allah (Peace be upon him) asked for an Ajwa date, chewed it until it was soft and placed a part of it into the baby's mouth. When the baby gleefully sucked the date, Messenger of Allah (Peace be upon him)

said, "Just look at the love that the Ansaar have for dates." Messenger of Allah (Peace be upon him) then passed his hand over the baby's face and named him Abdullah.

Because of her sacrifices for Deen, Allah Ta'ala had accorded her a position in Jannah. Messenger of Allah (Peace be upon him) once mentioned that he had heard footsteps in Jannah. When he asked the angels whose footsteps they were, he was informed that these were the footsteps of Umm-e-Sulaym (May Allah be pleased with him/her) the mother of Anas (May Allah be pleased with him/her). *[Muslim Vol. 2 Pg. 292]*

After reading these incidents, we should make this du'aa to Allah Ta'ala: "O Allah Ta'ala! Allow me to make sacrifices for Your Religion alongside my husband and allow me to be of assistance to him in the effort of Religion throughout the world just as You accepted Umm-e-Sulaym (May Allah be pleased with him/her) to participate in the expeditions of Jihaad, in the conquest of Makkah and the Battle of Hunayn. Guide us, assist us, grant us understanding and accept us for the propagation of Your Religion just as You accepted the Sahabiyaat (May Allah be pleased with him/her) for the same. Remove the love of the world from our hearts together with the desire of amassing the commodities of the world. Replace these inclinations with the love for You, the love for Your Religion and the love to see You. Turn our days into an effort to propagate the Religion to the Kuffaar of the world and effort to make the Muslims of the world proper practising Muslims. Also turn our nights into an effort of weeping before You and begging from You. I am making this du'aa for myself as well as for all Muslim men and women throughout the world. Use me as a vehicle for the guidance of every person on earth. *Aameen*."

'Commenting on the hadith which mentions the death of Umm-e-Sulaym's (May Allah be pleased with him/her) child, Moulana Muhammad Zakariyya (May Allah be Merciful on him/her) writes, "It took great patience and courage to endure the death of her child in a manner that her husband knew nothing about it. Because her husband was fasting, she feared that it would become difficult for him to eat if he learned about the child's death."

Every woman should learn a lesson from this incident. It is inappropriate to begin recounting every problem in detail as soon as one's husband steps through the door. Such an approach will have an adverse effect on any man's psychological well-being. The incident clearly highlights that extent to which the Sahabiyyat (May Allah be pleased with him/her) understood human psychology. Whereas people in today's times claim that they have mastered psychology, their practical lives indicate that they are children in the field when compared with the Companion of the Prophet y. When a husband enters the home, the burden of the day's problems should not be immediately dumped on his shoulders that are already sagging beneath the pressures of his occupation.

One should strictly abstain from telling one's husband about anything that would cause him to harbour ill-feelings towards another person. Always remember that if you create ill-feelings between him and his mother or sisters, the day will soon dawn when your beloved son's wife or your beloved brother's wife will cause a rift between you and your son or brother. This is the way in which fate takes its course. It should not be that you ever have to say: "As a daughter-in-law, I could not find a good mother-in-law. Now as a mother-in-law, I cannot find a good daughter-in-law."

If a daughter-in-law adopts the life of people like Khadeja (May Allah be pleased with him/her), Fatima (May Allah be pleased with him/her) and other pious women, Insha Allah Ta'ala she will not have to suffer the trouble of a difficult daughter-in-law. She should learn to be tolerant, loving and able to use flowers to repel thorns.

Another important principle that a Muslim wife should never forget is that she must not burden her husband with the day's problems as soon as he walks into the house because he could be even more stressed than her. A wife should first ask him about his day. If her husband is shocked because he has just narrowly escaped an accident or if he has just had some terrible experience, it will not only be inconsiderate for her to burden him with her problems, but it will be absolutely cruel. Therefore, if she needs to tell him something, she should tell him only after she is certain that he is composed and willing to listen. May Allah Ta'ala grant this understanding to all Muslim men and women. *Aameen*.

WOMEN WERE ALSO MUFTEES

An eminent scholar by the name of Imaam Abu Bakr bin Mas'ood Kaasani (May Allah be Merciful on him/her) has written a renowned masterpiece called "Badaai'us Sanaa'i", which is a commentary of his teacher's book titled "Tuhfatul Fuqaha". According to Allaama Shaami l, "Bada-ai'usSanaa'i" is a masterpiece that cannot be matched by any other book of Fiqh (Islamic jurisprudence). When he presented this book to his teacher Sheikh Ala'ud Religion Samarqandi (May Allah be Merciful on him/her) the Sheikh was so happy that he gave his daughter Fatima's hand over in marriage to Imaam Abu Bakr Kaasaani (May Allah be Merciful on him/her) By then she had already received many proposals from several kings and princes.

The lady was extremely well versed in Fiqh and had mastered the subject to thc extent that she was authorised to issue Fatwas. Therefore, the situation was not uncommon that when someone required a Fatwa, part of the Fatwa was written by her, a part by her father and another part by her husband.

FIVE QUALITIES OF A PIOUS WIFE

The mentor and guide of mankind Messenger of Allah (Peace be upon him) has condensed the qualities of a pious wife into four sentences in one hadith. Another hadith has mentioned a fifth quality. Before reading what these five qualities are, one should make an intention that one will do one's best to practise these qualities. At the same time, one should also make du'aa that Allah Ta'ala should grant oneself as well as all other Muslim women the ability to do this.

إن أمرها طاعته ونظر إليها سرته وأن أقسم عليها أبرت، وأن غاب عنها

نصحته فى نفسها وماله (ابن ماجه)

Messenger of Allah (Peace be upon him) said that a pious wife

"obeys her husband when he instructs her, she pleases him when he looks at her, she fulfils his oath when he swears an oath (that she should do something within the bounds of Shari'ah) and when he is out, she safeguards her chastity and his wealth."

THE FIRST QUALITY

The most important quality of a good wife is that she obeys every instruction of her husband that does not violate the commands of Allah Ta'ala. It is of course not permissible for a wife to obey any instruction that is against the

Shari'ah, such as attending mixed gatherings and going to places of sin. When a wife obeys all her husband's lawful instructions for the pleasure of Allah Ta'ala, she will win his love and trust. He will become her best friend and will do anything for her. Needless to say, this will happen only when the wife does everything to obey him. She should be prepared to sacrifice her rest and pleasures for him and always remember that any humiliation suffered in serving one's husband is actually an honour. When a bride adopts this attitude and remains steadfast, she will soon win over her husband's affection. The couple will then be like two hearts in one soul or like two minds in one body, doing everything together as a united body. They will plan and think as one person and work together to dispel any difficulty.

Whenever a wife senses grief in her husband's face, she should immediately share his feelings and sympathise with him. When he is happy, she should also share his happiness and not do anything to spoil it.

Abu Darda (May Allah be pleased with him/her) Advises his Wife

With great love and affection, Abu Darda (May Allah be pleased with him/her) once said to his wife, "When you see me angry, (affectionately) make me understand and I shall do the same when I see you angry. If we do not do this, we can never make any progress together."

A wife should wear what her husband wants her to wear, cook as he wants her to cook and do everything as he instructs on condition that his instructions do not violate the injunctions of the Shari'ah.

Every new bride should understand that things are going to be different after marriage. Before marriage, her sleep was sleep without worries, as were her moments of eating, drinking and playing. Her life after marriage will be one of responsibilities, a life in which she will be living under a new government. It is for this reason that the first lesson that girls of good upbringing receive when they marry is the lesson of being obedient. She is taught to sacrifice her own pleasures for the pleasure of her husband and to do everything as he wants it done. Married life, though enjoyable, has its own set of rules and restrictions. Whereas life was lived for oneself before marriage, life after marriage is lived for others. After marriage, a woman's dressing will not be for her, her sleeping will not be when she wants and she will not be waking up when she wants. Everything will be subject to the needs of her husband.

A bride should therefore proceed step-by-step into her new life, acclimatising to the changes as they occur. She will have to curb her desires as she goes along and she may have to eat after others have eaten, placing herself last. Her dressing and beautification will have to be to please her husband and when she has children, they will also demand her attention. As a result, she will again have to give precedence to their needs over her own because she will be directly responsible for the upbringing of this new generation.

Every wife should therefore not forget that the first requirement of a good wife in the words of Messenger of Allah (Peace be upon him) that she obeys her husband. Although the feat is not an easy one, she should remember that the rewards are tremendous. Umm-e-Sulayam (May Allah be pleased with him/her) narrates that she heard Messenger of Allah (Peace be upon him) say, "The woman who passes every stage of her life and finally reaches the final stage while her husband is pleased with her, she will surely enter Jannah. It is as if there is no barrier between Jannah and her. " The wife who keeps her husband happy and is always concerned about his feelings will therefore attain the ultimate goal of every person.

عن عائشة رضي الله عنها أن رسول الله ﷺ قال لوأمرت أحدًا أن يسجد لأحد لأمرت المرأة أن تسجد لزوجها ولو أن رجلا أمرا إمرأته أن تنقل من جبل أحمر إلى جبل أسود، ومن جبل أسود إلى جبل أحمر لكان حق لها أن تفعل (ابن ماجه ص ١٣٣ مطبوعه قديمی کتب خانه)

In fact, every Muslim woman understands that the Shari'ah has made it obligatory for her to obey the commands of her husband because of the great honour that Allah Ta'ala has granted the husband. The hadith has already been quoted in which Messenger of Allah (Peace be upon him) says, "If I were to command anyone to prostrate to another, I would have commanded wives to prostrate to their husbands. If a husband commands his wife to move a rock from a red mountain to a black mountain and then from the black mountain back to the red mountain, she is obliged to do as he says." *[Ibn-e-Majah Pg. 133]*

UNITING TWO HEARTS

Allah Ta'ala has appointed men as leaders of women in the couple's journey through life. Every post of leadership in this world is temporary. A leader today is soon an ordinary citizen. On the converse, a prisoner today may well be president of his country tomorrow. However, the leadership that Allah Ta'ala has granted a husband will last as long as he is married, which is often as long as he lives. In addition to this, his relationship with his wife is an intimate relationship by which their hearts are united, much unlike political leadership which is merely official. Because the husband remains her leader throughout the wife's life Messenger of Allah (Peace be upon him) has emphasised his position by stating that she would be commanded to prostrate before him if this was permissible for anyone besides Allah Ta'ala.

The worst difficulties of this world are temporary. Keep the final stages of your life in mind together with the bounties that Allah Ta'ala shall bestow on you for being an obedient wife. In this manner, every thorn will seem like a rose and nothing will be too difficult. Never make your husband angry and you will have no worries when Allah Ta'ala asks you on the Day of Judgement whether you had fulfilled the rights of your husband. You will be able to say that by pleasing your husband you sought Allah Ta'ala's pleasure, which you will have on that day.

May Allah Ta'ala make you the ruler of your husband's heart and include you in the ranks of people like Fatima (May Allah be pleased with him/her) who shall be the leader of the women in Jannah and in the ranks of people like Ayesha (May Allah be pleased with him/her) in whose lap Allah Ta'ala's beloved Prophet (Peace be upon him) passed away despite the presence of thousands of Companion of the Prophet y who would give their lives for him. *Aameen.*

THE JIHAAD OF WOMEN

Asma bint Yazeed Ansaa (May Allah be pleased with him/her) once said, "O Messenger of Allah (Peace be upon him) the other women have sent me to ask you something. Indeed Allah Ta'ala has sent you as a messenger to both men and women. We women have therefore believed in you and in Allah Ta'ala. However, we have to remain indoors, tend to our domestic chores, fulfil the desires of our husbands and bear their children. Despite all of this, men excel us in earning great rewards for things that we are unable to do. They perform their daily salah and Jumu'ah salah in the Masjid, they visit the ill, attend funerals, perform Hajj after Hajj and above all, they fight in Jihaad. When they go for Hajj, Umrah or Jihaad, we look after their property, raise their children and weave cloth for them. Do we not share their rewards?"

After hearing this question, Messenger of Allah (Peace be upon him) turned to the Companion of the Prophet y and said, "Did you ever hear a woman asking a better question?" "We never thought that a woman would ask such an excellent question," replied the Companion of the Prophet y.

Addressing Asma (May Allah be pleased with him/her), Messenger of Allah (Peace be upon him) then said, "Listen attentively and tell the ladies who have sent you that when a woman seeks the pleasure of her husband and carries out all her domestic chores to his satisfaction, she receives the same rewards that men receive for all their deeds." Asma (May Allah be pleased with him/her) returned very happily with this reply.

Obedience to and kind treatment of one's husband is an extremely great virtue which many wives are negligent in performing.

THE SECOND QUALITY

إن نظر إليها سرته

The second quality of a pious wife is that "she pleases him (her husband) when he looks at her".

Such a wife employs lawful means to look after her beauty and cleanliness so that she remains attractive for her husband. She also dresses lawfully in a manner that pleases him.

A GRAVE ERROR OF MANY WOMEN

Moulana Ashraf Ali Thanwi (May Allah be Merciful on him/her) has mentioned that it is indeed strange that many women look like street-sweepers and servants when at home with their husbands but dress up smartly when going out of the house. Is she dressing up only for others to see? She does not dress up for the husband for whose pleasure the clothes were made and for whom she made herself a bride, but she does this for others. She dresses shabbily before her husband and does not speak politely to him, yet she dresses exquisitely before others and speaks most sweetly with them. Others are therefore thrilled at the husband's expense. While

demanding her rights and maintenance from the husband, she spends the same to please others. Is this justice?
["At Tableegh wa Dawaa'ul Uyoob" Pg.91]

It is indeed improper for a woman to reserve her good clothes only for going out and to look shabby and untidy in the house with her husband. It is for this reason that Messenger of Allah (Peace be upon him) described a good wife as one who pleases her husband when he looks at her. If a wife takes pride in her appearance and beautifies herself, she will be the most beautiful woman to her husband.

THE THIRD QUALITY

The third quality of a pious wife that Messenger of Allah (Peace be upon him) described is that she fulfils her husband's oath when he swears an oath (that she should do something within the bounds of Shari'ah) e.g. he says on oath that she should visit his mother or that she should perform Tahajjud salah on a certain day. When this happens, she should do her best to ensure that she does exactly as he swore that she should. Of course, she should do this only when the act is permissible.

Such a situation usually arises because of the husband's love for his wife or because he takes pride in something she does. He will therefore take an oath that she does it so that he may see it happen or so that another may see it. It may also occur that he makes the wife take an oath that she will do as he says. When a wife has true feelings for her husband, she will do anything he wants her to do especially when an oath is involved.

RULING: According to the Shari'ah, it is normally not binding on someone to fulfil an oath that another person takes.

THE FOURTH QUALITY

Whenever the husband leaves the home for some reason (as most men do), it is the duty of the wife to safeguard her chastity and his wealth just as she would do when he is present with her. No honourable man would want his wife to be in the company of a non-Mahram man or that she should even make eye-contact with such a man. He wants his wife exclusively for himself.

When a woman marries, she becomes the focal point of his life and it is with her that he will satisfy himself and find solace. She holds this fundamental position in his life when he is with her as well as when he is not.

In addition to this, he also entrusts her with his wealth and possessions when he leaves the home. She should therefore safeguard his possessions when he is not at home. She should never waste his money or spend on others without his permission. Should she fail to take care of her chastity or his wealth, she will be guilty of breaching a trust. She should ask her husband for only those things without which some harm may come to them. Never should a wife insist that her husband buys her something merely because someone else has it. Irrespective of how attractive something may be, she should not ask for it if it is not necessary. By unnecessarily burdening the husband with such demands, she is guilty of extravagance as well as misappropriation of trust. Allah Ta'ala also describes a pious woman in the Quran when He says, "So the pious women are obedient and, in the absence of their husbands, are protective because of that which Allah Ta'ala has protected." *[Surah Nisaa (Surah 4), verse 34]*

المرأة راعية في بيت زوجها

Protecting her husband's home means that a woman should first ensure that she does not commit any sins. Thereafter, she should ensure that his wealth and other possessions do not fall into the wrong hands. In another hadith, Messenger of Allah (Peace be upon him) makes it clear that "a woman is a guardian over her husband's home." It is therefore clear that safeguarding her husband's wealth and possessions is not only a necessary quality of a good wife, but it is actually her duty.

A WIFE SHOULD BE GENUINELY CONCERNED ABOUT HER HUSBAND'S WEALTH

Moulana Ashraf Ali Thanwi (May Allah be Merciful on him/her) has mentioned in his advices that a wife's heart should pain when her husband's wealth is spent wastefully. It is her responsibility to be concerned about his wealth. She must never be liberal with his money or allow the servants to do as they please with it.

Whenever the desire creeps into one's heart to have something that another has, one should think about the following:

1. Death and the thought of what the less fortunate one has in this world, the less will one be accountable in the Hereafter. The more one has in one's home, the more will one have to account for.

2. The simplicity of the homes of Fatima (May Allah be pleased with him/her), Khadeja (May Allah be pleased with him/her), Zaynab (May Allah be pleased with him/her) and Ayesha (May Allah be pleased with him/her) The more one's home resembles the homes of these illustrious ladies, the closer will one be to them in the Hereafter.

By keeping these thoughts in one's mind, one will welcome death because the love for the material things of this world will not have permeated one's heart. Seeing the simplicity of one's home, others will also follow suit and the money saved can be invested for the Aakhirah.

We have not come into this world to amass wealth and possessions. We have come to carry out deeds that please Allah Ta'ala. The simpler we keep our homes; the more Allah Ta'ala shall love us. If we donate our excess ssessions to the poor, they will benefit tremendously while we will lose nothing. In fact, nearly every household has things in almost every room that are in excess of their needs.

LAVISH WEDDINGS

Women are inclined to waste a great deal of money in weddings. On such occasions, all matters are referred to women, almost as if men know nothing about spending. As a result of wastefulness on such occasions, many homes have been destroyed. Many people have remained indebted all their lives because of such lavish wedding ceremonies, causing them to age before their time.

HOSTING SIMPLE MARRIAGE CEREMONIES

If people really want blessings in their marriages and desire that the marriages should be filled with love and pious offspring, they should follow the advice of Messenger of Allah, who said, "The marriage with the most blessings is the one in which the least expenses are incurred."

خيرهن أيسرهن صدقاً .(ابن حبان حديث رقم ١٤٥٥)

Messenger of Allah (Peace be upon him) has also mentioned, "The best of women are those who ask for the least dowry." [Ibn Hibbaan]

من يمن المرأة أن تتيسر خطبتها وأن يتيسر صداقها وأن يتيسر صداقها

وأن يتيسر رحمها (كنز العمال ١٦: ٢٥٥٧٣ ك ٢:١٨١)

According to another hadith, Messenger of Allah (Peace be upon him) said, "The signs of a blessed woman is that her proposal comes soon, her dowry is small and her child is born soon." *[Kanzul Ummaal]*

One can well imagine that if the Shari'ah encourages the least expense for the dowry, which is a prerequisite of marriage, it will certainly encourage even less expenditure for the wedding ceremony and trousseau, which have no status at all in the Shari'ah.

Sufyan Thowri (May Allah be Merciful on him/her) has mentioned that when a bridegroom asks his bride what she brought with her, he is a thief. His wicked nature is indicated by the fact that instead of asking for mundane commodities from his in-laws, he should be grateful to them for giving him the light of their lives whom they painstakingly raised for so many years. By this token, it is also improper for a son-in-law to send a gift to his parents-in-law with the desire that they should also send him a gift.

Every woman will naturally say that she wants to incur the least expenses for her parents and will therefore not mind if her parents gave her little or even nothing when she marries. "However," she will concede, "I have no choice in the matter because my mother-in-law and sisters-in-law will ridicule me and people will look down on my family." It is the custom in many countries that the bridegroom's parents prepare a list of items that they want from the bride's parents. They even request what should be given to the bridegroom himself, what should be given to his father, to his mother and to each of his brothers and sisters. If this is not given in writing, it is made clear to the bride's parents in some other manner. This practice is unjust and violates the injunctions of the Shari'ah.

It is therefore imperative for every woman to bear in mind that she will soon be a sister-in-law or a mother-in-law when her brother or son marries. When the occasion arises, she should ensure that she or her mother do not impose on the parents of her son's or brother's in-laws. If her mother demands anything from her brother's in-laws, she should explain to her mother that the practice is unjust and that if she imposes on them, the time may come when her daughter's in-laws may impose on her. Favours should be sought only from Allah Ta'ala. Causing people unnecessary expenditure will invite Allah Ta'ala 's wrath.

THE FIFTH QUALITY

The Companion of the Prophet y once said to Messenger of Allah (Peace be upon him) that they would like to know what form of wealth is best to have. Messenger of Allah (Peace be upon him) replied,

أفضله لسان ذاكر وقلب شاكر وزوجة مؤمنة تعينه على إيمانه (ت ٣٠٩٢، ترغيب ٢: ١٩٨، ٣: ٢١)

"The best wealth is a tongue that engages in Dhikr, the heart that is grateful and a Mu'minah wife who assists her husband in his Imaan." ["At Targheeb wat Tarheeb" Vol. 2 Pg. 198 and Vol. 3 Pg. 41]

Wealth is generally referred to as something that is helpful to one and fulfils one's necessities. Whereas people generally regard money, businesses and property as wealth, Messenger of Allah (Peace be upon him) described three things as true wealth because of their immense benefits to man. Commenting on the above hadith, Mullaa Ali Qaari (May Allah forgive him) writes in his commentary of "Mishkaat" that a wife who assists her husband in his Imaan refers to a wife who is concerned about her husband's religiousness and reminds him when it is time to perform salah or fast, etc. In addition to this, she also ensures that he refrains from fornication and all other sins.

In our fast corrupting environment, we desperately need women who are concerned about the religiousness of their husbands and children. However, it is tragic to note that we are faced with a worsening situation because instead of encouraging their husbands to practise the injunctions of Deen, many women nowadays actually prevent their husbands from religious practices. Instead of encouraging them to be practical Muslims, such women tease their husbands and call them names because they wish to grow a beard or dress according to the Shari'ah.

The above hadith speaks about having a grateful heart. When a woman is blessed with such a heart, her life becomes one of contentment and happiness because she is grateful for whatever her husband provides. Ulama have therefore mentioned that when a wife is grateful for her lot, she will be blessed with a life that is almost free of arguments. In fact, religious thinkers maintain that ingratitude is the worst trait that anyone can possess. On the other hand, there can be no greater blessing than gratefulness. Allah Ta'ala asserts with great emphasis,

If you show"

﴿ لَئِنْ شَكَرْتُمْ لَأَزِيدَنَّكُمْ ﴾ (سورة ابراهيم ٧)

gratitude, then I will definitely give you more, and if you are ungrateful, then indeed My punishment is severe." [Surah Ibraheem (14), verse 7]

A FORMULA THAT WILL ELIMINATE DISPUTES BETWEEN COUPLES

Women should inculcate the quality of thankfulness within themselves so that they could be grateful for everything that their husbands provide. Even if their husbands can afford only simple foods, they should regard this as the most exquisite delicacy, bearing in mind that millions of people do not even have this privilege. Unfortunately, there are many women who are never satisfied with what they get. Whenever they are asked about their clothing, utensils, food, etc, they complain that they hardly have anything even though they have these things in excessive quantities.

A wife should express her gratitude for everything that her husband provides, irrespective of how little it is. When she views everything through the lenses of gratitude, she will see only the good in every item and no faults. A person once said that he cried for lack of shoes but when he saw someone without feet, he thanked Allah Ta'ala for blessing him with feet.

When a woman expresses her gratitude to her husband and to her in-laws, she will be expressing gratitude to Allah Ta'ala at the same time. One should accustom one's tongue to constantly say, "Al Hamdu Lillaah (all praises are for Allah). O AllahTa'ala thank You." When looking at every big and small item in the house, one should say, "Al Hamdu Lillaah. O Allah Ta'ala, I thank You." In fact, even when experiencing difficulty, one should say, "Al Hamdu Lillaah. O Allah Ta'ala, I thank You." For example, if one has a headache, one should think, "Al Hamdu Lillaah. O Allah Ta'ala, I thank You. At least my arms, my legs, my back, my stomach and the rest of my body are well." In this way, one's difficulties will also be alleviated. Always bear in mind that Allah Ta'ala promises to increase one's bounties when one is grateful. May Allah Ta'ala grant us all the ability to be grateful for everything. *Aameen.*

Messenger of Allah (Peace be upon him) once addressed a congregation of ladies and said to them that majority of the inmates of Jahannam were women. When they enquired about the reason, he said that this was on account of women being ungrateful to their husbands. This hadith makes it clear that showing ingratitude towards one's husband is a cause of landing a woman in Jahannam.

The wives of Messenger of Allah (Peace be upon him) are referred to as the mothers of the Mu'mineen and every Muslim is proud to be known as their children in Islam. Despite living lives of poverty and hardship, they never complained to Rasulullahs They neither had good clothing, exquisite jewellery, expensive furniture nor delicious food and never demanded these things even when the Muslims began conquering territories and wealth was streaming to Madinah.

After the demise of Messenger of Allah, Ayesha (May Allah be pleased with her) was once eating some food when she said, "Whenever I eat to my fill, I cannot help weeping." When one of her students asked the reason, she replied, "I recall the time when Messenger of Allah (Peace be upon him) departed from this world. By Allah Ta'ala! He never ate bread and meat to his fill twice in a day." Such was the life of the illustrious soul whom we claim to follow. Unlike us, he never regarded this world as his permanent abode. He understood that this world is a temporary place through which people pass as travellers.

The person who attaches herself to this world is like a foolish traveller who begins to furnish and decorate the waiting room of a platform while waiting for a train. Eventually, when the train (the angel of death) arrives and she has to leave the station, she begins to regret what she did. It will then be too late for one to make excuses and to say that one will no longer be extravagant and will no longer incur Allah Ta'ala's wrath by parading the streets in un-Islamic dress. When death comes to one, it will be too late for regrets. Therefore, one should not waste one's precious wealth on new curtains, expensive furniture and items for one's display units. Rather save the money to spend it for the propagation of Religion throughout the world. Give the money to your husband so that he can travel to spread Religion and also use it to support a needy relative or someone else who is poor. Endeavour to give charity in a manner that the left hand does not know what the right hand gives.

Ponder awhile about the home of the beloved wife of the most beloved creation r. All that she had in her room was a bed, a straw mat, bedding, a pillow stuffed with the bark of a date palm, one or two utensils to store dates and flour, a utensil for water and a cup to drink water with. She mentioned that months would go by without a lamp being lit in her room.

The Story of Prophet Isma'eel's (Peace be upon him) First Wife

We will presently relate the stories of two wives of Isma'eel (Peace be upon him), the son of Ibraheem (Peace be upon him). These two incidents make it clear that a grateful wife and an ungrateful wife cannot be compared. Whereas the first wife complained about poverty instead of being grateful for her lot, the second wife expressed thanks to Allah Ta'ala despite their poverty. As a result of her attitude, Ibraheem (Peace be upon him) made du'aa to Allah Ta'alato grant the couple blessings in their food and drink. As a result of this du'aa, the couple and their progeny (the Arabs) have enjoyed tremendous blessings. Gratitude therefore brought great blessings while ingratitude caused the first wife to lose her status as the wife of a Nabi u. This makes it clear that ingratitude was never tolerated in the pure homes of the Ambiya (Peace be upon him).

After Prophet Isma'eel (Peace be upon him) got married, his father Ibraheem (Peace be upon him) came to Makkah to visit him. Not finding his son at home, Ibraheem (Peace be upon him) asked his daughter-in-law where her husband was. Unable to recognise Ibraheem (Peace be upon him), she said that her husband Isma'eel (Peace be upon him) was out hunting. Ibraheem (Peace be upon him) then asked her about their condition. She complained to him that they were very poor and were experiencing great difficulty. After hearing her complaints, Ibraheem (Peace be upon him) told her to convey his regards to Isma'eel (Peace be upon him) and to tell him to change the threshold of his door.

When Isma'eel (Peace be upon him) returned, he asked his wife whether anyone had visited that day. She described Ibraheem (Peace be upon him), saying that he had come to look for Isma'eel (Peace be upon him). She also told him that the old man had asked about their condition, to which she replied that they were experiencing great difficulty. When Isma'eel (Peace be upon him) asked her if the man had left a message, she replied that he had instructed her to convey his regards to Isma'eel (Peace be upon him) and to tell him that he should change the threshold of his door. Isma'eel (Peace be upon him) then told his wife that the man was his father Ibraheem (Peace be upon him) and that the instruction meant that he should divorce her. The couple were subsequently divorced.

The Story of Isma'eel's (Peace be upon him) Second Wife

Isma'eel (Peace be upon him) later married another woman. When Ibraheem (Peace be upon him) visited the home after a long time, his son was out hunting again. Ibraheem (Peace be upon him) also asked this wife about their condition, to which she said that they were happy. When she offered him some food, he declined and asked her what they usually ate and drank. When she told him that they ate meat and drank water, he made du'aa to Allah Ta'ala to bless their food and drink. Relating the story to the Companion of the Prophet, Messenger of Allah (Peace be upon him) said that the blessings in food they saw was the result of this du'aa of Ibraheem (Peace be upon him) Ibraheem (Peace be upon him) then told his daughter-in-law to convey his regards to her husband and to tell him that he should keep the threshold of his door firmly in place.

When Isma'eel (Peace be upon him) returned, he asked his wife whether someone had visited them that day. She told him that an extremely kind and handsome old man had visited and enquired about their condition. She praised Ibraheem (Peace be upon him) and told her husband what reply she gave. When Isma'eel (Peace be upon him)asked her what message the man left, she told him that the man had left his regards and instructed that he should keep the threshold of his door firmly in place. Isma'eel (Peace be upon him) told her that the man was his father and that she was being referred to as the threshold. His father had instructed him to keep her in his marriage.

Although the second wife had meat only occasionally, she mentioned Allah Ta'ala's bounties to Ibraheem (Peace be upon him) without speaking about the many difficulties that came with it. Such an attitude was greatly appreciated by both husband and father-in-law. When a wife praises her parents-in-law as Isma'eel's (Peace be upon him) wife did, the husband is instantly impressed, his confidence in her is strengthened and he regards her as his own. If women could only understand this! When a daughter-in-law speaks only good of her in-laws, they will be very happy with her and even make du'aa for her and for her parents because they had raised her properly. They will feel that she has honoured them and is loyal to them. May Allah Ta'ala cast the shadow of Isma'eel's (Peace be upon him) grateful wife on the wives of the Ummah and grant them her excellent character. Aameen.

Every wife should therefore make an effort to express gratitude to Allah Ta'ala in every situation, favourable or not. One should constantly say,"

الحمد لله على كل حال

"(I praise Allah Ta'ala in every condition) Messenger of Allah (Peace be upon him) has mentioned that whoever does not thank people has not thanked Allah Ta'ala. One should therefore thank every person for the good they do to one."

The best method of thanking people is to tell them: (May Allah Ta'ala grant you the best reward). Mothers should also teach their children to say جزاك الله خيرًا whenever they are given something. Parents should also thank their children in this manner whenever their children do something for them.

Both Husband and Wife should Exercise Patience

Scholars throughout the ages are unanimous that Luqman (Peace be upon him) was an extremely wise man. In fact, some are of the opinion that he was a prophet. He was once working in an orchard when the owner of the orchard asked him to bring a cucumber. After peeling the cucumber, the owner sliced it and gave Luqman (Peace be upon him) slice by slice to eat. Luqman (Peace be upon him) ate every slice with relish. Seeing the enjoyment on Luqman (Peace be upon him)'s face the owner decided to eat the last slice himself. However, the taste was so bitter that he instantly spat it out.

"This tastes worse than poison, yet you were eating it with so much relish!" exclaimed the owner. "That's true," replied Luqman (Peace be upon him). "Why did you not tell me that it is so bitter?" queried the owner. "Why should I complain," replied Luqman (Peace be upon him)"when the same hand that always feeds me delicious food once gives me something bitter to eat?"

After relating this incident, Moulana Ashraf Ali Thanwi (May Allah be Merciful on him/her) comments that there will be no disputes between husband and wife if both remember the above rule. If the wife thinks that since her husband is always good to her, it matters little if he once behaves harshly towards her. At the same time, she should bear in mind that there are many times when he had to overlook things that she did. It is foolish to forget a lifetime of favours merely because of a single annoyance or scolding. Because of a single error on the husband's part, the wife should not blurt whatever she pleases by saying that she has only known hardship after marriage and would be better off dead. Such statements are unfortunately very common and should be avoided at all costs.

By the same token, husbands should remember that their wives do everything to serve them and should not be scolded merely because she once slipped up or did not do as desired. It is therefore imperative for both husband and wife to remember this principle that Luqman (Peace be upon him) demonstrated.

WHEN SOMETHING GOES WRONG

Whenever one is faced with hardship, the best recourse is what Allah Ta'ala has Himself advised in the Quran. By practising what Allah Ta'ala advises will earn Allah Ta'ala's pleasure and mercy. Once this is secured, every difficulty will become easy and every problem solved. Allah Ta'ala declares, "O you who believe! Seek help by means of patience and salah. Verily Allah Ta'ala is with the patient ones." *[Surah Baqara (Surah 2), verse 153]*

In this verse, Allah Ta'ala tells every Muslim male and female that whenever they face any difficulty, they should take support from the pillars of patience and salah. When this is done, Allah Ta'ala shall alleviate the difficulty because He always remains with the patient ones. It is understood that if Allah Ta'ala is in attendance of those who exercise patience, He will surely be with those who perform salah because salah is the greatest of all forms of Ibaadah.

A few verses later in the same Surah, Allah Ta'ala says, "So give glad tidings to the patient ones." Describing the patient ones, Allah Ta'ala says further, "(They are) those who, when any adversity befalls them, say, 'Verily to Allah Ta'ala do we (together with out wealth and children) belong, and to Him is our return.' These are the ones upon whom the collective and special mercies of Allah Ta'ala descend and who are rightly guided."

These verses make it clear that the truly patient people are those who are convinced that everything belongs to Allah Ta'ala. They know that if the Owner of something wants his property back, it is foolish to object. They also know that they will soon be returned to Allah Ta'ala where they will receive the rewards for exercising patience. Such people will be showered with Allah Ta'ala's special mercies reserved only for them. At the same time, they will not be deprived of the collective mercies that others will receive. Praising these people further, Allah Ta'ala says that they have truly been guided because they realise that Allah Ta'ala is in control of everything and that benefit and harm all proceed from Him.

One cannot imagine the great position of people who receive Allah Ta'ala's collective and special mercies, concerning whom Allah Ta'ala Himself has declared that they are rightly guided. Whenever one is faced with any difficulty, one should think that it is happening because Allah Ta'ala wants it to happen. None can avert the decree of Allah Ta'ala or protect one against Allah Ta'ala. Allah Ta'ala's system is unique and there is always a good reason for everything that happens.

One should always remember that life would not be so cherished had there been no death. Similarly, the day would not be appreciated had there been no night just as happiness would be a dull experience without grief and difficulty. This world is a blend of happiness and sadness and one will inevitably face both favourable and unfavourable conditions. The vigour and carefree nature of youth is dampened by the feebleness of old age and the joy of affluence is always threatened by the gloom of poverty. Such are the vicissitudes of this temporary life.

Those Muslim men or women are truly fortunate and wise who realises that every condition is from Allah Ta'ala and should turn to Allah Ta'ala at all times. Allah Ta'ala says in the Quran,

﴿ وَأَنَّهُ هُوَ أَضْحَكَ وَأَبْكَى ﴾ (سورة النجم:٤٣)

"It is certainly Him (Allah) Who makes (people) laugh and cry."

If Allah Ta'ala wills, He can make a crying person laugh in an instant and vice versa. Allah Ta'ala is constantly testing His bondsmen to assess their Imaan. One should therefore accept every hardship with a smile and seek Allah Ta'ala's assistance by exercising patience and by turning to Him in salah and du'aa.

When faced with a problem, no portion of one's heart and no drop of one's blood should turn to anyone besides Allah Ta'ala have the inclination to solicit assistance from someone else. Assistance should be sought only from Allah Ta'ala because only He has the power to assist one and He is Most Kind and Most Merciful. Every person wishes to be Allah Ta'ala 's friend like Ibraheem (Peace be upon him) was without realising that Allah Ta'ala makes only such a person his friend who is prepared to dive into the raging fire of Nimrood upon Allah Ta'ala 's instruction. Such a person cleanses his heart of all inclinations except his inclination towards Allah Ta'ala

﴿ فَعَّالٌ لِمَا يُرِيدُ ﴾ (سورة البروج آية :١٦)

He is convinced that everything that has happened, everything that is happening and everything that will happen in future takes place only by Allah Ta'ala's decree.

Advice to Women

In his famous work "Behisti Zewar", Moulana Ashraf Ali Thanwi (May Allah be Merciful on him/her) says that although it is seldom necessary for women to be told what is right from what is wrong, reminders are always beneficial. By understanding the following principle, many matters will become clearer. The husband and wife relationship is a lifetime relationship. If the couple's hearts are united, they can have no greater bounty. On the contrary, if their hearts are divided, they can suffer no greater calamity.

A woman should therefore win over her husband's heart and should be ready to respond to his slightest indication. Her success in both worlds lies in her readiness to do anything that he wishes. She will have the eternal bounties of the Hereafter in exchange for the temporary hardship of this world. She should do her best never to upset him. Even if he tells her that day is night, she should accept his word without hesitation. Difficult as this may be, it will make the couple inseparable.

KEEPING THE HUSBAND'S FEELINGS IN MIND

A wife should be vigilant over her husband's feelings and moods. She should joke and laugh with him only when his mood allows. The husband-wife relationship is not a hollow relationship. It is therefore necessary for the wife to realise that she should always maintain a high level of respect for her husband's feelings. It is incorrect for a wife to think that her husband is her equal.

A wife should refrain from asking her husband to do anything for her and if he affectionately wants to massage her arms or head, she should not shrug him off. Such behaviour is disrespectful towards one's father and is even worse towards one's husband because the husband's position is greater than that of one's father. A wife should always respect him in their conversations and should never overstep the limits of respect. *["Behisti Zewar"]*

AN UNPARALLELED RELATIONSHIP

Despite taunts of being a "wife-worshipper", a man could not be deterred from his devoted affection for his wife. When she was asked about this, the intelligent lady replied, "I regard my husband as my Jannah. The truth is that we are so much in love that we cannot bear separation for even a few moments. Although I am speaking to you presently, my heart is with him. Our love for each other is solely for Allah Ta'ala's pleasure. You may call me a besotted woman but I truly love him because he responds to my love with his own love. He is just as besotted about me and will do anything lawful for me. He takes me to Deeni lectures for ladies, from which I benefit tremendously. He rectifies my faults most affectionately and I do not feel offended in any way. When there is so much love between us, how can we not be besotted with each other?"

Such a relationship is not exclusive to the couple mentioned above. Every woman can harness her husband's love by submitting to him and doing everything he instructs. The proof of the pudding is in the tasting.

HOW I CONQUERED MY HUSBAND

The following is an account of a Muslim sister. She says: The hardships and difficulties I experienced during the years of my marriage are too many to discuss here. All I wish to express is the manner in which I became the darling of my husband.

At the beginning, my husband wanted nothing to do with me and was even prepared to divorce me. However, he changed his mind when some good people managed to persuade him not to do so. I bitterly regretted my decision to marry him and my heart would burn to ashes when I used to see happily married couples. My husband never spoke to me and refused to even drink the water I served. However, my parents-in-law possessed angelic qualities and were always trying to reason with my husband. Their efforts regrettably fell on deaf ears. They nevertheless sympathised with me and treated me well.

During a spare moment one day, I happened to read a book by Moulana Ahmad Muhammad Hatorni Saheb concerning Muslim husbands and wives. Together with this, I perused through some other books containing advices to brides and women a large. I found many factors in these books that applied to me and my life. My heart skipped a beat when I read the discussion about keeping one's husband happy. It occurred to me that I was also capable of conquering my husband as the book discussed.

I studied my behaviour and habits and focussed all my attention on my husband. I convinced myself that I could inculcate in myself all the qualities that my husband admired in women. I thought that if I am successful in this, my husband would certainly pay more attention to me. I therefore gave attention to the following three factors:

1. Determining the temperament of my husband.
2. Determining what qualities he admires in a woman.
3. Determining what he dislikes.

I then exerted all my faculties in studying his temperament, his likes and his dislikes. I managed to determine exactly what he admired in other women and I beautified myself accordingly. I also inculcated in myself the behaviour that he liked and cooked everything he liked. One day, he said to me, "You are becoming more beautiful each day." I gave no reply and thought to myself that by Allah Ta'ala's grace the arrow had struck its target. I could not stop thanking Allah Ta'ala as my heart swelled with joy. He then said, "Why are you looking so stunning?" I now thought that I would lose the opportunity if I did not reply.

I smiled and said, "When was I not attractive? I always looked like this but you took no interest." While saying this, I chanced to look him in the eye. I hit the mark and the prey had been ensnared in the trap. He affectionately responded, "No. You are extremely beautiful. I have behaved unjustly towards you and have hurt you unnecessarily. I shall mend my ways and will not allow you to leave my sight."

I have now become my husband's darling. In fact, he refuses to even eat another woman's food. He does whatever I ask and always confers with me before doing anything. My parents-in-law cannot believe what has happened and have congratulated me on my success. My advice to every woman who cannot make an impression on her husband is that she tries what I did. Insha Allah Ta'ala she will certainly succeed. Initially when my husband used to ignore my beauty, my youth and my enthusiasm, it seemed as if I was a widow living with my husband.

DO NOT DIVORCE ME

A married man struck up a relationship with a widow and wanted to marry her. However, she made it clear to him that she would marry him only if he divorced his wife. When he seemed determined to divorce her, she started making du'aa to Allah Ta'ala in earnestness. A friend of hers who was a pious lady gave her some advice. She told her to keep certain factors in mind so that she could win back her husband's love. She also wrote a touching poem for the lady to read to her husband which accurately portrayed her feelings. Al Hamdu Lillaah, this poem had a miraculous effect. The husband changed his mind about marrying the other woman and was saved from her lure. Hereunder follows a translation of the poem:

"I used to be proud of the one who is no
Longer in my fortune
What wrong did I do? Why was I no longer
Worthy of his love?
I am no longer the decoration of my own home
I am now a worthless object
Without reason, people have now made
Me a target of abuse
Today I swear on oath that I have always been loyal
A bud in season, I had been a lovely flower in my youth
Alas! Now a bird without wings
The house that we just built is now too small
Oh the grief! Who has become less accommodating?
The one who once regarded me as his thornless rose
The one who for years has been calling me the
Queen of bouquets
The one who has given me radiance and sunshine
Today he makes me cry, makes me appear like
A mere wall

Oh! Was my beauty not an elation for you?
Were you not my king and crown?
If you become annoyed, let it be with me for I
Shall calm you
As far as you may be from me, I shall call you closer
Do not stagger. Come forward and I shall accommodate you
I shall seat you in my eyes and in my heart
The wealth and assets of this world are trivial and
Can easily be lost
This entire world is trivial - but not my husband
Please tell me if I have erred
What crime can deserve such severe punishment?
Or are you hurting me for no reason? Then continue
My head is suspended in a noose, hit it as you please
I implore you in the name of the Magnanimous Rabb,
Keep me as your wife even if it be as a servant to
Your other wife
Why should I express what is in my heart?
I am happy with whatever pleases you
I am busy praying for you, my beloved
You have come to me and left me for carnal pleasures
The day will soon arrive when you will long for true love
Should I be a candle for the privacy of others?
Alas! To die for a woman!
Why did Zulaikha come out alive from Yusuf (u)'s room,
When she would have wished to emerge as a corpse (for shame)?
Others may see your familiar appearance
But my self-respect will never allow that
I see this calamity without tears flowing from my eyes
All I require is the drape of chastity (marriage)
It may be said that I will live taking Ž your name
I swear by the Rabb of honour and grace,
I shall give my life serving you
I shall remain loyal to you even though you are not
I shall remain in attendance as a sweeper
If I am unfit for the home, I shall be a wall
Keep me even if I have to be a servant

I shall at least have some support to dispel my grief
I remember how you used to sometimes
Decorate these plaits,
But never saw the tears (of joy) welling in these eyes
You would sometimes twirl these plaits over your arms
And this lap was often your pillow
I remember when you used to split my path
When you were a gardener, I was your
Flourishing garden
My bridal garland has not even withered away yet
Sitting here for you, from where has this
Calamity comes?
Who will now see this dejected face of mine
If I exercise patience, my heart will burn to cinders
Separation from you would make me weep forever
Nevertheless, my head is bowed and I submit to the one who issues the divorce."
[Translated from an Urdu poem]

NEVER ASK FOR ANYTHING ABOVE YOUR HUSBAND'S MEANS

A wife should be content with whatever her husband can afford to provide for her. If she desires something that he is unable to afford, she should not ask for it. Should she ask for such a thing, the husband will automatically think that she is inconsiderate. Of course, if the husband asks her what she would like to have, she may express her desire. She should not ask for it without his request because asking people for things lowers one in their sight. Ask only from Allah Ta'ala. Allah Ta'ala loves those who ask from Him and is displeased with those who do not ask of Him. On the other hand, people become displeased when asked for something. Remember that Allah Ta'ala has given people whatever they have and He can easily give you the same.

Dear sister! It is unfortunate that nowadays we tend to live beyond our means. Apart from the fact that the cost of living has soared, people tend to turn a blind eye to their necessities and keep buying things that they do not need. A man who is not in debt should be very grateful to Allah Ta'ala. One should remember that besides Allah Ta'ala, no one will be there for one if one is in a financial crisis. Never buy anything that one can do without and never spend beyond one's means. Having said that, you must lay stress on your husband to provide quality education to your kids because this is the best gift a father can give to his children. One must however, not forget that there is a world of difference between quality education and expensive education, read 'Misali Ustaad' by Baitul Ilm Trust and spell out its important points to your husband. You must though be careful that reading of Islamic literature must be in such a time that it does not hinder your duties, even five minutes reading will do if you can retain and practice upon what you read.

It is extremely imprudent of many "fashionable" women to waste their husbands' hard-earned money on unnecessary clothing and fashion accessories. Every wife ought to economise and save something every month for rainy days. Economising does not mean that one should be miserly. It simply means that one should not spend on things that are not necessary and that one should not pay more for something that can be bought for less.

HOW AN INTELLIGENT WOMAN RUNS HER HOME

"The first element of sound home management
is dexterity
Worry about others before yourself
Timeless practice dictates that the man shall
earn and provide
The wife's task is to use the money prudently
For peace of mind, the bedding should be only as
large as the material
How can a woman lacking this skill ever
enjoy prosperity?
The woman deficient in wisdom can only be
called a poor housewife
She can achieve nothing with the task of service entrusted to her
She will waste all their money in so many things
Her mother-and-sisters-in-law will then be
antagonistic towards her
Not one, but hundreds of calamities will strike
because of this
Her husband will regret his marriage with every breath
He will kill himself working without having

anything at home
She squanders everything that he brings home
Such behaviour is wrong, refrain from it dear sister
Spend in a avenues where spending is required
Your father-in-law will be happy, your husband will be happy and you will still remain as you are."
[Translated from an Urdu poem]

THE ETIQUETTE OF MEETING ONE'S HUSBAND WHEN HE RETURNS FROM A JOURNEY

Before leaving on a journey, a husband asked his wife what he should bring for her. She said, "May AllaaTa'ala bring you back safely because you are my greatest blessing in this world and the Hereafter. I need nothing but that you return to me safely." Any husband would be glad to hear such a reply because it indicates that she loves him more than material things.

When the husband returns, the wife should ask him how he is feeling and whether everything went well. She should show concern about what he ate and what he did. She should express gratitude to Allah Ta'ala for returning him home safely and should also tell the children to express gratitude to Allah Ta'ala. When her husband returns, the wife should never bombard him with all the problems she experienced in his absence and then follow this up with a barrage of questions like "What did you bring for me?", "What did you bring for the children?" and "Did you spend all our money?" Such questions will cause a wife to fall from the sight of her husband.

Of course, once he has settled at home, she may ask him everything about the journey. She should also show happiness with whatever he brings for her even though it may not be exactly what she wants. She should never tell him that he should have brought something in a different style, a different colour, etc. Saying such things will hurt his feelings and discourage him from bringing gifts in future. She should praise everything he brings and thank him profusely.

TAKE GOOD CARE OF YOUR HUSBAND'S POSSESSIONS

A wife should be particular about caring for her husband's possessions and keeping them in an orderly fashion. The room should always be neat, the bed should always made and the bedding always clean. It is useless if the husband has to tell the wife to keep the house tidy because things are more appreciated when they get done without a bidding. The wife should be even more particular about the tidiness of those things that her husband is fussy about. If he gives her something to put away, she should ensure that she keeps it safely. His clothes should be folded or hung neatly and not left strewn around.

There are women who will be found beating the children when the husband steps into the house. Whereas the man may be returning tired and frustrated, yearning for peace and quiet at home, he is confronted by wailing children and an irritated wife. The result: He cannot bear being at home and seeks an outlet in parks, clubs, restaurants and other company. He gradually begins to hate his family, regarding them as punishment for his sins. The incompetence of the wife therefore deprives the innocent children of their father's love and attention. A woman who is constantly screaming at the children and hitting them falls from her husband's eyes and he will soon begin to admire women who are calmer.

Picture this scene. The husband returns home tired. As he enters the door, he wife is chatting to her neighbour over the fence or talking to someone on the phone. Her dressing is shabby and her hair dishevelled. The house is in a mess, with flies buzzing about the dirty dishes scattered about the kitchen. Opening the refrigerator for some water, he finds it dirty, with no water in the water bottle. Picking up a glass to take water from the tap, he finds it sticky and greasy. Such a man is justly warranted to weep over his situation. Who can blame him for looking for another wife?

Women should also refrain from making excuses for things they do not do and from lying because this will reduce their husbands' confidence in them. It should not be that their husbands stop believing even the truths they say.

WHAT A WIFE SHOULD DO WHEN HER HUSBAND BECOMES ANGRY

When a woman's husband becomes angry or annoyed with something, she should not reciprocate his anger. She should rather hold his hand and apologise even though the fault is not hers. She should regard this apology and asking forgiveness as an honour because gestures like this save marriages. When the fault is hers, she would be foolish to become angry and to sit apart from him because this will drive them further from each other.

When one's husband is angry, one should never say anything that will aggravate him further. If he says anything unpleasant, she should exercise patience and not say anything in return. She should remain silent and ask for forgiveness. Once his anger has subsided, he will regret his behaviour and realise that his wife's conduct was excellent. In this manner, he will not become angry so frequently. If the wife says something during his moment of anger, the situation may erupt and reach dramatic proportions.

THE APPROACH OF A WISE WIFE

A man by the name of Waleed had to face a disciplinary hearing at work after being falsely accused of doing something. He was not even given the chance to defend himself. When he returned home, he was obviously upset and irritated. Despite his efforts to suppress his anger, he failed and he burst into a rage merely because he could not find his socks where they usually were. His wife was an intelligent woman and she immediately realised that her husband was not himself that day. She therefore did not interrogate him or rebuke him. She thought it inappropriate to discuss the mater until the couple has eaten and had time to themselves. She then gradually raised the subject and lovingly consoled him. As he spoke to her, the burden on his shoulders began to lighten and her felt much better. By the time he went to bed, he was completely at ease and felt pleased that his lifetime companion was so understanding and comforting.

WHEN A HUSBAND STRIKES UP AN EXTRA MARITAL RELATIONSHIP

A wife should never accuse her husband of having a relationship with another woman merely because of suspicion. If he is innocent of this, he will be deeply hurt by the accusation. If he is guilty of such a relationship, it will be useless for the wife to vent her anger on him or to make life difficult for him. Such behaviour will sink the wedge between them even deeper and obliterate the last vestiges of feelings he may have for her.

To make one's husband abandon such relationships and to win his complete attention, one should first stand up in salah during the late hours of the night and make sincere du'aa to Allah Ta'ala that one's husband should desist from such practices. At the same time, one should also tell him about the harms of such practices without offending him. Insha Allah

Ta'ala, he will soon mend his ways and become one's slave when Allah Ta'ala guides him. If this approach does not bear the desired effect, one should exercise patience and consult pious and learned people.

One should never expose him to others and disgrace him. Neither should one impose on him to stop him because this may make him more adamant. When a wife makes life more difficult for her husband and disgraces him by exposing his faults to others, she will be deprived of even the little attention he used to pay to her.

HOW TO LIVE AMICABLY WITH IN-LAWS

Together with blood relatives, Allah Ta'ala also speaks about the importance of in-laws. This makes it clear that there are rights due to one's parents-in-law just as there are rights due to one's own parents. It is the right of one's parents-in-law that one should serve them as long as they are alive. If one has to live with one's parents-in-law, one should regard it as one's honour to serve them. Constantly thinking about living by oneself will spoil one's relationship with one's parents-in-law.

Think awhile. A mother carried her son with immense difficulty and endured untold sacrifices and hardships in rearing him. The father also invested his efforts and money in raising his son. After all the effort in raising their son and getting him married, his parents entertained the hope that they will be able to live peacefully with their son and daughter-in-law in their old age and enjoy their grandchildren. How inconsiderate will that daughter-in-law be whose first concern when getting married is to separate this son from his parents? When the mother-in-law learns that the daughter-in-law is planning to separate them from their beloved son, matters begin to deteriorate and life becomes unbearable for all concerned.

A daughter-in-law should live amicable with all her in-laws. She should respect the elders among them, show compassion towards the children of their families and should not feel embarrassed to do what her mother-in-law or sisters-in-law tell her to do. She should never inform her mother about the wrongs that her mother-in-law does because this will lead to unnecessary disputes and will do no good whatsoever.

Some Advice

1. It should not upset you if your husband gives all his money to his parents and gives you nothing. In fact, if he hands the money over to you, you should decline the offer and suggest that he give it to them. In this manner, your parents-in-law will be impressed and will regard you as one of their own. Always obey your parents-in-law and never occupy your thought with leaving their house because this leads to a strained a relationship.
2. Never look down at or feel embarrassed about the work that your in-laws do. By assisting them in their work, they will have great love and admiration for you.
3. Never listen to gossip. Keep away from women who gossip and never add to their gossip.
4. Treat every instruction of your mother-in-law like an instruction from your own beloved mother. Give her pleasure precedence over everything else even though she may not treat one very well. Never contradict her instructions and never backchat when speaking to her. Speak to her with great respect and never address her as you would address an equal. Never say anything if she scolds you, and always remember that your mother-in-law is more important than your husband's mother-in-law. Never speak harshly to her and sip her harshness like a sweet drink. If she delegates a task to someone else, try to do it yourself.
5. Behave respectfully towards all elders like the wives of your husband's elder brothers. Always keep their ages in mind and do not speak to them as you would speak to women of your age. Treat them like your own sisters and you will soon notice that others will treat you likewise.

If they are younger than you, be loving and kind towards them and if you cannot do their work for them, assist them as far as possible. Adopt the same attitude towards your husband's sisters. However, you should adopt moderation in your approach because matters may become difficult once the limits of social relations are overstepped. Friendly relations with other women should never lead you to speak about others because anything said about another person whom she does not like is regarded as backbiting. Backbiting is a major sin.

6. In addition to this, you should also show love and affection towards the children of the family, such as the children of your brothers-and-sisters-in-law. Messenger of Allah (Peace be upon him) as mentioned that the person who does not respect elders and does not show mercy towards youngsters is not from among his followers. Our beloved Messenger of Allah (Peace be upon him) had great love for children. He once took a child in his lap and took no exception when the child wet him. In fact, he had so much love for children that he did not even approve of deceiving them. A woman once called for a child, telling the child that she would give him something if he came to her. Unlike many people who tell children this as a ruse, she had a date to give him. When Messenger of Allah (Peace be upon him) learnt that she actually had something to give the child and had not intended to deceive him, Rasulullah (Peace be upon him) told her that she would have been a liar if she had nothing to give him.
7. Never burden your servant with more work than she can manage. If additional work has to be given, you should assist her. Never behave harshly towards her and be sympathetic towards her if she is ill or experiencing some difficulty. Assist her in her work if she is not well. However, do not spoil her and make her lazy because she will then have to face the wrath of every employee she works for after you. If you have some delicacy to eat or drink, keep aside a share for her, even though it may be only a little.

NOTE: Moulana Ashraf Ali Thanwi (May Allah be Merciful on him/her) has written that although a woman should do her best to abide by the above, these are all moral teachings and she is not obliged to live with her in-laws. If she demands to live separately, her husband is obliged to provide separate quarters for her. In fact, moral conduct demands that if the parents-in-law do not need anyone to care for them, the husband should provide separate accommodati- on for his wife if he possibility is strong that she would not be able to live comfortably with his parents (as is the general case nowadays).

PONDER AWHILE!

In many cases where a daughter-in-law wants to live separately, it is the sisters-in-law (husband's sisters) who oppose the idea. However, the same sisters-in-law seem to forget that when they married, they made du'aa, asked others make du'aa and even had Ta'weezaat (amulets) made so that they could live separately. Despite the fact that they may have some difficulty in running their own home, women prefer to live on their own because they realise that living by themselves is the key to happiness. It is rather strange that when women become mothers-in-law and sisters-in-law, they forget the benefits of living separately and can suddenly prove to anyone that there is more harm in living separately.

Our Daarul Ifta regularly receives complaints from parents whose daughters are unhappy living with their in-laws. Many of them are even prepared to provide alternate accommodation because they realise the harms of living together. Regrettably, these are the same people who insist that their daughters-in-law live with them when their sons marry. One ought to realise that just as one's daughter finds it difficult to live with her in-laws, one's daughter-in-law is also someone's daughter and may also experience the same difficulty. One will be unjust to demand separate accommodation for one's daughter and insist on sharing accommodation with one's daughter-in-law.

If a man cannot afford to provide separate accommodation for his wife, the least he should do is provide her a kitchen of her own or allow her to cook by herself.

HOW A WOMAN CAN BECOME HER HUSBAND'S DARLING

Women often have to bear the brunt of their husband's ill-treatment as well as ill-treatment from their mothers-in-law. If they follow the advices that Messenger of Allah (Peace be upon him) outlined, Allah Ta'ala will soon place compassion for her into the hearts of her husband and her mother-in-law. As a result of this, she will be able to live happily and the entire family will also be able to live with happiness. May Allah Ta'ala grant every Muslim woman the ability to practise these advices. *Aameen.*

Here are four factors that will certainly create compassion in any husband's heart irrespective of his wife's level of intelligence. By employing these, the couple will be able to live with love and happiness. The four factors are:

1. The husband and wife should be pious.
2. The wife should understand the husband's temperament.
3. The wife should praise the husband and have true love for him.
4. She should cook good food for him.

The Couple Should be Pious and United

Unless and until the husband and wife both become pious, they cannot hope to be united. Allah Ta'ala says in the Quran, "So the pious women are obedient and, in the absence of their husbands, are protective because of that which Allah Ta'ala has protected."

﴿ فَالصَّالِحَاتُ قَانِتَاتٌ حَافِظَاتٌ لِلْغَيْبِ بِمَا حَفِظَ اللَّهُ ﴾ (النساء: من الآية٣٤)

This verse of the Quran describes the pious wife as one who accepts her husband as her leader, who obeys him and who safeguards her chastity and his wealth in his absence. Her behaviour should be chaste both in his presence and absence. She should also ensure that she manages the domestic affairs efficiently. "Saalihaat" (pious women) as described in the above verse also refers to women who are particular about their salah, fasting and all their other religious duties. Together with fulfilling Allah Ta'ala 's rights, she also fulfils the rights of her husband. A person who disobeys Allah Ta'ala cannot be expected to obey anyone else.

A woman should neither miss any salah nor delay it. She should begin preparing for salah as soon as the time for the salah sets in. In addition to the Faraa'idh, she should also be particular about the Sunnah and Mustahab acts. She should perform salah with so much concentration as if she is looking at Allah Ta'ala. If this is not possible, she should bear in mind that Allah Ta'ala is watching her. One will be able to perform salah with perfect concentration when one does not lose sight of the fact that one is standing in Allah Ta'ala's court.

Every wife should also make time to recite the Quran and to engage in Dhikr. Special attention should be given to abstaining from sin. One should ensure that no non-Mahram man sees any part of your body. Allah Ta'ala has granted every limb and every hair of the body as a trust. Every person is therefore obliged to safeguard this trust. A woman should undertake to screen her body from every person whom Allah Ta'ala has commanded that she veil herself, even from her cousins and brothers-in-law. She should guard against every sin and should she inadvertently commit a sin, she should repent immediately.

If you need to leave your house for some necessity, ensure that you are covered properly and that no non-Mahram can see any part of your body. Should he see any part of your body, he will be sinful for looking just as you will be sinful for exposing that part. You will therefore be guilty of sinning as well as for being a cause of another person sinning. If a woman emerges from her house without covering herself as she should and a hundred men look at her, she will be the cause of two hundred eyes becoming the prey of Allah Ta'ala's wrath. If she has been the cause of Allah Ta'ala's wrath, how can she possibly earn her husband's pleasure? How will her children be obedient to her? Because she has incurred the wrath of the Rabb of the universe, she can expect hardship to come her way. Of course, Allah Ta'ala 's wrath can be averted from her if she sincerely repents to Allah Ta'ala and resolves to abstain from all major and minor sins.

The woman who carries out the injunctions of the Shari'ah and who adopts the pure character taught by Messenger of Allah (Peace be upon him) will become worthy of being called a human being. Such a woman will be regarded as a cultured person and will be an embodiment of love and compassion. She will then be able to endure difficulty for the sake of others and tolerate others. The man who marries such a woman will remain a happy man. If a woman becomes pious, she can attain ranks higher than those of many men and will enter Jannah before them.

WOMEN ENTERING JANNAH BEFORE THEIR HUSBANDS

Addressing some women, Messenger of Allah (Peace be upon him) once mentioned that a pious woman shall enter Jannah before her husband. When her husband arrives in Jannah, she will have already taken a bath and applied perfume. She will be transported in red and yellow carriages and youngsters resembling scattered pearls will accompany her. Commenting on this hadith, Moulana Ashraf Ali Thanwi has mentioned that the only requirement needed for this honourable position is for a woman to become pious, which is not a difficult task at all. A poet says,

> "Bow in submission to the Shari'ah of
> Muhammad (Peace be upon him).
> By his mere indication, be prepared to kill yourself
> The head that does not bow to Allah Ta'ala 's commands.
> Will have to bow to powerless idols
> Kiss the Quran with respect as you place it
> on your forehead.
> Contentment is the capital of the heart,
> so place it in your bosom."
> *[Translated from an Urdu poem]*

THE PERSON WHO REFUSES TO BE A SERVANT OF ONE WILL BE THE SLAVE OF THOUSANDS

One should never think that the woman who roams the streets without dressing according to the Shari'ah is a free woman. Remember that the person who is not subservient to Allah Ta'ala has in fact chosen to be subservient to thousands of others. The person with the most freedom is the one who opts to pay servitude to One Allah Ta'ala. Allah Ta'ala will fill the heart of such a person with peace and contentment.

Ask any woman not dressed according to the Shari'ah what prevents her from dressing like a proper Muslim should. She will tell you that her relatives, her society or something else is preventing her. This reveals that she has opted to serve these people instead of the Wisest of the wise. Instead of serving Allah Ta'ala, she prefers serving her relatives, her manager, her director, her principal, her company's rules, her friends, the customers at the shop or restaurant where she works, the passengers of the airline that employs her, her boss for whom she plays the role of a private secretary or the clients who see her at the reception desk where she works.

In his book concerning the hoax of women's liberation, Mufti Taqi Usmani (May Allah be Merciful on him/her) has mentioned that the slogans of women's liberation have been used as a subterfuge to remove women from their homes and to parade them on the streets. To achieve this aim, women have been given posts as clerks, secretaries and typists. To boost sales in businesses, they have been made salesladies and models and every part of their bodies has been made an advertisement to promote products. The woman whom Islam has crowned with honour and chastity has been reduced to a lowly showpiece to sell cheap commodities and a toy to dispel man's boredom.

If one looks at the occidental countries of the world, one will notice that lowly jobs have been assigned to women. One will scarcely find a waiter in a restaurant, only waitresses. Hotel staff who clean rooms, people serving customers at businesses and receptionists are predominantly women. It is appropriate to quote a stanza from the above poem a second time:
"The head that does not bow to Allah Ta'ala's commands. Will have to bow to powerless idols."

THE STRANGE PSYCHOLOGY OF A NEW CULTURE

It is indeed strange that when a woman prepares food and serves it to her husband and children, enjoying their loving gazes and conversation, she is labelled as a backward and oppressed person. On the other hand, when she serves food to thousands of strange people as an air-hostess, becoming the target of countless lustful gazes, she is regarded as being a liberated and progressive woman. This is the warped philosophy of today's culture. The mentality of people has retrogressed to such ebb a woman thinks that she is respectable when she uses her charms to attract customers as a saleslady or a model or when she charms her boss into thinking that she is a good secretary.

﴿ إِنَّا لِلَّهِ وَإِنَّا إِلَيْهِ رَاجِعُونَ ﴾ (البقرة: من الآية١٥٦)

In the sight of Allah Ta'ala, a truly respectable woman worthy of immense rewards is that woman who remains indoors to diligently serve her family and manage their domestic affairs. Man's psychology has reversed. Instead of serving her family, each of whom will give their lives for hers, today's woman prefers to rather serve people she does not know, many of whom would not bat an eyelid to ravage her honour and chastity.

Instead of serving people who look at her with respect as their mother, she would rather serve people who look at her as a servant ready to jump at their bidding. This is really the disfigured psychology of people who dare to call themselves civilised.

TO SUMMARISE

To summarise what has been mentioned above, it may be said that no one is free in this world. A person is either subservient to Allah Ta'ala or to Shaytaan. While some choose to submit to the Shari'ah, others submit to their carnal desires or to social pressures. Every person therefore has the choice to choose which type of bondage s/he wants for herself/himself. Addressing faithful wives, a poet says:

> "When the dark night enshrouds the woman's world
> Your braided hair puts the morning to shame
> Dancing on the stage with their harps, many
> women are selling
> The charm of their eyes and the colour of their cheeks
> Before them every new opportunity is a showcase
> While your stage is the gaze of your husband."
> *[Translated from an Urdu poem]*

PROGRESS OR DESTRUCTION?

No one denies that bread can be eaten in a restaurant just as it can be eaten at home. Similarly, the night will pass whether it is spent in a nightclub or at home. A sick person can be cared for in a hospital as well as in a nursing home. By the same token, women can be bribed with money and other rewards to bear children for the state, who will be reared and cared for by paid nurses in state institutions (as is reportedly being done in Russia). However, one should remember that living in restaurants and dying in hospitals can never replace family life just as children raised by the state cannot make a nation.

There is a world of difference between rearing children and manufacturing shoes. If rearing children is treated like manufacturing commercial products, the end result will resemble a human being in looks but will be devoid of human qualities. Although a clone looks like the real thing, it can never be like the original.

Irrespective of how "free" women deem time up to the present day, women have never succeeded in overshadowing men. This proves that fate has already determined that women should exist under the leadership of men. This is because Allah Ta'ala has declared "Men are the leaders of themselves, they will always be subservient to man in some respect or another. From the beginning of women because of the virtue Allah Ta'ala has bestowed some of you over others."

﴿ الرِّجَالُ قَوَّامُونَ عَلَى النِّسَاءِ ﴾ (النساء: من الآية٣٤)

None can alter this decree of Allah Ta'ala and whoever attempts to do so shall meet humiliation and destruction.

Recognising the Husband's Temperament

The second factor by which the wife can win her husband's heart is by always taking his feelings and sentiments into consideration. She should take to heart everything he says and comply with his lawful desires. Pay attention to what he says and do not speak while he is speaking because this is disrespectful by any standard. If you need to say something, do so after he has spoken. It often happens that a person interrupts the speaker with a question before he has completed his piece whereas the question would have been answered during the course of the speech if the listener had been patient. Matters tend to become complicated and confusing with interruptions. Repeated questions also aggravate the speaker, leading to unnecessary problems. When your husband has said his piece, his instructions should be duly carried out.

Qaari Tayyab (May Allah be pleased with him/her) has mentioned that it is compulsory for a wife to do as her husband says. A wife should obey her husband even if he instructs her to do something that she dislikes. In such an event she should not behave arrogantly and backchat. The home will run smoothly when the wife obeys the husband and when he takes her feelings into consideration. However, she cannot win over his heart unless she obeys everything he says and regards him above herself. Obedience breeds obedience whereas disobedience will create dislike for her in his heart.

The wife who wants her husband to be her slave should first become his slave. As she obeys him, so too will be begin to obey her. Every wife should therefore always take cognisant of the things that her husband dislikes so that she may refrain from them. She should not do what he dislikes, should not cook what he dislikes, should not wear what he dislikes and should not go to places he disapproves of. In doing this, she will be doing the things that he likes and gaining his pleasure all the time.

It is also necessary for the husband to take his wife's feelings and desires into consideration. She has come to his home with a set of likes and inclinations. He should determine what these are and set out to satisfy them as best as he can. Besides him, there is none who can do this for her. When both partners play their role well, the show will run smoothly and all will be happy.

Praising the Husband and Having True Love for Him

The third factor effective in harnessing the affection of one's husband is to have true love for him and his family and to praise them in front of others. Many women have the bad habit of always trying to find out whether relations are good or tense between a woman and her in-laws. They will make every attempt to "fish out" the situation from an unsuspecting daughter-in-law. It is appalling that mothers actually train their daughters to backbite and find faults by asking them on the second day of marriage about their mothers-in-law.

It is unfortunate that when they return to their parents' home, women grossly exaggerate the faults of their in-laws and the hardships they experience. Hearing this, other women spice interpretation the stories and narrate them with great relish to everyone else. Eventually, an extremely ugly picture of the mother-in-law and her daughters is painted. When the story eventually reaches the mother-in-law, she is naturally upset beyond proportions.

The mother-in-law then tells her son what his wife is informing people about them. She also makes others witness to what has been said and often tells him that the narrator is truthful beyond doubt. The husband then begins to drift away from his wife, often without her even realising that she was the cause. The disputes and arguments between the couple then become uncontrollable and divorce or a lifetime of marital problems is often the end result.

It is therefore necessary for a wife to praise her husband, his parents and his relatives when speaking about them. She should not speak ill of them even when asked. This attitude will foster good relations between husband and wife and when her mother-in-law and sisters-in-law find out that she praises them in front of others, their love for her will grow and they will treat her well. They will even praise her in front of her husband, causing his admiration for her to increase. When the couple are happy, they will be able to prepare for their Aakhirah and concentrate on raising their children as good Muslims who will be a great asset to Islam.

In addition to being a major sin, speaking ill of one's husband and in-laws violates the sanctity of the home and does not behove a good wife.

If a husband's love for his wife is lacking for some reason, praising him will increase this love substantially. She should also tell him how much she loves him, emphasising that she loves him more than anything else in this world and that she cannot live without him. Ayesha Rused to recite the following couplets when Messenger of Allah (Peace be upon him) used to return home:

لنا شمس وللأفـــاق شمس
وشمسي خير من شمس السماء
فـــإن الشمس تطلع بعد الفجر
وشمسي تطلع بعد العشـــاء

"I have a sun and the horizon has a sun
But my sun is better than the sun in the sky
Because the sun rises after dawn
While my sun rises after Isha."

When a man hears words like this from his wife, not only will his love for her increase, but his health, his youth and every other faculty will gleam ever so brightly. Such sweet words are sufficient to cure any physical or mental ailment and to dispel any anxiety. There will definitely be a large place reserved for such a wife in her husband's heart. In fact, this was one of the reasons why Messenger of Allah (Peace be upon him) loved Ayesha (May Allah be pleased with him/her) the most. Every wife should attempt to study a biography of Ayesha (May Allah be pleased with him/her) to learn what the factors were that made her so beloved to Messenger of Allah (Peace be upon him) A comprehensive biography of this nature has been written by Moulana Sayyid Sulaymaan Nadwi (May Allah be Merciful on him/her). By emulating her pure lifestyle, every wife can become the focus of her husband's attention. He will then see to her every need and will not do anything without her.

The words of Ayesha (May Allah be pleased with him/her) were not mere words but true expressions of her feelings for Messenger of Allah (Peace be upon him). She also said, "If the women who taunted Zulaikha had seen Rasulullah (Peace be upon him), they would have cut their hearts instead of just their hands." These can only be the words of someone truly in love. They do not have to be taught to such a person, but will flow spontaneously.

لـو أمي زليخا لو رأين جبينه
لأثرن القطع بالقلوب على اليد

Another sign of love for one's husband is that the wife does everything to increase his happiness when he is happy. When he speaks to her with love and kindness, she should respond in a like manner. When the husband is distressed and worried, the wife should do what she can to relieve his grief.

Ali (May Allah be pleased with him/her) once light-heartedly said the following couplet:

أن النساء شياطين خلقن لنا
نعوذ بالله من شَرِّ الشياطين

"Women are certainly Shayaateen created for (misleading) us We seek Allah Ta'ala's protection for the evil of the Shayaateen."

In response to this, his wife Fatima (May Allah be pleased with him/her) replied using the same Arabic style of poetry:

أن النساء رياحين خلقن لكم
وكلكم يشمى شيد الرياحين

"Women are certainly fragrant flowers created for you

And each of you draws close to them, hoping to get a whiff."

After a tiring day at work, every man will be refreshed by the sweet and inspiring words of his wife.

Aatika (May Allah be pleased with him/her) was married to Abdullah (May Allah be pleased with him/her) the son of Abu Bakr (May Allah be pleased with him/her). When he was martyred at Taa'if, she was extremely grieved and said,

فأليت لاتنفك عيني حزينة
ولا ينفك جسدي أغبرا

"*I swear that grief shall never part from my eyes nor will dust leave my body.*"

These words truly express the intense love that she had for her husband. In fact, the Sahabiyaat possessed such extreme love for their husbands that the nations of the world fail to match.

Loving one's husband plays a vital role in Religion because it is a means of securing Allah Ta'ala 's pleasure. It is a means of safeguarding the chastity of society and ensuring the stability and happiness of future generations. It is an extremely effective solution to marital problems. The story of Ibraheem (May Allah be Merciful on him/her)'s daughter-in-law portrays an example of how a wife ought to be grateful and praise the good in her home without mentioning the difficulties. Her behaviour pleased her father-in-law and pleased Allah Ta'ala as well. In fact, this lady was so blessed that together with earning the du'aa of Ibraheem (Peace be upon him), Allah Ta'ala made his most beloved Messenger of Allah (Peace be upon him) a scion of her progeny.

Every bride should therefore express gratitude to her husband from the very first day of her marriage, irrespective of how little she gets. She should never find fault with anything in her new home and should rather praise whatever he gives her and be thankful to Allah Ta'ala. Through the blessings of such an attitude, her husband will be more compassionate towards her and pious people will be born in her progeny, who will be of great service to the Deen. It is not farfetched to expect that today's women can also raise children the likes of Khaalid bin Waleed (May Allah be pleased with him/her) , Umer bin Al Aas (May Allah be pleased with him/her), Umar bin Abdul Azeez, Aalamgeer, salahud Religion Ayoobi, Shah Isma'eel Shaheed, Moulana Muhammad Ilyas and Moulana Ashraf Ali Thanwi (A.R). However, it is necessary that women become exemplary role models for their children.

A LADY ONCE WROTE

"If you count yourself among the daughters of
this Religion of guidance
If you have value for the narrations of your predecessors
What are we, what is our veiling, our abstinence
and our piety?
Do not ask what the Mu'min women of the first
century have done
It was their love for their husbands and service
to their children
It was their smooth running of the home and
obedience to Allah Ta'ala
It was their donning the Hijaab, their modesty, their chastity and their loyalty
It was their chaste behaviour in adhering to Allah Ta'ala's command when He says
'Do not speak in lowered tones'
And it was their preparation for Jihaad."
[Translated from an Urdu poem]

A PRINCIPLE TO FOLLOW FOR A SOUND RELATIONSHIP BETWEEN HUSBAND AND WIFE

A woman once came to Umar (May Allah be pleased with him/her) and made it clear to him that she had no instinctive love for her husband. Umar (May Allah be pleased with him/her) explained, "Never make this known to your husband. Tell him that you love him very much (even though you have to pretend) because there are very few homes built on instinctive love. People live with each other on the basis of their status and Islam (i.e. people respect and obey each other because of their regard for each other's status and their being Muslims). The couple should accept and fulfil the responsibilities that Islam has detailed for each of them. This is the only way by which their relationship will become pleasant."

There are few couples blessed with perfect compatibility which enables them to have strong instinctive love for each other. The love of such people keeps growing despite numerous obstacles. Because everyone is not blessed with such a relationship, the Shari'ah has chalked out principles by which others can also develop their love. If a couple respect each other, are prepared to overlook each other's faults, keep expressing their love for each other, forget past mishaps and proceed with clear hearts, they will soon find themselves deeply in love. They will then become a united body, sharing everything, including each other's heartache. No obstacle will be insurmountable because they will be doing things together.

Another principle that Umar (May Allah be pleased with him/her) mentioned as recorded in another narration is that the couple should always express more love than their hearts contain. In this manner, their love will steadily grow and they will both be at peace with each other. They will then be able to carry out all their functions for this world as well as for the next.

A SIGN OF TRUE LOVE

Another manner of securing the attention and compassion of one's husband is to always apologise and ask for forgiveness after an altercation. This will remove any anger and dislike that may creep into his heart. A good wife cannot get any rest until her husband is happy with her. When people have rancour and enmity in their hearts, they are deprived of Allah Ta'ala's mercy and are vulnerable to calamities and hardships. People whose hearts are contaminated with such impurities can expect problems that are beyond their expectations. One should therefore cleanse one's heart from any ill-feelings towards others.

Allah Ta'ala has taught man the following du'aa in the Quran:

{TRANSLATION: "And do not place any impurity in our hearts against those who believe. O our Rabb! Indeed You are the Most Forgiving, Most Merciful."} *[Surah 59, verse 10]*

One of the bounties of Jannah will be that people's hearts will be cleansed of malice and hatred for each other. Allah Ta'ala says in Surah Hijr,

"We shall remove any animosity that may be in their breasts. As brothers they (the people of Jannah) will be seated on couches, facing each other." *[Surah 15, verse 47]*

The hearts of husband and wife should be as clear as mirrors for each other. Their hearts should exude love for each other at all times, whether in health or illness; happiness or sadness; youth or old age. They should always bear in mind that their disputes are not merely disputes between the two of them, but will affect perhaps hundreds of people when both families get involved. Their ripple effects of their disputes could run down to many generations.

It is therefore necessary that the couple always patch up their relationship after every dispute. They should immediately dispel any malice that may have crept into their hearts. Because the wife's heart is softer, she should be the first to ask for forgiveness even though the fault is the husband's. If she does not apologise, the husband should do so. They should then forget the entire episode. When such a situation arises, she should remember the following hadith.

THE WOMAN WHO WILL ENTER JANNAH

Imaam Tabrani (May Allah be Merciful on him/her) has narrated from Anas (May Allah be pleased with him/her) that Messenger of Allah (Peace be upon him) once asked the Companion of the Prophet (May Allah be pleased with him/her)

ألا أخبركم برجالكم من أهل الجنة؟ قلنا بلى يارسول اللّٰه، قال النبي في

الجنة والصديق في الجنة والشهيد في الجنة

والرجل يزور أخاه فى ناحية المصر لايزوره إلا للّٰه في الجنة

ألا أخبركم بنسائكم في الجنة

قلنا بلى يارسول اللّٰه قال الودود الولود إذا أغضبت أو أسيئ إليها أوغضب

زوجها قالت هذه يدي فى يدك لا أكتحل بغمض حتى ترضى

لا أكتحل بغمض حتى ترضى

"Should I inform you which of your men shall enter Jannah?" "Certainly," responded the Companion of the Prophet. Messenger of Allah (Peace be upon him) said, "Every prophet shall be in Jannah, every Sidique will be in Jannah, every martyr shall be in Jannah as well as every person who visits his brother in the far end of the city only for Allah Ta'ala 's pleasure."Messenger of Allah (Peace be upon him) then asked, "Should I inform you which of your women shall enter Jannah." When the Companion of the Prophet p begged to be informed, Messenger of Allah (Peace be upon him) said, "The woman who has tremendous love for her husband, who bears many children and when she gets angry or is ill-treated or when her husband becomes angry, she (takes his hand in hers and) tells him, 'My hand is in you

لا أكتحل بغمض حتى ترضى

I shall not line my eyes with sleep (I shall not have any rest) until you are pleased.'"

["At Targheeb wat Tarheeb" Vol. 4 Pg. 125]

This hadith makes it clear that a woman can earn her entry into Jannah by merely becoming uneasy when a rift is created between herself and her husband. If only women could understand this!

When a wife has true love for her husband, she will be unable to rest, eat or sleep after an argument. She will not find pleasure in anything until they make up have forgiven each other.

Cooking Good Food for Him

The fourth method by which a woman can capture her husband's attention is by learning how to cook well for her husband and being able to place a wonderful meal before him. This skill is exceptionally important for a good wife because it is a well-known fact that the way to a man's heart is through his stomach. The meals that a wife prepares affect the husband's heart as well as every limb of his body. The method and hygiene the wife employs to prepare his meals has a profound effect on the husband's love for her as well as on his opinion about her intelligence and skill.

Although serving bread, butter and jam for breakfast and simple dishes for lunch and supper will fill his belly, preparing sumptuous dishes is healthier and will increase the love he has for his wife. Every woman should master her culinary skills at her mother's home. She should learn to prepare tasty dishes from whatever means her husband is able to provide. She should also learn how to prepare the same meals in various ways so that it may taste different on various occasions. When a woman does this, her husband will fulfil her desires without her having to ask and will give her a choice in all matters. He will also ask her what du'aas she would like him to make for her.

When a wife cooks to please her husband for Allah Ta'ala's pleasure, she will earn the following three rewards:

1. She will be rewarded for pleasing Allah Ta'ala.
2. She will be rewarded for pleasing her husband.
3. She will be rewarded for the gratitude to Allah Ta'ala that every person who eats the food expresses. Therefore, if her husband, her

in-laws and her children enjoy the food, they express their gratitude to Allah Ta'ala for the good food. Because she was the cause of them being grateful to Allah Ta'ala, she will be rewarded for the gratitude that each of them expresses to Allah Ta'ala. Laying out the tablecloth is also something that every wife should learn. Whether she has only a plastic sheet to spread or whether she has a lace cloth, she should ensure that it is clean. If she has only plastic dishes instead of fine porcelain crockery, the most important factor is that it must be clean so that one is tempted to drink the water poured in because of its remarkable clarity. The person drinking will then be compelled to say:

الحمد للّٰه الذي سقانا ماء باردًا عذبًا فُراتًا ولم يجعله بذنوبنا ملحًا أجاجًا

{TRANSLATION: "All praise be to Allah Ta'ala who has provided cool, palatable and quenching water for us to drink without making it salty and bitter because of our sins."}

Together with all the dishes and cutlery being gleaming, the fruit and vegetables should also be clean. Even if you are making salad, arrange it in a tempting manner. According to your means, serve some sweet drink whenever possible to add extra flavour to the food. Hukamaa (plural of Hakeem- practitioner in alternative medicine) are of the opinion that looking at a fresh and green plan or tree early in the morning strengthens and soothes the eyes. This being the case, one cannot imagine how much more soothing to the eyes and comforting to the mind and body is the sight of a smiling wife with sweet words pouring from her lips at this time of the day.

Hukamaa also mention that when the tablecloth and eating area is spacious and clean, digestion is aided and the food supplies all the necessary nutrition by Allah Ta'ala's command. It is therefore beneficial to have a vase with roses or other flowers on the tablecloth. In addition to this, the dining area should be spacious and well ventilated. Of course, there is really no need for flowers when Allah Ta'ala has granted a couple real flowers in the form of wonderful and cheerful children who add a special ambience to the meal. The sparkling company that these flowers provide with their beaming faces are more conducive to good digestion than any medication.

It is unfortunate that lack of understanding and short-sightedness has led parents to feel that their children are a burden. They fail to realise that these children are the cure their illnesses and difficulties. Many women feel that they cannot do any constructive work with their children in the way; little realising that caring for their children is itself a great and noble work. They fail to realise that rearing their children and serving their husbands as great a virtue as reciting Quran and making Dhikr.

Girls should therefore be trained to cook from a young age. If, for example, a woman can prepare chicken in ten different manners, she will be able to serve ten different dishes. A simple dish prepared and served with flair is often much more enjoyable than an expensive dish. Similarly, serving a dessert, salad, sauce or drink lends opulence to even a simple meal.

However, one should remember that all one's time should not be used for cooking, leaving no time for Ibaadah, rest or tending to the children. It does not behove a Muslim woman to spend all her time in the kitchen. Every woman should therefore bear the following three factors in mind so that all her time is not squandered in the kitchen:

1. She should make wudhu and perform her Ishraaq salah. She should also perform Salaatul Haajah and ask Allah Ta'ala to grant her needs, especially on the days when she is expecting visitors. On such days, she should make du'aa to Allah Ta'ala saying, "O Allah Ta'ala! Only You can give taste to food, so add taste to my food. Create light in the hearts of everyone who eats this food so that they may become pious and beloved to You. You be pleased with me for preparing this meal for my husband's pleasure."
2. Be particular about cooking early in the morning immediately after the Ishraaq salah because Allah Ta'ala has blessed the mornings for the Ummah of Messenger of Allah (Peace be upon him). During this time, one can achieve in a single hour what would take three or four hours during any other part of the day. Women who do not begin early in the morning find no blessings in their time and often have to work late to complete their work. One should therefore engage oneself in Dhikr and recitation of the Quran after Fajr salah and then begin one's work immediately after Ishraaq. Everything will then get done

easily and in the shortest time.

3. Continuously make du'aa and Dhikr while doing your work. If one knows Surah Yaaseen or any other Surahs of the Quran, these should also be read if one is not in the state of impurity. However, the various forms of Dhikr, Durood and Istighfaar may be recited in any condition. This will also help in making the food tasty and getting the work done easily and quickly. By preparing the food in the state of wudhu and making Dhikr while cooking, Allah Ta'ala will fill the hearts of those eating the food with Noor (celestial light). The result of this will be that the person eating will receive spiritual nutrition together with physical nutrition. S/he will then be able to carry out more good deeds and stay away from sin.

May Allah Ta'ala grant every woman the guidance to carry out what has been mentioned. *Aameen*.

Imaam Ghazaali's (May Allah be Merciful on him/her) Advice to The Bride

In his masterpiece "Ihyaa'ul Uloom", Imaam Ghazali (May Allah be Merciful on him/her) has given the following advices to brides:

- A pious woman should stay indoors. It is unbecoming of a respectable woman to climb on to the roof of her home (in areas where people use the roofs of their homes as another storey) and to gaze out of the windows.
- Speak less to your neighbours and visit only when necessary. In fact, you should go out of the house only when necessary.
- Whether your husband is home or not, you should be concerned about his welfare.
- Make his pleasure the object of everything you do.
- Never be unfaithful to him.
- Always safeguard his property.
- Never go out of the house without his permission and if he does permit you, wear the simplest clothing and fulfil all the requirements of Hijaab. Use roads that have the least traffic.
- Do not become familiar with any non-Mahram and make yourself as least conspicuous as possible.
- Keep yourself occupied with the affairs of your home and caring for your property.
- Always be particular about your salah.
- If any friend of your husband visits while he is out, inform him of you husband's absence using the least amount of words.

A SPECIAL PRACTICE

One of the sterling practices of a pious wife is that she does everything she can for the home. The management of the affairs of the house rests on her shoulders and she should not neglect any of these duties.

Asma (May Allah be pleased with him/her) narrates that when she married Zubayr (May Allah be pleased with him/her), he possessed no land, no wealth and no slaves. All he had was a horse and a camel to carry water. She used to feed the horse, water it, and do everything to care for it. She also used to crush date stones for the camel to eat, fill the buckets of water, mend the bucket, knead dough, bake bread and carry date stones from a distance. It was only afterwards that her father Abu Bakr (May Allah be pleased with him/her) gave her a slave. After receiving the slave, she felt as if she had been released from bondage. *[Bukhari]*

THE REWARDS FOR CARRYING OUT ONE'S DOMESTIC CHORES

People are often given to thinking that the husband-wife relationship is a association confined to one's worldly affairs. They regard marriage as a mere medium of fulfilling one's passions. This notion could not be further from the truth.The husband-wife relationship is a union that is replete with religious benefits. If a woman gets married with the intention of fulfilling an injunction of the Shari'ah, understanding that her function is to please her husband a function which will secure Allah Ta'ala's pleasure. Whatever a wife does with this intention in mind will earn her tremendous rewards. Her every act from morning to evening every day of the year will earn Allah Ta'ala's pleasure and will be regarded as a form of Ibaadah. Each of these deeds shall be invaluable investments for the Aakhirah, even though it means cooking, cleaning the house, rearing the children or seeing to the comfort of her husband. These will be rewarded on condition that the intention is correct.

DOING THE HOUSEWORK

Allah Ta'ala has assigned the task of working and earning to men. The task of doing the housework, caring for the children and seeing to other domestic affairs has been assigned to women. This has been the practice of mankind since time immemorial.

Whether a woman is rich or poor, she will feel a sense of achievement and elation when she does her housework by herself. In fact, she will do better than a servant. Doing the housework is also an excellent form of exercise and every educated and uneducated person will agree that exercise is vital to the health of every person. Of course, a woman may employ the services of a servant if she needs to. However, the smooth running of the home will be jeopardised when everything is left to the servant. While servants may be able to carry out the menial tasks, the more important tasks should be done by the wife herself.

It is unfortunate that many women nowadays feel ashamed to do their housework and entrust their servants with doing everything. There are also many Muslim women who insist that they should have a maidservant to shirk their responsibilities even though their husbands find it difficult to employ one. Every woman should bear in mind that by doing no work besides issuing instruction, they will become inactive and lazy. Their health will be adversely affected and they may eventually reach a stage where they will be unable to do anything.

Just as men require exercise to maintain their health, women also require the same. Every woman has so much to do at home that she will get the required exercise merely by completing her tasks. Experience has proven that women who do their housework themselves are much healthier than those who have hired help. Women who are accustomed to having servants rapidly succumb to obesity and ill-health.

The Sahabiyaat (May Allah be pleased with him/her) did their own housework, as did Messenger of Allah (Peace be upon him) himself. Aswad (May Allah be pleased with him/her) once asked Ayesha (May Allah be pleased with him/her) what Messenger of Allah (Peace be upon him) used to do at home. She replied, "He used to assist his wife in her duties and then leave when it was time for salah." In another narration, Ayesha (May Allah be pleased with him/her) narrated that Messenger of Allah (Peace be upon him) would himself mend his shoes, patch his clothing and assist with the housework.

The Domestic Life of Fatimah (May Allah be pleased with him/her)

"In poverty, her condition was such,
shehad neither a maidservant nor a slave
Calloused both her palms had become
for daily the grindstone she turned
Carrying the waterbag across her chest
again and again
she had become pale even though from her face
the light still radiated
Dusty did her clothing remain
on account of her daily sweeping strain
She eventually approached the messenger of
Allah Ta'ala her father
but fate had it that he was then swamped by
another and another
Because they were not Mahram, she could not
say her part
Since modesty did not allow her there, hastily
did she depart
When Messenger of Allah (Peace be upon him) visited her after a day
he asked, 'What was it that brought you yesterday?'
Her bashfulness prevented words from reaching
her tongue
So her message did Ali (May Allah be pleased with him/her)

convey
The pure lady stood there silent
Boldness deserted her because it was an
occasion of respect
Such were the lives of the Ahlul Bayt
such was a scene from the life of the daughter
of the best of creation."
[Translated from an Urdu poem]

ACQUIRING SKILLS

Intelligent women do not waste their valuable time in play and entertainment. They invest their time learning new skills such as sewing, knitting, weaving and other crafts. A skill acquired as a child remains useful throughout one's life. People who have learnt a craft need never be dependent on others. A craft that one acquires is a companion in solitude and extremely useful when faced with financial difficulty. One will then not have to stretch out one's hands to others.

The Sahabiyaat also acquired skills. Sauda (May Allah be pleased with him/her) mastered the craft of curing and dying hides that she received from Taa'if. For this reason, she was always more financially independent that the other wives of Noble Prophet (Peace be upon him) Fatima bint Shayba (May Allah be pleased with him/her) mastered the art of sewing, weaving and stringing beads. Safiyya (May Allah be pleased with him/her) mastered the art of cooking. There were many other Sahabiyaat who spent their time weaving cloth. Umm-e- Ziyaad (May Allah be pleased with him/her) Umm-e-Shahjiyyah (May Allah be pleased with him/her) and a few other Sahabiyaat were skilled in spinning cloth and were of great assistance to the Muslim army that marched to Khaybar.

THE ROUTINE OF A PIOUS WIFE

"Early in the morn does the loyal wife rise
Beginning the day with the Fajr salah, no surprise
Here we have the servant lighting the stove
There we have the wife comforting the children
While one is on her lap, the other is tugging at her skirt
These stars are there roaming the garden

The one cries for a biscuit
Another cries to be dressed
She washes each one of them
She feeds something to all
When the husband washes and arrives
The food is before him to choose
With a smile and gleam he is out and away
She completes her meal, content to know that
she shall stay
Bringing the baskets, bringing the clothes
Sorting them out by herself
Grabbing the chance between her salah and Ibaadah
She reads avidly from 'Fadhaa'il A'maal' and
'Behisti Zewar'
When a friend without Hijaab passes by
She is grieved and almost begins to cry
Make Jannah your home if you wish
Increase the contents of Jahannam if you wish
Elevate our honour if you wish
Or plunge us into disgrace if you wish
Be a disgrace to your era if you wish
Or transcend the limits of honour if you wish
The progression of time makes it clear
The call is coming from everywhere, my dear
'Educating women about Islam is the door to progress'
'Educating women about Islam is the pride of progress.'"
[Translated from an Urdu poem]

Learning a Lesson from the life of Fatima (May Allah be pleased with him/her)

When Fatima (May Allah be pleased with him/her) married Ali (May Allah be pleased with him/her), the couple decided that he would work outdoors while she tended to all domestic affairs. She therefore fulfilled her tasks and served her husband with great enthusiasm and devotion. However, unlike today's times, the time in which they lived was a period of difficulty. Just to have bread, a woman of those times had to grind the wheat into flour by herself, gather wood to light the oven, kindle the fire and then bake the bread. Despite the hardship involved in this single task, she dutifully continued with all her chores without a word of complaint.

When the Muslims conquered Khaybar and a great deal of booty including many slaves fell to their lot, someone suggested to Fatima (May Allah be pleased with him/her) that she request her father for a slave to assist her in her work. Consequently, she went to the room of Ayesha (May Allah be pleased with him/her) and requested her to ask Messenger of Allah (Peace be upon him) for a slave on her behalf because her hands had become calloused as a result of grinding flour and her chest had developed blue lines because of the strain of carrying the water bag to and from the well. When Ayesha (May Allah be pleased with him/her) related what Fatima (May Allah be pleased with him/her) had told her, Messenger of Allah (Peace be upon him) sent for Fatima (May Allah be pleased with him/her). According toanother narration, she approached Messenger of Allah (Peace be upon him) directly but returned without placing her request because there were many people with him at the time. According to this narration, Messenger of Allah (Peace be upon him) came to her house afterwards and asked her what she had come for. Because she found it hard to relate her sufferings to Messenger of Allah (Peace be upon him), Ali (May Allah be pleased with him/her) explained the situation to Rasulullah (Peace be upon him). One can well imagine the grief that Messenger of Allah (Peace be upon him) felt when he heard about his daughter's hardship.

Addressing Fatima (May Allah be pleased with him/her) Messenger of Allah (Peace be upon him) said, "I deem it inappropriate that the daughter of Muhammad should be given a slave until every person in Madinah has own. However, I shall prescribe for you something that is better than a slave. When you lay down to sleep at night, say سبحان الله 33 times, الحمد لله 33 times and الله أكبر 34 times. his is better for you than any slave." She was after all the daughter of the best of creation. Therefore, without saying a word, she felt contented with what her father told her. This prescription is therefore called Tasbeeh Faatimi. *[Jaami'ul Usool Vol.6 Pg. 501]*

In this episode, Messenger of Allah (Peace be upon him) used his own beloved daughter to teach Muslims that irrespective of the rights that her husband owes to her from a technical perspective, a Muslim wife ought to care for her husband's home and regard this task as her own. *[Mufti Taqi Usmani in his book concerning the rights of husbands]*

RIGHTS PERTAINING TO WEALTH

The wife owes three rights to her husband with regard to his wealth. These are:

1. She should safeguard his wealth.
2. She should not ask for more than she needs.
3. She should be concerned that he does earn unlawful wealth.

It was therefore the practice of women of the past to remind their husbands every morning to stay away from unlawful earnings.

They would reassure their husbands that although they did not fear poverty and were able to bear hunger, they dreaded Jahannam and would be unable to bear its punishment. They were therefore contented with anything they received even though little, on condition that it was earned lawfully.

Every wife should bear in mind that the rights she owes to her husband take precedence over the rights she owes to even herself and over the rights she owes to all her relatives.

It is also among his rights that she keeps herself clean and neat at all times because he may need to fulfil his conjugal rights at any time.

Every wife should also treat her children well and display great love and mercy towards them. She should refrain from scolding them too often and should conceal their faults from others.

One of the most important responsibilities of a wife is that she should not waste her husband's wealth. In fact, it is not at all appropriate for a Muslim wife to waste money on unnecessary clothing, shoes, jewellery, etc. Money is often wasted on these things when extravagant functions like weddings, parties, etc are hosted. The object is then merely to show off.

She should spend only on those things that are absolutely necessary for personal self. Whatever is extra should be spend for the propagation of Deen, on pious people and the poor. We will now narrate a few incidents about some pious Muslim wives who spent generously in Allah Ta'ala's path.

Ayesha (May Allah be pleased with her) Spends on Others

Muhammad bin Munkadir (May Allah be pleased with him/her) once asked Ayesha (May Allah be pleased with her) for some money which he desperately needed. She said, "I have nothing to give to you presently. If I had ten thousand, I would have given it all to you. However, I have nothing at the moment." A short while after he left, Khalid bin Asadr sent ten thousand as a gift for Ayesha (May Allah be pleased with her). When the money arrived, she said, "It seems as if my word is already being put to test." She then sent for Muhammad bin Munkadirr and gave him the entire amount. With the money, Muhammad bin Munkadirr bought a slave girl for a thousand. From her, he fathered three sons whom he named Muhammad, Abu Bakr and Umar. All three were among the pious saints of Madinah. *[Tahdheeb]*

Being one of the causes for the birth of these three men, Ayesha (May Allah be pleased with her) will certainly share in the rewards that they all earned for their Ibaadah. It is not surprising that Ayesha (May Allah be pleased with her) was so magnanimous because she was after all the daughter of Abu Bakrr.

In his book "Stories of Companion of the Prophetr", Sheikh-ul-Hadith Moulana Muhammad Zakariyal, has quoted an incident in which Ayesha (May Allah be pleased with her) distributed two bags full of Dirhams. Although the bags contained more than a hundred thousand Dirhams, she forgot to keep aside even a single Dirham to buy meat with which she could break her fast that evening. Another narration is reported in which a similar incident took place with her while she was distributing a thousand Dirhams.

Tameem bin Urwar narrated that he saw his father's aunt viz. Ayesha (May Allah be pleased with her) distribute seventy thousand Dirhams to the poor while she wore patched clothing. *[It'haaf]*

A WIFE WHO USED TO SPEND ON ALLAH TA'ALA'S PIOUS BONDSMEN

A pious lady by the name of Raabi'ah bint Isma'eel sent a marriage proposal to a pious saint by the name of Ahmad Ibn Abil Hawariyl. He was an extremely pious person who was reluctant to marry. When he received the proposal, he declined saying that he did not want to get married because he was too engrossed in his Ibaadah and Dhikr. She sent him a reply stating that she was more engrossed in acts of devotion than him and herself did not need to get married. However, she wished to marry him so that his pious friends could benefit from a great fortune that her late husband had left for her. In spending on them, she felt that she would have a share in their efforts and be able to tread easily on the path to salvation.

Ahmad Hawariyl took leave to consul with his teacher Abu Sulayman Daranil, saying that he would marry her only if his teacher permitted. Although, Abu Sulaymanl had already prohibited Ahmadl from marriage, he permitted him to marry Rabi'ah saying, "Marry her for she is Allah Ta'ala's friend and her speech resembles that of the Siddiqeen."After marrying her, he mentioned that she hosted so many people for meals that they had a pond built in which the guests washed their hands. This pond was only for those who needed to rush and could not take the time to wash their hands properly. Despite this, the pond soon became damaged because many people who used it.

Ahmad Hawariyl narrated that he married three other wives after her but instead of getting angry, she was glad and would send him off to these wives after feeding him well. She was to Shaam what Rabi'ah Adawiyya was to Basrah. *[Ihya]*

A WOMAN WHO ENTERTAINED GUESTS

Abur Rabeel narrates that he was once visiting a village when he heard that the goat of a certain woman called Fiddah gave milk as well as honey.

Surprised at this, he bought a cup and proceeded to the lady's house. He told her what he had heard and said that he had come to witness this blessing for himself. When she made the goat over to him and he milked it, he found that it really did give milk and honey.

When he asked her how she came to own such an animal, she narrated her story to him. She and her husband were poor people who possessed nothing but one goat which produced the milk that they subsisted on. When the occasion of Eidul Adhaa arrived, her husband told her that he would have to sacrifice the animal. However, he changed is mind when she explained to him that the goat was their only livelihood and that it was not compulsory for them to sacrifice an animal because of their poverty. As it would be, they received a guest that very day. She said to her husband, "We have been commanded to entertain guests. Since we have nothing but this goat, you may as well slaughter it to feed the guest. When he set out to slaughter it, she thought that her children would be grieved to see it being slaughtered. She therefore told her husband to take the goat outside and slaughter it behind their wall. When he slaughtered the goat, another goat appeared on the wall and climbed down into their yard.

Thinking that the goat had escaped from her husband, the lady went out to see, but found her husband already skinning the slaughtered goat. When she told him about the other goat in their yard, he told her that Allah Ta'alamust have already replaced the goat for them. This goat was the very one that gave milk and honey. This was all because of the blessings of entertaining one guest. The woman then addressed her children saying, "This goat feeds on (what is in) your hearts. As long as your hearts remain pious and clean, the milk will continue being good. As soon as your hearts become tainted, the milk will also become the same. Keep you hearts good and everything else will also be good for you."

The Queen Zubaydah

Zubayda was the wife of the Khalifa Haaroon Ar Rasheed. The famous lady was the daughter of Khalifa Mansoor's son Ja'far. It was because of this son that Mansoor was called Abu Ja'far (the father of Ja'far). Zubayda was born in Mowsil while her father was the governor of the city. However, she was only two or three years old when her father passed away. She was then brought up by her grandfather the Khalifa Mansoor. Her grandfather loved her very much and although her name was Amatul Azeez, he affectionately called her Zubayda. This name stuck so well that people eventually forgot her real name. She married Haaroon Ar Rasheed when she was only fifteen or sixteen years old. No one expected Haaroon Ar Rasheed to become Khalifa because his elder brother Haadi was heir apparent to the throne. However, Haadi passed away before ascending to the throne and Haaroon Ar Rasheed became Khalifa with Zubayda as his queen.

The loving relationship of Haaroon Ar Rasheed and Zubayda is proverbial. Allah Ta'ala blessed her with piety, compassion and the rare ability to put things in order. She orchestrated the affairs of the royal palace like none other had ever done. Her generosity is also proverbial and no beggar left her door without receiving something. There were a hundred slave women in her palace, all of who had memorised the Quran. Each of them recited ten parts of the Quran daily, completing the Quran every three days. Whoever passed the palace could hear the Quran being recited.

She was very concerned with charitable community projects. In the year 208 A.H. (824), she left for Hajj and took a large contingent of engineers with her. Wherever she found people having difficulty with water or roads, she immediately arranged the means for addressing the difficulty. While travelling towards Baytul Muqaddas, she passed an area that experienced water shortages. She dispatched people to search for a suitable water source in the mountains to irrigate the area. Through this effort, water was channelled from a source which developed into a strong source of irrigation for the area as well as for many other areas.

She had hundreds of dams, Masjids and roads built for the benefit of the public. However, her most famous achievement was the engineering masterpiece known as "Nahr Zubayda" (the "Canal of Zubayda"), which for centuries provided water for the people of Makkah and for the millions of pilgrims arriving for Hajj. The source of the canal was a spring in a mountainous area approximately 25 to 30 km east of Makkah. Later on, another spring was joined to the canal. The canal passed by Arafat, Muzdalifa and Mina en route to Makkah. A major portion of this canal lies beneath the ground and it fills reservoirs built at appropriate places. The water used to supply hundreds of thousands of Haajis who stayed for many days at Mina and for a day at Arafat and Muzdalifa.

When the cost for constructing the canal was estimated, she was told hat it would be extremely expensive. She responded by saying, "Even if I have to pay a single labourer a gold coin for every strike of his spade, I shall happily do so but I shall never abandon the project." Zubayda spend no less than seven hundred thousand gold coins on community projects during this Hajj journey.

These were people who truly appreciated the Allah Ta'ala's bounties and spend as much as they could on Allah Ta'ala's creation. They understood that wealth is useless when squandered on the luxuries of just a few people. Zubayda passed away at the age of seventy and although centuries have passed since her demise, her name still lives on because of her noble deeds. The hand of death cannot erase the good works that people do.

It is the responsibility of every wife to utilise her husband's wealth for good causes. At the same time, she should be concerned about safeguarding his Imaan. These are important rights that she owes to him and she should never be negligent of these.

An Important Right of the Husband that Women are Heedless About

Jabirr narrates that Messenger of Allah's gaze once inadvertently fell on a woman. He immediately proceeded to his wife Zaynab (May Allah be pleased with her) and satisfied his need. He then addressed the Companion of the Prophet saying, "A woman appears as a Shaytaan. When any of you sees a woman who attracts him, he should immediately go to his wife because she has exactly what the other woman has." *[Tirmidhi]*

Messenger of Allah (Peace be upon him) has likened women to Sha- ytaan because the natural attraction they possess presents the ideal opportunity for Shaytan to deviate man. Their emergence from their homes is like the emergence of Shaytan himself. This fact makes it clear that women should not roam about and Muslims should make every effort to stay away from mixed gatherings.

Muslims men should guard their gazes because when their eyes meet those of a non-Mahram woman, Shaytaan exploits the opportunity to destroy their lives in this world as well as in the Aakhirah. One should always guard one's gazes because Shaytaan will develop sexual inclinations in people when they mix freely.

When a man satisfies himself with his lawful wife, his inclination to develop illicit relationships will be killed and he will be saved from the clutches of Shaytaan. It is therefore necessary for every wife to respond to her husband's need for intercourse, whether he asks directly or indirectly. Of course, she may excuse herself if she has a valid excuse to do so, such as menstruation. When a woman implements this attitude, she will be benefiting her husband from a physical, religious, mental, medical and spiritual perspective.

It is instinctive for the average man to look up at a passing woman, thereby creating an impression in his mind. It often happens that he may then become sexually aroused, plunging him into a state of uneasiness. When such as situation arises, Messenger of Allah (Peace be upon him) has instructed that the man should satisfy himself with his wife so that Shaytaan may not exploit the situation and cause him to sin. The solution is therefore simple and effective.

However, there may be rare cases when one wife may not satisfy a man's needs. In such cases, he may take up to three other wives on condition that he is absolutely certain that he can treat them all justly and provide adequately for them all. The Shari'ah has permitted these avenues because adultery is an intolerable sin. The chastity and moral fibre of society is highly coveted in Islam. Implementing the injunctions of the Shari'ah will safeguard these objectives and save society from the many illicit relations already existing such as affairs between brothers-and-sisters-in-law, cousins, etc. Women should therefore be particular about satisfying their husbands and should stop making excuses like saying that they will be unable to complete their tasks if they are delayed by taking a bath after intercourse. Muslim wives who make frivolous excuses of this nature should remember that if their husbands satisfy themselves in Haraam avenues, they (the wives) will also be liable for the sin because they had been the cause of it.

A WOMAN SHOULD RESPOND IMMEDIATELY

وعن طلق بن علي رضى اللّٰه عنه أن رسول اللّٰه ﷺ قال إذا دعا الرجل
زوجته لحاجته فلتأته وأن كانت على التنور

Talq bin Ali (May Allah be pleased with him/her) narrates that Rasulullaah (Peace be upon him) said, "When a husband calls his wife to satisfy his sexual need, she should respond even if she is busy at the oven." [Tirmidhi]

This hadith makes it clear that she should not refuse his call irrespective of how occupied she may be.

Nikaah is the Means of Securing Comfort

Allah Ta'ala has instilled passionate instincts in every man and woman. Allah Ta'ala has also prescribed the means by which man can fulfil these instincts. This means is Nikaah. The primary objective of Nikaah is to satisfy these instinctive passions in men and women. The husband should therefore do his best to satisfy the wife and she should do the same so that none of them has to resort to illicit means of sexual gratification.

REWARD FOR SATISFYING ONE'S DESIRE LAWFULLY

Messenger of Allah (Peace be upon him) once told the Companion of the Prophet that a person is rewarded for satisfying his sexual desire with his wife. When the Companion of the Prophet y expressed surprise that a person could be rewarded for satisfying a carnal passion, Rasulullah (Peace be upon him) asked them, "Will a person be sinful if he satisfies his desire unlawfully?" "Certainly," responded the Companion of the Prophet p. Rasulullah (Peace be upon him) said, "Therefore, if a couple refrains from unlawful relations and fulfil their needs within the command of Allah Ta'ala, they will be rewarded." *[Ahmad]*

THE WOMAN WHOM THE ANGELS CURSE

عن أبي هريرة رضى اللّٰه عنه قال: قال رسول اللّٰه ﷺ : إذا دعا الرجل

إمرأته إلى فراشه فأبت أن تجيئ لعنتها الملائكة حتى تصبح

(صحيح بخارى ص ٧٨٢، كتاب النكاح، باب إذا بات إمرأة مهاجرة فراش زوجها حديث

نمبر ٥١٩٣)

Abu Hurayrar narrated that Rasulullahs said, "When a man calls his wife to bed (for conjugal relations) and she refuses to respond (or does something by which his desire is left unfulfilled and he becomes angry with her), the angels continue cursing her until the next morning." [Bukhari Vol. 2 Pg. 782]

In the Arabic context, the meaning of a person being cursed is that the person is distanced from Allah Ta'ala's mercy. The husband sees to the needs of his wife and provides for her from his hard-earned wealth. In addition to this, he fulfils her many other rights as well. In return for all of this, she is expected to at least fulfil his sexual needs so that he may be saved from sin. She should bear in mind that the fundamental object of Nikaah is to protect the man's chastity and to save his eyes from roving. She should therefore not fail in this vital task because her failure would be disastrous for both of them. In addition to this, she would then also be subjecting herself to the curses of the angels.

Commenting on this hadith, Moulana Aashiq Ilaahi (Daamat Barakaatuh) says that because a mere indication is sufficient for an intelligent person, further elucidation is not necessary for this hadith. It is simple to understand and every woman who sees her failings in this regard should take heed.

Women who disregard this hadith find their husbands marrying other wives or (even worse) forsaking their chastity. The husband-wife relationship is extremely special because they can fulfil their needs with none other but themselves. It is therefore of paramount importance that their relationship should be one of love and understanding.

Our beloved Prophet (Peace be upon him) understood human psychology very well and identified all man's needs. His advices were therefore pertinent and effective. However, when one acts contrary to these advices, one will experience bitterness and conditions will worsen.

It is only by way of example that Messenger of Allah mentioned that the angels will curse such a woman until the morning. This does not mean that she will be exempt from these curses if she refuses during the day. It is necessary for her to respond to him at any time unless she has a valid reason like menstruation, etc.

Abu Hurayrar narrates that Our beloved Prophet (Peace be upon him) said,

إذا باتت المرأة مهاجرة فراش زوجها لعنتها الملائكة حتى ترجع
(بخاری ص ۷۸۲)

"A woman who spends the night away from her husband's bed (to avoid cohabiting with him) shall dwell under the curses of the angels until she returns."

[Bukhari Vol. 2 Pg. 782]

The above Ahadeeth make it clear that refusing to cohabit with one's husband is a grave sin that warrants the curses of the angels. Similarly, if a woman leaves her husband's bed against his wishes, she will also be subjected to the curses of the angels until she returns. Holy Prophet (Peace be upon him) had specifically mentioned all these things because these are factors that ruin families.

THE OPINION OF EXPERTS IN THE FIELD OF PSYCHOLOGY

Based on their vast knowledge and experience, experts in human psychology assert that the best wife is she who actively participates in love-making. It should be borne in mind that when one pan of the scale of love in empty, the other pan will empty by itself. When enthusiasm is lacking, the couple's sexual life begins to die. If the wife's attitude towards sex is cold, if she expresses reluctance towards it or if she oversteps the limits of bashfulness, the couple's relationship will be stifled and eventually killed.

On the other hand, when the couple enjoy a healthy sex life with both partners as eager participants, their love for each other will grow as well as their mutual trust. Such a couple will even have children who are active and intelligent. Such a couple will experience happiness and peace of mind.

A woman will be guilty of extreme laziness and insolence when she responds coldly to her husband's warmth, kind words and favours as he makes advanced towards her. This causes him to dislike her and to develop negative feelings towards her. In essence, the benefits of sexual relations are attained only when both partners are equally stimulated and when both enjoy their relationship.

By employing her intelligence, gentle nature, beauty and other methods of attraction, a bright woman can maintain hers and her husband's youth and their period of sexual activity without resorting to extreme measures. When couple's sexual activity contains receptiveness, attraction towards each other and fulfilment coupled with the intentions of pleasing Allah Ta'ala, fulfilling their duties towards each other and being parents of pious children, they will experience unparalleled pleasure.

Allama Ibn Qayyim writes that the sign of such pleasure will be that every limb of the body will be at ease and the mere sight of one's spouse will delight one's eyes. In addition to this, his words will be a song to the ears, his fragrance wills the most precious in the world, his kiss will sweeten the mouth and the touch of his hand will generate a powerful emotion, giving contentment to the entire body. However, if anything is lacking in the relationship, the contentment will be incomplete and wanting.

[Rowdhatul Muhibbeen Pg. 216, 217]

When a person enjoys doing something permissible, he will be rewarded for it on condition that he does the act to please Allah Ta'ala because it is a command of Allah Ta'ala and a practice of Messenger of Allah.

لعن الله المسوفات التي يدعوها زوجها إلى فراشه فتقول سوف حتى تغلبه عيناه

Messenger of Allah also said, "May Allah Ta'ala's curse be on the woman who says, 'I'm coming, I'm coming.' When her husband calls her to bed, she keeps saying, 'I'm coming, I'm coming,' until he falls asleep."

Muslim narrates a Hadith from Abu Hurayrar in which Messenger of Allah (Peace be upon him) says, "By the Being in whose control is my life! When a husband calls his wife to bed and she refuses, He in the heavens becomes angry with her until her husband is happy with her."

The reason for this is that Shaytan becomes extremely pleased when he separates the couple and they become enemies instead of benefiting from each other's love and company. Another hadith of Muslim mentions that Shaytaan sets up his throne on water and then disperses his disciples to cause mischief. The closest to him is the one who causes the most evil and strife. When the disciples gather afterwards, one of them says, "I worked on so-and-so until he committed adultery." Another says, "I did not rest until separated a couple." Hearing this, Shaytaan congratulates the disciple and seats him closest to him, telling him, "You are the one! You are the one!"

This narration makes it clear that Allah Ta'ala's enemy is most pleased when a rift is created between two hearts containing the love of Allah Ta'ala and His Rasul. Therefore, when a husband calls his wife to bed and she thinks that he thinks only of sex or that she will have to take a bath in such cold weather, she should immediately tell herself that these thoughts are from Shaytan. She should then recite thrice "A'oodhu Billaahi Minash Shaytaanir Rajeem" and thrice "Laa Howla wa Laa Quwwata Illa Billaah". She should then go immediately to her husband. Insha Allah Ta'ala, this will disgrace Shaytan and he will leave the house. Allah Ta'ala will then make such a wife beloved to her husband.

Nafil Fasts may be Observed Only With the Husband's Permission

وعن أبي هريرة رضي اللّٰه عنه أن رسول اللّٰه ﷺ قال: لايحل للمرأة أن تصوم وزوجها شاهد إلّا بإذنه ولا تأذن في بيته إلّا بإذنه

(صحيح بخارى، كتاب النكاح، باب لأتأذن المرأة فى بيت زوجها ، حديث نمبر ٥١٩٥)

Abu Hurayra (May Allah be pleased with him/her) reports that Rasulullah (Peace be upon him) said, "It is not permissible for a woman to fast (an optional fast) in the presence of her husband unless he permits her. She may not also allow anyone into his house without his permission." [Bukhari]

Although the Ahadeeth have mentioned many virtues of observing optional fasts, a woman may not observe them without her husband's permission because fasting would deny him his conjugal rights. Of course, a good husband would never prevent his wife without good reason. He should not deny her the virtues merely because he is upset with her on some other account. However, should he refuse her permission, it is not permissible for her to fast because obeying him takes precedence over Nafl fasts.

OBEYING ONE'S HUSBAND IS MORE IMPORTANT THAN NAFL ACTS OF WORSHIP

The above hadith makes it clear that obeying one's husband takes precedence over all Nafl (optional) acts of worship. Therefore, when a woman obeys her husband, she will receive rewards greater than what she would receive for Nafl acts of worship. For this reason, a woman should never feel that her husband has deprived her of rewards if he refuses her permission to observe Nafl fasts. She should reflect on her reasons for fasting. It is obvious that she is fasting to be rewarded and to attain Allah Ta'ala's pleasure. These being the reasons, she should bear in mind that by obeying her husband's instruction not to fast, she will receive greater rewards and in pleasing her husband she will attain Allah Ta'ala's pleasure because Allah Ta'alawill not be pleased with her until her husband is pleased with her. The obedient wife will therefore receive a greater reward for eating and drinking than she would receive for fasting.

A Mother's Advice to her Daughter

Parents should give their children a proper upbringing by adorning them with the jewels of sound Islamic education, the gems of managing a household, the garments of fear for Allah Ta'ala, the bangles of Taqwa and the trousseau of obedience to Allah Ta'ala and engaging in His Dhikr. These are real gifts.

It is especially important for mothers to display respect for their husband in front of their daughters because their daughters will treat their husbands exactly how they see their mothers treating their fathers. There are many good mothers who raise their daughters so well that their sons-in-law and their families consider it their good fortune that these fine ladies have married into their families. Men marrying such women have attained kingship even though they may be living in shacks. They are wealthy with the sweet words she speaks and her ever-endearing smiles. The children born to such a couple will also be righteous servants of Allah Ta'ala blessed with intelligence and keen aptitudes because they have been brought up in the lap of an excellent mother.

Among the ranks of such mothers was Asma bint Khateeja Fazaariyar who gave the following golden words of advice to her daughter. These words are an inspiration to very bride.

"Beloved daughter! You are now departing from this home where you spent the days of your childhood and where you first set your foot upon the threshold of adolescence. You will now be the decoration of a bed that exudes a fragrance which will be unfamiliar to you. You will be treading step-by-step with a lifelong companion who is still a stranger to you."

"Dear daughter! Become the ground for your companion so that he may become your heaven. Become his cradle and he will become your supporting pillar. Become his slave and he will become yours. Never nag or force him into anything because he will then despise you. Never stay away from him because he will then forget you. If he draws close to you, draw even closer to him. Show concern for even his nose, ears and eyes (i.e. never cause him even the slightest harm). Be particular about using perfume because it comforts his mind via his nose. Keep watch over your tongue becase your sweet words gives him comfort via his ears. Keep your appearance attractive because so that you may be the delight of his eyes and his source of contentment. Let him always see you in a good condition with your hair combed, with kohl in your eyes, with neat clothes and a scarf on your head."

"My precious daughter! If you are particular about practising these advices, your home will be reminiscent of Jannah no matter how small it may be."

May Allah Ta'ala grant every Muslim wife the ability to practise the advices given above. It should never be that a bride dresses well and beautifies herself only while her marriage is new and then begins to resemble a maidservant after a few months, dressing up only when going out. A wife should never appear shabby in front of her husband because this will destroy his love for her.

A GROOM'S GIFT TO HIS BRIDE

An Arab groom lovingly presented to his bride four golden lines of poetry when they met the first night. We shall quote this as advice for the benefit of every new bride as well as for every married woman because it is never too late to practise. May Allah Ta'ala grant every woman the ability to practise. *Aameen.*

خذ العفو مني تستديمى مودتي
ولا تنطقى في وقت حين أغضب

"Overlook my errors and my love for you will be eternal
Never backchat when I'm angry for this will be infernal.

ولا تنقريني نقرك الدف مرة
فإنك لا تدرين كيف المغيب

You should never beat me like a drum you beat
For you know not what sound you will meet

ولا تكثري الشكوى فتذهب بال هوى
وياباك قلبي والقلوب تتقلب

Never complain incessantly because this destroys affection.
My heart should then never accept you because hearts are quick to change with every new attraction
I have seen that when love and annoyance unite in one heart
Love does not stay but has to depart."

In the second couplet of the poem, the poet tells his wife that she should never chance to backchat and retaliate when he is angry because this could produce a reaction that both of them will regret. In the final couplet, he warns her that by backchat, complaining and annoying him in any other way, his love for her may soon depart.

A BRIEF ANALYSIS OF THE POEM

1. If a woman wants the love of her husband, she should forgive and forget his faults and errors.
2. She should remain silent when he is angry. She should rather admit her fault and ask for forgiveness instead of defending her wrong. In fact, she should ask for forgiveness even if the fault is his. In addition to this, she should do whatever he asks.
3. Never complain. Rather be grateful to Allah Ta'alafor whatever you have. Patiently bear the difficulties that come your way from your sisters-and-mother-in-law. Of course, there is no harm in telling your husband your difficulties, but never chose to do so at a time when he is tired and unwilling to listen.
4. Incessant complaining irritates the husband and this will diminish the love he has for his wife in his heart.

Some Golden Principles for Every Bride to Follow

We will now present some extremely precious principles for every wife to follow so that she may live happily with her husband and her mother-in-law. These principles appear in the book "Tuhfatul Khawateen" (A Gift to Women), which was written by Moulana Muhammad s Ahmad Surti Saheb in the Gujrati language and has been translated into Urdu by Moulana Sulayman Saheb. May Allah Ta'ala grant us all the ability practise these principles and to make du'aa for the author of this book and the translator.

Beloved daughters! Remember that you have not been made to live forever in your parent's home. Their home was merely an inn for you. Allah Ta'ala had intended that you will soon leave this home. Has any visitor stayed forever at your house? Just as every visitor has left after a short while, you will also soon be leaving. Your parents will have to see you off when you have come of age and groomed for marriage. You will then have to leave to be with your in-laws. This is why a daughter is often referred to as a fleeting treasure. Your parents are doing nothing wrong because this is the command of Allah Ta'ala and the practice of our beloved Rasulullah (Peace be upon him).Such is the practice of people throughout the world, whether they are princes or paupers.

Precious daughters! Today you live with your parents and have shade beneath the roofs of their homes which are filled with love and affection. You are being reared here without experiencing any difficulties and without worrying about preparing food and sewing clothes. Here you have only peace and contentment. Whatever harm you do is quickly forgotten and your parents gently correct your mistakes. Your parents want only comfort for you and do not want to burden you with any worries.

However, dear daughters! Have you ever thought that you will one day be living with your in-laws? Will they also turn a blind eye to your iniquities? Never! They do not have the accommodating nature of your parents. There you will have to work to establish your self-respect and your honour. You will have to prove that you are competent and resolute. Without this, you cannot expect to have peace and happiness.

I shall first tell how to live with your parents, much of which you may have already experienced. Thereafter, I shall tell you how to live with your in-laws and you will become aware of everything. If you practise what you are about to read, you will be able to transform any home into a garden of paradise. Everyone will then embrace you with open arms and congratulate your every trait. People will congratulate your parents and no one will dare to do you any harm. The entire family will be compassionate towards you and your husband will boast about you. Young and old will respect you.

It is commonly understood that a woman's ability to cope with her housework is the first test she is put through when she starts living with her in-laws. It will also be seen whether you can run a home, whether you can keep your home clean, whether you can entertain guests and whether you behave well with relatives. If you are found lacking in any of these fields, it will be said that you know nothing. Today there is someone to correct you, afterwards there will be none to advise you. Then you will have to do things by yourself. If you do nothing today, how will you be able to cope then? Even if you do manage to cope then, it will be extremely difficult without today's training. If you are accustomed to being lazy, others will look down on you. How then can you expect respect? How can you then be happy?

I therefore have the desire that today you acquire the skills and expertise that will be a shield against future difficulties and which will navigate you through troubled waters. You will be mistaken to behave proudly and say that you know everything and will be able to manage by yourself. You should not rest assured merely because you can cook a few dishes, can stitch on a button, can decorate a few things, can recite the Quran or have read a few books. You will then be no better than a person who spent the entire night reading the story of Yusuf and Zulaikha and cannot even say the following morning whether Yusuf was a man or a woman.

It is therefore necessary that notwithstanding the tediousness of any task, you should never leave it incomplete. You also have to develop the ability to complete your tasks without any assistance. You should be independent of your mother- or- sisters- in-law as well as of any other helper. You should do things with such rapture and competence that the men of the house of are left gaping. Continue your housework together with tending to the children and bringing them up properly. It should never be that a single problem should cause you a hundred other problems or that a single need should cause you to forget a hundred others. Be cognisant of everything and never sway to extremes. Be moderate in all that you do. When you keep these things in mind, you will be able to correct matters whether they are done mistakenly or purposely.

Regard you friends as friends and enemies as enemies. Think before doing anything and you will save yourself and others from harm and inconvenience. This will also avert squabbles and disputes. If you behave in this manner, people will overlook your errors because when a sensible and careful person slips up, people are forgiving. On the other hand, people mock a fool even when he makes sense. Remember that all the good of this world and the Hereafter can be acquired by utilising one's intelligence correctly. Intelligence and modesty are two invaluable gems because modesty saves people from evil. I shall begin with mentioning those factors that will prove to be guiding lights for the future.

How to Live in your Parent's Home

Serve your parents with heart and soul and never cause them any grief. Have their meals ready on time as they prefer it. Listen attentively to what they says and dutifully carry out their instructions. Never disturb them when they busy and have things done as they are accustomed to doing it. Never nag and never demand. Arrange their clothing in an orderly fashion and always put soap, towels, etc in their place. Keep their home clean.

Wake up early in the mornings, quickly fulfil your needs and perform your Fajr salah. Recite the Quran, perform Ishraaq salah and then begin your work, bearing in mind that you should be ready to serve them at any time. Apologise and seek forgiveness when they become angry with you and never try to confuse them. Never even say, 'Oof!' to them in protest. Never be ungrateful to them and always remember their favours to you. If you do them a good turn, never remind them about it. Do everything by yourself and always put your stationery, clothing and other things away. If you all of this, I can truly say that you know something. If not, you should never think that you are capable.

Dear daughters! Remember that if your faults are not ironed out early, they will soon show their colours. Bad character, insolence, immoral behaviour, stinginess, pride and stubbornness are such evils that you may be unaware of and which your parents may brush aside, attributing them to your young age. They may turn a blind eye to these traits thinking that they will disappear by themselves. However, these traits will only thrive with age and prove to be your downfall. They will then only be identified and corrected when they cause one to stumble and fall.

An intelligent person is one who employs evasive measures long before the floods come. In time, your intelligence will show you the road, modesty will save you from evil and Allah Ta'alawill ease the difficulties that are headed your way. This world is fuelled by intelligence and the person whom Allah Ta'ala has blessed with the most intelligence shall be able to manage affairs most wisely. The stability of every structure pivots on the amount of intelligence employed.

THE MANNER OF LIVING WITH ONE'S HUSBAND

Dear daughters! I will now explain to you the manner in which you should live when you move in with your in-laws. Always remember that the relationship between husband and wife is not like loose threads that can be separated whenever one wishes. Marriage is a lifelong commitment. It takes nothing less than death to sever this union. If the couple's hearts are united, they can share no greater bounty and it is as if Jannah has come down to earth for them. On the other hand, if their hearts are not united, they can experience no worse tragedy and will not be blamed for thinking that Jahannam has come to earth.

Every woman has the ability to make her marriage work. It is imperative for a wife to win over her husband's heart by dying herself in his colours and doing everything he wants her to do. She should convince herself that if he commands her to fold her hands and stand all night long, her success lies in doing as he says. Success in the Hereafter should be sought even if it means enduring some hardship in this world.

CAPTURING YOUR HUSBAND'S HEART

A marriage can be successful when the couple are compatible and united. Without this, their lives will be incomplete and troubled. It is therefore imperative that every wife does her level best to learn the method of capturing her husband's heart. Without learning this method she can never be successful irrespective of how educated, attractive or wealthy she may be.

Wise people have mentioned many methods of harnessing one's husband's love. A woman who regards serving her husband and loving him as an important aspect of her Imaan has no option but to practise the guidelines which will be mentioned hereunder.

- Regard your husband as a wealthy man even though he may be poor.
- Consult with him in all matters and do as he advises.
- Never do anything against his wishes and always give precedence to the things that please him.
- Always be concerned about his peace of mind and never do anything that will cause him grief.
- Accept whatever he gives you with a happy heart.
- Do whatever he asks you to do in a manner that he is left without a worry.
- Always be happy and smiling so that all his worries can disappear merely by looking at you.
- Fulfil his needs before your own.
- Feed him as best as you can.
- If he cannot afford to buy clothes, sew them yourself.
- Try to do everything by yourself.
- Never ask him for something that he cannot afford otherwise he will be saddened if he cannot give it to you. If you are destined to have it, you will surely get it without asking.
- Do not ask him to do anything that you can do by yourself.
- Never tell him all your problems as soon as he arrives because his mind may already be inundated with other problems.
- Speak of good things while eating because when a person is happy, even the simplest meal is as tasty as the best delicacy. On the other hand, a delicious meal will seem dull to a troubled mind. When a woman begins telling her husband all her day's problems as soon as he walks in; his eating, sitting and resting will become difficult. In fact, he may even lose his appetite. Together with upsetting him, such behaviour is also displeasing to Allah Ta'ala.
- If Allah Ta'ala grants you the ability, assist him in his work.
- Share his problems and console him whenever he has a problem so that the burden may be raised from his shoulders.
- When he is in debt, assist him to settle it by earning some money without violating the laws of the Shari'ah. If you have some money of your own or some jewellery that can be sold, give this to him if he needs it so that he may appreciate the fact that he is more valuable to you

than these things. Never remind him about such favours afterwards and do not even make an effort to remember such things.

- Never neglect your duties to him and always do things that are in his best interests.
- Try to do all your housework by yourself. Insha Allah Ta'ala, Allah Ta'ala will soon show you easier days.
- Spend as little as possible and try to save as much as you can. If your savings are meagre, never stop saving with the thought that it is too little. Whatever you save will come in handy during rainy days because when days are dark friends are always few. You will then be saved from the humiliation of stretching your hands out in front of others. Your husband will then be amazed at your prudence and farsightedness.
- Sew your clothing by yourself, cook by yourself and look after the children by yourself.
- Reply gently when he asks a question.
- Be gentle when he is angry.
- Continue fulfilling his rights even if he is unhappy with the way you do things. This will please Allah Ta'ala:
    - Do your share even though it may be difficult.
    - Be content with whatever he is content with.
    - Spend his wealth with care and with a conscience.
    - Whatever your husband brings home is in your care. You may either apply your inventiveness and capabilities to make your home valuable or you could behave like a slovenly and lazy wife by laying everything to waste. Your poor husband will have no say in the matter. Your home is what you make of it. A skilled and capable wife is never distressed.
    - Everyone seeks refuge from a disorderly and chaotic home. Although difficulties will arise from time to time, sometimes depriving you of food and rest, you must make an effort to keep the house in order because a man will not be able to bear a chaotic home for long. When he cannot find peace and rest at home, he will be forced to find it elsewhere. He may then begin to regard his home and his children as calamities.
    - A good wife is always making an effort for her home to be an

example of Jannah. Together with herself being at ease in her home, she does her best to make every occupant of the house comfortable as well.

- Men appreciate women who are competent and who are able to organise affairs well. It is unfortunate that many beautiful women lack these qualities and have thus become worthless in the eyes of their husbands. It should be borne in mind that most men appreciate inner beauty more than outer beauty. Irrespective of how unattractive or imprudent a woman may be, she will certainly win over her husband's affections if she is obedient.

It is not difficult for every wife to apply all the above principles in her life, thereby earning the devoted love of her husband. However, it is tragic that most women fail to understand this and wrongly think that they will be able to force their husbands into submission by behaving harshly and temperamentally. It is really the women who strive to please Allah Ta'ala and who serve their husbands with love and gentleness who become the beloved of their husbands and whose husbands would give their lives for them. The husbands of such women will do anything to please them and are proud of them. Such couples are the ones who live happily ever after. Intelligent women avail themselves of such behaviour while foolish women are deprived of it.

As an intelligent woman you should always bear the following in mind:

- Forsake your egotism and your temperamental behaviour.
- Do not allow pride and selfishness to approach you.
- Do not speak to a strange man in private.
- Do not speak ill of your husband in front of another.
- Do not breathe a word against him.
- Do not eat before him.
- Do not discuss matters that do not appeal to him.
- You can even win over a temperamental husband by diligently serving him.
- Be as he wants you to be and do what pleases him.

- Keep his secrets safe within your heart.
- Beautify yourself as he prefers.
- Stay away from the company of evil and ill-mannered women.

By keeping all the above in mind and practising accordingly, you will enjoy good fortune and your husband will be yours forever.

Every Woman's Wish

It is the natural desire of every woman to have a husband who does what she wants, who consults with her before doing anything and who hands all his money over to her so that she may run the home as she desires. Despite having this desire, many women fail to make any efforts to realise this desire. Without having any respect for their husbands, they become furious about the littlest thing and storm out of the house at the slightest provocation. They are constantly arguing with their husbands about clothing and jewellery and still expect their husbands to do as they say. Not only are such women disrupting the homes of their husbands, but they are destroying the lives of both their families.

LEARN TO LOVE YOUR HUSBAND

Every woman should learn to love her husband. Irrespective of how evil, ill-mannered or dim-witted her husband may be, the wife holds in her hand the keys to set her husband straight. There are numerous examples of women who have successfully changed their husbands for the better. There are no obstacles for the patient woman. To purge her husband of bad habits and to make him receptive and sympathetic towards her, she should narrate to him anecdotes from the lives of the pious, she should encourage him to participate in religious gatherings and she should also read good books of Ahadeeth at home so that he may hear. In addition to this, she must also do what pleases him and serve him with sincere devotion. When a woman sincerely loves and serves her husband, it is impossible for him to stray away from her.

CONQUER HIS HEART

Your husband's heart will be conquered by the resounding throb of love emanating from the deepest recesses of your heart. Always keep your home clean and ensure that everything of beauty in your home is well arranged. Keep your loving gazes fixed on him and always meet him with a smile. Obey whatever he tells you instead of arguing. Insha Allah Ta'ala, this will ensure a happy marriage.

"YOU MIND YOUR OWN BUSINESS AND I'LL MIND MINE"

When there is enmity and dissention between a couple and they lack love for each other, the words "You mind your own business and I'll mind mine" will be commonly heard. Happiness will rue visiting such a home and the buds of joy will wilt. Eventually, every hope the couple entertained will be rubbed into the dust.

SECURE FASTEN THE BOND OF LOVE

Allah Ta'ala has created the bond of love between people and this bond can only be secured with the injunctions of the Shari'ah. This bond is not a loose one and will not break with a slight jostle. When a couple get married, they have pledged their loyalty to each other and the wife is always in a position to fasten the bond more securely. By doing everything to please him and by sharing his joys and problems, the bond will be cemented. In this transaction, profits are accrued when everything is given without anything taken in return.

IDENTIFY HIS PREFERENCES

To conquer her husband's heart, a wife should ensure that she introduces into herself everything that her husband likes. It is imperative for her to know exactly what to do to please him. She should therefore cook what he likes and wear what he likes. In fact, she should bring her pleasures to coincide with his.

Sadly, there are many men whose wives are extremely attractive, yet they will be found in the company of women much less beautiful. Beauty, wealth and a good education are not sufficient to keep one's husband for oneself. What is required is the art of knowing what pleases the husband. A wife should know how to capture her husband's interest. She should know what he likes so that she could keep his gazes fixed on her.

WHAT DO MEN LIKE?

Because every man is different, it is not possible to specify exactly what every man likes. While some men prefer women with make-up, others prefer women without it. While some men prefer fashionable women, others prefer simple women. While some prefer extroverts, others do not. In this manner, tastes vary from man to man. It is therefore necessary for women to inculcate such qualities within themselves which their husbands would value and appreciate. Some of the qualities that men adore are as follows:

1. One of the primary features men love is beauty. Even though a woman may not be naturally beautiful, she can make herself look beautiful by dressing well and making themselves up. Of course, she may adopt only those means of beautification that the Shari'ah permits and these are more than sufficient.
2. Men also look for innocence and an appreciative nature in women. They would dare not approach women who harbour malice in their hearts, who deceive and whose hearts bear ill-feelings against others. Women should therefore make every effort to make innocence and gratitude of paramount importance in their lives. In fact, these qualities develop modesty and inner beauty. When a woman's heart is filled with malice and ill-feelings against others, her husband loses confidence in her and other people also lose their respect for her.

3. Men do not want their wives to be more intelligent than themselves. When an ordinary man marries a graduate, he remains uneasy because he feels weaker and inferior to her, causing him a considerable degree of embarrassment. A wife should therefore not extol her academic achievements when these would make her husband feel inferior.
   In addition to this, she should not make him feel less intelligent in any other way. A man may stand in awe of a highly educated woman, but he can seldom love her. By the same token, women also do not like men who assert their authority and who want their wives to dance at the snap of their fingers.
4. The most effective manner of harnessing the undivided attention of one's husband is to be humble before him and to serve him diligently.

Men feel content when their wives are obedient and their love for them grows tremendously. Men detest women who are impudent, immoral and stubborn.

5. Men also like women who are forgiving and who love them despite their faults.
6. Men love women who are compassionate towards others; women who are naturally tender and who would take orphans into their laps because they feel them sorry. Men do not like women who are selfish and who feel nothing to insult and abuse others. They also do not like women who withdraw into spells of silence because they feel dejected and without hope.
7. Men adore women who are lively and happy because such an attitude makes others also feel happy. Such a woman lifts her husband's spirits when he is feeling under the weather and also dispels his tiredness, providing him with peace and contentment. She should therefore always make an effort to do and speak about things that make him happy. The proverb is famous that says: Laughter is the best medicine. Women should always bear this proverb in mind and she will be her husband's best doctor.
8. The most cherished quality in a woman is her chastity. A woman's beauty sparkles with added radiance when she is chaste. Only such a woman can remain loyal to her husband. A woman lacking chastity will be worthless to her husband even if she is bestowed with immense physical beauty.

When a woman does as she pleases without caring how others feel, she will fall from her husband's esteem. Obey your husband and the world will obey you. Secure his confidence and you will earn the confidence of the entire family. Conquer your husband's heart and your home will be reminiscent of Jannah.

A Dialogue Between Mother and Daughter

"Look, the carriage has come
Let me weep till my heart is done
If I cannot weep as much as I would like
Just allow my heart to become light
I suppose I will have to leave
Leave the ties of love that seem impossible to
retrieve What shall my abode be?
When I have to leave the affection and
love showered on me
Leave the doting, attention and affection
Leave my parents, sisters, brothers and their attraction
I am breaking away and leaving them all
I am taking leave from them all
I was the little chirping bird of the garden
Oh has it really passed by, I beg your pardon
I was a little doll toone for me
Out of your home you have cast me
A disgrace of fate
What banishment of late!
Your generosity for me seems a thing of the past
Out of your home have I been cast."

THE MOTHER'S REPLY

"Listen well, O my broken-hearted one
All that has happened is your turn has come
This period dawns on every child
This bridge has to be crossed by everyone
meek and mild
This time of separation does arrive
For all people in the world alive
Such is the custom of the world in which we have mirth
Such are the practices of our earth
The one whom you call mother with such love
Was also someone's daughter, their turtledove
She was also the beloved child of her mother
Showered with the affection of her sister and brother
Those who have raised you, with whom you have grown
Never shall you be separated from them to
be on your own
Theirs you shall always be and they yours
Then whatfor do you grieve, always open
are their doors
On a throne they always gave you a seat
Showed you happiness most complete
Despite hardship, they gave you comfort and ease
They never held anything against you, so
should you, please
Never speak against them an ill word
Not even 'Oof!' or something unheard
The reputation of your family you now hold in your hand
Honour it, do not rub it in the sand
You are the product of my efforts and toil
You are the fruit of my love, from my very soil
You will find everything with us here
So leave with happiness, have no fear
There shall be difficulty and strain
There shall be effort and pain
There will be heartache, but every tunnel ends with light

You will also have love, happiness and delight
By no behaviour, by no manner, not at all
Should you ever allow this to topple and fall
Those who have nurtured and raised you so
Still love you and are letting you go
This enjoyment, this pleasure
This blissful life, this leisure
This carefree life without sorrow
Are all fleeting by, not there tomorrow
May Allah Ta'ala grant you happiness
where you are headed
Even more than you had here where your
roots are embedded
May Allahs grant you everything you
want and need
Love, contentment, happiness and all on which
your heart can feed
Not by error or by something you earn
For the home of your parents should your heart
never yearn
From every mother comes this advice so sincere
Never forget it, never disregard it my treasured dear
Always serve your husband well
Fulfil his wishes before he can tell
You will flower and bear fruit too
If you remember what I have just said to you
What my mother used to say was true
Her advice was good I always knew
In certain ways the husband is unto his wife
Like her Rabb, the Giver of her life
He will always keep her happy and content
If she devotedly remains his, doing nothing
without his consent
Her world will be like Jannah so near
Her Aakhirah will be Jannah without fear
True were the words of my mother dear."
[Translated from an Urdu poem]

Disputes Between Mothers- and- Daughters-in-Law:

It has become common among many people to keep their sons with them after marriage because their sons are too young to earn or to run a home by themselves. The daughter-in-law therefore has no option but to live with her parents-in-law. This practice has become so popular that a man is frowned upon when he decides to live by himself. People then start labelling him, calling him a naïve and stupid person. In fact, his parents feel hurt to think that they raised him for so many years and now he suddenly wants to leave them. They feel that once their son has married, they will be able to enjoy their grandchildren growing up in front of them.

As a result, the entire family lives together and the mother-and-daughter-in-law are separated from each other only when one of them leaves this world. When the two live together, it is impossible for harmony to prevail. An Urdu proverb rightly says that when two dishes are put together, they are bound to clatter. There is scarcely a bride who is spared this route.

The disputes and problems between mothers-and-daughters-in-law will continue until the custom of living together is abolished. Until this happens, it will be futile to even write about creating harmony between them.

THE EVIL OF DISPUTES AND ARGUMENTS

Nobody needs to be told that an argument between two persons is unpleasant irrespective of who the persons are. It destroys any peace and harmony that exists between them and the two will always be apprehensive of each other. This is especially serious when the argument is between mother-in-law and daughter-in-law. Living in such a home eventually becomes unbearable for everyone. Everything one of them says or does will be a thorn in the other's side and each will search for the other's faults.

The husband then becomes caught in an impossible situation. If he sides with his mother keeping her rights in mind, his wife becomes upset. Of course, he does not want this because he has still the rest of his life to spend with her. On the other hand, if he sides with his wife, his mother becomes upset, calling him an ungrateful traitor. The husband is now torn apart. Whereas upsetting his wife will ruin the relationship for the rest of his life, his mother is his ticket to Jannah and it was she who raised him with great difficulty and who spent many sleepless nights for him.

To save a man from such a situation, it is necessary to search for a solution that would eradicate disputes between mothers-in-law and daughters-in-law altogether. It is necessary to identify the factors leading to such disputes so that their hearts are cleansed from hatred, jealousy and other ill-feelings towards each other. If a woman does this, she will be saving herself from much grief and heartache. To achieve this, it is also important for the husband and the father-in-law to read books like "A gift to the husband and wife" by Maulana Ashraf Ali Thanwi (May Allah be Merciful on him/her) and "The rights of wives" by Moulana Muhammad Taqi Uthmaani (Daamat Barakaatuh).

DISPUTES CAUSED BY THE MOTHER-IN-LAW

One of the greatest causes of disputes between mothers-and-daughters-in-law is he absence of religiousness in the home. When the consciousness of Religion dominates a household, it will be purged of problems and arguments. As for the disputes generally caused by mothers-in-law, seven of the most common ones are discussed below.

The First Cause: The natural jealousy in the heart of the mother-in-law who thinks that someone new has taken control of her beloved son whom she reared and cared for with great pain and difficulty.

The Second Cause: The mother-in-law plays the role of a ruler. She asserts her authority to ensure that everything happens only as she wants. When her daughter-in-law enters the house, she feels that her domination will be threatened and that she will be overthrown.

The Third Cause: The mother-in-law demands control of not only her husband's money, but also wants to control her son's money. Problems arise between her and her daughter-in-law when the daughter-in-law also expects her share of the money.

The Fourth Cause: Some mothers-in-law become suspicious that their daughters-in-law are sending things from their husbands' homes to their mothers.

The Fifth Cause: Mothers-in-law seem to forget that they were also daughters-in-law at some stage of their lives. When they keep this in mind, they will realise that their daughters-in-law are also women with desires and feelings.

The Sixth Cause: When a single suspicion is created, a chain of unwarranted suspicions crowd the mother-in-law's mind, eventually forcing all good thoughts of her daughter-in-law to vanish from her mind.

The Seventh Cause: Because many women have a harsh and uncompromising nature, they treat their daughter-in-law very cruelly. They assassinate the character of their daughters-in-law for every little reason, giving them no peace to do anything properly. When the poor scapegoat has become frustrated, she eventually retaliates and all hell breaks lose.

DISPUTES CAUSED BY SISTERS-IN-LAW

When a man marries, his sister begins to find life difficult because she is not as free as she always was in her home. She dreads touching or doing anything for fear that it should upset her sister-in-law. As a result, she begins to abhor the new bride, making things difficult for the poor woman. She then leaves no stone unturned to search for her sister-in-law's faults and to stir trouble between her brother and his wife and between her mother and her sister-in-law.

DISPUTES CAUSED BY THE DAUGHTER-IN-LAW

A daughter-in-law is generally naïve and inexperienced. She fails to realise how trivial matters can spiral into a furore and fails to value the benefits of remaining silent. She wants her husband to instantly become her slave and cannot tolerate taking instructions from her mother-and-sisters-in-law. She had been indoctrinated with the belief that her mother-in-law will be policing her every action and monitoring her every move. She feels that just as she has entered the home as a daughter-in-law, her mother-in-law was also in the same situation some day. She therefore regards herself equal to her mother-in-law and believes that she can wield as much authority in the house as her mother-in-law can. She tells herself that she is not a slave and that she will tell her mother-in-law a mouthful if the lady tells her anything. Her friends have by then brainwashed her into thinking that if she once bows to the sway of her mother-in-law, she will always be oppressed. "The first impression is the lasting impression", they told her. She will therefore never tolerate being an underling.

Of course, there may be several other causes and these may vary from situation to situation, but I am convinced that the causes mentioned above are really responsible for creating baseless suspicions and ill-feelings between daughter-and-mother-in-law. These well up within their hearts and when they become impossible to contain, they burst forth like a raging volcano. Mother-and-daughter-in-law are then at loggerheads and are continuously fighting, providing free entertainment for neighbours and relatives.

If both the mother-in-law and daughter-in-law realise their positions and reflect upon these causes which are really fuelled by being naïve, selfish and intolerant, they will be able to overcome the situation. They should educate themselves in Islam and develop a sound understanding of Deen, which will go a long way to eradicate all problems.

How Every Mother-in-Law Should Think

A mother-in-law should always bear in mind that her daughter-in-law is also a human being with aspirations and feelings. She has made the sacrifice of leaving her parents home to be with her husband forever. The mother-in-law should therefore treat her daughter-in-law like her very own daughter. She should be gentle with her and think that if she behaves harshly towards her, the poor girl will have no one to turn to because she has left her family behind. She is not a slave and her husband owes her many rights, which have been ordained by Allah Ta'ala and His Rasul s. Just as the mother-in-law was once also a daughter-in-law, she should not forget that her daughter-in-law also enjoys the things that she once enjoyed. She should treat her daughter-in-law as she wanted her mother-in-law to treat her. While the mother-in-law has already enjoyed good times in her life, he should now give her daughter-in-law the chance.

When the mother-in-law harasses her daughter-in-law and behaves sternly with her, she should bear in mind that this behaviour is futile because the daughter-in-law cannot run away and will continue living there. All that will be achieved is that others will have free entertainment and will have ample gossip to keep them busy. In addition to this, the honour of the family will be dragged through the mud.

Every mother-in-law should therefore be as accommodating as possible. She should forgive and forget her daughter-in-law's errors knowing that she is not doing them purposely but because she is still inexperienced and naïve. In all probability, the mother-in-law also made the same mistakes when she was a young daughter-in-law. When she adopts this attitude, life will become pleasant for both mother-and-daughter-in-laws.

A mother-in-law should bear in mind that she may not expect her daughter-in-law to do everything in the house. The daughter-in-law should never think that when her mother-in-law first met her to chose her as a wife for her son, she was extremely sweet and pleasant. However, her charms seem to have disappeared after her son's marriage.

I personally feel that it is best for the mother-in- law to hand over all the affairs of the home to her daughter-in-law and occupy herself with Ibaadah, taking care not to heed the instigations of her other daughters-in-law. If her daughter-in-law makes serious mistakes, she should be corrected with affection and forbearance. She should not be reprimanded for every little error as is done with one's own children. With all these factors considered, the home will be like Jannah for all.

HOW THE DAUGHTER-IN-LAW SHOULD THINK

Every daughter-in-law should bear in mind that if her mother-in-law is really her enemy, she would never have allowed her son to marry her and would have never allowed her to live in her home. All mothers-in-law are not bad. It has often occurred that the foolishness of the daughter-in-law has led to problems in the family, causing a rift between mother and son. Many daughters-in-law cause tremendous difficulty for their mothers-in-law, especially in situations where the mother-in-law is dependent on her son and daughter-in-law. Such daughters-in-law often behave most insolently towards their mothers-in-law, shunting them around the house and not allowing them any say in even their own affairs. Some of them even extract services from their mothers-in-law. The poor old lady is then stricken with grief and often curses her daughter-in-law.

There is many daughters-in-law who makes mountains out of little molehills and elaborates these to her husband so that the man should be antagonistic towards his parents and sympathetic towards her. Unaware of the truth, the man falls for her ploy and argues with his parents and sisters while his wife watches from a distance. There have been many oppressive daughters-in-law who have suffered terrible diseases because of their tyranny.

Every daughter-in-law should remember that although she is not a slave, Allah Ta'ala has made it compulsory for her to serve her husband. She should also not forget that there should be none more honoured in her husband's sight than his mother because his Jannah lies beneath her feet, as Rasulullahs has explicitly mentioned in the Ahadeeth. If a husband becomes blinded by his love for his inconsiderate wife and behaves disrespectfully towards his mother, how will he ever enter Jannah? Being the cause of his entry into Jahannam, how will his wife stay alone in Jannah? It is therefore imperative for every wife to keep in mind the fact that her husband's entry into Jannah hinges on his behaviour towards his mother.

A woman will be doing a great service to her husband if she cares for his mother. She should not lose sight of the fact that her mother-in-law is much older than her and may soon be leaving this world. Thereafter, the daughter-in-law will assume control over household affairs. There is therefore no reason to hasten the situation. If her mother-in-law has ill-feelings against her, she should overlook these and bear in mind that she will soon be a mother-in-law herself and may be exposed to the same feelings.

Every daughter-in-law should also remember that her mother-in-law has always been the queen of her home and expects everyone young and old in the household to respect her authority, to do as she expects and to consult with her before doing anything. She is therefore unable to tolerate rebellion and impertinence from her daughter-in- law. The daughter-in-law should respect her mother-in- law and bear in mind the difference in their ages.

If Muslim women were religious and if they possessed sound Islamic knowledge, we would not experience the problems we have today. Even if these problems did arise, it would neither be as widespread nor as serious as it is presently. It is therefore necessary for women to daily read books like "Fadhaa'il A'maal", "Fadhaa'il Sadaqaat" at home and accompany their male Mahram relatives on Tableegh visits. With Islamic knowledge, a person will be able to differentiate between right and wrong and both mothers-in-law and daughters-in -law will respect each other and live amicably.

A daughter-in-law should treat her mother-in-law like her own mother. In fact, she should respect her even more because while her mother is her mother, her mother-in-law is her husband's mother and she should regard her husband higher than herself. When a daughter-in-law treats her mother-in-law well, the old lady will make du'aa for her and it is with du'aas like this that people are saved from calamities and tragedies in their lives. The patience that the daughter-in-law has to exercise with her mother-in-law, will save her from having to exercise patience in much more trying times. She should remember that the du'aas of her mother-in-law shall prove to be an impregnable fortress for her children. Serving her mother-in-law on a cold winter's night will earn her such rewards that she will treasure once she leaves this world.

If a woman wants to bear luminaries like Rabia Basriyyah (A.R) and Rasheed Ahmad Gangohi (A.R), she should exercise patience with her irritable mother-in-law and her instigating sisters-in-law and forgive them. She should refrain from backbiting them; she should make du'aa for them during her Tahajjud salah and ask her mother-in-law for forgiveness even if the fault is not hers. By doing this, her offspring will become great people who will be the cause for the guidance of many others.

A daughter-in-law must never speak ill of her in-laws when visiting her parents. Just as she is loved and respected in her parent's home because of her sterling attributes, she should employ the same attributes to win the respect of her in-laws. A truly respectable woman is one who is respected by both her parents and her parents-in-law.

If a daughter-in-law employs the approaches mentioned above, her mother-in-law will have no reason to harass her irrespective of how harsh and uncompromising her mother-in-law may be. By the same token, if a mother-in-law practises the advices given above, her daughter-in-law will not clash with her even though her daughter-in-law may be impertinent and stubborn. All the members of the family will then be able to live in peace and harmony.

A House Burned Down By Its Own Lantern

We will now present to you a drama which depicts the state of affairs when a man lives with his mother, his wife, his sister/s and sister/s-in-law. You will notice that many characters in the drama are people who are not conscious about the obligations they owe to Islam and do not have a sound knowledge of Islam. It is hoped that this drama will assist the reader to understand many things. If you are a daughter-in-law, you will learn that it is important to respect your mother-in-law and to abstain from behaving insubordinately with her.

If you are a mother-in-law, you will learn that it is unwise to have two daughters-in-law living with you. If you are forced to even keep one daughter-in-law with you, you will realise that you should not interfere in her matters that you should not persistently go to the kitchen when she's busy and should not ask too many questions. If your daughter-in-law is prepared to cook for you, you will be doing yourself and her favour by leaving the kitchen in her capable hands. You may then keep yourself busy in Ibaadah and in assisting people in Allah Ta'ala's path. You will then be served three good meals with respect and honour.

If you are a sister with married brothers, you should be very diplomatic and tactful in ensuring that you do not have to live with your brothers' wives. If you are the elder sister-in-law and your husband's younger brother's wife insists that she wants to live on her own, you should not oppose her decision. May Allah Ta'ala guide us all to practise Religion properly.

The cast of the drama is as follows:

It is evening and Afdhal Ahmad is returning home from his shop when he meets his friend Muhammad Waseem. After greeting each other, Muhammad Waseem asks how his friend is keeping.

Afdhal Ahmad: What can I say? I have such a backlog of work that I can hardly being to explain. I have to cancel a few orders because the strikes seem endless.

Muhammad Waseem: The workload nowadays is becoming overwhelming and we can barely meet our payments. In fact, I was just about to leave today when my boss called me back for more work at the office.

Afdhal Ahmad: The strange thing is that even after overcoming the work at the business, you have to face a series of other problems at home.

Muhammad Waseem: Oh yes! I have no fear for the complications at work, but those at home! May Allah Ta'ala protect us! Those things can reduce a man to dust.

Afdhal Ahmad: You have hit the nail on the head. Since I got married I have a new crisis staring me in the face every time I reach home. I have my mother relating one story to me and my wife relating another story altogether different.

Muhammad Waseem: Your situation is not unique. Everyone is having this problem nowadays. I feel that we should all engage in Taubah and Istighfaar.

Afdhal Ahmad: I don't think so. In fact, I don't think that anyone's situation can be as pitiable as mine. I have lost every desire for life. Before marriage I used to hear about disputes between mothers-and-daughters-in-law who are at loggerheads every day. I now have first-hand experience. The constant bickering between daughter-and -mother-in-law causes friction between husband and wife. I blame the mothers-in-law for all these problems. Too many times have I seen my mother admonish my wife for every little thing. It seems as if my mother's full-time occupation is to watch the poor lady like a hawk and haul her over the coals for everything she does wrong.

Muhammad Waseem: I am having the same problem. Every day my wife begs me to either get her a house of her own or to send her back to her parents. I have no idea what to do any more!

Afdhal Ahmad: What can the poor wife do? I am most surprised to see that it is the mother-in-law who looks for a daughter-in-law and then suddenly becomes the lady's arch enemy. She doesn't seem to realise that the woman is after all her son's wife. When the daughter-in-law does anything commendable, she gets no praise, very unlike the scolding she gets when she does anything wrong. Irrespective of who does something wrong in the house, a mother-in-law thinks of no one else's name but that of her daughter-in-law.

Muhammad Waseem: Dear friend, we seem to be in the same boat.

Afdhal Ahmad: We are not the only ones suffering. Today, there is scarcely a Muslim home that is free from such problems. Wherever, a mother-and-daughter-in-law share a house, they turn it into a pit of Jahannam. Among the primary causes for the suffering new brides experience are jealous and evil sisters-in-law.

Muhammad Waseem: What can be the solution?

Afdhal Ahmad: The only visible solution is to live separately from our parents. Of course, the difficulty will be that people will point fingers at us and call us sinners. In addition to this, our parents will regard us as unfaithful and disobedient sons. However, I have now made up my mind to get myself a house of my own. Although my wife and I do not watch television and videos, these are still present in my father's house. As my wife says, we are also affected by its evil presence because Allah Ta'ala's curse falls on the house. Besides this, it is practically impossible to stop our children from watching. Everyone knows that today's movies are a major cause of promiscuity, leading our children to fornication. They also contribute substantially to crime and all other sorts of evil. Especially for the sake of the children, I have therefore decided to live by myself even if I have to rent a house somewhere.

It is unfortunate that nowadays an obedient and good person is said to be the one who allows matters to proceed as they are. In doing this, he is destroying his life and dragging his defenceless wife through hell, whereas Allah Ta'ala has placed her in your mercy and protection. Perseverant as the two may, the attitude of the mother-and-sisters-in-law will never change. As a result, the upcoming generation will suffer, falling prey to negative emotions like fear, mistrust and cowardice.

Muhammad Waseem: Anyway, are you attending the Moulana's lecture at the Jamia Masjid tonight?

Afdhal Ahmad: Of course. In any case, I will have to go to the Jamia Masjid tonight to make arrangements for some people going out in the path of Allah Ta'ala You carry on home, I'll meet you later.

(Afdhal Ahmad goes home where he hears the following):

Aamina Bibi: Maryam! Maryam! What are you doing? Is the tea not ready yet? I've told you a hundred times to work quickly!

(Maryam arrives with the tea).

Aamina Bibi:	Where have you left the cake?
Maryam:	Zubayda is coming with it, mother.
Aamina Bibi:	Couldn't you do it yourself? Did your hand break? If this is the case, why didn't your parents send a servant with you so that you wouldn't have to do anything?
Afdhal Ahmad:	Who baked this cake?
Zubayda:	Maryam did.
Aamina Bibi:	Will she never learn anything?
Afdhal Ahmad:	Zubayda, take this tea away; I shall rather have some at the restaurant.
Aamina Bibi:	Why Afdhal Ahmad? What is wrong with the tea?
Afdhal Ahmad:	There is no difference between drinking this tea and drinking hot water.
Aamina Bibi:	What can I do son? I am at my wits end with this woman.
Unays:	Mister Muhammad Waseem is at the door.
Afdhal Ahmad:	It is already eight 'o clock. I'm late. I will have my tea at the restaurant. (He then leaves the house).
Aamina Bibi:	I have not seen a woman as stupid as you. Did your parents not teach you anything? You cannot even make tea. My poor son had to leave without having his tea.
Maryam:	But mother, it's not my fault. Zubayda told me that the tea was done and you were rushing me.
Aamina Bibi:	Oh dear! Are you not ashamed to put the blame on others?
Maryam:	No mother. I never pass on the buck.
Aamina Bibi:	Be quiet! You talk too much!

(A cough is heard as Bhai Sulayman enters the house. Maryam and Zubayda disappear into their rooms.)

Bhai Sulayman: Where is Afdhal Ahmad's mother? (He sees her sitting.) What are you doing sitting here?

Aamina Bibi: I am lamenting over my ill fortune.

Bhai Sulayman: What is there to lament about? Allah Ta'ala has granted you sons, daughters and daughters-in-law. What more can one ask for?

Aamina Bibi: What else? Our precious daughter- in-law gives me endless grief. Her tea tastes like hot water and my beloved Afdhal Ahmad had to go without tea.

Bhai Sulayman: What was wrong with the tea?

Aamina Bibi: She threw the tea leaves in before the water could boil.

Bhai Sulayman: You must have been rushing her again. You are none the better. You fuss about every little thing. You want to be in charge of everything that happens in the house and blame everything on our daughter-in-law. I do not at all approve of your behaviour!

Aamina Bibi: Oh! So your daughter-in-law is faultless, is she?

Bhai Sulayman: You have finished with her and it seems like its now my turn to suffer the brunt of your anger. See how you become angry at the slightest provocation. Nobody says that daughters-in-law are perfect. Is it her fault that she has become your daughter-in-law?

Aamina Bibi: Get away please! She will never have a mother-in-law like me even if she has to have another life.

Bhai Sulayman: After this life I do not think that she would want another.

Aamina Bibi: Oh dear! You are adding fuel to the fire by siding with that useless woman. My entire body is alight. How sad that my precious son had to go without tea!

Bhai Sulayman: You must try to control your tongue. You have no idea how many pots of tea Afdhal Ahmad empties with his friends in restaurants. You have no need to worry about him not having a cup of tea here.

Aamina Bibi: You have no love for your son.

Bhai Sulayman: How can you say such a thing? Why would I be standing here defending his wife if I had no love for him?

Aamina Bibi: Now you are presenting evidence like a lawyer. This is all your fault. I was always reluctant to propose for Khadija Aapa's daughter.

Bhai Sulayman: What wrong did Khadija Aapa do to? She did us a favour by bringing to our home a bride who dons Islamic Hijaab and is well educated in Islamic knowledge.

Aamina Bibi: In that case, I would rather have an illiterate daughter-in-law!

Bhai Sulayman: Please tell me why you do nothing else all day besides following the poor lady like a shadow?

Aamina Bibi: You would like to say that I am doing this because I am insane.

Bhai Sulayman: I cannot understand why you have changed so much.

Aamina Bibi: How have I changed?

Bhai Sulayman: Do you not remember the time when my mother was alive? Do you not remember how many times you asked me to either get us a house of our own or send me back to your parents? Remember how you used to complain about the things that my mother used to tell you and how you used to get tired of serving her? Did you not feel that that my mother used to scold you even though you were capable of doing everything? Was this not hurtful?

Aamina Bibi: Not at all.

Bhai Sulayman: Alright. If it was not hurtful, why were you always complaining to me? You know well that you were hurt, but you do not want to admit it because you have now become a mother-in-law instead of a daughter-in-law. Think awhile. Does your constant nagging and scolding not hurt your daughter-in-law as well? Will she not be complaining to Afdhal Ahmad about your harshness? Do you not think that she also must be wanting to have a house of her own? Why do you behave like this when you have experienced the same situation? A surprised that women forget that they were daughters-in-law once they become mothers-in-law. Imagine what your reaction would be if your Zubayda was in this situation.

Aamina Bibi: I would never marry my Zubayda in a family where the mother-in-law behaves like an executioner.

Bhai Sulayman: While you would not tolerate the harshness of a mother-in-law for your daughter, you see nothing wrong in ruining the life of someone else's daughter.

Aamina Bibi: Who is ruining her life?

Bhai Sulayman: You are doing worse than ruining her life because you are practically enslaving her. You rebuke her at every step and keep insulting her. This is worse than a slow lingering death. There are too many vibrant young brides who have withered away and entered their graves as demoralised souls because of the bitter remarks and insults of their mothers-in-law.

Aamina Bibi: You seem to be intent on lecturing today. Leave all this for now and let us eat. Zubayda is coming with the food.

Bhai Sulayman: I shall not eat until you promise that you will not tell our daughter-in-law anything in future.

Aamina Bibi: Alright! Alright! Let's eat. In future I shall say nothing to Afdhal Ahmad's wife. Are you happy?

Bhai Sulayman: I shall be happy only when you keep your word. Otherwise, you two will have to live separately.

NOTE: You should read this drama as a sister-in-law so that you would refrain from causing harm to your brother's wife or the wives of your husband's brothers. As a mother-in-law, you should ensure that your daughter-in-law is comfortable if she has to live with you and never listen to what others have to gossip about her. If your mother has daughters-in- law, you should ensure that you restrain her from behaving unjustly towards them. May Allah Ta'ala guide us all to the right path. *Aameen.*

Parting Advice

When a young woman leaves her home as a bride
It is as if Qiyamah has arrived
Giving some parting advice to her departing daughter, the mother said
Greet your mother-in-law with salam when you arrive
Show respect to your father-in-law so that none may say
This is a girl without respect
Always honour your husband
And your life will be one of distinction and merit
Be happy and friendly to everyone in your house
You will then be their illuminating lantern
Never speak in high and harsh tones
And live with simplicity and good character
Take care not to walk about bare-headed
Keep your hair always covered and concealed
You are most fortunate to have your marriage made
Remember that you should now remain chaste forever
Sleep the earliest and be the first to wake upKeeping your attention fixed on your heart
I understand well your uncertainties and fears
These are part of heat of your spark of love
When the sharp rays of the sun extend from you
Remember to show the glow and serenity of the moon as well
Do not hesitate to do the housework
Because this is the practise in the world throughout

When you apply yourself to the housework
You will gain respect and honour from all at home
Do the work of everyone young and old
And, our daughter, you will make a name for yourself
Never backchat with your husband
So that you may never be disgraced in the Hereafter
I have rendered my parting advice
I have taught you everything you need to know
I would sacrifice gold, silver, anything for you
Now marriage has come, waiting for you
May Allah Ta'ala bless this hour
Now that our parting has come so beautifully.
[Translated from an Urdu poem]

The Precious Parting Gift of a Father to his Daughter Hafsa

The time has finally arrived when hearts
are embellished and hurt
This hour of helplessness was waiting you for
a long time
Now you will be leaving your sisters and brothers
Leaving your father, your home, your family
and your town
I have accepted this and have imagined the heartbreak
It bores a hole in the heart and breaks it to pieces
This is Allah Ta'ala's command, the practice
of the world
A girl will leave for her husband's home,
leaving this temporary one
That is your real home, so proceed there
From this day on, your living and dying shall be there
This is not the time to weep, take it from me
Hear well what I say and make no mistake
You are going only to your real home
Do what is honourable and the respect will be immense
Fulfil the rights of one and all
Serve your husband through every pitfall
You understand well the status of your husband
Should he be displeased, Jahannam shall be your end
Be steadfast on the Shari'ah, O my beloved

And be aware of the rights of all
The life of a happy couple is itself Jannah
So always bear in mind the prophetic life the Sunnah
Higher than your mother is your mother-in-law
And higher than your father, your father-in-law
Serve and respect them at all times
As long as you live, for always
Hold fast to the Shari'ah of Deen
Even if you have to give your life and be killed
I have much to say, but what can I do
I have no control of my heart, no strength to contain
I am restraining my emotions, what about you?
Dear daughter, you have exhausted an ocean of tears
You do not weep so when someone leaves on a journey
Things will remain as they are, nothing will change
Exercise patience, for the status of the patient
one is high With the patient one is his Rabb, what more can he want?
Enough now, my beloved, everyone is making du'aa
Stand up and express gratitude to Allah Ask whatever you need from Allah Ta'ala
Your father is also asking Him for you
O Allah Ta'ala, O Merciful and Kind
Wherever Hafsa goes, let happiness not be far behind.
[Translated from an Urdu poem]

The Etiquette of Leaving Home

A good wife prepares herself to leave long before the time that her husband fixes for leaving so that they may leave in time. With a bit of extra effort from the wife, she will be able to assist her husband so that he should not forget anything in the rush. If often occurs that the husband may forget something and remember it only long afterwards, because of which he has to turn back or make alternate arrangements. This causes undue difficulty for both husband and wife.

When rushing to leave home in the mornings, the husband may forget something that he was to take with him or he may forget something in the pocket of the trousers he changed out of. Before her husband leaves in the morning, a good wife will ensure that all his things are kept together and that his breakfast is prepared on time. In this manner, her husband can leave without worries. He will then leave every day making du'aa for her and will even be able to perform two Rakaahs salah before leaving. With peace of mind, he will also be able to recite the Sunnah du'aa for leaving the home. The du'aa is:

بسم اللّٰه توكلت على اللّٰه لاحول ولا قوة الا باللّٰه

I leave with the name of Allah Ta'ala and I trust only in Allah Ta'ala because there is no power to do good and no might to resist evil except from Allah Ta'ala

In response to this du'aa, the wife should say:

أستودعك اللّٰه دينك وأمانتك وخواتيم أعمالك

I entrust your Deen, your safety and your final deeds in the care of Allah Ta'ala

Shaytan will be unable to cause a rift between such a couple who are in the care and protection of Allah Ta'alaInsha Allah Ta'ala, Shaytan will be unable to even enter their home.

A woman can therefore earn her husband's du'aas and pleasure by carrying out simple deeds like this. By doing this, she will also attain Allah Ta'ala's pleasure and she will be able to bring up her children under the shade of Allah Ta'ala's mercy and benevolence. May Allah Ta'ala grant all women the ability to carry out such rewarding deeds. *Aameen.*

THE DU'AAS THAT WOMEN MAKE FOR THEIR HUSBANDS EVERY MORNING

An Arabic newspaper once interviewed several women and asked them what they do every morning when their husbands leave for work and what du'aas they make for them. The following were some of the replies:

A. "I look towards the heavens and say:

يا رب أعده لي سريعا وأعده لي سليما

O Allah Ta'ala! Return him to me quickly and return him safely."

B. "I greet him warmly and say:

يارب إحفظه لي، إنه زوج مثالي، وأب لايعوض لأطفالي

O my Rabb! Protect him for he is an excellent husband and an irreplaceable father to my children.

C. "I always make the following du'aa:

متى تجعلنا أغنياء حتى لا يضطر هذا الرجل العجوز إلى أن يكدو يعمل

كل يوم ثماني ساعات

O Allah Ta'ala! When will you make us wealthy enough so that this ageing husband of mine will not have to work eight hours a day.

D. "When he leaves, I always say to myself:

هل سيعود لي ثانية؟ أو إستحمله لي سيارة الموتى كما حملت زوج جارتي

Will he return to me safely or will an ambulance bring him back home like it brought back the corpse of my neighbour's husband.

E. "I look at the clock after he leaves thinking to myself:

متى تدق الساعة السادسة مساء حتى أرى زوجي مرة أخرى

When will the clock reach 6 PM so that I may see my husband again.

F. I get busy cleaning the house and preparing food for my husband and my children

فالرجال لا يعودون إلى بيت قذر، ولا إلى طعام لايهضمونه

Because men do not return to dirty homes and unpalatable food

إطبع على فمه قبلة أخرى، ويبقى هذا الشعور على شفتي، إلى أن يعود

G. "When he leaves, I tell myself, 'Should I not perhaps kiss him again (or once more) so that the feeling remains on my lips until he returns?'"

لما أستطعت أن أغسل ملابس أطفالي، ولا أعد طعامهم

H. I try to forget about him because if I think about him, I will be unable to wash my children's clothes or cook food.

لماذا أوقعتنى يارب فى هذا الرجل وهنالك ملائين أحسن منه؟ ونالت

الجائزة الأخيرة

I look towards the heavens and say, "O Rabb! Why did You throw me to this man when there are millions of men better than him."

The last woman mentioned won the prize.

You have read all the above replies and may have liked some of them. If you were the tenth woman in this competition, you would do well to give the following reply:

"I first greet him with salam, adding 'Fi Amaanillaah.'

When he leaves reciting the du'aa

بسم اللّٰه توكلت على اللّٰه لاحول ولا قوة إلا باللّٰه

I say to him:

إتق اللّٰه فينا، ولا تطعمنا إلا حلالا

Fear Allah Ta'ala concerning us and feed us nothing that is unlawful.

This is a reminder for the husband not to employ any means of earning that violates the injunctions of the Shari'ah. A pious husband ensures that he does not indulge in transactions involving interest, lying, bribery, etc. He is particular about performing his salah with Jamaa'ah in the Masjid and encourages others to do the same. If he employs other Muslims, he allows them also to perform salah with Jamaa'ah in the Masjid.

A good wife also reminds her husband that man has been sent to this world not only to earn a living. He should therefore spend some time in the Masjid with others to make an effort that everyone practises total Deen. She should tell him that he must not invest all his valuable time to earn this temporary world but he must invest time to secure salvation in the Hereafter.

We shall now relate the incident of an Arab Bedouin woman so that every reader my glean something from it. By inculcating the same devotion she possessed, a woman can transform her home into a garden of Jannah.

إن زوجي إذا خرج يحتطب أحس بالعناء الذي لقيه فى سبيل رزقنا، وأحس بالحرارة عطشه في الجبل تكاد تحرق حلقي، فأعدله الماء البارد

حتى إذا ما قدم وجده

The Bedouin lady relates, "When my husband goes out in the woods to gather firewood, I feel the fatigue he feels while earning for us. I feel the blazing heat beating down on him as he works on the mountain and it seems as if the thirst he feels will soon scorch my throat even though I am sitting in my hut. I therefore ensure that the house is clean, change into clean clothing and wait for his return with cold water in my hand. When he enters the door after collecting the firewood, I welcome him as a bride deeply in love welcomes her bridegroom. I give him all my attention and make him most comfortable. If he wants my company, I make myself available to him just as a little child plays and frolics with her father."

The Etiquette of Conversing with One's Husband

Whenever the youngest wife of Abu Darda (May Allah be pleased with him/her) related any Hadith from her husband, she would begin by saying, "My master narrated to me" The Arabic word "sayyid" (translated as "master") is used to denote extreme respect. When the speaker attaches the word to himself/herself such as saying "Sayyidi" ("my master") or "Sayyidina" ("our master"), the phrase denotes love and admiration as well.

When speaking with her husband, a wife should bear the following in mind:

1. She should listen attentively to what he says without speaking between his sentences. After he has spoken his piece, she may ask him something only to clarify what she does not understand. She should be silent when he is speaking because any doubts she has will most probably be explained during the course of his talk. By interrupting his speech, she may cause him to omit some important detail or to dwell on some unimportant subject.

If a wife needs to tell her husband to do something, she may tell him to do so without referring to what other men do. For example, instead of saying, "Why don't you take us out once a week like how my sister's husband does?" she should rather say, "We would really appreciate it if you could take us out once a week."

2. When referring to her husband in conversations with others, a wife should not use the pronoun "he". She should refer to her husband as "my husband" or by a title people use for him. She may also refer to him as someone's father e.g. "Muhammad's father", "Saabera's father", etc.
3. A wife should always speak softly with her husband. She should never allow anger to make her raise her voice when speaking to him.
4. She should refrain from interrogating him with words like "Why?" "What?" "When?" "What for?" etc. For example, she should never question him disrespectfully by saying, "Why have you come late?" or "Why do you beat the children like an animal?" or "What on earth did you do that for?" or "We never know where you are. Why don't you ever tell us where you are off to?"

Instead of phrasing her questions like this, she should adorn them with sweet words and gentle tones so that his heart is softened and he will respond kindly to the questions. She will then have the answers she requires without hurting her husband. For example, instead of saying, "Why have you come late?", she should say, "We waited very long for you to return. I cannot rest until you return. Neither the kids nor I could eat without you."

Similarly, instead of saying, "Why do you beat the children like an animal?" she should say, "You hit Rasheed very hard last night on his ear. Children sometimes lose their hearing when struck so hard. We should then not fall prey to Allah Ta'ala's wrath." She may also say, "When children are beaten, they begin to regard their parents as oppressors. They start forming the idea in their minds that their parents hit them merely to vent their anger and have no feelings for them. They convince themselves that they will be hit whether they do right or wrong. Such children then become stubborn and disobedient. We should therefore exercise patience when the children misbehave. In this way, we will be greatly rewarded. It is things like this that make parenthood a most rewarding experience. Instead of beating them, we should try to reform them in other ways. They will soon realise the error of their ways and change their habits."

In a like manner, instead of rebuking him for coming late, she should say, "I would be so happy if you could inform me exactly when you expect to return so that I could prepare myself beforehand and have things ready for you." Instead of ranting and raving about being unaware of his whereabouts, she should merely express her concern for his safety, telling him that she would feel at ease if he kept her informed about where he was.

Whereas interrogating the husband would only have negative effects and create animosity; phrasing her questions with wisdom and love will win his respect and love together with addressing the problem at hand. The incorrect approach will make matters worse and if the husband is not a considerate man, he may purposely do things to aggravate the situation. He may start returning home even later or start beating the children more brutally.

When the wife phrases her questions more wisely, her husband's heart will soften and he will regret his ways. He will always take heed not to repeat his mistakes and will be proud of his wife's intelligence and diplomacy.

Irrespective of the situation, the wife should maintain her composure and take care never to raise her voice when speaking to her husband. She should respect him at all times and never allow herself to fall prey to backchat. By behaving respectfully and courteously, even the most tyrannical husbands can be moulded like wax.

Remember that the slip of a tongue at an inopportune moment may have implications that can plague one for a lifetime. Always adopt a soft tone when speaking so that no feelings are hurt. If this world fails to rewards you for this approach, do not forget that the Hereafter will not be so miserly to reward.

A harsh approach will definitely cause harm at some stage. If one has been harsh towards one's husband, one should lose no time in apologising and doing one's best to make him happy by serving him diligently.

Remember also that regardless of how wealthy your parents may be, you should never be fooled to think that you may leave your husband at any time to live with your parents. Although it may seem easy to call your father or brother to fetch you, it will be most difficult to return when the time comes. Leaving your husband is to leave him in the hands of other women. If he ever returns to you after sharing the company of others, he will never be the same person who was exclusively yours; he can never be. Although your mother and younger brothers will support you in your separation, you will rue your decision as time passes, especially once your brothers marry and you have sisters-in-law to contend with. The occasion should never arise when they tell you, "You could not live in harmony with your own husband and mother-in-law, it is no surprise that you cannot live with us as well!" Such a tacit remark is sufficient to instantly wilt the most blooming flower. Whereas a woman can bear a thousand insults from her husband, she cannot withstand a single insult from her sister-in-law. Dry bread and water in your husband's home is much better than eating Biryani in your brother's home.

Ladies of the past were often heard saying, "The sedan came as a wedding procession and left as a funeral bier." A couplet from a poem quoted earlier reads:

"Others may see your familiar appearance
But my self-respect will never allow that
I see this calamity (of separation) without tears flowing from my eyes."

Her husband's home is the only home for a woman and she should make every effort to ensure that life therein remains pleasant for all. She should accept every hardship with a smile because these will all pass by with her still living in the same home. She should turn her attention to Allah Ta'alawhenever she encounters any difficulties and cry before Him to alleviate them. However, she should never think that she will be better off somewhere else. Insha Allah Ta'ala, the time will soon arrive when Allah Ta'ala will make her home reminiscent of a garden of Jannah.

5. Another important factor that every woman should consider when addressing her husband is that she should not phrase any sentence as a command. Human nature dislikes being commanded, especially when a harsh tone is used. A person commanded in such a manner will either flatly refuse or grudgingly comply. Jurists have even mentioned that a father should not use a commanding tone when instructing his child to do something because if the child refuses to do as told because of the tone, he will be sinful. The father should rather say, "Son, I think that it would be best if you did that."
["Khulaasatul Fataawaa Vol. 4 Pg. 340]

Therefore, instead of telling her husband, "Bring this", "Do that" or "Tell him this", a wife should rather say, "It will be best if you did this" or "I would like you to do that" or "I would really appreciate it if you could bring that."

If every wife could act on these pieces of advice, they will certainly see the positive difference it brings to their lives. May Allah Ta'ala guide all Muslims women to act accordingly. *Aameen*.

What a Wife Should Never Do

1. A wife should never force her husband to do things that he simply cannot manage to do, e.g. she should not pressurise him to spend more than he can afford. Women often compare what their husbands give them to what their husband's brother/s give their wives so that their husbands may spend more on them. They also compare what their children get to what other fathers give their children. In doing so, they pressurise their husbands to spend beyond their means, often causing their husbands to fall deeply into debt. Even if the husband is wealthy, they deprive the poor and needy of his charity because they are interested in serving only their own desires.

The eminent Sahabi Mu'aadh bin Jabal (May Allah be pleased with him/her) counted such women as one of the greatest tests for men. May Allah Ta'ala save every man from such women and every woman from becoming such. Rajaa bin Hayaar has narrated that Mu'aadh bin Jabal (May Allah be pleased with him/her) said,

أنكم إبتليتم بفتنة الضرآء فصبرتم وإني أخاف عليكم من فتنة السرآء وهي النساء إذا تحلين بالذهب ولبسن ريط الشام وعصب اليمن فاتعبن الغني وكلفن الفقير مالا يطاق

(المرأة المثالية فى أعين الرجال ص ١٣)

"*You people exercised patience when you were tried with the test of hardship. However, I fear for you the test of prosperity, which is the test of women who beautify themselves with gold, who wear the fine garments of Shaam and the crowns of Yemen. They make wealthy husbands tired of spending on them and burden poor husbands with more than they can bear."*

It is with reference to such a woman that an Arab poet wrote:

أن كلفتنى مالم أطق

سائك ما سرك منى من خلق

"If you burden me with more than what I can bear
Remember that you will suffer more difficulties than the ease I gave you thus far."

2. A wife never should repeatedly complain to her husband about his mother.

الضيف الذي سيرحل عما قريب

A guest who will soon be leaving

If a person is displeased with his mother, there is no way that he can ever change her for another. A good wife should regard her mother-in-law as her own mother. By exercising patience and treating her mother-in-law well, a woman can attain the valuable du'aas of the old lady, which will prove beneficial in this world as well as in the next.

Every woman should also bear in mind that her mother is also ageing and it should never occur that her sister/s-in-law ill-treat her mother if she ill-treats her mother-in-law. The principle is clear that one will be treated as one treats others. By the same token she should also bear in mind that she will herself become an ageing mother-in-law one day. It should not be that her daughter-in-law ill-treats her because she did the same to her mother-in-law.

At the same time, she should also remember that people become more like children as approach the age of senility. Therefore, just as one would not abandon one's two-year old child who is impossible to live with, one may also not abandon an old person.

Therefore, if your husband is the only son or if he has other brothers who refuse to care for their mother, do not deprive yourself of the tremendous reward of caring for an old lady. Never pester your husband to provide separate accommodation for you unless the relationship between yourself and your mother-in-law is so strained that it jeopardises your mental and spiritual welfare in this world and in the Hereafter. Under such circumstances, it is best for you to live by yourself. However, even then you should ensure that you serve your mother-in-law so well that she does not even have to get a glass of water by herself.

Whether you are living with your mother-in-law or not, you should make it clear to your husband that when he is with his mother, he should give her more attention. In this way, his mother will not feel that he has forsaken her for his wife.

3. When travelling by car, allow your mother-in- law to occupy the front seat with your husband. Whereas you always have the opportunity to sit in the front seat, you will make her happy by sharing the privilege with her. By pleasing her, you will also be pleasing Allah Ta'ala and when Allah Ta'ala is pleased with you; you will be short of nothing in both worlds.
4. Always give your mother-in-law the first choice whenever the two of you have to choose between two things. For example, if there is a choice to make between two types of materials, give both in her hand so that she may choose which one she likes best. When she has made her choice, take the other one happily. If there is a fear that the mother-in-law will deprive the daughter-in-law of her share and give it to her own daughter instead, the husband should give his wife her share in private. If the mother-in-law has to object, she may be told that her daughter-in-law's mother or another relative had sent the item as a gift for her.
5. Especially if your mother-in-law is a widow, never leave her alone at home when you go out with your husband unless she is happy to stay behind. By refusing to take her along with you, unnecessary ill-feelings may develop in her heart towards you.
6. When a mutual relative phones, allow your mother-in-law to speak to the person as well. Because some mothers-in-law are anxious to know who phoned and what is being discussed, it is best to call them to the phone to speak whenever possible. Of course, if the husband can afford to do so, it will be best if he could arrange a separate phone

for his wife in her room and another for his mother so that each could have her privacy.

Remember that the sign of a good wife is that she is able to tolerate every difficulty that her in-laws give her. Fire will never extinguish fire. It is water that will do this. Whenever an act is done with gentleness and composure, the act is beautified and multiplied in value.

Another right that the wife owes to her husband is that whenever he brings a gift for her, she should tell him to get the same for his mother. If he cannot afford to do so, she should tell him to give it to his mother and give her the same whenever Allah Ta'ala gives him the means. She should remind him that he is deeply indebted to his parents and that even his hardest efforts cannot repay this debt. The wife who turns her husband against his parents should bear in mind that she is merely littering her relationship with her husband with thorns.

There are many women who refuse to forget even a slight altercation with their mothers-in-law. While their husbands are at work, they compound the matter in their minds, inflating it beyond proportions. Eventually, when the husband returns tired from work, the wife bursts into tears. When the concerned husband tries to pacify her and enquires the reason for the outburst, she brushes off the issue by saying that he should not worry. This she does purposefully to stimulate his concern further. After begging her to express her feelings, she eventually tells him that she would be better off dead because she cannot tolerate the misery of living with his mother. Accentuating the episode with false tears, she reports the incident to make her mother-in-law seem like an ogre. If the husband is a shallow-thinking person, he may scold his mother and speak to her harshly, thereby attracting Allah Ta'ala's wrath to his home.

Women should therefore try to forget the little arguments that ensue with their mothers-in-law and face the night with new vigour when their husbands return so that the men do not have to return home with the dread that all hell is soon to break lose.

Again, we should not overlook the fact that if arguments between a mother-in-law and daughter-in-law are a daily occurrence, making life miserable for all at home, the only solution is to arrange separate quarters for the two. If this is not possible, the least that can be done is that separate kitchens be arranged for the two because most arguments erupt over the stove. Of course, arrangements could also be made that the kitchen be the exclusive domain of the daughter-in-law, who would be free to do as she pleases with the mother-in-law coming in only to eat meals.

One should always remember that the status of parents is indeed extremely high. An excellent wife is the wife who encourages her husband to maintain good relations with his parents, brothers, sisters and other relatives. We shall now quote a letter from the book "Tuhfatul Uroos" that a new mother wrote to her mother after giving birth to her first child. She wrote:

To my mother, my beloved mother:

I love you very much and I need you today more that I have ever needed you in my life. Everything around me is causing this love for you to burst forth from my heart like it has never done before. I have never before realised the great intensity of this love. Although I have always loved you, but I have never before felt the depth of this love as I do now. It is indeed strange that I feel like this now whereas I have never experienced this feeling when I was a little girl on your lap.

I have always noticed your intense love for me and the attention you showered on me. I sensed your love for me as I grew from a little infant, to a young girl and then a young lady. When I eventually became a bride, I started living a new life, a life that was strange from the life I was used to with my parents, and family. When I noticed the favours and attention you showered on my brothers and myself, I was astonished to discover that there could actually exist a being as magnanimous as yourself who would be prepared to sacrifice her life for the comfort and happiness of her children. I then began to wonder exactly who this great person whom I call mother is. I wonder which mine has produced such a gem and what kind of heart you had to be able to exude only love and gentleness.

Dear mother! The first scream of my newborn daughter has exposed the secret to me. Her innocent gurgling has taught me volumes and a discovered a great deal when I took her in my lap and wiped away her warm tears. I then had the answers to every question that had plagued my mind for so long. Today I can appreciate your feelings and see through your eyes. Your graces are being showered upon me even to this day without ever desiring repayment. Today I have realised what it means to be a mother because I have just become one. I can see your radiance in this little child and I can see my entire life in her, my infancy, my blossoming, my marriage and my becoming a mother.

Dear mother! The moments of labour were extre- mely severe. During the moments every mother experiences, I wished that you had been near. However, I have now forgotten the pain and only have memories of the little pounding heart that has now occupied my world. From a distance I recognised my child as the nurse carried her to my bed to lay her down. I had been carrying her in my belly for nine months as she grew and was nourished with my blood. I had been eating and sleeping as normal and carrying out my tasks while carrying the world's greatest treasure.

Dear mother! She is now my life. She is everyth- ing to me. She is my cherished bud. She is my daughter. For a long time I had been cherishing the kiss of your affection. Now I feel your presence with us whenever I kiss your little granddaughter.

Your loving daughter.

This touching letter clearly expresses the deep love that every mother has for her child and the love that every child has for his/her mother. It is therefore imperative for a wife not to complain to her husband about his mother. Even though your mother-in-law may insult you, rebuke you or even hit you, you should always remember that she is after all the mother of your husband. She is the mother of your lifelong companion, the mother of your beloved. She is the same woman who carried your husband with difficulty for nine long months. It was she who cared for him as an infant, who used to sacrifice her rest and sleep to nurse him when he was little and who had to endure countless difficulties when raising him. Is it just to get him to fight with her merely on account of a little altercation she had with you?

May Allah Ta'ala never show me nor anyone else the day when a woman makes a man fight with the one who bore him, making him forget the difficulties and hardships she endured for him. Even the Quran pays tribute to the hardship that mothers endure for their children. When delivering her child, every mother puts her life at risk. Every wife should picture this supreme sacrifice that her mother-in-law made for the life of her husband. It does not behove a Muslim to forget the sacrifices that his mother made for him by scolding her or by speaking to her harshly, especially when siding with his wife. Similarly, it does not behove a Muslim wife to pitch a son against his mother merely because of a little injustice done to her.

The life of this world is but a life of a few days. Just as day follows the night, difficult conditions will soon give way to good times. People spend many decades in prisons with hard labour and still emerge alive. A few years with one's mother-in-law will then surely not kill a person.

If you are not living with your mother-in-law, do try to send some cooking or baking to her regularly. Always phone her to enquire about her welfare and keep sending your children to visit her. It is tragic that association with the Kuffaar has made our Muslim women disassociate their children from their children's paternal grandparents and paternal aunts. As a result, the children have little regard for their paternal relatives and associate only with their maternal grandparents and maternal uncles and aunts. Whereas children will readily take to their maternal relatives, they are afraid of their paternal relatives, almost as if they are a different creation. Remember that just as you have sisters-in-law from whom you turn your children away, you may also be a sister-in-law to some woman who may do the same to you.

You should therefore repent for your shortcomin- gs and abstain from destroying your good deeds by backbiting about your sisters-in-law. Doing this, will be giving them all your good deeds and burdening yourself with their sins. May Allah Ta'ala save all women from conniving sisters-in-law who will leave no stone unturned to cause trouble for their brother's wife. *Aameen*.

The Formula for Avoiding All Types of Trouble

One should always bear in mind that the bond between husband and wife is among the signs of Allah Ta'ala's immense power. A man is closer to his wife than he is to any other person. In a like manner, a woman is closest to her husband. When another person steps into this relationship, no good can be expected from it. Problems between couples are caused mostly by the interference of relatives. To achieve his sinister end of separating husband and wife, Shaytan sometimes uses the wife's relatives and sometimes the husband's relatives. This topic has been delt with in a comprehensive way in "Pariaishaan Rehna Chor Digiay" by Darul Huda, the book is currently available only in Urdu. However, there is another small book in English "A Brief Guide To A Distressfree Life" by DarulHuda Publishers that spells out guidelines for living a life with minimum worries and tensions.

It is therefore important for a woman not to complain to her husband about her mother-in-law or sister-in-law. She should also conceal such matters from her mother as well and always speak favourably of her in-laws. However, she may reveal the reality of the situation if circumstances are so grave that the couple's relationship is at stake. Always remember that you should never reveal the faults of your in-laws to your family because this will only cause harm.

Messenger of Allah (Peace be upon him) said that on the Day of Qiyamah Allah Ta'ala will conceal the sins of the person who conceals the shortcoming of others. On the other hand, when a person discloses the faults of another, Allah Ta'ala will expose his faults to the extent that he will be disgraced sitting in his own home. Messenger of Allah (Peace be upon him) has also mentioned that the worst form of usury is to embarrass a Muslim.

It therefore does not behove a Muslim woman to disclose every fault of her in-laws to her family. Many women have the evil habit of telling their family and friends everything that the husbands say and do as well as whatever his family does at home. Muslim women have to refrain from such practices to safeguard their years of Ibaadah from being registered in the accounts of the people whom they backbite or slander.

An intelligent wife should excuse herself to tend to some activity when an argument is brewing between her husband and herself. She should interrupt the altercation to pretend to see to the food cooking on the stove or she may excuse herself to put a child to sleep. In this way, she will be leaving the place of dispute. She should also try to get her husband away from the place because this is an extremely effective manner of cooling tempers. Doing this will also confirm with the Sunnah, practices of Messenger of Allah (Peace be upon him), each of which holds tremendous benefits and mercy for the Ummah. Practising the Sunnah of Messenger of Allah (Peace be upon him) is a great source of creating love, blessings and harmony between people. It is because Muslims today have neglected the Sunnah practices of Messenger of Allah (Peace be upon him) that they are tasting the punishment of disputes and discord.

Bukhari and Muslim narrate a Hadith from Sahl bin Saadr in which he says that Messenger of Allah (Peace be upon him) once visited his daughter Faatima (Mat Allah shower His blessings on her). Upon arriving at her home, he did not see her husband Ali (May Allah be pleased with him/her). When Messenger of Allah (Peace be upon him) asked where Ali (May Allah be pleased with him/her) was

أين ابن عمك؟

Faatima (May Allah be pleased with him/her) informed him that she and Ali (may Allah be pleased with him/her) had an argument because of which he left the house.

When Messenger of Allah (Peace be upon him)

أنظري اين هو؟

sent some one to look for Ali (May Allah be pleased with him/her), he was informed that Ali (May Allah be pleased with him/her) was sleeping in the Masjid. When Messenger of Allah (Peace be upon him) came to the Masjid, he found Ali (May Allah be pleased with him/her) lying on the ground with some sand on his exposed shoulder. Messenger of Allah (Peace be upon him) said

يا أبا تراب قم يا أبا تراب

to him, "Rise, O Abu Turaab (Father of Sand)! Rise, O Abu Turaab!"

Sahl (May Allah be pleased with him/her) says that the title of Abu Turaab became Ali's (May Allah be pleased with him/her) favourite title.

The behaviour of Messenger of Allah (Peace be upon him) with his son-in-law teaches a lesson to the relatives of all women, making it clear to them that they should never overreact and side with the woman when a problem arises. Many people take their daughters/ sisters away to their homes after she has had an argument with her husband, forcing the husband to go there and beg for his wife.

The other important lesson that the incident teaches us is that a person should leave the place of an argument and lie down somewhere else until his anger abates. This is imperative because a person is likely to say or do something regrettable when he is angry. Remember that if you cause trouble you too will be troubled. More details can be found in "Kisi ko Takleef Na Digiay" by Baitul Ilm Trust. Once one has regained one's composure, Shaytan will not be able to manipulate the situation. This Hadith therefore contains the following three important lessons:

a. When tempers flare, the couple should leave the place where the dispute is taking place.
b. The couple should not elaborate on the details of their dispute in front of relatives. They should be especially cautious not to make mountains out of molehills. Domestic problem should be confined to the home where they should b resolved internally with the help of du'aa to Allah Ta'ala.
c. The person resolving the dispute should try to lighten the atmosphere

and not dwell on the dispute, as Messenger of Allah (Peace be upon him) did when he raised Ali's (May Allah be pleased with him/her) spirits by telling him,

قم يا أبا تراب قم يا أبا تراب

"Rise, O Abu Turaab (Father of Sand)! Rise, O Abu Turaab!"

In a like manner, when Messenger of Allah (Peace be upon him) separated himself from his wives for a month, Umar (May Allah be pleased with him/her) lifted the spirits by jesting, "O Messenger of Allah! We men of the Quraysh were always dominant over our women. Since we arrived in Madinah it seems as if our women have been influenced by the Ansaar women who dominate their men." This remark made Messenger of Allah (Peace be upon him) smile.

These incidents teach us that the person attempting to reconcile disputing parties should begin by lightening the atmosphere so that anxiety and anger are dispelled before proceedings commence.

EVERY WOMAN SHOULD THINK FOR HERSELF

There are many brides who are reluctant to apply their minds and who prefer to behave like children who do only what they are indoctrinated to do and say. You will find that they cannot do anything without first consulting their mothers or friends. As a result of this, even their marital lives are governed by others. Although it is wise to seek advice from one's pious mother, she may fail to understand the complete situation at home and the temperament of the husband. As a result, her advice may be detrimental to the couple.

In addition to this, every husband expects his wife to be his confidante and close companion without having an intermediary. He cannot tolerate it if even his blood relatives interference in this relationship. It is therefore imperative for a wise wife to tread carefully every step of the way, taking assistance from du'aa without repeatedly referring to her mother for advice. She should use the natural intelligence that Allah Ta'ala has granted her and not become dependent on the advice of others.

A WOMAN SHOULD NOT DISCLOSE HER FAMILY'S SECRETS TO HER HUSBAND

A secret remains a secret as long as it is not disclosed. Although parents may not specifically tell their children that certain matters are confidential, they expect their children not to disclose them. It is therefore expected that a person should not disclose family secrets to his/her spouse after marriage. The first harm of disclosing family secrets is that it is tantamount to betraying one's parents. This is a grave matter because one's parents have always showered one with countless favours and one cannot ever repay them for what they did. They will be extremely grieved to know that the child whom they painstakingly raised for twenty years is now disclosing their secrets to a stranger.

The second harm of this is that a person's feelings and attitudes are susceptible to change. In fact, the heart is called "qalb" in Arabic because it is so prone to changes. Therefore, if the couple have to separate at some stage, these secrets may be made public, causing untold embarrassment to the entire family.

The third harm of disclosing family secrets is that your spouse may use it to tease you if ever the opportunity arises. These secrets are dormant weapons that can be used against you at any time. When you could not stop these secrets from escaping your one mouth, how will you stop it from escaping your husband's mouth as well? He will soon disclose the secret to his parents, brothers and sisters, who will in turn reveal the same to their in-laws and relatives. When the news spreads as a secret, it travels faster and will not reach the ears of the people who form the subject matter.

An Incident To Illustrate How Molehills Become Mountains

Khalid's company is sending him to Australia for a week. He calls his wife from work to tell her to pack their bags because she could stay with her parents for the week while he is away. She immediately phones her sister to tell her to come over to their parent's home for a few days so that the sisters could spend some time together. The sister secures permission from her husband Ahmad and also starts packing. When Ahmad meets Khalid at Asr time, he asks, "When do you intend leaving for Australia?" Khalid is stunned to know that his brother-in-law already knows about his journey whereas hardly two or three hours had passed since his company told him about it. He returns home angry with his wife for telling "the whole world" about his trip and a storm erupts. That night, his wife again calls her sister and scolds her for informing her husband, who in turn received a tongue-lashing from his wife for "opening his mouth when he knows how sensitive his brother-in-law is". As a result, two homes are alight and Ahmad has to beg Khalid for forgiveness.

Situations like this cause many men to lament about their wives, just as an Arab poet once wrote:

تنحي فاجلسى مني بعيدا أراح اللّٰه منك العالمينا أغربالا إذا أستودعت

سرا وكانونا على المتحدثينا حياتك ما علمت حياة سوء وموتك قد يسرا

الصالحينا

"Stay far from me! Stay away! May Allah Ta'ala protect the world from you. Are you like a sieve that sifts secrets only to pass them on to others? In my opinion, your life is one of sin and your death a relief to the righteous ones."

May Allah Ta'ala save all Muslim men and women from developing such habits. *Aameen.*

We shall now relate a true incident from an article written by Sheikh Muhammad Rasheed Al Aweed, entitled "Risaalah ila Hawa", which appeared Arabic journal called "Jareedatul Qabs". The article reports an incident related by a Dr. Lancaster who served for many years as a marriage counsellor in New York. In support of her opinion that couples should not disclose all their family secrets to each other, she reports a case where a couple experienced serious marital problems after being happily married for ten years.

When the cause was investigated, it was discovered that the wife disclosed to her husband that her father always loved in fear of her mother because she was an extremely ill-tempered person. However, he patiently tolerated her behaviour until she mellowed as the children grew. He was then relieved of his anxiety. She revealed this secret to her husband in confidence little realising that whenever the two were embroiled in an argument, her husband taunted her by saying that she followed in her mother's footsteps. He would also tell her that if he had known that her family was like that, he would have never landed himself into the snare. Another one of his statements was that she should never think that he is a softie like her father. In this manner, their relationship deteriorated very drastically.

The same advice is given by Dr. Kenneth, a leading psychologist. She says, "The harms of being explicit to one's spouse about one's feelings are greater than its benefits. A typical example of something you should never tell your spouse is: 'I cannot understand why I can't seem to love you.' In a single year, I have witnessed 184 cases in which the harms of being explicit and candid with one's spouse are manifest. A wife should therefore never disclose her secrets to her husband and if her husband discloses his secrets to her, she should place her hand over his mouth, making it clear to him that he should tell her anything of the sort. Similarly, they should also not disclose their deepest feelings to each other."

Instead of being frank about the absence of love between them, the couple should make it seem to each other that their love is undying and strong, even though this may require sheer flattery. Therefore, instead of candidly stating that you did not miss him in his absence, you should say, "I could not sleep without you" or "My food would not digest until you returned."

Just as you should not disclose your secrets and the secrets of your parents to your husband, you should also not disclose the secrets of your brothers and sisters to him. For example, you should not inform him about the problems that your sister is having with her in-laws or about the reasons for your brother's broken engagement, etc. You should rather take these secrets with you to your grave and never disclose them to anyone whether you are asked about them or not. As a faithful slave of Allah Ta'ala and follower of the Messenger of Allah (Peace be upon him), you should bear the principles of the Shari'ah in mind and protect the honour of you family by keeping such secrets a secret. May Allah Ta'ala guide all Muslim women to do what is right and to remain steadfast on the truth. *Aameen*.

The Couple Should Never Reveal Their Private Lives to Others

The Noble Prophet of Allah (Peace be upon him) has strongly prohibited Muslims from revealing the details of their private lives to others. It is extremely shameless of a bridegroom or a bride to tell his/her friends about their meeting with each other on their first night of marriage. When Messenger of Allah (Peace be upon him) was informed that people revealed such matters to others, he said,

فلا تفعلوا فإنما ذلك مثل الشيطان لقي شيطانه فى طريق فغشيها والناس ينظرون

"Never do this! It is like a male and female devil having intercourse on the road with everyone watching." [Musnad Ahmad]

Describing the pristine traits of righteous women in the Quran,

حفظت للغيب بما حفظ اللّه

Allah Ta'ala mentions, "So the pious women are obedient and they safeguard the private affairs (that take place between them and their husbands)..."

It is also important for women not to describe the beauty of other women to their husbands because this may cause their husbands to be attracted to the women described. The incidents of hurt caused by unfaithful husbands are too numerous and well known and therefore do not need elaboration. It is also improper for women to tell their husbands about intimate details relating to non-Mahram women, such as their pregnancies, etc.

Messenger of Allah (Peace be upon him) said:

لاتباشر المرأة المرأة فتنعتها لزوجها كأنه ينظر إليها

(بخاری کتاب النکاح ۹/۳۳۸ وابوداؤد ۳۱۵)

"*A woman should not associate with another woman and then describe her to her husband as if he is looking at her.*" *[Bukhari & Abu Dawood]*

You may have heard several incidents of men divorcing their wives to marry the associates or family members of their wives. Such relationships have often started when the man's wife introduced him to the other woman or when she spoke about her to him. It is primarily because of the absence of Shari Hijaab that such illicit relationships have destroyed many marriages. More devastating are the cases where men foster illicit relationships with their domestic servants and other employees. It is therefore vital for women to observe the Shari injunctions concerning Hijaab whether their families approve of it or not. Among the men they should conceal themselves from are all their cousins and brothers-in-law.

Many women make the mistake of regarding their cousins (especially the sons of their maternal aunts) as their brothers whereas such men are definitely not Mahram. Women should ensure that they conceal themselves from such men at all times. In addition to this, every woman should ensure that her husband is not exposed to non-Mahram women such as her sisters, her sisters' mature daughters and his cousins.

It is not futile to reiterate that women should not praise the beauty of any non-Mahram woman to her husband. She should not make statements like "she was looking stunning in that red dress" or "she does not even 'show' even though she is in her sixth month". It is Haraam to reveal such details to one's husband or to one's brother.

GUARDING THE HUSBAND'S SECRETS

A wife should not disclose any of her husband's secrets. Among his most confidential secrets are the details of their love-life. Not only is it Haraam to disclose these details, it is also Haraam to ask another woman about it. Messenger of Allah (Peace be upon him) has classified people who reveal these details as the worst of people. He said,

أن من أشر الناس عند الله منزلة يوم القيامة الرجل يفض إلى إمرأته
وتفضي إليه ، ثم ينشر سرها (مسلم رقم ٢٥٩٧، ٤٦٤ ج١)

"Verily the person in the worst condition on the Day of Qiyamah shall be person who engaged in sexual relations with his/her spouse and then revealed these secrets to others."

A wife may not reveal these details at any stage of her life. Although there may be many other secrets that are not as confidential as the above category, it is still unbecoming of a good wife to reveal these even to her adult children. She ought to guard his secrets up to her grave and not become the target of statements like that of an irate husband who once said, "No secret remains safe in a woman's custody except her age."

The incident leading to the revelation of Surah Tahreem (Surah 66) is well documented and you must have read it somewhere. If not, you should refer to an authentic commentary of the Quran and try to acquire one to read at home. Among such commentaries are Mufti Shafi's "Ma'aariful Quran" and Mufti Aashiq Ilaahi's "Anwaarul Bayaan", both of which have been translated into English. The incident tells us about a secret of Messenger of Allah (Peace be upon him) that Hafsa (May Allah be pleased with him/her) knew about and which she disclosed to Ayesha (May Allah be pleased with him/her). This angered Allah Ta'ala and He revealed the following verses of Surah Tahreem to chide them:

"If the two of you repent to Allah Ta'ala, then your hearts have surely turned. However, if you two assist each other against him [Messenger of Allah (Peace be upon him)] then his protecting friends are Allah Ta'ala Jibra'eel and the pious believers. Besides these, the angels are also aides to him." *[Surah 66, verse 4]*

Harmonising One's Sentiments and Preferences With Those of One's Husband

Every person has his own set of likes and dislikes. A good wife makes every effort to harmonise her likes and dislikes with those of her husband. Of course, she should not subscribe to those inclinations and sentiments of his that oppose the laws propounded by Allah Ta'ala and the Messenger of Allah (Peace be upon him). In fact, she should be so closely associated with him that she can fulfil his wish even before he can mention it to her. She should do things as he wants them to be done and should also conduct herself as he wants her to conduct herself. This is one of the most important ingredients to ensure that the couple's love for each other remains sturdy and everlasting. Whereas beauty and wealth are fleeting commodities, inculcating valuable qualities can never bore one's husband and cannot be lost overnight.

The souls and thoughts of the couple should be united and they should do things in unison. Each one should like what the other likes and dislike what the other dislikes. Such a relationship will ensure that the couple live happily together and together see to the healthy upbringing of their children. When a couple lives in this manner, their children will have a happy life which will lead to the sound development of their capabilities and character traits. Such children will prove to be confident and capable, making excellent leaders for humanity.

Made-up beauty is false and even real beauty is contentious and temporary. However, a wife who is in harmony with her husband remains praiseworthy even after her death.

Ayesha (May Allah bre pleased with him/her) reports that she was once drinking water during her menstrual cycle when Messenger of Allah (Peace be upon him) took the cup from her and drank the left-over water, placing his mouth on the same place where hers had been. When a husband and wife drink each other's left-over water from the same utensil, they will be practising a Sunnah of Messenger of Allah (Peace be upon him). You should remember that when you are candid and free with your husband, your relationship with him will be more lasting, your love will be deeper and your honour maintained.

If even the most foolish man on earth gets a wife who is pleasant and eager to please him, he can easily join the ranks of the wisest of men. On the other hand, if a wise man has the ill-fortune of marrying a disobedient and foolish wife, it is only a matter of time before he is relegated to the ranks of the foolish. One of the fortunate men to be blessed with an excellent wife was the famous Chief Justice Qadhi Shurayh. When Imam Sha'bi once asked him about matters at home, he replied, "My wife has not displeased me for the past twenty years." When Imam Sha'bi asked the reason for this, Qadhi Shurayh replied, "From the first night of our marriage, our personalities united and up to this day we are like one soul in two bodies. When I met her, the first night and saw how beautiful she was, I performed two Rakaahs salah to express gratitude to Allah Ta'ala. When I turned my head to end the salah with Salam, I saw her also ending her salah with salam beside me. When I stretched my hand towards her after completing my du'aa, she said, 'Be patient, O Abu Umayyah.'"

"She then said, 'All praise is due to Allah Ta'ala. I praise Allah Ta'ala; I seek His assistance and invoke His choicest mercies on Rasulullahs and his family. I am a simple lady who is unaware of your personality. Do tell me what you like so that I may carry it out and tell me what displeases you so that I may forsake it. There are many women from your people whom you could have married. Similarly, there are many men from my people to whom I could have been married. However, when Allah Ta'ala decrees a matter, it comes to pass. You have now become my master, so do as Allah Ta'ala has commanded every Muslim husband, i.e. that his wife should either be "retained in good faith or released in kindness." Thus do I terminate my speech. I seek forgiveness from Allah Ta'ala for myself and for you.'"

Qadhi Shurayh continued, "When I heard this speech, I was compelled to reply. I therefore said to her, 'I praise Allah Ta'ala, seek His assista- nce and invoke Allah Ta'ala's choicest mercies and peace on Rasulullahs and his family. You have indeed spoken such words that will be a source of good fortune to you if you remain steadfast by them. However, if you have to detract from them, they will be held against you.' I then proceeded to mention everything I liked and everything I disliked. I then said to her, 'Whenever you see anything good, spread the word around and whenever you see anything evil, conceal it.'"

"She then asked, 'What love do you have for my family?' I replied, 'I do not want to visit them so frequently that they get tired of me.' She proceeded to ask, 'Which of your relatives do you approve of so that I may allow them into the house and which of them do you disapprove of so that I may make some excuse.' I then informed her of those of my relatives who are pious and those who required du'aa for guidance so that she may avoid them.'"

Qadhi Shurayh then said to Imam Sha'bi, "She has lived with me for twenty years and I have never needed to reprimand her for anything. I only once reprimanded her for something, but was wrong to do so." *[Extracted from "Al-Mar'atul Mithaaliyya fi A'yunir Rijaal" Pg. 34]*

It is therefore necessary for a wife to act and think according to her husband tastes. It is in the marriage of such women that people as great as Qadhi Shurayh can be of service to humanity. Despite being a pauper, a person with a wife like this will have a life better than that of a king. May Allah Ta'ala make all women icons of compatibility for their husbands. Aameen.

The above incident makes it clear that the couple should ask each other about their likes and dislikes from the beginning so that they may adopt what the other likes and abstain from whatever the other dislikes. If the adage is true that there is a woman behind every successful man, then the life of Qadhi Shurayh is an excellent example of its accuracy.

A Good Wife is Content With What Allah Ta'ala Decides

Another sterling attribute of a good wife is that she is pleased with whatever Allah Ta'ala decides, whether the decision is in her favour or against it. Whatever her condition, she is always grateful to Allah Ta'ala.

Imam Isma'eel reports that he once visited a town where he saw an extremely beautiful woman in the marriage of a very unattractive man. When he asked her how she could be pleased to be married to him, she replied,

أسكت، فقد أسأت فى قولك، لعله أحسن فيما بينه وبين خالقه فجعلنى ثوابه، أو لعلني أسأت فيما بيني وبين خالقي فجعله عقوبتي أفلا أرضي بما رضي اللّٰه لي؟ فأسكتتني (المرأة المثالية ص ٣٧)

"Be silent! You have uttered a very unpleasant statement. In his relationship with his Creator, my husband may have pleased Allah Ta'ala so much that He has made me his reward. On the other hand, in my relationship with my Creator, I must have displeased Allah Ta'ala so much that He has made him my punishment. I am pleased with Allah Ta'ala's decision for me." So saying, she silenced Imam Isma'eel *["Al Mar'atul Mithaaliyya" Pg. 37]*

A similar incident is narrated in the book "Aqdul Fareed". An extremely unattractive man by the name of Imraan bin Hittaan was married to a very beautiful woman. She once said to him, "We are both definitely destined for Jannah." When he asked her the reason for this, she said,

لإنك أعطيت مثلى فشكرت وإبتليت بمثلك فصبرت، والصابر والشاكر

في الجنة (زهرات من الروض، المرأة المسلمة ص ٢١)

"You were given a wife like myself and you were grateful to Allah Ta'ala while I have been granted a husband like yourself and I have exercised patience. The patient ones and grateful ones are certainly destined for Jannah."

HOW AN INTELLIGENT WIFE SHOULD DEAL WITH A FOOLISH HUSBAND

It often happens that when a foolish man's mother or sisters instigate him against his wife, he starts insulting her parents or other relatives, telling her that they are bad people. Because a woman has natural love for her relatives and especially for her parents, she is bound to retaliate by insulting his family. When she retaliates in this manner, matters get out of control and Shaytan has a field day and ravages the marriage which may have been a happy one for many years.

An intelligent wife does not retaliate in this way. When her husband insults her brother for example, she should say, "I seek forgiveness on my brother's behalf. If my parents or any of my relatives have hurt you in any way, I seek forgiveness on their behalf and I shall tell them not to hurt you in this manner again. Please do forgive them. I feel that if they have caused hurt to you or to anyone else, we should not allow their wrong to disrupt our home. The wrong they did will not be corrected by us arguing. Instead, two wrongs will be perpetrated and two relationships will be destroyed. We should therefore first resolve one problem before creating another."

We shall now narrate an incident from every reader will learn invaluable lessons, Insha Allah Ta'ala. Addressing a relative of his, Khalid bin Yazeed once spoke ill of his wife's brother Abdullah bin Zubayr (May Allah be pleased with him/her). Khalid's wife Ramla bint Zubayr (May Allah be pleased with him/her) was sitting nearby and overheard what was being said. However, she said nothing and kept her head bowed. After saying whatever he wanted to say, Khalid's anger had not yet abated. He then turned to his wife and said, "You have said nothing. Did you remain silent because you agree with whatever I have said about your brother or was your silence due to your disagreement?"

لاهذا ولا ذاك! ولكن المرأة لم تخلق للدخول بين الرجال إنما نحن

رياحين للشم والضم فمالنا وللدخول بينكم؟

She replied by saying, "It is neither this not that. A woman has not been created to interfere in the dealings men have between themselves. We are merely fragrant flowers who have to be admired and smelt. We have no reason to interfere in your matters."

Hearing this remarkable reply made Khalid stand up and kiss his wife's forehead. Every trace of anger and malice that dominated him a while ago was forgotten.

It is because of women like this that Sulayman (May Allah be pleased with him/her) remarked in one of his judgements,

المرأة العاقلة تبني بيتها ، والسفيهة تهدمها (مأخوذ از المرأة المثالية ص ٢٦)

"An intelligent woman builds a ruined home while a foolish woman ruins a built home."
["Al Mar'atul Mithaal- iyya" Pg. 26]

Such a woman mends tattered hearts with her intelligence and du'aas. She irrigates dead hearts with the water of her love and heals burnt hearts with the balm of her sincere affection. If Ramla (May Allah be pleased with him/her) had defended her brother or agreed with her husband, matters would have worsened considerably. Instead, the intelligent lady extinguished the flames of her husband's anger in an instant without hurting anyone. Neither did she blot her brother's image by siding with her husband nor did she infuriate her husband by defending her brother. It is sincerely hoped that every Muslim woman will learn from this incident and adopt the ways of their pious predecessors.

By employing her natural intelligence and sweet tongue, a woman can conquer the hardest man. All she needs to do is to comfort him when he is grieved, be devoted to him and win a place in his heart. It is because of the magic in her voice that the Quran has forbidden women from speaking to non-Mahram men in sweet tones. Her voice is sufficient to entice a man to commit sins. A woman should therefore treat her husband's foolishness with a dose of love, gentleness and kind words. This will effectively stem the tide of his anger and calm his fury. We shall now quote some Arabic verses which eloquently described the manners of speech. By employing these manners of speech, many wives will Insha Allah Ta'ala solve many of their domestic difficulties.

Praising his wife's manner if speech; the famous Arab poet, Bashaar bin Bard says:

وقد تكون بها سلمى تحدثني
تساقط الحلي حاجاتي وأسراري

"When with her, Salma's words fall like pearls off a necklace, each one dispelling my every concern and deepest worry

حديث لو أن اللحم يصلى بحره
غريضا أتى أصحابه وهو منضج

Her speech is so warm that if people left meat with her, they would find it roasted when they returned

وكـــــان رجع حديثها
قطع الرياض كسين زهرا

The echoes of her words are like sections of a garden filled with fragrant flowers."

Every bride should emulate the excellent manner of speech that Bashaar's wife employed. Her manner was always cordial and friendly, instantly dispelling his every worry and concern.

It has been reported that when a slave girl was brought to the Khalifa Haaroon Ar Rasheed, he commented,

فلو لأكنف فى وجهها، وخنس في أنفها لأشتريتها

"If it were not for the blemishes on her face and pigmentation on her nose, I would have purchased her."

Hearing this, the lady requested permission to speak. When she was permitted to speak, she recited the following couplets:

ما سلم الظبى على حسنه
كلا ولا البدر الذى يوصف
الظبى فيــــــه خنس بين

والبدر فيـــه كلف يعرف

"Despite its good looks, the beauty of the deer is not perfect, never!
Neither is the beauty of the full moon that people laud
The deer has blemishes on its nose
And the full moon has blemishes that all are aware of.."

Hearing the eloquence of her words, the Khalifa purchased her and she became one of his most favoured slave girls. Even though she lacked physical beauty, this woman won the Khalifa's favour purely on account of her intelligence. She taught the Khalifa and all those present that although the moon has obvious blemishes, these do not affect its radiance and overall beauty. She indicated that although Allah Ta'ala had not blessed her with physical beauty, Allah Ta'ala had blessed her with the gem of intelligence by which she could be of sterling service to her master.

It is praiseworthy of a woman to beautify her physical self without the use of jewellery and to beautify her inner self with attributes such as:

1. Intelligence coupled with diplomacy
2. Maintaining a clean and tidy home
3. Obedience to her husband
4. The concern to beautify herself for her husband so that he could be attracted to her without burdening him with expenses.

The Khalifa Mu'tadid once fell asleep while resting his head on his wife's thigh. She gently placed a pillow beneath his head and left. When he awoke, he was upset to see that she had left. He asked her what the reason for her behaviour was, because he felt that her action stemmed from pride. She denied this and said, "We were taught never to sit near a sleeping person and never to sleep near someone who is sitting." Mu'tadid was satisfied with this reply.

Every woman should be grateful to Allah Ta'ala for every quality that Allah Ta'ala has blessed her with, whether the quality be related to her inner self or her physical appearance. By being ungrateful for these blessings, they will gradually diminish and she will begin to lose confidence in herself. She will then doubt her abilities and the value that others attach to her.

A woman should do everything with foresight and a conscious mind. In

this manner, she will be respected and admired. It will not be redundant to again quote the statement of Sulayman (May Allah be pleased with him/ her) who said,
"An intelligent woman builds a ruined home while a foolish woman ruins a built home." Whereas an intelligent woman will introduce orderliness to a chaotic home and will be able to understand the personality of her husband, a foolish woman will disrupt an orderly home, replace its love with enmity and its tranquillity with agitation. May Allah Ta'ala save every home from such a woman. Ameen.
A poet once said:

المرأة العاقلة تبني بيتها، والسفيهة تهدمها (مأخوذ از المرأة المثالية ص ٢٦)

"O beautiful lady! Harness your loose tongue!
Do not taint your beauty with your words.

يــا حسنة الوجه توقت الخنا
لا تبدلــــن الزين بالشين
ويا قبحة الوجه كوني محسنة
لا تـجـمـعــــن بين قبـحين

O unattractive one! Be righteous!
Do not join two negative traits within yourself (i.e. unattractiveness as well as impiety)."

Whereas a man can tolerate unattractiveness, he will not be able to tolerate a woman who does not control her tongue.

A GOOD WIFE IS ALWAYS LOYAL TO HER HUSBAND

A good wife always stands by her husband's side regardless of circumstances. Whether he is experiencing prosperity or whether he is suffering hardship, she never leaves his side. A man is most unfortunate when he has a wife who is actually married to his wealth. Such a woman will remain loyal to her husband only while he is wealthy.

A true wife loves her husband only for Allah Ta'ala's pleasure. She has no obsession for the things of this world and her only obsession is pleasing her husband. She ensures that he is never displeased with her and treats him equally well whether he is healthy or ill. True love dictates that even once a woman's husband has passed away, she still adheres to the lifestyle she lived while he was alive. Just as she did nothing to displease him during his lifetime, she will do no such thing after his death. Such was the behaviour of Umar bin Abdul Aziz's (May Allah be pleased with him/her) wife. After he passed away, her brother asked here whether she wanted back her jewellery which her late husband had deposited in the state treasury. She replied, "How can I be happy with it now when I was not happy with it during my husband's lifetime?"

It is in praise of his loyal wife that a Bedouin suffering starvation once recited the following couplets:

يا رب أني قاعد كما ترى
وزوجتي قاعدة كما ترى
والبطن مني جائع كما ترى
فما ترى ربنـــا فيما ترى

"O my Rabb! I am sitting here as You see
Sitting with me here is my wife as You see
My belly is empty as You see
What is Your opinion about what You see?"

If a woman refuses to stand by her husband's side when he is in difficulty, his grief will be doubled. When a man suffers a setback like loss of employment, a good wife will wipe away the perspiration of anxiety from his forehead. She should comfort him by telling him that wealth comes from Allah Ta'ala and that He takes it away only for good reasons. She should advise him to regularly perform his salah and to constantly recite "Yaa Mughni" and in addition to this, he should also recite the following du'aa:

اللّٰهم إكفني بحلالك عن حرامك وأغنني بفضلك عمن سواك

"O Allah Ta'ala! Grant me sufficient Halaal sustenance so that I may save myself from Haraam and, by Your grace, make me independent of everyone besides You."

She should tell him that she does not mind living, eating and dressing simply for as long as they need to so that he may not have any financial burden. With such support from his wife, no difficulty is insurmountable for a man. Her inspiring attitude can lift him out of any gloom and convert any illness to glowing health.

On the other hand, when a woman regards her husband only as a means of fulfilling her needs, she will rebuke him in his difficulties instead of comforting him. She will tell him things like, "Did I not tell you not to do business with so-and-so?" or "I warned you against investing there! Now you have lost everything just as I told you!" or "Now how will we pay the children's fees, the lights and water? How will I do without our domestic servant? I will now have to bear the brunt of your foolish dealings!"

It is with reference to such women that the famous Arab poet Abu Amr Ibn Alaa wrote:

فإن تسألوني بالنساء فإننى عليم بأدوآء النساء طبيب إذا شاب رأس المرء

أو قل ماله فليس له في ودهن نصيب

If you ask me about women, I have profound knowledge of their behaviour and am also a physician to treat them
When a man's hair whitens or when his wealth diminishes, he will have no place in her heart."

A GOOD WIFE HAS EYES ONLY FOR HER HUSBAND

Another outstanding feature of a good wife is that she loves only her husband and this love is solely for the pleasure of Allah Ta'ala. She has no ulterior motives for this love. Messenger of Allah (Peace be upon him) has mentioned that a woman will enter Jannah if she passes away when her husband is pleased with her. *[Tirmidhi Vol. 1 Pg. 219]*

When a woman's love for her husband is not related to his wealth, his beauty, his position, his qualifications or anything else, she will win a prized position in his heart which none can wrest from her.

One of the traits of the women of Jannah is that they will be قاصرات الطرف "*maidens with lowered gazes*" This means that these women have eyes for none besides their husbands. Another of their qualities is that they are "damsels sheltered in tents". This verse means that they are women who do not beautify themselves and roam about for others to admire. They reserve their beauty exclusively for their husbands. A good wife should therefore have eyes only for her husband and she should not look at non-Mahram men. At the same time, she should go out of her house only when absolutely necessary so that she does not become the admiration of every other man.

The famous king Haaroon Ar Rasheed had a black slave girl whom he loved very much and who also loved him very much. She was his favourite slave girl. Because of his attachment to her, the other slave girls became extremely jealous of her and they were always scheming against her so that the king may devote less attention to her. As a lesson to them all, the king once spread out a tablecloth filled with jewels, gold and silver. He then made an announcement that every person can take whatever s/he can lay his/her hands on. When they heard this, all the king's servants and courtiers started taking whatever they could. However, his favourite slave girl stood where she was, intently looking at the king. When the king asked her why she was not taking the jewels and treasures, she asked, "Is the announcement true that a person can keep whatever she lays her hands on?" When he confirmed this, she calmly stood up and, placing her hand on the king's shoulder, said, "I desire the master of this gold and silver. If I have him, I shall have all of this and if he is not mine, I shall have nothing." The king presented this as an example to the rest, making it clear to them that although she did not possess the beauty they had, she more than made up for it with her love for the king.

The lesson that every Muslim should learn from this incident is that we should seek to please Allah Ta'ala at all times regardless of what people say. When we have secured Allah Ta'ala's pleasure and have won Him over, the contents of the heavens and the earth shall be at out disposal. However, if He is displeased with us, we shall be perpetually worried and depressed even though we may possess the riches of the world. May Allah Ta'ala make every Muslim His sincere bondsmen and bondswomen who follow in the footsteps of His beloved Prophet (Peace be upon him) *Aameen*.

A Mother's Advice to her Daughter on the Night of her Marriage

When the leader of Kindah Amr bin Hajar was married to Ummu Iyaas bint Awf bin Muslim Shaybaani, her mother Umamah bint Haarith called her aside on the night of their marriage and gave her the following pieces of advice. Every new bride should heed these valuable pieces of advice, which outline the rights that every wife owes to her husband.

She said, "Dearest daughter! You are now leaving the environment in which you grew up and you are turning your sights onto a horizon which you are unfamiliar with. Your companion there will be someone with whom you are not acquainted. Today, all of you shall be under his authority.

فكوني له أمة يكن لك عبدًا وشيكًا، وأحفظى مني خلالًا عشرة يكن لك زكرًا وذخرًا

You should therefore become his slave girl and he will become your conscientious slave.

Adopt ten attributes which will cause your husband and other people to speak favourably of you and which will be a treasure for you in the Hereafter.

These attributes are:

The first and second are that together with being content with whatever he gives you, you should humble yourself before him. Listen attentively to whatever he says and obey his instructions.

The third and fourth are that you should always be conscious about how your husband likes to see you and smell you. Whenever he sees you, his opinion of you should not be tainted and whenever he smells you, he should never smell anything besides a pleasant fragrance.

وإن الكحل أحسن الحسن الموجود، والماء أطيب الطيب المفقود

Kohl is the best, easiest and least expensive form of beautification while water is the best fragrance because taking a bath regularly and making wudhu often ensures that the body remains clean and does not exude an unpleasant odour.

The fifth and sixth attributes are that you should always take his times of eating and sleeping into consideration because the sparks of anger are usually ignited by hunger and lack of sleep. Have his meals prepared before time and if you get delayed, feed him something light while the meal is being prepared. If he gets angry when the meal is delayed, apologise and present your excuse. However, you should never use anger to reply to anger.

The seventh and eighth attributes are that you should always safeguard his wealth as well as his family and his status. His wealth is best safeguarded by sound financial management and his family is best safeguarded by good supervision.

The ninth and tenth attributes are that you should never disobey his instructions and never disclose any of his secrets. Disobedience will fill him with rage and disclosing his secrets will make you vulnerable to any plot he may scheme against you. He will then have no confidence in you and will never regard you as his own. Never express joy when he is grieved but rather share his grief and comfort him. On the other hand, you should also take care never to express grief when he is happy.

وإعلمي يابنية! إنك لا تقدرين على ذلك حتى تؤثري رضاه على رضاك وتقدمي هواه على هواك فيما أحببت أو كرهت، والله يضع لك الخير واستودعك الله

Remember, my daughter dear! You will never be able to conquer his heart until you give preference to his pleasure over your own and until you like what he likes and dislike what he dislikes. We now leave you in Allah Ta'ala's care. May He grant you every good and save you from every evil." *["Silsilatul Usratil Muslimatis Sa'eeda" Vol. 1 Pg. 45]*

May Allah Ta'ala grant every Muslim wife the guidance and ability to implement all of the above in their lives. *Aameen.*

A FATHER'S ADVICE TO HIS DAUGHTER

It is Mustahab (commendable) for a father to advise his daughter on the occasion of her marriage. Anasr narrates that whenever the Companion of the Prophet (Peace be upon him) sent their daughters as brides to their husbands, they would emphasise the importance of serving the husband and fulfilling his rights. *["Tuhfatul Uroos" Pg. 77]*

Abdullah bin Ja'farr bin Abi Taalib gave the following advice to his daughter:

"Avoid jealousy and pride because these are the keys to divorce. Avoid rebuking because this creates enmity and resentment. Use kohl because this is the best means of beautification and the best perfume is water."

When Farafasa bin Ahwas gave his daughter Naa'ila in marriage to Usman (May Allah be pleased with him/her), he advised her in the following words:

"Dearest daughter! You are going to be in the company of women of the Quraysh who have better access to perfumes than you have. Therefore, remember these two pieces of advice that I am giving to you. Use kohl and apply the perfume of water (i.e. bath regularly) so that you may smell as fresh and fragrant as rain water."

["Tuhfatul Uroos" Pg. 122]

In addition to the advice given above, Abul Aswad advised his daughter thus:

"Pay attention to your physical appearance and remember that kohl is the best means of beautification. Always apply perfume and remember that the best perfume is to perform wudhu properly."

In fact, even many non-Muslims have identified that washing the face several times with cold water is an excellent manner of maintaining one's beauty.

The above quotations make it clear that Islam strongly recommends women to beautify themselves for their husbands. Whether a woman is rich or poor, young or old, at home or travelling, she should bath at least once daily. During summer, she may even bath twice a day. Of course, this depends on her health. Otherwise, she will be making wudhu several times for her five daily salah. Besides these times, she should wash her hands and face after completing her work in the kitchen.

Women should also ensure that they use kohl, which is inexpensive means of beautification that does not require much time to apply. In addition to this, it does not have to be removed when making wudhu or when taking a bath. If women could adopt these simple but highly effective means of beautification, the Muslim Ummah will save millions which could be utilised for more worthy causes.

It is commonly said that women are men's dolls. It is therefore necessary for every husband to provide the means of beautification for his wife so that her added beauty may attract him to her and increase their love for each other.

Abdul Faraj Isfahaani has mentioned that even beautiful women need to beautify themselves and keep themselves clean to win a place in the hearts of their husbands. These factors enhance her beauty. In addition to this, she should also dress attractively. Of course, a woman may only use those types of clothing and means of beautification that the Shari'ah permits. She should be cautious that her husband should not see her in an unkempt condition and that he should not get an unpleasant odour from her.

A wife should remember that she will suffer the consequences of her failings in this regard. If she does not take care of herself and allows herself to fall prey to shabbiness and obesity, her husband will detect her indifference and he may be attracted to other women.

Women should also be cautious not to allow their clothing to get soiled. They should immediately remove any stain that falls on their clothing. It is commonly mentioned that when a person keeps his/her clothing free from stains and dirt, Allah Ta'ala will keep his/her heart free from the stains of sin.

The importance of personal hygiene cannot be overemphasised. One's teeth and mouth should always be clean and nails always neatly pared. Although this is especially important for a wife, the husband should never neglect the same for himself. The details of this will Insha Allah Ta'ala be mentioned in the book "Gift to a husband". When the men of the Bani Israa'eel neglected personal hygiene, their women resorted to adultery.

The Advice of Maulana Muhammad Ahmad Surti to His Daughter

Dearest daughter! You are now leaving for your husband's home. Leave happily. May Allah Ta'ala bless your new home. May you spread light wherever you go and may Allah Ta'ala grant you the understanding and foresight to brighten your future. May you find happiness with your husband. May Allah Ta'ala grant both of you such great love for each other that lights the way ahead and which provides comfort for your in-laws as well.

Dearest daughter! May Allah Ta'ala guide you to uphold the honour of your parent's home when you live with your in-laws. Never allow disgrace to come to your parents or your parents-in-law. Our honour is now in your hands. Never allow anyone to criticise the careful and loving upbringing that your mother gave you.

Dearest daughter! May Allah Ta'ala grant you the ability to tackle every difficulty with courage and determination. May He also grant you the ability to cross every intricate and delicate situation with dexterity and skill. Keep away from arguments and disputes and Allah Ta'ala will grant you the traits of a respectable woman.

Dearest daughter! From the day you were born, we realised that you were not meant to stay with us always but would be leaving us for another. You were destined to live as a guest in our home and we raised you until you developed the ability to run your own home. We are now handing you over in the safe custody of your in-laws.

Dearest daughter! You are now leaving your parents, your brothers and your sisters. What a painful moment indeed! Women have come from near and far to attend the wedding and children are all dressed in excellent Islamic dress, all beaming with excitement. All your father's friends are here as well as friends and relatives from our families and associates. Some are weeping openly, others are sobbing silently while the eyes of so many are welling up with tears, each one of them trying to lighten the grief burdening their hearts. Looking across the spectrum of people young and old, a strange form of gloom seems to have enveloped them all.

Dearest daughter! Look at your mother! Her grief is inexplicable. She bore you in her womb for nine long months, feeding you with her own blood. She would sleep on the wet portion of the bed, keeping you snug on the dry part. She then kept her gazes fixed on you for eighteen years. How will her tears every dry? She sacrifices her rest for you and forfeited many nights of sleep during her youthful days for your sake. When it came to you, she neither knew day as day or night as night. How will her days and nights now pass without you?

You cannot imagine the difficulties she endured for your education and for raising you. A slight frown on your face would eliminate all her happiness and your single tear would ignite a thousand sparks in her heart. You are now leaving this warm lap of your mother. She fed you the best food without desiring it for herself and dressed you in the best clothing without wishing that the money had been spent on her. Her heart always told said, "When my daughter eats well, it is as if I am eating and when she dresses well, it is as if I am dressed."

To alleviate your single worry, she would take a thousand worries upon her head. Can you remember how many good nights your mother passed in anxiety for you? She would sit at your bedside for hours when you were ill and would pay no heed to her own health because of her concern for your health. Alas! What must be passing through her heart at this moment? She will now have to bear this separation. Only Allah Ta'ala can grant her the ability to bear it.

Dearest daughter! You are leaving your beloved sisters behind as well. Together with being your sisters, they were also your close companions. You were always together and did nothing without each other. You played and enjoyed yourselves together and were so close that you even thought the same thoughts. They love you dearly and were always ready to do what you told them. Your happiness was their happiness and your grief was theirs. They laughed when you did and trembled when you showed the slightest sign of displeasure. You played together on the swings and sat together through long nights listening to the stories of the pious. You slept together and woke up together.

How depressed are they today? Although they will continue their activities, their tearful eyes will always be searching for you. They simply cannot forget you.

If only you could see your friends today! One stands in the corner weeping while another is sobbing silently somewhere else. If they did not see you for two consecutive days, they would become restless and find an excuse to come looking for you. They would attend and host Islamic programmes for ladies to be with you. Now they will be unable to meet you for weeks. Perhaps only you know the grief that they will experience during these times.

Daughter! Today you will also be leaving me. I always desired that you should be and educated and knowledgeable young lady with refined manners and donning Islamic dress with Hijaab. Together with ensuring that you have the best food and clothing, I always wanted you to be blessed with excellent morals and a noble character. You are now the sterling example I always envisaged. I also entertained the hope that you would become a wife from whom good wives learn to better themselves and from whose behaviour bad wives correct themselves.

You will recall that I was never harsh with you in your upbringing, yet I never ignored any bad habit. I always prohibited you from reading books and novels that promoted immorality and I always brought home for you such books to read that taught good morals and valuable lessons. I also protected you from the filth of television, video and cinema because it is these things that have destroyed many noble homes and brought disgrace to honourable families.

Dearest daughter! You know well that I have always given preference to your comfort over my own. I have always chosen the best teachers for you and safeguarded you from the corrupted secular syllabus. I have always been taking you and your mother to Islamic programmes and have always devoted special attention to your education. I have always regarded my home and children as a trust which Allah Ta'ala has placed in my care so that I may teach you good manners and conduct. I realise that I will be answerable to Allah Ta'ala if I were to fail in teaching you Islamic morals and conduct After having done all of this, I now place you in the custody of another good family.

Light of your father's eyes! You are really leaving us today. Separation from you is truly heartbreaking. However, this day is an extremely momentous day for you. Although it appears as if you are merely moving from one home to another, this move is really an enormously significant one. To this day you were free to do as you pleased in your parent's home. However, from today you will have to do things with dexterity and skill. To this day, you were free to desire whatever you pleased. From this day onwards, you will have to foresee the consequences of your aspirations before setting your sights on them. Whereas you could previously ask others for the things you desire, you will now have to play a role in fulfilling the hopes of others.

Up to this day, you were issuing instructions for others to follow. Now you will have to take instructions from others. Without first being a slave, you cannot become a queen.

Dearest daughter! Today your entire world will be changed. The ways and procedures you were accustomed to will have to be altered. You will even have to change your ways of speaking. Every facet of your life will take a new meaning and new angle.

I remember well how you used to behave stubbornly and throw tantrums until we were all forced to give in to you. I accept that these occasions were rare, but remember that you should think carefully before you express your desires in future. You should first try to ascertain what the reaction of your husband and his family will be. Remember that you will be unable to control the hearts of others until you are able to control your own.

Your life has now taken such a momentous turn that it resembles a vehicle turning into a different road. Your thoughts and tendencies are sure to change, just as your hopes and aspirations will. You will experience such a personal revolution that you will begin to forget the past. Your attitudes, outlook, pace of life and pattern of life will change so dramatically that even you will be surprised.

Dearest daughter! My sense of duty urges me to tell you certain things today that will be of use to you and which will save you from many difficulties and complications in future. Failure to adhere to these guidelines has already destroyed many marriages.

The first factor to understand is the meaning of marriage. Marriage is not a contract to enter into slavery. Marriage is a contract of mutual assistance. Marriage is a contract whereby a couple agree to spend their lives together according to the principles stipulated by the Shari'ah. A couple therefore have to share a mutual bond of love and concern for each other. They need to be loyal to each other and have to regard each other as their own. Marriage is the shackle that binds the couple so that they may lead their lives together in harmony and solidarity. To make this relationship work, either party has to make sacrifices.

There is no doubt about the fact that Allah Ta'ala has given men superiority over women and has allowed men to lead women. This does not allow men to dictate to women, but is intended to entrust men with the responsibility of protecting and providing for women. If this were not the case, men would not have been enjoined to fulfil the innumerable rights they owe to women. To maintain harmony between the couple, women have also been commanded to fulfil numerous rights that they owe to men. When the two fulfil the rights due from them, they will enjoy a pleasant and harmonious life.

Since marriage is a relationship of mutual support and assistance, the couple are dutibound to formulate principles and blueprints by which they will be able to provide maximum comfort to each other. Each of you should understand what duties you have to fulfil. The definition of these duties will depend on your existing circumstances. However, I would like to point out some factors in this regard.

Dearest daughter! We are seeing you off from our home with flood of tears. On the contrary, when you arrive at your in-laws, you will be received with smiles, laughter and happiness. There it will be different world. The atmosphere will be filled with joy and every person's face will be lit with glee. Everyone will be speaking fascinating words and they will embrace you happily. You will be the star attraction and everyone's attention will be focussed on you. Every lady will be waiting anxiously to see you and a thousand praises will be expressed at your every step. This attention and adoration will last only a few weeks but you must be cautious and alert during this while because your every movement will be scrutinised. A slight error will be magnified and inspected. However, you are intelligent enough because you have seen many women become brides. I am confident that you will pass this period of scrutiny carefully without giving anyone the opportunity to smear your name.

Dearest daughter! The first person to acquaint yourself with is your husband. He is the person on whom the prosperity or damnation of your future depends. Therefore, your most important duty is to understand him and to harmonise your thoughts and desires with his. In this manner you will be able to avoid clashes. When a couple's desires and thoughts are incompatible, they are prone to disputes, which eventually ruin their lives. I shall not discuss the duties of the husband because I am presently concerned with addressing you. I am sure that your husband's parents have fulfilled their responsibilities by informing their son about his duties. Since they will be living with him, they will certainly advise him from time to time.

Remember that Allah Ta'ala has described the husband as clothing for his wife and the wife as clothing for her husband. If a person is wearing no upper garment and has a wound on his shoulder from which puss is flowing, people will certainly be repulsed. Similarly, they will also be revolted to see filth on his body when he is wearing no clothes to conceal it. However, if a person has such a wound or filth on his body but covers it with clothing, none will have the opportunity to speak ill of him. In this manner, each partner will conceal the defects of the other.

A poet once said, "I have become you and you me. If I am the body, then you are the soul."

Just as clothing protect people from the elements, the wife protects the husband and vice versa. Regard your husband as your own self and guard him likewise. The one who serves is really the master. You can only win people over by regarding them above yourself.

Always pray to Allah Ta'ala saying, "O Allah Ta'ala forgive my sins, allow me to die in a good condition, allow me entry into Jannah and accept my progeny to spread Religion throughout the world." People are prepared to give their lives for Jannah. However, I am convinced that you will be able to achieve this great prize by fulfilling the requirement stipulated by Prophet (Peace be upon him). Umm-e-Salma (May Allah be pleased with him/her) has narrated that she heard Prophet of Allah

(Peace be upon him) say that a woman will enter Jannah if she passes away when her husband is pleased with her. In another Hadith, Prophet of Allah (Peace be upon him) told women that their husbands are their Jannah or Jahannam. The lofty gardens of Jaanatul Firdous are waiting for every woman and the maidens and servant of Jannah are anxious to welcome them. However, the condition is that she has a certificate to certify that her husband is pleased with her.

Dearest daughter! Remember that diligently serving your husband is as easy as it sounds because you will have to reduce yourself to nothing. However, Allah Ta'ala has made it easy for woman to earn Jannah. While He has commanded men to remain pleased with their wives, He has also made the husband's pleasure a means for every wife to enter Jannah. Every woman should therefore grab the opportunity and leave no stone unturned to keep her husband pleased. Even if a woman has a husband who is foolish, he will still be the most important person in her life because most of her time will be spent with him. Because the couple will almost always be doing things together, you should remain loyal to your husband and bind yourselves together.

Remember that you will only be able to win a place in the hearts of others once you have won a place in his heart. The woman who has fallen from the sight of her husband has really lost this world as well as the Hereafter. A woman can rule her husband's heart only once she has won his love and affection. If a husband has no love for his wife, her status in his home will be simply like that of a maid servant.

Every husband is but a human and desires love and doting. He expects to find love and comfort after marriage and if his wife provides these blessings for him, he will have to be a fool to seek them elsewhere. When a husband steps into his home, he will be delighted to find his wife at the door to welcome him home. Her gleaming face and her happiness to receive him is enough to dispel his every worry. When she follows this reception up with a sincere desire to fulfil his every need, there will be none more beloved to him in the entire world.

A person employing servants will be most pleased with the servant who serves her the best and who is most concerned about her comfort. If such a servant has to leave, she will be sad and will miss her all the time. However, if a lazy and uncooperative servant leaves one's employment, one will be more relieved than sad. Similarly, when a wife wins her husband's heart with diligent service and after making many sacrifices, her husband will be unable to bear separating from her for even a minute. On the other hand, if a wife does nothing to please and comfort her husband, her presence in the home is as good as her absence. Such a woman cannot expect her husband to have any love for her and cannot expect him to miss her when she leaves. Whereas a lazy servant can be changed at any time, the marriage contract which is entered into after much deliberation cannot be dissolved as easily. Marriage is a union that is made to last a lifetime.

It is therefore only a foolish woman who will forfeit entry into Jannah merely because she does not want to serve her husband to please him. It can only be such a woman who would sell the everlasting bliss of the Hereafter for a few days' rest in this world. It is indeed unfortunate that there are so many women who are so short-sighted that they cannot appreciate the love of their husbands. It is for this reason that they remain adamant and refuse to do what their husbands tell them. As a result, they have not only destroyed their lives in this world and the Hereafter, but they have also destroyed the lives of their posterity.

Dearest daughter! Do you remember a time five years ago when a respectable man became our neighbour. Although his parents lived with him, they were always happy with their daughter-in-law and there were no disputes between her and his parents. He was earning well and they always lived comfortably. However, it always appeared that the couple were perpetually ill. Although they were physically well, their health was always poor. The only reason for this was that the two could not get along together. They lacked love and devotion to each other. Their opinions always conflicted and they fought endlessly. He was adamant about his views while she refused to give in to his standpoint. Little realising how this was ruining their lives, neither would allow the other's opinion to dominate.

Such disputes are devastating indeed. If one has to analyse such disputes, one will find no tangible reason for them. However, disputes require no important matter to hinge upon. They will readily spring from the most insignificant differences and they are bound to happen in the lives of every couple. It is therefore necessary to adopt humility and give in when necessary. This will resolve all disputes and ensure harmony between the couple.

Dearest daughter! You may have seen that couples fight for hours only because someone moved the husband's chair slightly forward or simply because a little extra salt fell into the food by mistake. Such rows sometimes last the entire night, forbidding sleep for the neighbours. Word soon spreads throughout the town that the couple's marriage is on the rocks, giving every person the opportunity to add delightful titbits to the story. The town is then flooded with rumours like, "Did you hear that she has been by her mother's place for the last six months and her husband does not even bother to call her back? When he is forced to call her back, he does so reluctantly." The wife's name is eventually smeared and she is disgraced.

An example of this was the marriage of your cousin. You know how much she suffered when her husband separated from her without divorcing her and without giving her any maintenance. Even she admits that she failed to appreciate the love he showered on her when they married. Instead, she never did what he instructed her. Matters were not too serious at the beginning because he exercised a great deal of patience then. However, when she refused to mend her ways, the couple were forced to separate. She always opposed his views and contested everything he said. The couple did not understand each other's disposition and did not even make an effort to do so. Eventually, they contested everything and she was soon off to her parent's home. Although his brother is presently supporting her and her children, signs of friction are already starting to surface between her and her brother's wife. After all, a woman who has no concern for what her husband says cannot be expected to have concern for what her sister-in-law says.

Every man gets married for happiness and comfort. No sensible person marries a woman merely to plague her life with difficulties. Even a person with a little sense will not want to make life miserable for himself and his wife by arguing with her for every trivial matter. He will not want the life of his children to be ruined by parents who are always at loggerheads.

Remember that a man is at liberty to marry another woman whenever he pleases. Even if he does not remarry, he is not forced to tolerate an impudent wife. It is the woman and the children who suffer the worst effects of a broken home.

You also have the example of your aunt's son. While he is a man brought up in a modern society, he married a girl who hailed from a simple, but noble background. While he adored modernism, she hated every bit of it. She refused to do anything different and would even get a headache when he asked her to cook something new. Although he did not insist that she becomes an icon of modern fashion, he wanted her to forsake the Shari'ee way of dressing. To his dismay, she refused to yield. Eventually, matters deteriorated and she started taking exception to everything he said. Life became intolerable for both and, as you know, the only way out was divorce.

He was wrong to expect her to forsake the Shari'ee injunction of Hijaab to parade the streets like the shameless Kuffaar. He also tried to force her to forsake her salah. His attitude is not a modernist approach, but insanity. He failed to realise that he was inviting Allah Ta'ala's wrath to himself. He failed to realise that in the words of Rasulullahs, a wife who practises the injunctions of the Shari'ah is the greatest bounty a man could possess.

An intelligent wife will realise that no man will undertake the many responsibilities of marriage merely to cause problems for himself and his wife. She should therefore convince herself of his love for her and she should not be stubborn. Therefore if a woman does not want her marriage to break, she should not oppose him openly. She will never succeed in contesting an issue as soon as he proposes it, especially if he is in a bad mood. She should seek the perfect opportunity to discuss every matter with him in an amicable manner, stating her point of view without offending him.

When a couple differ about any matter, you should discuss your differences with love and concern for each other. You should both present your motivation and a final decision should be taken at the end to decide which course you will be following. Remember that you will both have to alter your opinions a little before a decision is reached. In this manner, each will be making some sacrifice for amicability to prevail. Although you will both suffer some difficulty in altering your opinions, remember that this is much better than being embroiled in a vicious circle of ego-trips and endless bickering.

If you ever feel that your husband is treading a path that may lead to harm for your family or relatives, you should explain the danger of the situation to him with love and sincerity. If you approach the matter with love and if you make sincere du'aa to Allah Ta'ala to make your husband understand, I am certain that Allah Ta'ala will reconcile his views with yours and conflict will be avoided. You should make du'aa to Allah Ta'ala for this after every Fardh salah and at the time of Tahajjud. If he fails to understand your opinion the at once, Insha Allah Ta'ala he will understand it at a later stage. When a woman adopts humility, wisdom and diplomacy, she will be able to avert disastrous consequences."

The Importance of Keeping the Children Clean and Tidy

We often receive mail from men who complain that after their children were born, their wives have become extremely slovenly in their dressing and personal hygiene. In addition to this, they also neglect their children. As a result, staying in the house becomes unbearable for these men. Every woman should avoid such a situation because it should never occur that a father's heart is divorced from his children. By depriving her children of their father's love, a woman is harming only herself. She will be destroying the morale and courage of these innocent souls who will soon be tomorrow's leaders. She will be the cause of her children growing up with an inferiority complex which will certainly stunt their confidence and ultimately their progress. What chance will such children have of becoming valuable sons and daughters of Islam like Umar bin Abdul Azeez, salahuddeen Ayoobi and Raabiya Basriyya?

We recommend monthly Zouq Shouq for quality upbringing of your kids. The magazine is available in Urdu, details can be sought out from www.mbi.com.pk and writers_panel@yahoo.com.

A mother should therefore never destroy their children in this manner. She should always keep them clean and neat so that any person in the house will readily pick them up and love them dearly. These people will also be pleased to make sincere du'aa for such children. One will then see that when the child's grandmother sees the child, she will be saying,

اللّٰهم إني أعيذها بك وذريتها من الشيطان الرجيم

"O Allah Ta'ala! I beseech You to protect this child as well as her progeny from the accursed Shaytan."

Seeing such a child, she will also pray to Allah Ta'ala saying:

اللّٰهُمَّ إجعلها صالحة

"O Allah Ta'ala! Make her pious and righteous."

Picking up such a child, the grandfather will say:

اللّٰهم تقبلها بقول حسن وأنبتها نباتاً حسنا

"O Allah Ta'ala! Accept her (for all good) in a most beautiful manner and raise her in all safety and prosperity."

Seeing the child smiling and laughing, he will also say:

أضحك اللّٰه سنك

"May Allah Ta'ala always keep you smiling."

When taking such a child in his arms, words of du'aa will automatically emerge from the father's lips:

اللّٰهم إجعلها قرة أعين لنا

"O Allah Ta'ala! Make her the coolness of my eyes."

Even the mother will be inspired to pray for the child saying:

اللّٰهم نور قلبها وأجعلها مقيمة الصلواة

"O Allah Ta'ala! Illuminate her heart and make her one who establishes salah."

Instead of scolding the child when she cries, the mother will say:

لا أبكاك اللّٰه أسعدك اللّٰه في الدارين

"May Allah Ta'ala save you from crying (out of grief and regret) and may He bless you with good fortune in both worlds."

Hugging the child with love, the uncle will say:

اللَّهم أجعلها خادمة لدينك وداعية إليك وإلى رسولك

"O Allah Ta'ala! Make her one who will serve Your Religion and one who will always be calling people towards Your Deen."

Kissing the child affectionately, the aunt will say:

اللَّهم فقهها

"O Allah Ta'ala! Grant her the understanding of Your Deen."

When the child is ill in bed, the mother will say:

لا بأس طهور إن شاء اللَّه

"Do not worry (Allah shall soon cure you). This illness is a means of purification, Insha Allah."

She will also add:

اللَّه يشفيك من كل دآء يؤذيك

"May Allah Ta'ala cure you from every illness that may affect you."

It goes without saying that a child who receives so many du'aas from family and relatives is truly fortunate and will certainly be protected from Shaytan, Jinn, black magic, etc. Allah Ta'ala will also make such a child a good Muslim and servant of the Deen.

NOTE: All the above du'aas apply to females. When they are made for males, the Arabic pronoun "haa"

اللَّهم إجعلها

should be changed to "hoo". Therefore, the phrase should be read as:

اللّٰهم إجعله

Whereas the clean and tidy will receive all these and more du'aas, a dirty and unkempt child will only hear comments like, "What an unfortunate child you are to have such a neglectful and slipshod mother!" May Allah Ta'ala guide all mothers who have this terrible attitude. *Aameen.*

Every mother should adhere to the following guidelines:

1. Bath the children at least twice daily during the summer months.
2. Change the children when their clothing becomes soiled.
3. Never allow the children to get used to being dirty or shabby.
4. Do not delay in washing the children's soiled linen. Never allow any soiled linen of garments to stay in the house because these things allow the Shayaateen an opportunity to occupy the house and cause dissent and problems. One should therefore not suffice by merely allowing linen or garments to dry after a child has urinated on them. One must ensure that these are thoroughly washed. For further details on this subject, one should refer to books dealing with the Islamic upbringing of children.

Every mother should devote all her attention to the upbringing of her children. If she has the means, she should hire a servant to attend to the domestic chores while she gives her undivided attention to the children. Mothers should also ensure that every child is not born too soon after another so that each child can be given due attention. Together with ensuring that there is no deficiency in the child's physical and educational instruction, care should be taken that the child's spiritual instruction also received special attention. By having several children in rapid succession, the mother becomes weak and the children are also born physically weak. In addition to this, the children are deprived of their mother's attention and their father's affection. Such children usually suffer from an inferiority complex and lack self-confidence and courage. As a result of receiving inadequate attention, they are prone to bad company.

You should make available important books like Students' Bahishti Zewar, Authentic Mamoolat for morning and evening, and Shara-e-Asma' ul Husna by Baitul Ilm Trust for better upbringing of your kids.

It is advisable for a woman to conceive a child only after the previous child has been weaned off breast milk at the age prescribed by the Shari'ah. By this time, the mother would have regained her strength and the child will be healthy and confident enough to pass through the various stages of his life. By this time, the mother may start preparing for another child if she has no Shari'ee excuse preventing her from this. Experienced Muftees are of the opinion that the spacing of a few years between children is permissible on condition that the intention of the parents is not wrong. For example, family planning is not permissible when the parents are doing it out of fear for poverty. Of course, permanent methods of contraception are permissible only under special circumstances.

We shall now present some poems of Ibraheem bin Saalih concerning the upbringing of children. May Allah Ta'ala instil in the heart of every mother the importance of raising her children well so that they can serve the Religion brought by Messenger of Allah. It will be beneficial for anyone who understands Arabic to memorise these poems.

عـوك بنيك علـى الأداب في الصغر
فإنمـــــا مثل الأداب تجمعهما
كيمـــــا تقربهم عيناك فى الكبر
في عنفوان الصبـأ كالنقش فى الحجر

"Acquaint your children with good manners from young So that they may be a delight to your eyes when they grow up
Educating them in childhood is like an inscription upon a rock."

The poet emphasises the fact that when children are taught good habits from a young age, these habits remain with them permanently.

Hereunder are a few verses from Sheikh Qattan, taken from his book.

لزوجة مطيع عينك عنها راضية
وطفلة صغيرة محفوفة بالعافية
وغرفة نظيفة نفسك فيها هانية
ولقمة لذيذة من يد أغلى طاهية

خير من الساعات في ضل القصور العالية
تعقبها عقوبة يصلى بنار حامية

"Delighted are the eyes of her husband when he sees his obedient wife.
The modest little child is hail and healthy.
She keeps the room clean so that he feels comfortable.
He eats a delectable morsel prepared by a most precious woman.
His simple home is better than hours in lofty palaces Better than these places which sinning has exposed to a flaming punishment."

NOTE: Although keeping the children and the home clean is extremely important, a woman should not spend so much time cleaning that she has no time to prepare meals or to do anything else.

الوصية

وللتعهد لموقع عينيه .... والتفقد لموضع أنفه ... فلا تقع عينه منك على قبيح ... ولا يشم منك إلا أطيب الريح .

Using Perfume for the Husband

A woman should regularly apply a perfume that her husband likes because perfume makes her more attractive and enhances their love. It is effective in dispelling any animosity that may exist between the couple. Perfume creates a sense of vigour and it is also pleasing to the angels. Just as the eyes are messengers of the heart, which have direct access to the heart, the nose also shares the same privilege. Therefore, when a person sees or smells something pleasant, he takes an immediately liking to it. On the other hand, when he sees something unpleasant, like the sight of his shabby wife, he develops an immediate feeling of aversion. It is for this reason that wise women are always cautious that their husbands should never see them unkempt and that their husbands should never smell an unpleasant odour from them.

Perfume has such an attraction that Messenger of Allah Ta'ala prohibited women from leaving the home after applying perfume. This is because the perfume will attract men. While men's perfume has a strong smell, women's perfume ought to have a light fragrance. Messenger of Allah Ta'ala mentioned that the things of this world that he liked most were his wives, perfume and salah, which was the coolness of his eyes. *[Haakim, Nasa'ee, Bayhaqi]*

Women should not apply perfume at all when leaving their homes for any purpose whatsoever because the fragrance of their perfume may attract non-Mahram men. She may apply perfume only at home for the pleasure of her husband. As mentioned earlier, the best perfume is water because regular washing, making wudhu, bathing and paying attention to one's oral hygiene will ensure that no foul odours leave the body. Women should be especially particular about applying perfume during their periods of menstruation.

Ayesha (May Allah be pleased with him/her) narrates that a woman once asked Prophet of Allah (Peace be upon him) about the method of taking a Fardh Ghusl (bath). After explaining the procedure to her, Prophet of Allah (Peace be upon him) added, "Then purify yourself with a swab of musk." When the woman asked how would she be purified with a swab of musk, Prophet of Allah (Peace be upon him) told her that she would be purified with swab of musk unable to understand the hint, she repeated her question. Prophet of Allah (Peace be upon him) said,

سبحان اللّٰه

"SubhaanNAllah! Purify yourself with it."

At this stage, Ayesha (May Allah be pleased with him/her) drew the woman aside and explained to her that she should use the swab of musk to apply some musk to her pubic area so that the smell of menstrual blood may be eliminated.

By applying perfume regularly, a woman can strengthen the love between her and her husband. May Allah Ta'ala make the use of perfume a common feature in every Muslim home and free every home from physical and spiritual filth. Aameen.

It is also important for the wife to ensure that their bedroom always has a pleasant fragrance. A wife should also apply perfume on her husband because this was one of the Sunnah practices. By doing this, their love will grow and they will earn the rewards of practising the Sunnah. Ayesha (May Allah be pleased with her) says,

طيبت رسول اللّٰه ﷺ لحرمه حين أحرم، ولحله قبل أن يفيض بأطيب ما وجدت .(رواه مسلم صفحة ٣٧٨ ج١)

"I applied the best perfume I could find to Prophet of Allah (Peace be upon him) when he entered into the state of Ihraam (i.e. just before forming the Niyyah for Ihraam) and after emerging from the state of Ihraam (i.e. after he had completed all the rites of Hajj besides the Tawaaf Ziyaarah)." *[Muslim Vol. 1 Pg. 378]*

According to another narration, she said, "I personally applied perfume to Prophet of Allah (Peace be upon him) when he entered into Ihraam."

When Ayesha (May Allah be pleased with him/her) was experiencing her menstrual cycle and could not enter the Masjid when Prophet of Allah (Peace be upon him) was in I'tikaaf, he would lean his head into her room (which was adjacent to the Masjid) so that she could wash and comb his hair.

These Ahadeeth teach us how a woman can express her affection for her husband. It is therefore wise for a woman to sometimes apply perfume to her husband's body and clothing, especially before the Friday salah or even before other Fardh salahs. She will also be rewarded for practising a Sunnah if she combs his. At least once in her lifetime, she should practise the Sunnah of washing her husband's hair. By doing these things, Insha Allah Ta'ala, the couple will also share the strong bond of love that existed between Ayesha (May Allah be pleased with him/her) and Prophet of Allah (Peace be upon him).

Honeymoons

I appeal to all readers to imagine themselves as sisters-in-law (i.e. sisters of a married man) when reading this chapter instead of regarding themselves as wives. In this manner, they will employ the advices here to benefit their sisters-in-law (brothers' wives) instead of using it as an excuse to burden their husbands with the expense of an exotic holiday.

Here is no harm done if a newly married couple spend some time by themselves after their marriage, especially if they are to share a home with the husband's family afterwards. In fact, it is necessary for them to spend time together so that they may acquaint themselves with each other. By learning each other's disposition and preferences, they will develop trust and love for each other. In this way, they will be able to fulfil their purpose of being comforts and supports for each other. This time to develop their mutual love and concern is their vehicle for attaining the good of both worlds. As a result, they will be able to earn great rewards by carrying out good deeds and by refraining from evil.

By understanding each other, the couple will be saved from harbouring ill-feelings against each other and they will behave mercifully towards each other. By doing this, they will be earning Allah Ta'ala's pleasure because as they look at each other with love, Allah Ta'ala will look at them with love and mercy.

Allama Ibn Qayyiml wrote, "When two hearts are united in their love for Allah Ta'ala and His Prophet (Peace be upon him) they become the favourite target for Allah Ta'ala's enemy, who will everything to create discord between them. It is therefore extremely important to be on guard for Shaytan's plotting to disunite married couples.

Newly married couples should therefore take some time to journey somewhere by themselves. If possible, they should spend the major portion of their honeymoon spreading the Religion of Allah Ta'ala so that the beginning of their new lives together can commence with a beginning that is in Allah Ta'ala's obedience coupled with the concern of Messenger of Allah. They should share Prophet of Allah's (Peace be upon him) concern for every individual to be saved from Jahannam and become a worthy resident of Jannah. When a relationship germinates from the seed of this concern, its branches can only yield blossoms of the likes of Hasan and Husayn (May Allah be pleased with them), with fruit the likes of salahuddeen Ayoobi, Umar bin Abdul Azeez, his wife Faatima bint Abdil Malik and Zubayda the wife of the Khalifa Haroon-ur-Rasheed.

If the couple have the means to view some scenery, they should do so. However, my personal opinion is that minimum expenses be incurred during the honeymoon, as well as during the Walima and other marriage expenses so that the couple may rather spend the money on Hajj, Umrah or on things that they require. If the couple have the means, they may also use the time to perform Umrah so that they can make du'aa for themselves and their progeny in Makkah and Madinah. They may make the following du'aa:

اللّٰهم ألف بيننا كما ألفة بين محمد ﷺ وخديجة رضي اللّٰه عنها اللّٰهم ألف بيننا كما ألفت بين محمد ﷺ و عائشة رضي االلّٰه عنها

"O Allah Ta'ala! Create between us the love that You created between Muhammad and Khadeja. O Allah Ta'ala! Create between us the love that You created between Muhammads and Ayesha."

They should also make du'aa to Allah Ta'ala to bless them with pious children. We will presently quote a letter that a Kuwaiti bride wrote to her mother after her honeymoon. May Allah Ta'ala bless every couple with the happiness that He blessed this couple with and may every couple heed the lessons taught in this letter. *Aameen.*

My dearest Mother
As salamu Alaykum wa Rahmatullahi wa Barakaatuh

After spending a wonderful honeymoon, I have returned to my little home that my husband had built. I wish that you were nearby so that I could tell you all the new experiences I have had with my husband.

My husband is a wonderful man who loves me as dearly as I love him. Of course, I am still unaware of many of his habits. I sometimes feel as if I have known him for years, while the feeling also returns often that he is a complete stranger. Although I had no contact with him at all in the little world where I was brought up, yet I wish to do my utmost to please him because this is what you have taught me. Because you had always emphasised these teachings, I am convinced that I am able to remember every piece of advice that you gave me. I am also practising everything you taught me. I remember especially well the advices you gave me with tears in your eyes and with a smile that betrayed shuddering lips. Today I recall every word that emerged from your lips. They are still ringing in my ears as I think of how you said them to me as I sat on your loving lap clinging by your heaving chest. With your words in my mind, today as a daughter-in-law, I see every situation you described then.

Dear mother! Today I have your sterling example to look up to. I have before me the exemplary manner in which you treated my beloved father and your children, myself included. I shall do as you did. You taught us the meaning of love through your life of sacrifice and planted the seed of love in out hearts with your own caring hand. You even taught us how to walk.

I received your sweet letter in yesterday's post. Mom, as I read your letter filled with love, every line was ringing with your wonderful voice, opening every sinew in my ears. I searched through every word but was unable to find your warm kiss that you have addicted me to.

I have just finished preparing a meal for my husband who must be on his way home by now. Dearest Mom! Rest assured, I have am now very capable perform preparing a meal. I am exceptionally pleased with myself because my husband thoroughly enjoys the food I cook and he never forgets to thank me for a wonderful meal afterwards. It was you who taught me this skill and who reminded me that the way to a man's heart is through his stomach.

I am performing my five Fardh salahs regularly and do not delay in taking a Ghusl immediately after my monthly period. In addition to this, I observe my Qadhaa fasts as quickly as possible after Ramadhaan. I am paying the full Zakah due on my jewellery and we daily read the books "Riyadus Saaliheen" and "Fadha'il A'mal" at home. I am also doing my best to encourage my servant at home, my neighbours and my acquaintances to be particular about their salah and about observing the hijab.

I can now hear the keys in the door. It must be my husband. He would also like to read this letter. He ought to know what we are communicating about. He also wishes to share the moments when my soul is lost in thinking about you. He now wants the pen from me and wants me to leave space on the paper so that he could also write something.

I am blowing kisses to you, to father and to all my brothers. I leave you all in Allah Ta'ala's care.

Was salamu Alaykum wa Rahmatullahi wa Barakatuh

Your daughter

Your Husband is Either Your Jannah or Your Jahannam

عن الحصين بن محصن ان عمة له أتت النبي ﷺ فى حاجة ففرغت من حاجتها، فقال لها النبي ﷺ إذا تزوج أنت؟ قالت: نعم، قال: كيف أنت منه؟ قالت: ما ألوه إلا ما عجزت عنه قال فانظري أين أنت منه فإنما جنتك ونارك (أخرجه احمد٤١٩/٦ والحكم ١٨٩/٢)

Husayn bin Mihsinr narrates that his aunt once came to Prophet of Allah (Peace be upon him) to address some need. When her need was addressed, Prophet of Allah (Peace be upon him) asked her whether she was married. When she replied in the affirmative, Prophet of Allah (Peace be upon him) asked her about her relationship with her husband. She told Prophet of Allah (Peace be upon him) that she did everything her husband asked from her except those things that she was incapable of doing. Prophet of Allah (Peace be upon him) said to her,

أنظري أين أنت منه فإنما هوجنتك ونارك

"Consider well your relationship with him because he is either your Jannah or your Jahannam."

[Ahmad Vol. 6 Pg. 419 and Haakim Vol. 2 Pg. 189]

When a woman fulfils the rights of her husband, she will become worthy of entering Jannah. On the other hand, when she neglects her duties towards him, her negligence could be a cause of her entering Jahannam. May Allah Ta'ala save all women from such misfortune. *Aameen.*

What are the rights that a wife owes to her husband? We have prepared a list of these rights at the end of this book. Read these well and ensure that you are not found lacking in any of them. If you have neglected any of them, ask your husband for forgiveness and make up for the hurt you have caused to him. Seek forgiveness from Allah Ta'ala as well.

One of the greatest rights that a wife owes to her husband has been outlined in the following hadith. Prophet of Allah (Peace be upon him) said,

إلا أن لكم على نسائكم حقا ولنسائكم عليكم حقا، فإما حقكم على نسائكم فلا يوطئن فرشكم من تكرهون، ولا يأذن في بيوتكم لمن تكرهون رواه إبن ماجه والترمذي ص ٢٢٠

وقال: حديث حسن صحيح وذهب الخطابي إلى أن معناه "إلا يأذن لأحد من الرجال فيتحدث إليهن، فلما نزلت أية الحجاب وصار النساء مقصورات، نهى عن محادثتهن والقعود إليهن

"Take heed! You have rights over your wives and they have rights over you. Among the rights your wives owe to you is that they never allow on your bed anyone whom you dislike and that they never allow into your homes anyone whom you dislike." [Tirmidhi Pg. 220]

It is not permissible for any Muslim woman to talk with any non-Mahram man without concealing herself. They should never speak openly to even the sons of their neighbours when these sons come of age. When a woman's husband is not at home, she should never allow any non-Mahram into her house irrespective of who he is. A woman should avoid the company of non-Mahram men just as desperately as she would avoid snakes and other dangerous creatures. There have been many chaste women who have been divorced because they had neglected these important injunctions of the Shari'ah.

If a husband comes home to find his wife with a non-Mahram man, he will be plagued with suspicion throughout his life even though she was completely innocent. A woman who practises the teachings of Prophet of Allah (Peace be upon him) will have honour in this world as well as in the Hereafter.

A Comparison Between Two Women

During my years as a Mufti, I have dealt with thousands of marital problems. To solve the crisis in their marriages, people have asked questions and many have requested for Ta'wezaat (amulets). We shall present the causes of these problems as examples of two women, so that every woman can do her best to emulate the example of the first woman and avoid being like the second woman. If every woman adopts the practices of the first woman, she will save her marriage from problems in the future. May Allah Ta'ala guide all Muslims wives to do what is right. *Aameen*.

THE FIRST WOMAN: She wakes up early to perform her Fajr salah. If her husband has fallen asleep after Tahajjud, she gently wakes him up. After briefly reciting Quran and making Dhikr, she starts preparing breakfast for her husband and children.

THE SECOND WOMAN: After a great effort, her husband manages to wake her up and she performs her Fajr salah with great difficulty just as the sun is about to rise. She then goes straight back to bed.

THE FIRST WOMAN: She wakes up her little children, ensuring that they recite all the morning du'as. She uses a Miswaak or something else to brush the children's teeth and then feeds the family with love and affection. With every morsel of food she feeds the children, she gives them valuable advices such as observing the etiquette of attending school and Madrasah, obeying the instructions of their teachers, not being mischievous, etc.

She then dresses according to the Sunnah, reciting the relevant du'as and putting on each garment from the right. She then sends them off to school and greets her husband with a beaming face.

THE SECOND WOMAN: She wakes up late and rushes because it is almost time for the children to start school. From the kitchen, she shouts at the eldest child to wake up. When the child does not wake up after many shouts, she hits the child shouting, "It's almost seven and you're still not up!" Then turning to the smaller child, she screams, "Get up! Your transport will arrive at any moment!" Distressed by her temperament, the entire family starts conversing with the heavens. However, her bellowing voice and their fear for her does not allow them to procrastinate. With broken hearts, the stumble out of bed, getting no inspiration from their father's gloomy face. They eventually find their way out of the house without even eating properly. Leaving the door, the youngest child shouts, "Mom, I've forgotten my lunchbox." The reply comes, "You idiot! That is why I tell you to wake up early!" She then rushes out of the door to give him his lunchbox without bothering about her unkempt appearance. Seeing her shove the lunchbox in her child's hand and looking most bedraggled, the neighbour takes pity on the husband and children. He thinks to himself, "How did this poor man get saddled with such a shrew?"

THE FIRST WOMAN: After seeing everyone off, she makes wudhu and perfirm four Rakaahs of Ishraaq salah. Thereafter, she recites Quran and Wazeefah books like "Munaajaat Maqbool", "Hizbul A'zam" or "Dharee'atul Wusool". She makes sincere du'aa to Allah Ta'ala and then engages in Dhikr. Hearing her littlest daughter cry, she hurries to see what has happened. She sees that the child has fallen. Taking the baby in her arms, she says:

نور اللّٰه وجهك يا فاطمة

"May Allah Ta'ala illuminate your face, O Faatima."

She then sees to the child. When the domestic servant arrives, she gives her the dishes and clothing to wash. She then cleans their bedroom herself. Noticing that her husband has forgotten to take his wallet with him, she immediately phones him to tell him that she has it with her and has put it away safely. She then perfirm her Chaast salah (Salaatut Duha) and busies herself with the cooking.

It is not long before the children start arriving from classes. She therefore prepares a light but wholesome meal for them. She thinks to herself that when they arrive, she will warmly greet them with salam and serve the food to them with water to quench their thirst.

THE SECOND WOMAN: After everyone has left the house, she sits down to drink her tea without bothering to clear the kitchen. Hearing the baby cry, she shouts from the kitchen, "Now what? Am I supposed to die for you lot? You children extract every drop of blood from me. An I have no rest at all?" She then gulps down her tea and proceeds to the child's room. She scolds the child for waking up so early and playfully slaps the child's bottom. However, the child howls even more. She changes and washes the child, but the crying does not cease. She then grabs the bottle that was used the previous night and fills it with milk without washing it. The child drinks the milk happily and stops crying. Although the child is satisfied, only Allah Ta'ala knows what germs and bacteria may have entered his stomach with the milk.

She then hurries to clear the kitchen. When she takes the tablecloth out to dry, she meets her neighbour who is also outside. "I heard the baby crying a lot today," the neighbour asks. "I cannot understand these children," she replies, "The one has to be at school early and this one wakes up so early in the morning. Then instead of helping me by calming the child or preparing the breakfast, my husband demands that everything should be done quickly." In this manner, she spends half-an-hour chatting to her neighbour.

She then starts cleaning the bedroom and cooking. By then the servant arrives, late as usual. She spends ten minutes scolding the servant for arriving late; "Is this the time to come? It is almost time for the children to return from school! Hurry with your work!" She then hurries to prepare food, not caring whether it is cooked well or not. She then dumps the food in a lunchbox and leaves the kitchen. When the children arrive home and ask the servant where their mother is, they receive the reply, "She is in the room," or "She is at the neighbour's place."

THE FIRST WOMAN: She greets the children with salam as they arrive and kisses each one of them. At the same time, she reminds them to recite the du'aa for entering the home,

اللّهم إني أسيء لك خيرالمولج وخيرا المخرج بسم اللّه ولجنا وبسم اللّه خرجنا وعلى اللّه ربنا توكلنا (أبوداؤد ص ٣٣٩ ج٢)

Giving the child a biscuit to eat, she tells him to bath, to change out of his school uniform and to get ready for Madrasah. When the child tells her that he received a star in school for his work, she expresses her pleasure and reminds him that he should thank Allah Ta'ala for granting him the ability to complete his homework the previous night and for making him get a star as a reward for his efforts.

When her husband arrives from work for Zuhr salah, she greets him with a wide smile as he enters the door and cheerfully says, "As salamu Alaykum wa Rahmatullaahi wa Barakaatuh." The tablecloth was already laid for his meal, but he has to perform his salah first. She has his sandals ready for him to make wudhu and a fresh towel as well. After returning from the Masjid, he eats a hearty meal and rests for a while before returning to work.

THE SECOND WOMAN: After hastily dressing the children for Madrasah, the scene at her house is as follows: "I do not want to go to Madrasah because the Ustadh hits me too much!" cries the young son. "He hits you only because you never learn your work," comments the elder sister. "Not true!" the little rascal retorts, "He hits me for nothing!" "I shall tell your father about this and he will give you a beating," the mother threatens. "You may tell him. I am not afraid of him." Eventually, after a great deal of scolding and shouting, one child attends Madrasah while the other does not.

THE FIRST WOMAN: After neatening the bedroom and spraying some fragrance, she closes the door. Because the family will be visiting the father's parents that evening, she busies herself with ironing the children's clothing for the evening. When the children arrive from Madrasah, she washes them, gives them some juice and biscuits to eat and prepares to perform her Asr salah. Giving the baby some toys to amuse herself, she tells her eldest daughter to look after the baby while she performs her salah. The daughter happily agrees and asks, "Are we visiting grandmother and grandfather today?" "Yes my dear," she replies, "Insha Allah Ta'alawe will all be visiting them this evening."

THE SECOND WOMAN: The eldest daughter returns from Madrasah. Because she neither took a bath in the morning nor in the evening, her body is dirty and her hair dishevelled. As soon as she returns, she starts playing. As the mother is busy speaking to her neighbour, the son starts crying for money to buy something. Swinging around, she slaps the child and says, "Can't you see that I'm speaking?"

Eventually, she manages to hastily perform her Asr salah, make tea and give milk to the baby. She hardly completes preparing the children's clothes for the next day, when it is time for Maghrib. Her husband is returning home and dreading making an appearance because he expects to meet a wife who is screaming at the kids. He therefore returns home only after performing his Maghrib salah in the Masjid.

When he returns home and enters his room, he smells something awful. The child was drinking milk and spilled it all over the bed. Here are also biscuit crumbs all over the room and toys scattered about. The kitchen is its usual mess and as soon as his wife arrives, she starts her usual verbal assaults; "Just look at our opposite neighbour's husband! He takes the family out every day. They are visiting the children's grandparents today. When will you ever take us out?"

Exhausted, the husband falls on the bed asking, "When will supper be ready?" "You will get your supper just now," she replies and heads for the kitchen. Twenty-five minutes pass without a call to the table and he again calls out, "When do we suppper?" The husband is now irritates and, seeing the children fighting, he seizes the opportunity to vent his anger. Hitting both of them, he shouts, "Can't you see that I'm tired? Can't I have even a few moments of rest?" When the family is eventually called to eat, they have to consume a meal that was too hastily prepared to be tasty. Forcing the food down his throat, the husband laments his ill-fortune.

THE FIRST WOMAN: After performing her Maghrib and Awwaabeen salah, she tells her eldest daughter to show her what homework she has for the night. She then supervises what her daughter is doing and assists her where necessary. She then proceeds to make the rotis before her husband arrives home. When she is about to begin with the rotis, she hears the doorbell ring. As the children run to the door, she fills a jug of water to place on the tablecloth. As the husband walks through the door, one child holds his hand while the other takes the basket of fruit from his hand and gives it to their mother. Seeing his beautiful and clean children, the husband is forced to kiss them both.

Taking her father to her room, the elder daughter shows him what lessons she has learnt for the day. As he is sitting to revise some work with her, they hear the mother's sweet voice calling them to eat. Engrossed with the children, he fails to sit down immediately for the meal. When she comes to room saying, "Come on now, the rotis are getting cold," he apologises for not coming immediately and they all sit down to eat. After reciting the du'as for eating, the family start enjoying a delectable meal, observing all the etiquette of eating. "We are going to my mother's today, have you made anything?" he asks. "Yes," she replies, "I have made the custard you brought because she enjoys it. I have also cooked some knuckles which your father loves." "Excellent," he smiles, "we shall leave after salah Insha Allah Ta'ala." Although he is bust eating, he thanks Allah Ta'ala for the excellent wife and children that Allah Ta'alahas granted him. Sincere du'as in her favour pour forth from his heart with every morsel he eats.

Every reader is a liberty to decide which of the two women is the better one. Of course, the decision is not a difficult one. May Allah Ta'ala grant every woman the guidance to emulate the example of the first woman. *Aameen. [Adapted from "Silsilatul Mar'atil Muslimatis Sa'eeda" Vol. 1 Pg. 45]*

A man who is hard at work all day and who has to bear the strain of travelling home afterwards needs a wife who has completed all her daily chores and is waiting for him at home. He needs her to be looking good for him, with fragrance decorating the air about her. His fatigue and the frustration he suffered with his employers, customers or clients will all vanish when he sees her cheerful smile and warm welcome. However, his fatigue and frustration will only be increased when he returns to a wife who is angry with the children and who fills his ears with stories of the arguments she had with neighbours and tales about her sisters-in-law.

How Can One Tired Person Comfort Another Tired Person?

If both the husband and the wife are tired and frustrated, neither can offer any comfort to the other. Neither will be able to smile with the other to ease the fatigue. If the parents cannot laugh and brighten life for the children, their lives will be merely an unfortunate existence. This scenario is common in the lives of couples who are both employed. Such people become like machines, whose lives are reduced to programmed drudgery. How can contentment and happiness ever find their way into the lives of these people? Their lives revolve around their work and their homes lack contentment and peace. Such an automated existence defies nature, defies logic, defies Religion and defies civility.

Allah Ta'ala has created couples so that they provide love, comfort and compassion for each other, thus leading to the survival of humanity on earth in a manner that is promising for all concerned. When a woman provides for her husband the necessary love and compassion, she will not only be a his toy in bed, but his valued advisor and trusted confidante as well. By assisting each other through life, the couple will be able to easily fulfil their worldly duties as well as the responsibilities they owe to the Deen.

An Urdu book dealing with the status of family life in Islam mentions that when love exists between a couple, they will be able to taste the flavour of Ibaadah and find pleasure in obeying Allah Ta'ala and remembering Him. They will be sources of comfort for each other when they have concern for each other. Therefore, a good wife should ensure that she keeps herself neat and clean before her husband arrives from work so that she may alleviate his fatigue and so that he may feel comfortable and relaxed. The secret formula for making children good and obedient is for the mother to have a light meal ready for the children when hey return from school. The mother who starts scolding and shouting at the children as soon as they return home is indeed extremely foolish. She should never welcome them with remarks like, "Why is your clothing so dirty?" or "Why do you throw your books around?" etc.

The mother should not think that the child has been away from home for six hours, but she should think that the child has been deprived of motherly compassion for six hours. She should think that for the past six hours, they have been deprived of feeling their mother's delicate touch on their cheeks and from having their mother's warm gaze on their faces. She should therefore shower her love on them because their fatigue and hunger cannot bear the burden of a scolding. After feeding them their meal, she may advise them against certain untoward behaviour and encourage them to do good. The advice taught in childhood remains with a child throughout his/her life.

THE PERFECT WIFE

Arabic is such a beautiful language that no other language can match it. Its beauty is magnified when expressed in the words of an eloquent Arab Bedouin. We shall now present the reply of one such Bedouin who was asked to describe the perfect wife. With wisdom and in an advising manner, he points out that the most important trait of a perfect wife is humility. If you understand Arabic, you should analyse his words and derive direct benefit from them. You should also not deprive your children and younger sisters and brothers from the opportunity to learn Arabic.

The Bedouin says:

فضل النساء أطولهن إذا قامت، وأعظمهن إذا قعدت،وأصدقهن إذا قالت

"*The best of women is she who appears to be the tallest when she stands, the most outstanding when seated and is certainly the most truthful when she speaks.*"

التي إذا غضبت حلمت وإذا ضحكت تبسمت وإذا أصنعت شيء

جودت

When she becomes angry, she subdues her anger, she smiles instead of laughing and whenever she does something, she does it well.

التي تطيع زوجها، وتلزم بيتها العزيزة في قومها الذليلة في نفسها الودود وكل أمرها محمود

She obeys her husband and prefers to remain indoors. She is honourable in the eyes of her people while remaining unassuming without any pride.

She loves her husband dearly, expresses her love and is very fertile. In fact, everything about her is praiseworthy.

In his book "Al Mar'atul Mithaliyya", Sheikh Uthmaan narrates from Abu Ma'shar that a person once took an oath that he will not marry until he had conferred with a hundred people. After conferring with ninety-nine people, he decided that the hundredth person will be the first person he sees coming up the road. It so happened that the first person he saw was someone who appeared to be a madman. After greeting the person, he said to him, "I have experienced many problems with women and have taken an oath not to marry until I have conferred with a hundred people. You are the hundredth person. What do you advise me to do?"

The man replied, "Women are of three types. The one is exclusively yours, the other has been appointed over you and the third is neither yours nor appointed over you. You should marry the one who is exclusively yours. She is the one who is young and friendly, whom no man has ever touched.

If she sees any good in you, she is grateful and praises you. On the other hand, if she sees anything bad in you, she merely says, 'All men are like that.'"

فإما التي لك فتشابه ظريفة لم تمسها الرجال إن رأت خيرا حمدت وأن رأت شرا قالت: كل الرجال كذا

Such a woman never complains about her husband and never laments her fortune by comparing her husband's faults to the strengths of other men. She should think that everything is from Allah Ta'ala and if her Shari'ah has any shortcomings other men also have shortcomings of their own. We will not describe the other two types of women because their description is of no use to you. All we wish to do is to present to you this wonderful trait; whenever you experience anything good, praise and thank Allah Ta'ala and your husband and whenever you experience anything bad, console yourself by thinking that every home has its problems.

TRUE LOVE BETWEEN HUSBAND AND WIFE

A woman can have her husband eating out of her hand by expressing her love for him and obeying him. By being his servant, he will become her servant, will love her tremendously and make her his confidante. To attain this status, a bride will have to make some sacrifices during the early part of her marriage. You are already familiar with an example of such sacrifice which was displayed by the daughter of Prophet of Allah (Peace be upon him) Zaynab (May Allah be pleased with him/her). Her mother taught her how to serve her husband diligently, thereby making him loyal to her.

فارق صاحبتك ونحن نزوجك أي إمرأة من قريش

When the Quraysh told him that if he divorced her, they would allow him to marry any woman of the Quraysh he desired, he said to them,

لا: والله إني لا أفارق صاحبتي، وما أحب أن لي بامرأتي إمرأة من قريش

By Allah Ta'ala! I shall never leave my wife. I would not like any other woman of the Quraysh in exchange of my wife."

Although he was not yet a Muslim then, his love for Zaynab (May Allah be pleased with him/her) had sunk so deep in his heart that he could not leave her despite having the choice to marry any other woman. There is a lesson in his words for every Muslim woman. The lesson is that even though a man was not a Muslim, he appreciated the loyalty and service that his wife showed. He realised that although he had the choice of marrying any beautiful woman, he would never find someone as loyal and diligent as she.

An Arab Bedouin from the Bani Udhra tribe once married a beautiful woman. When he suffered poverty, the woman's father forcibly kept her in his home, refusing her permission to return to her husband. When the husband approached the governor Marwan about the matter, Marwan summoned the woman and her father. When Marwan saw the woman, he fell in love with her and forced the husband to divorce her. After her Iddah, Marwan bribed her father and he married the woman.

However, the Bedouin was still very much in love with his wife and he travelled to Syria to plead his case before the Ameer. The Qaadhi (judge) summoned the woman and sternly reprimanded Marwan after the facts were made clear to him, Marwan begged for pardon and pleaded that when he saw her, he fell helplessly in love with her and could not help himself.

When the Ameer summoned the husband and wife to appear before him, he also fell in love with her and wanted to marry her. He therefore asked the husband, "What do you say if I marry her?" The Bedouin refused to permit the marriage and recited the following couplets:

والله ، والله، لا أنسى محبتها
حتى أغيب فى قبري وأحجاري
كيف أسلوا وقد هام الفؤاد بها
فإن فعلت فإني غير كفار

"By Allah Ta'ala! By Allah Ta'ala! I cannot forget my love
for her until I disappear in my grave and decompose
How will I ever console myself after leaving her when every my love
for her has permeated my every sinew? If I ever have to leave her, I shall never be able to repay the good she has done for me."

ياسعدي أينا أحب اليك: الأمير في عزه وشرفه
وقصوره؟ أومر وأن في غضبه وإعتدائه
أو هذا الأعرابي في جوعه وأطماره؟

The Ameer then asked the wife what she thought about the proposal. He asked her, "Which of us do you love most?

Do you love the Ameer so that you may live with respect, with honour, with jewels and in palaces? Or do you love Marwan who acquired your hand oppressively? Or do you prefer your Bedouin husband with his poverty and little shack?"

The lady replied in eloquent Arabic verse. If only every reader could understand Arabic! Although her words are being translated, no language can justly express the depth and effect of Arabic. Every Muslim should have the enthusiasm to learn Arabic. If you cannot learn Arabic, you should at least encourage your children or little brothers and sisters to do so. Her reply was as follows:

هذا وإن كان فى جوع وأطمار
أعز عندي من أهلي ومن جاري
وصاحب التاج أومرو أن عامله
وكل ذي درهم ومنهم ودينار

"Despite his poverty and his little shack, he have given me so much love and affection, that he is more noble to me than all my family and relatives. As for the ruler (the Ameer) and his governor Marwan, they merely have silver coins and gold coins i.e. all they can give me are gold and silver coins without true love and affection."

May Allah Ta'ala bless every Muslim couple with the love and loyalty he blessed this couple. May he bless them all with selfless devotion for each other and with the fervour to assist each other in carrying out good deeds such as performing Tahajjud salah and making an effort for the Religion to spread throughout the world. *Aameen.*

Who is a Beautiful Woman?

In the words of an Arab poet, a beautiful woman is not one with whom a man falls in love at first sight, only to find out later that her character is not as beautiful. However, a truly beautiful woman is one whose beauty

بل الجميلة التي كلما كررت بصرك فيها زادتك حسنا

(مأخوذ از من أجمل ماقرأت ص٣٢)

Increases each time a man looks at her and each time he observes her various attributes. Such a woman will be found smiling whether she is experiencing good conditions or whether circumstances are trying for her. She is a comfort for her husband during prosperity and during poverty. Her husband is unable to detect any difference in her attitude when the children are crying, when he is away on a journey or when she is ill. Regardless of the circumstances the couple face, she is always pleased with Allah Ta'ala's decision for them. During prosperity, she is always grateful and during difficult times, she exercises patience.

When a young woman asked beautiful old lady what she used to preserve her radiant beauty,

إستخدم لشفتي الحق، ولصوتي الذكر، ولعيني غض البصر، ولبدني الإحسان، ولقوامي الإستقامة، ولقلبي حب الله، ولعقلي الحكمة ولنفسي الطاعة، ولهواي الإيمان

she replied, "For my lips I use the lipstick of truth, for my voice I use the Dhikr of Allah Ta'ala, for my eyes I use the kohl of lowering my gazes (thereby refraining from looking at things that are forbidden), for my body I use the training programme of doing good deeds, for my posture I use dedication, for my heart I use the love of Allah Ta'ala, for my intelligence I use wisdom and foresight, for my soul I use obedience and to control my desires I use the conviction that Allah Ta'ala is watching."

Read the above statement once again and make du'aa to Allah Ta'ala that He should bless you and every Muslim with the same excellent qualities.

Remember that the true beauty of a woman lies in her obedience to her husband. In gratitude for the effort that he makes to support her, she should at least serve him diligently and fulfil the many rights she owes to him. Advising women about the rights of their husbands, Ayesha (May Allah be pleased with him/her) once said:

يا معشر النساء، لو تعلمن بحق أزواجكن عليكن، لجعلت المرأة منكن

تمسح الغبار عن قدمي زوجها بخد وجهها

"O gathering of ladies! If you knew the rights that you owe to your husbands, you would use your cheeks to wipe the sand off their feet." [Ibn Hibbaan and Bazzaar]

The beauty of obedience attracts love. When a home is filled with love and affection, a woman will enjoy true happiness because it is impossible for her not to enjoy the fruits of the devotion and dedication she showers on her family. Women are the fountains of love and compassion and their mere presence exudes radiance and affection, bringing warmth, blessings and prosperity to the entire family. A husband will be overjoyed when he merely looks at his obedient wife and his love for her will increase all the time. It is the duty of every woman to create an atmosphere of love in her home so that her husband may never have to use the option of divorce which lies exclusively in his hands.

The foundation of every happy family has always been built on mutual love, compassion and loyalty. With such a foundation, every member of the family can carry out his/her functions effectively without anyone getting frustrated and bored and without feeling uneasy.

The more obedient a wife is, the more beautiful she will appear to her husband. Despite her abilities to manipulate situations and her powers to attract men, a woman still remains weaker than a man. She will therefore have to submit to her husband's superiority at some stage and desist from opposing him. A husband cannot value his wife's beauty and attractiveness when she is disobedient. It is therefore wise for every wife to remain obedient to her husband and walk the path of their life with him instead of against him.

Prophet of Allah (Peace be upon him) has sternly warned women against disobeying their husband when he said that the salah of two types of persons will not even pass their heads. The first person is the slave who runs away from his master. His salah will not accepted until he returns to his master. The second is a wife who disobeys her husband. He Ibaadah will also not be accepted until she starts obeying her husband. *[Tabraani and Haakim]*

OPENING THE LOCKS TO YOUR HUSBAND'S HEART

Irrespective of how indifferent a man may be towards his wife, every woman has been blessed with faculties that will force him to turn all his attention towards her. She has been blessed with natural looks, a melodious voice, a charming smile, graceful manners, a sweet tongue, delicate lips, smouldering eyes and a soft touch. Using these qualities, she will easily be able to conquer her husband's heart. These traits are such that they are more effective than any magic potion available. It is therefore surprising when any woman asks for a Ta'weez (amulet) to build her husband's love for her.

A man may still be excused for asking for a Ta'weez so that his wife's love for him may increase. He may even be advised to try some formulas. However, in her natural physique, her appearance, her voice and, above all, in her obedience to her husband, a woman has the most effective love potion. With these things, she will be able to conquer her husband's heart very easily.

It is commonly said that if a woman is standing on top of a 130 storey building, a man passing beneath will naturally look up to see her. The attraction that a woman has on a man is stronger than the attraction a magnet has on apiece of iron. In fact, psychologists state that if a man's

bone and a woman's bone were thrown on an open field, there will be a force of attraction between them.
["Tuhfatul Uroos"]

It is for this reason that jurists state that it is not permissible for even an extremely old woman to travel without a Mahram. Regardless of her old age, there is bound to be an old man who will be interested in her. A woman's body and her ways find their way into a man's heart very quickly and she can easily make him fall for her.

Not even a picturesque island or breathtaking scenery will capture a man's heart as effectively his good and obedient wife when she smiles at him and speaks to him sweetly. When she does this, he will readily respond to anything she says. A woman therefore has no need to resort to radical means of winning over her husband unless she happens to be married to a man whose heart is locked away from charm or if she needs something extra. For such drastic situations, we shall present five keys to the locks of a man's heart. By using these keys, a wife will be able create an atmosphere of true love in her home, thereby her happiness in both worlds. The five keys are:

(1) البصر Sight:

Among the most important factors that conquer a man's mind and heart are the things that he sees. One something appeals to the eyes, the heart readily takes a liking to it. On the contrary, once the eyes dislike what they see, the heart confirms the dislike. Therefore, when a woman's appearance appeals to her husband, his love for her settles deep within his heart.

فلا تقع عينه منك على قبيح

She should therefore ensure that he never sees her in a condition that may repulse him.

Together with her personal hygiene and beauty a woman should also ensure that she maintains a high degree of cleanliness when tending to her children and home. In this manner, her husband's opinion of her will not be tainted.

A survey conducted by psychological researchers has revealed that in the opinion of most men, a clean and tidy bedroom with flowers, with pictures of scenery and with clean linen all tastefully arranged is extremely effective in creating a restful and peaceful environment. These factors create such an idyllic atmosphere even though the bedroom is small. Irrespective of how insignificant something may seem, its importance is increased significantly when cleanliness and tidiness are added.

(2) السمع Hearing:

A woman's sweet voice is sufficient to melt a man's heart. When a woman uses her naturally endowed voice to tug at the chords of her husband's heart, she will never complain about her husband beating her, about him neglected her, about him not listening to her, etc. By addressing him sweetly, he will be ready to fulfil her every desire. Her voice will be a source of comfort and jubilation for him, even reviving his dead spirits.

A woman should therefore develop her understanding to be able to realise what to say on which occasion. She should know when to be silent and when to speak softly. She should also remember that whatever enters the heart through the doors of the ears very seldom leave the heart. May Allah Ta'ala bless the poet who said:

"The injuries of swords and spears can heal but the injuries caused by the tongue cannot."

It is therefore imperative for a couple not to hurt each other by the things they say. A husband should never hear statements like, "You never take us anywhere!" or "Look at our house! We have nothing here. You should see the curtains and furniture in the neighbour's home!" or "You spend so much on others (your parents) while your own wife and children are living in poverty!" By making statements like this, the wife will drive her husband further away from her instead of drawing him closer. After statements like this, she will not even have the curtains and furniture she desires because he will have no love for her. However, once she wins his love, she will have whatever she desires and he will be happy to give it to her. He will then ask her what she desires so that he could fulfil her wishes.

(3) الشم Smell:

Many people do not realise the powerful effect that smell has on a person. Philosophers have always maintained that the effect that the sense of smell has on personal relationships is profound indeed. They say that a woman's sweat glands produce an extremely subtle fragrance which can drive a man wild. The more fragrant a woman is, the stronger attraction she has on men. Of course, Allah Ta'ala only knows the truth of this theory.

Because the sense of smell strongly influences a person, every woman should ensure that she always applies perfumes that her husband likes. However, she should take care not to apply perfumes that have a strong smell. Because women have a keener sense of smell and know which perfume should be used for which occasion, a wife should apply her husband's perfume to his body. As was previously mentioned, Ayesha (May Allah be pleased with him/her) applied perfume Prophet of Allah's (Peace be upon him) body.

Many people think that staying away from women is an act of Ibaadah and sacrifice. This notion is erroneous because while performing I'tikaaf in the Masjid, Prophet of Allah (Peace be upon him) used to allow Ayesha (May Allah be pleased with him/her) to wash and comb his hair. This hadith has been quoted earlier. Since Messenger of Allah (Peace be upon him) is the best example for mankind, his exemplary behaviour teaches us that staying away from one's wife is not an act of piety. If it were, Prophet of Allah (Peace be upon him) would have been the first to do it. May Allahs grant every Muslim the guidance to practise every Sunnah of Prophet of Allah (Peace be upon him). *Aameen.*

Every wife should ensure that her husband never smells an unpleasant odour on her. She should therefore keep her body and mouth clean and smelling good at all times. She should see to it that toilet is never dirty and foul-smelling. For this, the use of an air-freshener is extremely useful. In short, she should make sure that her husband does not smell anything unpleasant at home. In this way, their love will grow and Shaytan will have much less opportunity to create animosity between the couple.

In this regard, every wife should remember the words of Umamah bint Haarith, who said to her daughter, "whenever he (your husband) smells you, he should never smell anything besides a pleasant fragrance. Kohl is the best, easiest and least expensive form of beautification while water is the best fragrance because taking a bath regularly and making wudhu often ensures that the body remains clean and does not exude an unpleasant odour."

THE IMPORTANCE OF ORAL HYGIENE

Islam has placed great emphasis on hygiene. A Muslim should always bear in mind that the cleaner and purer she is, the closer she will be to Allah Ta'ala. The angels will then also remain in her constant attendance. On the other hand, when she is dirty and unclean, Shaytan and his companions keep in her company.

If a woman performs salah while her mouth is dirty and foul-smelling, the angels are revolted and stay far away. It is appalling for a person's mouth to be foul-smelling when the same mouth is used for Allah Ta'ala's Dhikr and for the recitation of the Quran. The true measure of a person's cleanliness is not her fragrance or make-up. A person will be said to be an icon of cleanliness when her mouth does not emit a foul smell, when her teeth are clean, when the unwanted hair on her body is removed, when her nose is clean, when her nails are short, when her hair is neatly combed and when her fingertips and soles of her feet are clean and sparkling. If a woman claims to be clean, it is by scrutinising these aspects that she can be given the title. In addition to these determining factors, it will also be seen whether her kitchen, her refrigerator and her bathroom is clean. When a woman is particular about maintaining the cleanliness of all the above, she can truly say that she has love for cleanliness. A woman would also be doing herself a favour by asking another woman to tell her of her shortcomings in this regard so that she may correct herself.

It will not be redundant to repeat that the woman who is particular about all the above can truly be called a clean woman. Perfume and make-up alone do not constitute cleanliness.

Islam has emphasised the importance of oral hygiene. It is unfortunate that many women regularly eat sweets, chocolates or "paan" and then sleep without first brushing their teeth. Let alone neglecting their own teeth, they also allow their children to sleep without brushing. It is indeed tragic that we have lost the teachings of our Deen. In a hadith of Bukhari, Urwar states.

وسمعنا إستنان عائشة أم المؤمنين في حجرته

That he would hear his aunt Ayesha (May Allah be pleased with her) brushing her teeth with the Miswaak while he was in another room. A narration of Muslim also mentions that she could be heard using the

Miswaak.

Ayesha (May Allah be pleased with her) narrates that whenever.

أن رسول اللّه ﷺ كان لا يرقد ليلا ونهارا فيستيقظ إلا تسوك قبل أن يتوضأ

Rasulullahs woke up from his sleep during the day or during the night; he would brush his teeth with a Miswaak before making wudhu. [Ahmad and Abu Dawood]

Rasulullahs was extremely particular about oral hygiene. When someone asked Ayesha (May Allah be pleased with her) what was the first thing that Rasulullahs did whenever he entered the house, she replied that he first used the Miswak. *[Muslim]*

فقالت "السواك" (رواه مسلم)

Every person should ponder whether she makes any effort to revive the Sunnah of Messenger of Allah. Did you ever encourage your husband, brothers or sons to use the Miswaak as soon as they enter the home? By encouraging others, you will be receiving their rewards as well as the reward of enjoining a righteous act. You should also ensure that you are as particular about brushing your teeth as Ayesha (May Allah be pleased with her) was. The following points should always be kept in mind:

1. According to your preference, get yourself a thin or a thick Miswaak. Keep your Miswaak clean and trim the bristles often. If possible, change your Miswaak regularly, just as you would change your toothbrush when necessary.
2. Brush your teeth thoroughly after every meal, especially after eating foods that leave an odour. In fact, after eating or cutting such foods, you should wash your hands thoroughly as well.
3. Use dental floss in front of a mirror so that all traces of food remaining between the teeth are effectively removed. It is such pieces of food that often cause diseases and bad breath.
4. Try to brush your teeth while looking at a mirror.
5. Abstain from eating "paan" and prevent your children as well because it is harmful and has very few benefits.

6. Ensure that you brush and floss before going to bed because germs breed easily on the food particles in a sleeping person's mouth, giving rise to plaque, tartar and various oral diseases. This is especially important after eating sweet things. Remember: "sweets eat teeth".
7. At least once a year you should visit a female dentist or a doctor who could examine the condition of your teeth. The healthier your teeth, the healthier will the rest of your body should be. When one's teeth are healthy, one will be able to chew one's food well, thereby facilitating easier digestion and a healthier stomach. A healthy stomach is the foundation of better overall health.

The importance of oral hygiene cannot be overemphasised especially because it goes a long way in strengthening the love between husband and wife. Its importance can be gauged from the following two directives that Rasulullahs gave Ummu SulaymR when he sent her to assess another woman for marriage. He told her.

شمي عوارضها وانظري الى عرقوبيها

(أخرجه أحمد فى المسند ٣/٢٣١ المستدرك ٢/١٦٦)

To smell the woman's mouth to gauge whether she is particular about oral hygiene and to observe the area around her Achilles tendon to see whether it is clean or not. *[Ahmad Vol. 3 Pg. 231, Haakim Vol. 2 Pg. 122 and Bayhaqi Vol. 7 Pg. 87]*

This hadith makes it clear that Messenger of Allah (Peace be upon him) attached great importance to oral hygiene and would first have this assessed before taking a woman into his marriage. Cleanliness of the mouth is necessary because even a woman is beautiful, all her beauty will fade when she opens her to reveal an incomplete set of decayed teeth. When her mouth is foul-smelling because of neglecting her teeth, no one will want to be near her.

In fact, Islam so much discourages women from appearing unkempt and unattractive before their husbands that Messenger of Allah (Peace be upon him) told the Companion of the Prophet never to return home from a journey at night without first informing their wives of their return. He emphasised that if they should return suddenly, they should first inform their wives of their return "so that a woman with dishevelled hair may comb her hair and remove unwanted hair." *[Bukhari]*

لكي تمتشط الشعثة وتستحد المغيبة (رواه البخاري ص ٥٢٤٧)

Islam disapproves of a wife allowing her husband to see her in a condition that will make him dislike her because their love for each other is the foundation of their relationship. It is after all the strength of this relationship that will assist them to attain success in both worlds. The relationship of a couple can be likened to a little kingdom with the husband as king and the wife as queen. The stronger their love and compassion for each other, the more good and blessings spread in their kingdom. It is therefore necessary for a wife to ensure that she does nothing to taint her husband's love for her. This is the reason why the Shari'ah instructs men to give their wives time to prepare themselves before returning home from a journey.

This principle also teaches us that if a wife expects her husband home by a certain time and he happens to return sooner than expected (even if it be from his workplace), he should try to inform her beforehand.

(4) اللمس Touch:

After marriage, every couple realises that the greatest factor which joins their hearts is when their bodies touch. The heat of each other's body is sufficient to quell their fears, comfort their hearts and cure their illnesses. A wife should therefore assist her husband in taking pleasure from touching her. Instead of drawing back when he touches her, she should advance towards him and encourage him to touch her. Doing so, she should make the intention that he will be reminded of the pleasures of the Hereafter when he experiences this pleasure. In this way, he will be encouraged to prepare for the Hereafter. He may then also realise that just as the pleasures of this world are temporary, the nature of his life is the same. He will realise that he will soon be leaving for the Hereafter where the bounties are eternal. To attain those bounties, it is necessary to repent and to make a concerted effort.

(5) التذوق Taste:

The first medium with which a person tastes is his mouth. Because the mouth is the most sensitive part of a person's head, its response is extremely quick. The first avenue to this mouth is a kiss. Without the need for proof and substantiation, a kiss effectively expresses the love that a couple share. Although a kiss is without words, it speaks volumes about the depth of a couple's love. It reveals the innermost contents of the heart in the sincerest and most convincing manner. There is scarcely anything more effective then a kiss to consolidate a couple's love.

A kiss is more effective than a thousand advocates in convincing a man that his wife loves him. When a wife kisses her husband affectionately, he truly believes that she is exclusively his.

There is no specific time for kissing, neither does it require a special occasion. When one's love is overwhelming, one is forced to express it with a kiss or a few kisses so that the flood of emotion subsides. It is extremely unfortunate that many women neglect this important factor and kiss their husbands only when they engage in sexual relations. The Sahabiyaat (May Allah be pleased with him/her) used to kiss their husbands often. Among the many occasions when they kissed them was whenever they left home. To express their love and respect for their husbands on this occasion, they kissed them on the forehead.

One should also make a point of kissing one's husband when he leaves the home and whenever he returns. When one's husband kisses one on one cheek, one should offer the other cheek as well so that a second kiss would cement their love for each other. Unfortunate is the wife who deprives herself and her husband of this extremely sweet and enjoyable expression of love. An intelligent wife showers kisses on her husband because she knows that this is a most effective key to the locks of her husband's heart.

When a woman employs all these means of conquering her husband's heart, she will have no need to pay exorbitant fees for Ta'weezes and love potions. A study of cases where husbands have either divorced their wives, separated from them or married a second wife against their wishes will reveal that most of the women involved were negligent of using the above five keys to find their way into the hearts of their husbands. They lacked the ability to express their love for their husbands.

The less couples kiss, the less will their love for each other grow. If the couple kiss each other for Allah's Ta'ala pleasure, they will also be rewarded in the Hereafter.

اللهم أرضنا وأرض عنا

Of course, attaining the pleasure of Allah Ta'ala is the greatest reward.

The Etiquette of Writing a Letter to Your Husband

Writing a letter is half as good as meeting a person. However, when a wife is writing a letter to her husband, the matter receives added importance. A husband greatly values a letter from his wife when he is out on a long journey and his children are small. Such a letter is a great comfort and companion. We will therefore present some guidelines to observe when writing to your husband.

1. Begin the letter with "Bismillaahir Rahmaan nir Raheem".
2. Thereafter, write your name, followed by the name of the person to whom the letter is addressed. Next comes "As salamu Alaykum wa Rahmatullaahi wa Barakaatuh" and then the Islamic date.
3. Thereafter, you should praise Allah Ta'ala, convey Durood and salams to Rasulullahs. However, if you are writing to someone about whom you fear that she will disrespect the name of Allah Ta'ala and Rasulullahs, you may recite the Bismilla verbally as you write.
4. Instead of taking your husband's name, address him with terms such as "My beloved husband", "The joy of my life", "Sweetheart", etc.
   An example of such a letter is as follows:
   "Bismillaahir Rahmaanir Raheem"
   To my most beloved husband and most honoured companion.
   From your loving wife

As salamu Alaykum wa Rahmatullahi wa Barakaatuh

6 Rabi-ul-Awwal 1422

I praise that Allah Ta'ala besides whom there is none worthy of worship, Who is our Creator and Sustainer. May Allah Ta'ala shower His special mercies,blessings and peace on Muhammads after whom there shall be no prophet.
I hope that this letter finds you in the best of health. I have just received your letter. It lit up my day and was a comfort and blessing for me. It saw me through my daily chores and was a companion in my loneliness. However, my joy cannot be perfected until I see you and speak to you directly. I wish that I had wings so that I may fly to meet you. Whenever our little one hears a car, he runs to the door expecting you to arrive.

5. Try not to give him any bad news in the letter. If you feel that you have to tell him something of this nature, first think to yourself how you would feel if someone conveyed such news to you while you were on a journey.
6. Always express your love in your letter and tell him how much you are missing him. You may say things like:

- "Although our bodies are far apart, our souls and thoughts are always together."
- "There has not been anyone who missed their travelling companion as much as I am missing you. May Allah Ta'ala make the hours of our separation pass by quickly."
- "I shall bear this separation from you for the pleasure of Allah Ta'ala because you are making an effort for His Religion to spread. Otherwise, no soul will be able to bear being separated from a person as kind and beloved as you."
- "I hope that our time apart passes by quickly and that we are soon reunited with good health and happiness."

7. Always ask your husband to make du'aa for you and your family. You may say, "I make du'aa for you after every salah and the children also make du'aa for you. Please do not forget us in your valuable du'as."

8. Do not ask him to bring gifts for you and the children if you fear that he may not have enough money. Tell him that all you require from his trip are his du'as because according to the Ahadees, the du'as of a Musaafir is readily accepted.
9. Ask him for forgiveness in your letter. You may say, "We have been married for ten years and I have made many mistakes. I beseech you for forgiveness for everything that I may have done which has offended you or hurt you in any way. I shall do my best never to repeat these mistakes again."
10. If your husband is away on business, remind him about his obligations to the Deen. You may say, "I read an interesting Hadith last night and though that is should it with you. The hadith states that ... I also hope that you are taking your friends along with you to the Masjid for you five salahs and that you are encouraging them to also participate in the Deeni gatherings taking place at the Masjids."
11. If your husband has left to spread Deen, give him encouragement to remain steadfast.

YOU MAY CONCLUDE THE LETTER AS FOLLOWS

I am now reluctantly taking leave from you. Please lower your forehead that is always prostrating before your Rabb in the Masjid and at home so that I may place a kiss on it. I shall extent my sinful hands to you so that you may kiss them as well even though they do not serve you as well as they should. The children also wish to kiss you because they are missing their father's loving shadow over them.

May Allah Ta'ala keep you safe wherever you are and may He return you safely home very soon.

Yours and only yours truly,

Was salamu Alaykum wa Rahmatullahi wa Barakaatuh

Your loving wife

A Letter to a Beloved

I am sitting her all by myself, in silence and
with heartache
My heart is grieved and my eyes are wet
It seems as if the world's anguish has enveloped me
I a therefore writing this sorrowful poem
O my beloved, my most loved one!
Thoughts of you keep coming to me
Wreaking havoc in my heart and soul
I am shaking and shuddering
In the downpour of distress showering on me
O my beloved, my most loved one!
My heart has lost hope and my home is lifeless
Where is the spirit that once occupied it?
Everything has become rudderless
And the pain of bereavement has overtaken me
O my beloved, my most loved one!
I am now weary of loneliness,
Frightened to be swamped by heartache
However, my heart consoles me by saying
That we shall soon be reunited one day
O my beloved, my most loved one!
Our day of meeting shall be one of great jubilation
Every pleasure will be up and dancing
Every evening will be colourful and every
morning cheerful

It shall be a grand day, the day we will be reunited
O my beloved, my most loved one!
You steadily made me exclusively yours
By being vibrant, by winning my heart
Have you now forgotten me since you went
to South Africa?
Has your love for me been lost?
O my beloved, my most loved one!
No letter of yours has yet reached us
By which our could have taken some support
For Allah Ta'ala's sake, do not be so forgetful
Otherwise my life will be destroyed
O my beloved, my most loved one!
Please explain to me the reason
For depriving me of your communication
Are you upset about something, dear love
Do give me a reply, tell me something
O my beloved, my most loved one!
[Translated from an Urdu poem]

Pinning One's Hopes Only in Allah Ta'ala

A Muslim should not pin any hopes in people. It is especially important for a good Muslim wife not to pin her hopes in her husband, her father, her brothers, her mother-in-law, her sisters-in-law or anyone else. She should not expect anything from them. Remember that no one can give anything without Allah Ta'ala's command. Allah Ta'ala is the only One Who gives and He is the only One in Whom a person may pin her hopes.

Everything that any person possesses is from Allah Ta'ala. People are merely the temporary custodians of the wealth they possess. Their possessions are a test for them and while they may have it today, tomorrow it will be with someone else. The basis of almost every domestic dispute is that the husband or the wife expects something from the other and when this expectation is not met, an argument erupts.

It often happens that a woman marries a wealthy husband and expects to receive many things from him. However, it is often the case that people seem wealthy but are really not so. It is therefore wrong to pin hopes in the wealthy just as it is incorrect to lose hope in the poor.

Even worse than pinning hopes in people is to ask them either directly or indirectly. One should ask all one's needs only from Allah Ta'ala. If Allah Ta'ala grants something, none can withhold it and if Allah Ta'alawithholds something, none can grant it. If one does not receive something after asking Allah Ta'ala for it, one should rest assured that not having it is better for one.

Imaam Ahmad used to make the following du'aa:

اللّٰهم صن لساني عن غيرك كما صنت وجهي عن غيرك

"O Allah Ta'ala! Save my tongue (from asking from others) just as You have saved my face (from turning to others in worship)."

A poor man once came to the Khalifa Haroon Ar-Rasheed to ask for something. However, he found the Khalifa engaged in salah. After completing his salah, the Khalifa made du'aa to Allah Ta'alabefore turning to the poor man. When he asked the poor man what he wanted, the person said, "My need has been seen to. I have received what I came here for." When the Khalifa asked him to explain what he meant, the man said, "I came to ask you for some money for my daughter's wedding. However, I have seen you extend your hands to ask from someone else. I then decided that I should rather ask my needs from the One whom you ask. You are a beggar just like me and also have to stretch your hand to someone. What can one beggar give another? I shall therefore ask directly from the Independent One whom you ask and Who gives you."

When a wife constantly asks from her husband, she falls from his esteem. A wife should abstain from asking her husband for things and should tell him that his du'as are sufficient for her. She should tell him that his smile alone is priceless for her because it makes Allah Ta'ala pleased with her, and when Allah Ta'ala is pleased with her, her du'as will be answered very quickly. When she refrains from asking from her husband and from expecting things from him, Allah Ta'ala will inspire him to ask her what she needs. When he sincerely asks her what she wants, she should not disappoint him by denying that she wants something. She may then inform him of her needs.

A wife should also bear in mind that if her husband brings her something she dislikes, she should not ask him why he brought it or that he should not have wasted money on something she does not need. Whatever the gift, she should take it happily and say, "Jazaa Kumullaahu Khayran" ("May Allah Ta'ala reward you abundantly"). She should thank him profusely and praise the choice of gift.

If it does occur that a wife desperately needs something which the husband is not providing, she may suggest to him saying,"I feel that this is needed in our house. What do you think?" or "Do you also feel that we need this?"

Rasulullahs has mentioned.

إذا سألت فسأل اللّه.
وإذا إستعنت فاستعن باللّه

"When you need to ask for something, ask from Allah Ta'ala and when you ask for help, ask only from Allah Ta'ala."

Imaam Raazil has written the following, which are worth their weight in gold. Every Muslim should read them often until the message they contain penetrate the innermost recesses of the heart. He says that it appears as if Allah Ta'ala is addressing man saying:

قلبك لي، فلا تدخل فيه حب غيري
ولسانك لي، فلا تذكر به أحدا غيري
وبدنك لي، فلا تشغله بخدمة غيري
وإذا أردت شيء فلا تطلبه إلا مني

TRANSLATION: "Your heart is Mine so do not enter the love of another into it
Your tongue is Mine so do not make the Dhikr of anyone but Me
Your body is Mine so do not use it to serve anyone but Me
When you require something, do not ask it from anyone but Me."

If one does not immediately get what one wants, one should not be disappointed and should neither ask nor desire that someone should give it to one. Allah Ta'ala provides for everyone and will certainly provide for someone who begs from Him. Even if one's need is something small, one should ask it only from Allah Ta'ala. Allah Ta'ala gives and never tires of giving.

A GOOD TURN IS NEVER FORGOTTEN

It is commonly said that someone who does a good turn to another may forget the good that he did, but the one to whom the good turn was done never forgets it. It is also understood that a person becomes the slave of someone who does him a favour. These two statements should encourage every wife to serve her husband diligently. A wife should think that when she leaves this world, her husband will not forget the service she gave him and will always make du'aa for her. He will remember her sterling service throughout his day and night and the du'as he will make for her could well be the cause for her salvation.

Ayesha (May Allah be pleased with her) would say that from all the wives of Rasulullahs, she envied Khadeja (May Allah be pleased with her) the most even though she had never seen her. The reason for this was that Rasulullahs always spoke fondly of Khadeja (May Allah be pleased with her) and whenever he slaughtered a goat, he would search for her friends to give them a piece of the meat. When Ayesha (May Allah be pleased with her) told Rasulullahs that he speaks of Khadeja (May Allah be pleased with her) as if there is no other woman like her, he extolled her virtues and added, "My children were also from her. The best woman of previous times was Maryam bint Imraan and the best woman of our period is Khadeja bint Khuwaylid."Saying this, Rasulullahs pointed towards the heavens and the earth. *[Bukhari, Muslim, Tirmidhi]*

Ayesha (May Allah be pleased with her) also narrated that she envied Khadeja (May Allah be pleased with her) more than any other wife of Rasulullahs because he thought of her so often. Once, when Messenger of Allah (Peace be upon him) spoke of Khadeja (May Allah be pleased with her) Ayesha (May Allah be pleased with her) asked him why he thought so often of her when Allah Ta'ala had given him better wives. Rasulullahs replied, "By Allah Ta'ala! The wives Allah Ta'ala gave me after her are not better than her. She brought Imaan when others were Kuffaar. She believed me when others refused to believe. She sacrificed her wealth for me when people denied me theirs. Allah Ta'ala has given me children through her and not through any other wife."
[Bukhari, Ahmad, Tabraani]

The life of Rasulullahs clearly displays the saying that a good turn is never forgotten. Rasulullahs remembered her very fondly, which is clear proof of her loyalty, noble character and sound intellect. Although Khadeja (May Allah be pleased with him/her) was fifteen years elder than Messenger of Allah, he did not marry another woman during her lifetime even though it was customary among the Arabs then to do so. This is also ample testimony of the value that Rasulullahshad for her. His loyalty to her and her devotion to him are perfect examples for every Muslim couple.

May Allah Ta'ala grant these sterling qualities to every Muslim couple in this period of time when disobedience has become the order of the day and people no longer seem to value the good that others do for them.

Without doubt, the lives of any couple will be truly blissful when the husband and wife behave compassionately towards each other, when they value each other's company and when they provide comfort for each other. Such a relationship will change the lives of many for the better in our current environment where people are living like animals, without any direction whatsoever. It is to every couple that we present as a gift the beautiful example of Khadeja (May Allah be pleased with her)'s relationship with Rasulullahs. It is for every wife to emulate the love, service, obedience, respect, gentle speech, self-sacrifice, patience and gratitude that she displayed.

We plead to every woman to string the pearls of these qualities into a necklace which should never be taken off her neck. She should apply all of these qualities to her relationship with her husband so that she could become worthy of the highest echelons of Jannah. May Allah Ta'ala assist every woman to abstain from every sin and to hasten towards good deeds. *Aameen.*

There is a Great Woman behind Every Successful Man

You may have heard this cliché many times already. However, you should apply yourself to be such a great woman. You should be the driving force behind the success of your husband, your brother/s and son/s. Of course, you should also motivate your daughter/s and sister/s equally. You should empower all these people around you with firm Imaan, unshakeable conviction in Allah Ta'ala, resoluteness, courage, the best of morals and noble character. However, you will be unable to imbue them with noble character if you have not acquired it already.

If you shout at the children whenever they make a mistake, calling them all sorts of names and being harsh with them, all they will learn is harshness. One should rather be gentle and compassionate with them so that these qualities penetrate their hearts.

When dealing with her husband, a wife should be loving, gentle, patient, vibrant, methodical, resolute and smiling. This will give him courage and confidence to face any hardship with ease. It will also give him peace and comfort whenever he enters the home. These qualities will also assist in the upbringing of the children, will bring honour and respect to the home, and will prepare the husband and children to accomplish great feats in future. They will thus become worthy of leading the Ummah successfully and become worthy sons of Islam. At the same time, a woman should make every effort to remove the love of this world from the hearts of all those around her. Such women are themselves great leaders.

If we analyse the accomplishments of Rasulullaah we will definitely find the input of Khadeja (May Allah be pleased with her) and his other pure wives. Similarly, the women of the Ansaar played a significant role in the spread of Islam just as the women of the Muhaajireen were an indispensable ally in the Hijrah and efforts of their men. Fatima bint Abdul Malik was a shareholder in the achievements of Umar bin Abdul Azeezl just as Zubayda played a key role in the empire of Haroon Ar Rasheed. In the same fashion, the wife of the eminent Chief Justice Qaadhi Shurayh must also receive credit for his accomplishments.

Just as the expression in the heading holds true, it is also true to say that behind every lazy and ill-tempered man there is a woman just like him or one who is an immoral and corrupt "intellectual". Whereas many women of the past were a calamity because of their ignorance, today's college and university graduates are egotistical, self-centred and arrogant. It is tragic that they are consumed by the desire to amass the pleasures and comforts of this world. The Western culture that they have imported into their lives has removed them from the safety and chaste environment of their homes and made them parade the streets and catwalks only to attract customers. They have thus forsaken their families and children, who suffer the worst repercussions of such an immoral society.

Because mothers are too busy in offices and businesses, they are depriving their children of breast milk and raising them on powdered and tinned milk. In doing this, they are not only depriving the children of the nutrition they need, but they are also misappropriating a valuable trust that Allah Ta'ala has placed in their custody. Whereas Allah Ta'alahas granted breasts to women for the purpose of suckling their children, today's women have corrupted its role by using them as showpieces in night-clubs and on the streets.

Remember that the benefits of breast feeding are not only restricted to filling the child's stomach, but it is via this means that Allah Ta'ala transfers the character traits of the mother and her family to the child. It is also by this means that the child absorbs the mother's love, which cannot be found anywhere else. It is also possible that a child could develop animalistic instincts when fed the milk of animals. However, the details of this are lengthy. Those who wish to read about this may refer to books concerning the Islamic upbringing of children.

A great mother is required to raise a great child. A great mother is one who gives the child her own milk, who showers the child with her love and whose children have complete confidence in her and complete reliance on Allah Ta'ala.

A wife should run her home so well that the husband does not have to worry about anything pertaining to these affairs. In this way, he will be able to use his time to serve Allah Ta'ala's Deen. She should also encourage her children to learn the Quran, the various aspects of Religion and Arabic. At the same time, she should create within them the urge to spread the Religion throughout the world. Equipped with the knowledge of Deen, the Quran and the Ahadees of Rasulullahs they will be tremendous assets to the Ummah and whatever good they do will accrue to the account of their parents even after the parents have left the world. In addition to this, if they are a means of guiding others to do good, the parents will even attain the rewards that these other people do throughout their lives. It is with regard to such women that a poet said:

ولو كان النساء كمن فقدنا لفضلت النساء على الرجال

"*If our women were like those women who passed, women would have been better than men.*"

The Description of a Perfect Wife

We shall now present the description of a perfect wife in the words of Ulama and wise men with vast experience who have studied various times and aspects of life. We appeal to all women to add the qualities described here to their practical lives instead of just adding them to their registry of general knowledge. To bring something into one's life, it is necessary to first make an intention. When a person resolves to lead a pious life, Allah Ta'ala makes it easy for her. You should therefore make an intention now to implement everything you are about to read. If possible, perform two Rakaahs salah before continuing so that Allah Ta'ala may make it easy for you. Make du'aa to Allah Ta'alasaying, "O Allah Ta'ala! Grant me the ability to adopt all the good qualities of an excellent wife that are pleasing to Your Rasul (May Allah be pleased with him/her) and the pious saints. Allow me to practise these so that I may please my husband and my family and become a source of comfort for them all. Aameen."

The perfect wife is she who provides encouragement for her husband, she who behaves intelligently, she who turns her husband's attention towards her, who wins his heart and who showers her love and compassion on him.

It is said that Shaytan addresses women saying, "You are half my army and are my arrow which never misses its target." This makes it clear that half of Shaytan's armament is in the form of carnal desires. The remaining half is in the form of anger and frustration. When a husband does not find comfort with his wife, Shaytan will turn his attention towards other women.

Whereas women can be extremely simple and unpretentious, they can also be very difficult and hard to handle. While they have the qualities of purity and virtue, they are also capable of causing enmity and corruption. If they chose, they can bind a broken family just as easily as they can divide a united family. An irreligious woman is a scourge to her family and to her progeny to come. No one can give happiness to her family and they will always remain deprived of comfort. On the contrary, a good and pious woman is the light of her home and enjoys the status of a queen in her home.

The perfect wife is resolute and follows the path that Islam has chalked for her. She refrains from adopting the practices and modes of dressing of the Kuffaar. In fact, she even abstains from buying perfumes and other articles that the Kuffaar manufacture so that her wealth is rather spent on articles that Muslims manufacture. This she does so that her money can benefit the Muslims instead of their enemies.

She neither apes the West in their fashion, their domestic lifestyles or in their ways of living. She realises that the blessings of life and the blessings of the home are derived from the love and understanding that a couple develops between themselves. She knows that these blessings are neither acquired by wearing expensive clothing nor by decorating the house with exclusive furniture, appliances and curtains. These things are after all merely for show.

The perfect wife is she who encourages her husband to carry out good deeds. Addressing all men, a woman once said, "The true hero among you is the one whom us women cannot entice towards sin." In fact, it was because of a woman that the son of Aadam ecommitted the first murder on earth when he killed his brother.

The perfect wife has the deep-rooted fervour within her to assist her husband and to cooperate with him. In fact, the husband and wife should both share this commitment and should be prepared to make sacrifices for each other. They should both have the inclination to give rather than to take.

The perfect wife is prepared to dedicate her life to her husband. She has made up her mind to live for her husband's pleasure instead of for her own pleasure. Whatever she does should be according to her husband's liking. When she does this, the time will not be long before her husband will do the same for her. However, she will have to make many sacrifices during the early years of marriage.

The perfect wife is one who detests pandering to the desires of her Nafs (carnal self). She does not allow her Nafs to beguile her, thereby causing her to either barter her family's honour, to compromise on the children's proper upbringing or to neglect her husband's rights. This quality of a woman is sufficient to win her husband's heart and to give him peace of mind.

إياك وكسب الحرام، فأنا نصبر على الجوع، ولا نصبر على النار

Such a wife advises her husband to abstain from earning money via Haraam means, assuring him that the family are prepared to tolerate hunger rather than the fire of Jahannam. She constantly reminds him that he should not usurp the rights of others, he should not lie or cheat in business, he should not infringe on the rights of his employees, he should not miss his salah with Jamaa'ah and should do nothing else by which his earnings become tainted, thereby exposing the entire family to fire of Jahannam.

Advices for a Bride

Allah Ta'ala has passed a decree that the person who disobeys Him shall never have a life of contentment even though she/he seems to be living a life of affluence and luxury. Despite these pleasures, his/her heart is filled with worries and anxiety. Such a person cannot really enjoy any of the pleasures available to him/her. As for the life of the Hereafter, only worst can be expected. May Allah Ta'ala save us all from such damnation. *Aameen*.

It is therefore necessary for every bride to make up her mind to lead her life in harmony with the injunctions of the Shari'ah. She should resolve that she will not earn the wrath of Allah Ta'ala regardless of the pressures that others apply on her. We shall therefore present the following valuable advices for every bride to practise.

SALAH

Steadfastly perform every salah as soon as the Adhaan is called out. Prolong your salah and ensure that the limbs of your body are at rest during your salah so that you resemble a tree or a pillar. Pause after every verse of Surah Faatiha.

HIJAB

Every Muslim woman should be particular about keeping her body concealed from non-Mahram men. She should ensure that no part of her body and no hair are exposed to them. In fact, she should even ensure that no non-Mahram man hears her voice.

If ten non-Mahram men look at a woman walking about without

covering her hair, twenty eyes have been subjected to Allah Ta'ala's wrath. The woman has thus become a cause of attracting Allah Ta'ala's wrath her way. A bride should therefore ensure that she dresses properly when visiting her in-laws. It is unfortunate that many Muslims actively attract Allah Ta'ala's wrath by encouraging the custom where women are expected to shake hands with their brothers-in-law, the uncles of their husbands and other non-Mahram members of the family. A new bride should refuse to shake the hands of any non-Mahram, making it clear to all that the act is Haraam. It is therefore best for a woman to clarify such matters with the person proposing. She should tell them that she should not be asked to do anything contrary to the Shari'ah.

The wife of Dr. Muhammad Ridhaa has written an article in an Arabic magazine about the harms of disregarding the Shar'ee hijab. In it she writes, "When a bride walks out of her house in attractive clothing, she is actually inviting every young and old, cultured and uncultured man to have a good look at her. She is actually saying to them, "Will you not look at this stunning lady? Are you not tempted to get close to me?" Walking in the streets and commercial centres, she is really like a hawker peddling her wares. She is just like the sweetmeat merchant who decorates his sweetmeats with various colours, wraps them in attractive silver foil and places them in appealing containers so that passers-by may ogle at them and get tempted to buy them. By doing this, there is soon a string of customers waiting to have their share."

Rasulullahs has mentioned that among the inmates of Jahannam shall be women that are naked despite being dressed. In addition to attracting men to themselves they are also attracted to men. They parade the streets with their heads swollen (with pride) like the humps of camels. Rasulullahs made it clear that let alone entering Jannah, such women will not even smell the fragrance of Jannah even though the fragrance of Jannah can be smelt from a very great distance. *[Muslim]*

It is Haraam for any Muslim woman to wear clothes that are thin enough to reveal the limbs of her body, her complexion or even her hair. Similarly, it is Haraam for her to wear clothing that is so tight-fitting that it reveals the shape of her body. Such clothing attracts men and rouses their desires. Of course, she is permitted to wear this and any other type of clothing in front of her husband because he is the person she ought to entice. Such clothing will cause him to focus all his attention on her, excluding all other women.

When women do observe hijab, it is necessary for them not to wear clothing that attracts the gazes of men. Their garments should therefore not be colourful or made attractive in any way. It should be as least attractive as possible. Every woman walking the streets without hijab is perpetrating a grave injustice to every other woman because even if a man looks at such a woman by mistake, the thought of her being his wife may enter his heart. These types of thoughts are very common when sisters-in-law and brothers-in-law mix. The consequences of this are, needless to say, disastrous because when the thought enters the mind as a seed, Shaytan ensures that he nurtures and cultivates the seed until it develops into a large tree.

When this thought takes root in a man's mind and he happens to see his wife in a dishevelled state, his heart becomes more detached from her. This is an excellent catalyst to such an explosive situation because he soon starts reprimanding her for even the littlest fault. If she makes the mistake of behaving insolently, the situation may become violent. Eventually, he may lose all hope in her and decide to end the marriage, thinking that he should have married the other woman who is always attractive when he sees her. However, he fails to realise that the other woman looks much worse than his wife when she removes her elaborate make-up. It is only a heartless and cruel woman who would parade in front of another woman's husband to attract him.

When a wife allows her husband to mix freely with other women, she is exposing the family to ruin. It could seem as innocent a situation as his uncle's daughter-in-law congratulating him on the opening of his new business, but the thought lingers long in his mind, "She spoke so sweetly. I wonder if..." The tongue is one of Shaytan's most efficient agents and a woman speaking in alluring tones can easily seduce a man. Shaytan's efforts are concentrated on the eyes, hearts and genitals. It is therefore necessary for every Muslim to be on guard when these organs are involved.

One can well imagine a situation where a young woman is entertaining non-Mahram family men such as her brothers-in-law, her cousins and others, causing them to become attracted to her ways and talks. By doing this, she is actually ruining the marriages of her sisters, her sisters-in-law and other relatives. She will be inciting arguments and problems in all these homes when these men return to their wives still thinking of her. Women like this should bear in mind that people who cause disputes in the homes of others will be unable to save their own homes from disputes. Such a woman should beware that her husband does not become attracted to another woman, leaving her as a divorcee. May Allah Ta'ala save all Muslim homes from such problems and may He grant every Muslim woman the guidance to don the Shar'ee hijab. Aameen.

The harms of men looking at women are too numerous to mention. A poet writes about a woman who beautified herself and stepped into a shop. Seeing her just once caused the shopkeeper to instantly hate his wife, it destroyed the spirituality of his salahs and fasts, and soon led him to sin. An Arabic couplet reads:

نظرة فإبتسامة فسلام

فكلام فموعد فلقاء

A look, a smile, a greeting, a word, a promise and ultimately the meeting.

One will be horrified to hear about the incidents reported to our Daarul Ifta. There are incidents about men married to young and pretty women who blacken their faces by having relationships with their servants, with beggars and with middle-aged divorcees who have already been divorced twice. As mentioned earlier, a person who earns Allah Ta'ala's wrath cannot expect contentment in her life.

It is unfortunate that when people get their daughters married, they are advised not to indulge in Haraam activities such as videoing the function, hosting functions where sexes intermingle and being extravagant. However, they disregard these advices, saying that the Ulama merely want to put dampers on their fun. They also say that they will do as they please because such functions take place only once in a lifetime. It is not long after the marriage that things start going wrong. They then learn that the man is interested in someone else and had no concern for his wife. Otherwise, the bride is experiencing great difficulty with her in-laws. The same people who then wanted to do as they please, rush to some Ulama, begging for a Ta'weez to make up the marriage.

It should be borne in mind that no Ta'weez and no du'aa can remove Allah Ta'ala's punishment. It is only Taubah that will benefit a person then.

A woman has to repent for her sins, especially for the sin of discarding the hijab and the sin of being extravagant. Insha Allah Ta'ala, Allah Ta'ala will alleviate her difficulty.

ABSTAINING FROM PHOTOGRAPHING AND VIDEOING

The third advice to every bride is that before the marriage she should make the condition that she will not tolerate photographing and videoing at her marriage. She should make it clear that she will not attend any function where these two activities take place because such a function is sure to attract Allah Ta'ala's wrath. In act, it has happened that a person taking a video of a function kept a copy of the video with him and managed to alter the footage. He then blackmailed the family to pay him a large sum of money to prevent him publicising the video.

Apart from such an occurrence, the harms of photographing and videoing are numerous. If a woman decides to change her life and done the hijab, her days of flaunting her assets and flouting Allah Ta'ala's commands will be preserved on paper or on film. In fact, this will still be there for all to see long after she has left this world. Any man who then sees this will take pleasure in doing so. Although she may be dead, her sins will still live on. Because a woman was filmed, she will become the cause of thousands of men sinning during her lifetime as well as long afterwards.

Every bride should therefore do herself a favour and avoid taking videos and photographs. She should also refrain from using make-up that prevents her wudhu and salah from being valid.

Remember that love and peace in a home can be attained only by pleasing Allah Ta'ala because every person's heart is in Allah Ta'ala's control. By attending a beauty parlour, a woman will be breaking Allah Ta'ala's commands because the parts of her body that ought to remain concealed are then exposed to others. Although a woman may think that she is pleasing her husband in this way, the ill-effects of such places will soon drive the couple apart at some stage of their lives if not sooner.

A woman should not go to beauty parlours or private beauticians but should rather do what they can for themselves at home. The hearts of mankind are completely in Allah Ta'ala's control. When a woman adopts the permissible means of beautification, Allah Ta'ala will cement the love for her in her husband's heart from the very first night. However, when she exposes the most private areas of her body to others (even though the others may be Muslim women), she will be committing a major sin and earning Allah Ta'ala's wrath.

May Allah Ta'ala grant all Muslim women the guidance to practise the teachings of Religion by carrying out every deed they ought to carry out and by abstaining from everything what the Shari'ah forbids. *Aameen.*

BEAUTY PARLOUR

The desire to be beautiful is a natural instinct within every woman and it is the right of every to be given the opportunity to beautify herself. Islam does not dispute this instinct. In fact, Islam encourages this instinct on condition that it is carried out only for one man viz. the husband. A woman is at liberty to use all types of perfumes and make-up for her husband as long as the ingredients are permissible.

Rasulullahs has mentioned that a woman is akin to an adulterer when she applies perfume and leaves her home, passing by people who can smell her fragrance.

Islam does not permit a woman to walk about out of her home wearing perfume, especially when she has to pass men. This is so because perfume is a subtle but exceptionally effective invitation to men. Whereas physical beauty can be concealed, a sweet fragrance cannot be hidden. It moves ahead of a woman and lingers in the air long after she has passed by, stirring desire within the men who smell it.

Neglecting the advice given above will certainly cause many marital problems and could eventually lead the couple to divorce. A woman should therefore be very cautious about her behaviour. Although she must maintain her beauty, she should not overspend. She must always be mindful of her husband's budget and should avoid burdening her husband with expenses such as unnecessary jewellery and fashionable clothing.

It is unfortunate that many women are fanatical about clothing. A man in Bangladesh distributes free saris to women every year. It so happened that 19 women once died in a stampede as others were rushing to grab hold of a sari. The poor women left their homes to get saris but returned only in their Kafns (burial shrouds). It is necessary that every woman realises that she has to be conscious about her husband's financial situation when spending on clothing and jewellery. Even if a woman's husband is wealthy, she should spend as little as possible on herself and use the rest for the causes of Deen.

Another harm of visiting beauty salons has been mentioned in an article written by Dr. Abdul Mun'im, who is the dean of the Faculty of Medicine at the Cairo University. He writes, "To have the hair set, cut, dyed, uprooted and implanted according to western fashions requires the use of many unnatural methods which cause hair loss. The many instruments, machines and chemicals used are extremely harmful to the hair. It is therefore not advisable for any Muslim woman to visit such places."

When a woman has her styled, undue pressure is exerted on the hair roots, causing the roots to be deprived of their required blood supply. As a result, they become brittle and start falling off. When women become accustomed to visiting beauty parlours for their facials, hairdos, threading, waxing, bleaching, etc, they appear very beautiful for a while. However, the toll is soon taken on their skin and bodies when a 25-year old woman starts looking like a 40-year old.

Women who visit beauticians and salons are generally women who are not conscious about their Deeni obligations. They are heedless of their salah and engage in various deeds that earn Allah Ta'ala's wrath. Eventually, the effect of their sins causes their husbands to lose interest in them. They then become like the many Kaafir women who attend to them at such salons, who neither have any interest in their husbands and whose husbands have no interest in them. They lead separate lives and share only the same home. How can such women make a new bride attractive for her husband when they have not succeeded in winning their own husbands? Muslim women should not allow such women to lay a hand on them.

If the salon is staffed by men or if men visit as well, there can be no doubt that the Muslim woman visiting there is causing Allah Ta'ala's wrath and curses to shower down on herself.

A Muslim woman should care for her beauty by herself at home. She should remember that it is not only the accessories and make-up that attract her husband to her, but it is her piety. As already mentioned, Allah Ta'ala creates the attraction within the husband's heart and it is He who unites their hearts. This He will not do if the woman is disobedient to Him.

We will now quote some Arabic poetry which was translated from

Persian by Sheikh Basheer Al Ghazzi. It is extracted from the book "Tarbiyatul Banaat" by Sheikh Ali Fikri. Every woman should try to memorise these couplets. She should avoid the company of evil women and women who are extravagant. She should also not allow beauticians and women at beauty salons to touch her body. The poet says:

فقلت له: أمسك أم عنبر لقد صيرتني بالحب مغرم أجاب الطين أني

كنت ترابا صحبت الورد صيرني مكرم ألفت أكابرا وأزددت علما كذا

من عاشر العماء يكرم

"I said to the sand: 'Are you musk or ambergris? Your fragrance has certainly made me fall madly in love with you.'

The sand replied by saying, 'I was just ordinary sand (being trampled upon) but my association with a rose has made me fragrant and honoured (so that I am now applied to the head).'

In this manner, I have associated with many pious and knowledgeable ladies and have had my knowledge increased.

Such will be the condition of any woman who associates with such women; she will also have status and honour (and be the pride of her parents and husband)."

Remember that any "friend" who pressurises you into visiting salons and beauticians is destroying the hard-earned money of your father or husband in a single sweep. This money could have been better used on your little brother/sister or little children. Even if they do not need anything, keep in mind that every Muslim in the world is your brother or sister and there are millions who could have used the money for more important things. You should never let your love for luxuries blind you from the more important aspects of life. In fact, it was recently reported that a boy from Lahore committed suicide recently because his parents did not buy him new clothing for Eid. His desire for new clothes was so intense that it blinded him from seeing his parent's poverty.

There are millions of people whose money finishes before even spending half the month. They can barely afford food, let alone school and Madrasah fees for their children. Therefore, if any woman forces her "friend" to spend a few hundreds if not thousands in vanities, she is not worth having as a friend. She is obviously unsympathetic to the plight of others. When the money spent at a beauty parlour in a few hours could provide food for a family for an entire month, it would be foolish to even consider going there; especially when one will be incurring Allah Ta'ala's wrath as well. When a woman is pressurised into such a situation, she should remember that she is not just an ordinary woman. She is the daughter of illustrious souls like Khadeja (May Allah be pleased with her) and Ayesha (May Allah be pleased with her). She is cast in the same mould as people like Zaynab (May Allah be pleased with her) and Zubaydal. She is also the mother of people who will follow in the footsteps of Umarr and Khaalid bin Waleedr. She cannot lower herself to emulate people who have no regard for Allah Ta'ala and His Rasuls.

Remember that just as fragrant flowers cannot flourish in barren ground and just as beautiful song-birds do not perch on thorny bushes, someone as great as a future salahud Religion Ayoobil will not be found cradles in the arms of some beauty salon product who is flaunting her charms for public approval and flouting the commands of Allah Ta'ala. No child as great as Khansa (May Allah be pleased with her) or Zaynab (May Allah be pleased with her) bint Jahashr will suckle from the breasts that have had their size and shape exhibited to every passer-by. Children of worth, who will be assets to the Ummah, cannot emerge from the homes of such women. Such women cannot be mothers to the illustrious souls of the past, whose names Muslims are proud to take and to use for their own children.

Of course, it is not farfetched to expect such people from today's Muslim Ummah. All that is needed is that Muslims apply themselves diligently to Islam and do their utmost to ensure that the Religion reaches every person on earth. Every Muslim mother should have reliance only in Allah Ta'ala and devote herself to her husband. She will then be a cause of happiness and joy for every member of her family, encouraging them to emulate the examples of Islam's great heroes and heroines.

May Allah Ta'ala grant every Muslim adult and child the ability to practise Religion in its totality and spread it throughout the world. *Aameen*.

Avoiding Ta'weezat That do Not Conform With the Shari'ah

Every Muslim woman should take care not to ever consult any astrologer, fortune-teller, palm-reader, exorcist, witch doctor, faith healer or others of the type. They should also not advise other women to consult such people. The Ahadees have strongly condemned visiting fortune-tellers and believing them. Also included in the ambit of this hadith is consulting any of the other persons mentioned above. People who visit them will also be deprived of Rasulullahs's intercession in the Hereafter.

One should remember that all conditions come from Allah Ta'ala and Allah Ta'ala sends conditions to people according with their deeds. Therefore, when one faces any difficulties, one should immediately mend one's ways and make an attempt to please Allah Ta'ala. Instead of seeking help from these people and looking for amulets to wear and incantations to read, the best cure is attaining the pleasure of Allah Ta'ala. Rather than solve problems, such people only create dissention in families and contribute to a person's anxiety. In fact, many men have divorced their wives because their wives were secretly having Taweezat (amulets) made for them.

Of course, if the need truly arises for a person to receive treatment, she may consult a reliable Aalim with her husband's consent. If he does permit her, she should have the treatment done through the means of her Mahram. However, it must be stated that a Ta'weez is a du'aa. Therefore, it is more important and more effective than a Ta'weez for a person is to make du'aa to Allah Ta'ala. The most effective prescription to ward off evil is to recite the "Manzil". One should keep a copy and also make one's children and little brothers/sisters memorise it. It should be recited regularly every morning and evening.

AVOIDING JEALOUSY

A woman should never be jealous of her sisters-in-law, be they her husband's sisters, her brothers' wives or her husband's brothers' wives. Jealousy is a malady that harms the jealous person more than the victim because the jealous person's heart is always on fire.

Shaytan always assaults a woman's mind with thoughts about the good fortune of her sisters-in -law, making her forget what she has or what she had. He makes a woman believe that her sister-in -law (husband's brother's wife) receives more from her in-laws than she does and that her in-laws listen to her sister-in-law more than they listen to her. Shaytan also makes her jealous of the way that her sisters-in-law are treated by their husbands. In this manner, he plagues her mind with hundreds of thoughts so that an inferno of jealousy eventually consumes her.

To be safeguarded from such deception, a woman should console herself with the thought that whatever people have comes from Allah Ta'ala. She should think that if she needs something that others have, she should ask Allah Ta'ala for it instead of burning her heart. Allah Ta'ala will soon grant her what she wants. In this manner, she will not be causing difficulty to herself and to her family and she will not be guilty of showing ingratitude for Allah Ta'ala's bounties to her. Her success in this world and the Hereafter will therefore not be jeopardised.

If one must envy another, it should be because the other person is actively engaged in acts of virtue such as Tahajjud salah, recitation of the Quran, etc. May Allah Ta'ala save every Muslim from jealousy and from every other spiritual diseases. *Aameen.*

WHEN A WOMAN HAS THE III FORTUNE OF BEING MARRIED TO A CONSTANTLY WARRING INGRATE

There are many women who have the misfortune of being married to men who have no love for them, who do not appreciate anything they do for them and are constantly at loggerheads with their wives. To solve a problem like this, it is necessary to pinpoint the cause of his behaviour, a feat which requires a great deal of skill and experience.

It is often the case that besides the apparent cause, the source of the couple's differences is a factor that deeply embedded within the lives of the couple and which only the couple themselves will be able to identify through mutual understanding and mutual trust. The root of the disputes may be that they did not acquaint themselves with each other's habits from the beginning or that a mother-in-law, sister-in-law or someone else is creating the division between them. It may therefore be necessary to refer the matter to a trustworthy Aalim who has experience in marriage counselling. However, one should never be despondent. If one person's advice does not solve the problem, other people should be consulted, even if they are family members.

There are times when the couple realises from the outset that their marriage may be short-lived. This often occurs when the husband is displeased with his wife's looks. The reason for this is often that the husband does not see his wife before marriage and the proposal for marriage is extended on the basis of what his mother, sister or another relative tells him. It is therefore necessary that the man is taken to see the woman he intends marrying so that both are satisfied with each other's looks. In addition to this, each one should make enquiries about the other, consult with reliable Ulama and make Istikhaara.

However, if one is already married, there is no need to lose hope. The thought of separating should never enter your mind. If from the beginning the couple strongly feel that they will be unable to make up their marriage, the woman should be cautious to avoid falling pregnant. This is necessary because if the couple are divorced, it is the innocent child who will suffer the consequences of their divorce. Such a child will be emotionally scarred.

There have been many couples who detected problems from the beginning but continued along the rocky path until several children were born. When they were eventually forced to separate, the children began to develop many psychological and emotional problems. It is such children who grow up into adults with low self-esteem, lack of confidence, weak-heartedness and a range of other emotional problems in addition to many physical illnesses as well. Those couples who unsuccessfully force themselves to stay together pass years of daily arguments making life a hell for themselves as well as for their innocent children.

However, the period of birth control should be brief. It is therefore best to consult with reliable Ulama after a while to decide what course to take because it also happens that the birth of a child bonds the couple and transforms their disparities into pure love.

The problem is not uncommon where a couple have been married for a long time and may even have children. However, they are always arguing and love seems to be lacking between them. In a situation like this, the wife should analyse the problem by asking herself questions like, "During which times does he get most angry?" "Concerning which matters does he get most angry?" "What reduces his anger?" "Why were there no arguments today?" By asking such questions, the couple will be able to solve their own problems without eternal intervention. Of course it is necessary for both to be committed to resolving their differences. It should not be that one is doing everything to resolve the differences while the other has no interest in the matter.

It is a fact that most married couples are capable of leading peaceful and amicable lives, happily navigating through the rough tides of life and enjoying the blessings, strength and fortunes of married life. When there is a problem, the responsibility rests more heavily on the wife's shoulders to identify the root of the problem. She should then employ her feminine subtlety and ingenuity to amicable solves the problem. In doing this, she may have to make a few concessions, but she should never regard this to be a difficulty because every hardship and difficulty that she endures will be amply rewarded. The great extent of this reward can be gauged from the fact that obedience to one's husband is second only to obedience to Allah Ta'ala and obedience to Rasulullah (Peace be upon him).

The most important priority is to identify and eradicate the root of the problem without the intervention of close family members because when close family members intervene, they are prone to take sides and further complicate the problem. In such situations, every wife should implement the following:

1. Always speak in soft and gentle tones.
2. Remember that man is a slave to favours i.e. people adore those who do them favours and are morally indebted to them. The best favour a wife can do for her husband is to do what he pleases.

3. Endure his reprimands and constantly make du'aa to Allah to cement the love between you and your husband. You may also recite "Bismillahir Rahman nir Raheem" thrice followed by Surah Faatiha once before blowing on his food and drink. Make du'aa to Allah Ta'ala to improve his character as well as your own so that you two may live in harmony.

We will now narrate a true-life account from which every heart-broken wife may take comfort, knowing that the dark night will soon give way to a bright morning. This incident is narrated by Sheikh Mahmood Istanbuli and the central figure of the story is a friend of his. He says that his friend was a short-tempered but simple man. He had hardly completed his studies when he got married. As a result, he was totally unaware of the etiquette and conduct of treating women. Therefore, the day soon came when he behaved in a harsh and impolite manner.

His wife complained to her mother about his behaviour. Fortunately, her mother was a wise and pious woman. She said to her daughter, "Dear, your husband is still young and very inexperienced. However, the signs of piety and amiability are apparent on his face. You should therefore bear with him and gradually lead him aright. Gently explain things to him and he will soon treat you as he should." The daughter took her mother's advice and she did not have to wait long before her mother's prediction was realised.

A Muslim wife should therefore never lose hope in Allah Ta'ala's mercy. All she has to do is fulfil her duties and make du'aa to Allah Ta'ala to mend their relationship. Allah Ta'ala has so often bonded people who were arch enemies, making them bosom friends. It is therefore easy for Allah Ta'ala to bond a couple who have committed themselves to living with each other.

Many disputes between husband and wife arise when one of them does not respond immediately to the other's call. Therefore, when one of the couple calls for the other or asks for something, the other should respond immediately. Among the people who Rasulullahs cursed are the "Musawwifat". These are those women who say "sowfa" ("soon") when their husbands call them to bed i.e. instead of responding immediately, they say, "I am coming soon." Eventually, when they do arrive, their husbands are already fast asleep. *[Ibn Hibbaan]*

Of course, it is necessary to bear in mind that whereas men are quickly aroused, women need time and foreplay before she is ready for intercourse. Every couple should understand this natural difference. It is therefore necessary for every newly-wed man to study books like "Tuhfatul Uroos" or "A Gift to a Husband".

When a couple are sincerely committed to pleasing each other, it will be very easy for them to respond immediately to each other's call. They will be prepared to make sacrifices for each other, thereby solving countless potential problems in their lives. This commitment will transform grief into happiness and selfishness into self-sacrifice.

It often happens that although the couple are happy and compatible, financial or other difficulties cause their relationship to be strained. As a result, they drift apart and have little time for each other. They will lie on the bed facing opposite directions, showing little or no interest in each other. Such a situation should not be misinterpreted as personal dislike or enmity. It is merely the stress and tension of the situation which creates this temporary rift. During such periods, the wife should treat the situation with caution and make every attempt to understand the problem. She should say and do nothing that may aggravate the problem. She should remember that even sweet things taste bitter to a sick person.

She must try her best to put him at ease and make things comfortable for him. For example, if he is tired and worried and goes straight to his room to lie down when he returns home, she should ensure that the children are quiet so that he may rest in peace. She should not allow her children to suffer the brunt of the problems he encountered while at work. The food should also be prepared on time so that he is not further disturbed and the situation not further inflamed. Although the husband realises that he will be wrong to make his wife or children suffer for his anxiety, he may still scold them because of the strain he is suffering. The wife should ignore this outburst and remain silent because any response from her will transform a spark into an inferno that may be extinguished only by divorce.

Here are a few guidelines to alleviate your husband's worries. Of course, every woman understands her situation better and may use any other method that she deems appropriate.

1. Ask Allah Ta'ala to forgive yours and your husband's short comings

every morning and evening. Also encourage your husband to do the same.

2. Recite the various du'as and Aayats prescribed for alleviating worries. Encourage your husband to do the same.
3. Besides the five Fardh salahs, you should perform two Rakaahs of Salaatut Taubah often and make du'aa to Allah Ta'ala begging Him for assistance.
4. Give whatever Sadaqah (charity) you can afford and urge your husband to do the same. This Sadaqah should be given secretly.

Dissention between a couple is commonly caused by mothers-in-law and sisters-in-law. From the numerous cases of divorce, separation and disputes between couples that have been reported to the Daarul Ifta, it has been noticed that most of them have been caused by interferences from a woman's mother-in-law or sisters-in-law viz. her husband's brothers' wives or her husband's sisters.

In my humble opinion, the most effective solution for this problem is for a couple to live by themselves, even though in a rented apartment. In this manner, their lives and the lives of their innocent children will be saved from ruin. In fact, breaking a marriage is the most loved act in the sight of Shaytan. The Shayaateen make tireless efforts to separate husbands from their wives and they have a remarkable level of success. However, they are unable to influence the lives of those couples whom Allah Ta'ala showers with His mercy.

If a daughter-in-law is having problems with her mother-in-law who is dependant on her, arrangements should be made so that the daughter-in-law is able to cook by herself and provide three meals for her mother-in-law. Of course, if the mother-in-law is happy to live with another daughter-in-law, she may do so if the other daughter-in-law is also happy with the arrangement. However, even in this case, every other daughter-in-law should at least send some dish regularly for the mother-in-law. In this manner, every daughter-in-law will receive the du'as of their mother-in-law and their relationships will remain cordial.

May Allah Ta'ala grant happiness to every couple and transform every strained situation in their homes into joy and pleasure. *Aameen.*

A Valuable Lesson for Every Good Wife

A man bought a slave and, after bringing her home, the following conversation ensued:

"What is your name?"

"A slave has no name. Whatever name my master prefers, that shall be my name."

"What food do you like?"

"I like whatever my master likes for me."

"What clothing would you like me to buy for you?"

"I am pleased with whatever clothing you buy for me."

"What work can you do?"

"I shall do whatever work you need me to do."

"Tell me what you enjoy."

"Of what significance are the pleasures of a slave compared to the pleasures of her master. I enjoy whatever you enjoy."

Hearing these replies of the slave, the master began to weep because it made him realise that his relationship with Allah Ta'ala ought to be the same. He said to her, "You have taught me what my attitude with Allah Ta'ala should be." The slave then focussed her attention to Allah Ta'ala and said, "O Allah Ta'ala! What bounty can I have that is better than the ability to diligently serve one of Your bondsmen. So by Your infinite grace, forgive my sins and shortcomings for I know that You are the Most Kind and the Most Merciful."

It is the duty of every Muslim to behave like the slave in the above incident and to have no desire that is opposed to what Allah Ta'ala and Messenger of Allah (Peace be upon him) want. Just as the slave woman expressed loyalty and obedience to her master, so too should every wife do everything to please her husband, even though she may have to sacrifice her own pleasures in doing so. She should do everything with the thought in mind that pleasing her husband pleases Allah Ta'ala. When Allah Ta'ala is pleased with a person, no difficulty is insurmountable.

COURTING AFTER THE ENGAGEMENT

It is our plea to every Muslim sister that she should not allow her fiancé to court her after the engagement because he is still regarded as a non-Mahram. It is therefore Haraam for the two to see or speak to each other. Allowing this will lead to ruin in this world as well as in the Hereafter.

The disastrous consequences of courting that have been reported to our Daarul Ifta are too painful to mention here. The harms of courting are sufficiently illustrated by the opinion of expert psychologists who state that if a man's bone and a woman's bone were thrown on an open field, there will be a force of attraction between them. Shaytan's claim is famous. He said, "If Rabia Basriyya and Hasan Basri were alone together, I will be able to lead them to sin." If he can lead these two great saints astray, what chance do others stand?

Allowing a strange boy to accompany a girl to a place where there is none to watch them is like placing fresh meat in front of a hungry wolf. In such a situation, there is little if no chance at all that the girl will ever be able to protect her chastity. Eventually, the family is embarrassed when the girl falls pregnant. They can then not find anywhere to hide their faces and many parents even subject their daughters to the trauma of an abortion.

It is unfortunate that many foolish girls fail to realise that such behaviour will taint their family's name and smear their honour for generations to come. In addition to this, the ill-effect of their sins remain with the couple well into their marriage. There have been many cases where a boy and girl have been dating for a very long time, sometimes even for years. They would be seen together everywhere and would spend hours on the phone speaking to each other. However, their marriage does not last. People are astonished to learn this and no one can make sense of it. The girl's name is then spoilt for life and no one wants to marry her because they know that he her husband has divorced her. We therefore plead to all women not to incur Allah Ta'ala's wrath by courting and dating. They should avoid such relationships like they would avoid snakes and scorpions. If the couple feel that they have to be together, they should be married as quickly as possible. May Allah Ta'ala save every Muslim from perpetrating Haraam. *Aameen*.

One should also remember that the engaged couple should not even communicate by telephone because this always goes further. They will eventually meet and become intimate. The couplet has already been quoted earlier where a poet says:

نظرة فابتسامة فسلام

فكلام فموعد فلقاء

"*A look, a smile, a greeting, a word, a promise and ultimately the meeting.*"

After the couple meet alone it is only a matter of time before they perpetrate the ultimate sin. When one makes a resolution to refrain from sin, Allah Ta'ala assists one all the way.

NEVER SHAKE HANDS WITH NON-MAHRAM MEN

The intrinsic quality of a good woman is that she never raises her gaze to look at non-Mahram men, never greets them and certainly never shakes their hand. It is only when absolutely necessary that she will have to say few words, and then too, the barest minimum. It is most unfortunate that in many parts of the world, Muslim women are forced to shake hands with their husbands' family on the day of Eid. She is also compelled to kiss the hands of these non-Mahram men even though she opposes the custom. They are also required to shake and kiss the hands of their cousins and brothers-in-law. Such acts serve only to attract Allah Ta'ala's displeasure and curse.

Women should always bear in mind that a perfect lifestyle can be ruined when Allah Ta'ala is displeased with one just as a ruined lifestyle can be made perfect when Allah Ta'ala is pleased with one.

The situation will arise that when a sensible woman refuses to shake the hands of non-Mahram men or when she refuses to speak with them, other members of the family will mock her. However, she should ignore their mockery and make du'aa to Allah Ta'ala that He should guide them. She should encourage such women to attend Islamic programmes for ladies so that they may be inspired to practise the injunctions of the Shari'ah. Remember that when Allah Ta'ala's commands are violated, the home will be deprived of love and blessings.

A woman should only try to explain her reasons to women who are willing to understand. If they are not willing, she should rather maintain silence. She should explain to these women that the least harm of shaking hands with non-Mahram men is that they will find her hands softer than those of their wives. In addition to this, they may also find her more attractive than their wives, especially when she is dressed up and beautified on the day of Eid and on other occasions. As a result, they will lose interest in their wives and start wishing that they had married her instead. Displeased with their wives, they will start arguments at home and ruin the entire family's life. Therefore, by shaking the hands of non-Mahram men, a woman will be doing a great injustice to the wives of these men. Although the act seems good, the consequences are disastrous.

On the other hand, when a woman shakes the hands of these men, she may find them more attractive than her own husband. She may fall for his smile, his perfume or his looks, thereby becoming discontented with her husband. She should also explain to them that such acts incur Allah Ta'ala's wrath and when Allah Ta'ala is displeased with anyone, they can expect only difficulty and hardship. When a woman explains this to those who are mocking her, they will also realise the harms and see the truth.

Insha Allah Ta'ala, when a woman convinces others about this and they begin implementing all the injunctions of the Shari'ah, she will receive the rewards of all their deeds even after she passes away.

Prophet Muhammad's Advice to Women

تصدقن يا معشر النساء

Addressing a gathering of women, Messenger of Allah (Peace be upon him) said, "O assembly of women! Spend abundantly in charity (Sadaqah) because I have seen that a large number of women are in Jahannam." When the women enquired the reason for so many women entering Jahannam, Messenger of Allah (Peace be upon him) replied, "Because women curse often and are ungrateful to their husbands." *[Muslim]*

In this hadith, Rasulullahs advised women to avoid falling into Jahannam by spending abundantly in charity. In another hadith, Rasulullah (Peace be upon him) mentioned that Sadaqah cools Allah Ta'ala's anger just as water extinguishes fire.

Ayesha (May Allah be pleased with her) narrates that Messenger of Allah once delivered a sermon for the women. He said,

يانساء المؤمنين! تهادين ولو فرسن شاة فانه ينبت المودة ويذهب الضغائن

"O believing women! Give gifts to each other, even though it may be the hoof of a goat because giving gifts develops love and eliminates enmity."
[Muslim Vol. 2 Pg. 714]

A Muslim woman should therefore give gifts to the women of her husband's family, even if it means preparing a dish for them. However, her intention should be to please Allah Ta'ala.

HE EARNS BUT SHE REAPS THE REWARD

عن عائشة رضي اللّٰه تعالى عنها قالت: قال رسول اللّٰه ﷺ : إذا أنفقت المرأة من طعام بيتها غير مفسدة كان لها أجرها بما أنفقت ولزوجها أجره بما كسب وللخازن مثل ذلك لا ينقص بعضهم أجر بعض شيء .

(متفق عليه كذا في المشكوة ص ٧٢، ج١)

Ayesha (May Allah be pleased with her) reports that Messenger of Allah said, "When a woman gives the food in her home as charity without spoiling her act (by ostentation, extravagance, etc), she will receive the rewards of what she spent while her husband will receive the reward for earning it and the treasurer shall have the same reward. The rewards of each of the three shall not diminish because of the rewards of each other."

["Mishkaat" Pg. 72]

According to another hadith, Allah Ta'ala will enter three persons into Jannah because of a morsel of food or a handful of dates. The first is the owner of the house (i.e. the husband), the second is the wife who cooked the food and the third is the servant who took the food to the beggar.

Ayesha (May Allah be pleased with her)'s sister Asma (May Allah be pleased with him/her) asked, "O Rasulullahs! I have nothing to give in charity except that which my husband Zubayrr gives me. Rasulullahs replied, "Spend generously and do not hold back, otherwise provisions will be held back from you."

Ulama have written that giving Sadaqah will safeguard a person from Shaytaan when he is on his deathbed. It also saves him from uttering words of ingratitude when suffering severe illness and from dying a sudden death. In brief, giving Sadaqah ensures a good death. Another hadith states that Sadaqah saves one from heat in the grave and that a person will rise on the Day of Qiyamah beneath the shade of his Sadaqah.

It has been reported that once, while leading the Salaatul Kusoof, Rasulullahs was shown Jannah and Jahannam. He noticed that most of the inmates of Jahannam were women. When the Companion of the Prophet asked the reason for this, Messenger of Allah (Peace be upon him) told them that it was because women forget the good done to them and are ungrateful to their husbands. Rasulullahs also said to them, "If you are good to them (women) all your life and there comes a time when she is upset with you, she will say, 'I have not seen a single good day with you!'" *[Bukhari and Muslim]*

This trait that Rasulullahs described is commonly seen among women. Despite the good treatment many of them enjoy, they are often heard telling their husbands, "I have only experienced hardship since I arrived in this house!" Although this phrase and statements of this nature have become clichés in the female world, they should be avoided.

Because Rasulullahs saw so many women in Jahannam, he did prescribe a solution for the women of his Ummah. The solution is to spend generously in charity. It is for this reason that when Rasulullahs informed the Sahabiyat about this, he took Bilalr with him to the place where the women were seated to collect their Sadaqah from them. After hearing what Rasulullahs had to say, the women generously gave away their earrings, necklaces and other jewellery in Sadaqah.

It is unfortunate that today's women do not heed the stern warnings mentioned in this hadith. Even if they do, they make their husbands spend on their behalf. It is therefore their husbands who have to give zakah and Sadaqah for them. If a woman does spend herself, she often takes the money from her husband rather than use her own wealth. A woman's jewellery may get lost or stolen or she may sell or pawn it to pay for an unnecessary function, but it is very unlikely that she will ever donate it as Sadaqah for Allah Ta'ala's pleasure. If nothing of the above occurs, they leave their jewellery behind as inheritance without it being of use to her in the Hereafter. They keep changing their jewellery, having them always remodelled until the value is scarcely what it was because of labour costs. In this manner, they are wasting a great deal of money that could be used in better avenues.

The Virtues of Sadaqah

The hadith of Rasulullahs is famous in which he stated, "Save yourselves from Jahannam even though it is by means of half a date." Nabi has mentioned that Sadaqah extinguishes sins just as water extinguishes fire and that every person will rise in the shade of his Sadaqah on the Day of Qiyamah. *[Ithaaf]*

According to the amount of Sadaqah that a person gives in this life, his shade on the Day of Qiyamah will be correspondingly greater. On the Day of Qiyamah, every person will require shade because the heat will be so intense that many people will be drowning in their own perspiration.

A hadith of "Mishkat" states that Sadaqah extinguishes Allah Ta'ala's anger and saves one from a sudden death. A narration in Ihyaa mentions that Luqmane advised his son to give Sadaqah whenever he committed a sin. The incident is famous about an immoral woman who was forgiven because she did the charitable act of giving water to a thirsty dog.

Abbaad bin Umarr has mentioned that people will be extremely hungry, thirsty and naked on the Plains of Resurrection. However, Allah Ta'ala will feed those who fed the hungry in this world, He will give drink to those who gave a drink to the thirsty in this world and He will clothe those who gave clothing to the poor in this world.*[Ihyaa]*

According to another narration, the people destined for Jahannam will be standing in a row when a pious Muslim destined for Jannah will pass by them. Seeing him pass, one of the people headed for Jahannam will ask him to intercede on his behalf. Turning to him the pious Muslim will ask, "Who are you?" "Do you not recognise me?" the person heading for Jahannam will ask, "I am the one who gave you water to drink on a certain day." The pious person will then take this person by the hand and plead to Allah Ta'ala saying, "O Allah! I owe this person a favour." Allah Ta'ala will then forgive the person and enter him into Jannah as well.

According to another hadith, the people destined for Jannah will form rows and the people destined for Jahannam will also form rows on the Plains of Resurrection. A person from the row of people headed for Jahannam will recognise someone from the row of people headed for Jannah and will call to him, reminding him of a favour he did to him. as a result, the person headed for Jannah will take this person by his hand and secure forgiveness for him from Allah Ta'ala.

Rasulullahs has also mentioned that the following announcement will be made on the Day of Qiyamah: "Where are the poor people from among the Ummah of Muhammads? Let them rise and search the Plains of Resurrection for anyone who for My sake has given them a morsel of food to eat, a sip of water to drink or a garment to wear. Let them take such people by the hand and lead them to Jannah." Consequently, the poor people will identify all such persons and take them along to Jannah.

It is therefore necessary for Muslim women to open their hearts and to stop refilling their refrigerators all the time. The least they should do is to give away everything that they do not require, while the best will (of course) be to give to others what one needs for oneself. One should remember that although the food that one selfishly keeps away from the poor will not rot in the refrigerator, it may rot in one's stomach and harm one's health.

THE HARMS OF HOARDING

When someone once sent a piece of cooked meat as a gift to Ummu Salma (May Allah be pleased with her), she kept it aside on a niche in the wall because she knew that Rasulullahs liked meat. A while later, a beggar came to her door saying, "Give something for Allah Ta'ala's sake. May Allah Ta'ala bless you." The beggar received the reply, "May Allah Ta'ala blesses you too," indicating that there was nothing to give him. The beggar therefore left. When Rasulullahs arrived and asked if there was something to eat, Ummu Salma (May Allah be pleased with her) sent her servant to get the meat from the niche. However, instead of finding the meat, the servant found only a white stone. When Rasulullahs was informed about this, he told them that Allah Ta'ala had transformed the meat into a stone because the beggar was denied it.

Commenting on this hadith, Sheikhul Hadithl writes, "This incident teaches us that the food that is not given to the needy and which one refuses to give to them is actually like a stone because instead of giving one the benefit it should, it creates hard-heartedness. Therefore, despite having the food, a person is deprived of its benefits and virtue. This is why we enjoy the many bounties of Allah Ta'ala without receiving their benefits."

People nowadays say that things no longer have the effect and benefits they used to have. This is not because of any fault in the things themselves but because our intentions are no longer sincere.

Every woman should therefore develop the habit of spending generously in charity. This should be done in a manner that the left hand does not know what the right hand gives. Instead of keeping leftover food in the refrigerator, they should give them to the poor. Similarly, it is fruitless to amass wealth in banks when it can benefit others much more. One should remember that anything given to others for Allah Ta'ala's pleasure is regarded as Sadaqah, irrespective of how little it is. Whatever one gives to relatives, friends and neighbours are regarded as gifts rather than Sadaqah.

Whenever Allah Ta'ala blesses someone with a bounty, the manner of expressing gratitude is to give the old bounty away. For example, when someone gets new clothing, he should give his old clothing away either as a gift or as Sadaqah if he will not be needed them any longer. Similarly, if Allah Ta'ala grants one a motorcycle when he has only a bicycle, he should give the bicycle away if he can afford to do so. The same applies if one has a motorcycle and Allah Ta'ala grants him a car.

It is sad that when a person buys a new refrigerator for a few thousands, he prefers selling the old one for a few hundreds or even less instead of giving it away to someone deserving. By giving it away, one will attain tremendous rewards each time someone uses it. One will also attain their invaluable du'aa, which could be a means of one's salvation in the Hereafter.

Even more distressing is the fact that many women sell their old clothing and old dishes when they receive something new. Some even go to the extent of selling the empty paint tins they used when painting their homes. Such behaviour is not necessary when Allah Ta'ala has granted these people in abundance. They would earn much more by giving things away to others for Allah Ta'ala's pleasure.

The best way to spend in Sadaqah is to clear out your cupboards every week or at least every month. You should then give away everything that you do not need so that whatever Allah Ta'ala has in store for you is not delayed in reaching you because you are retaining what you do not need. When you give something away for Allah Ta'ala's pleasure, Allah Ta'ala replaces it by at least ten fold. Therefore, spending one coin for His pleasure will earn you ten coins and if these ten are also spent for his pleasure, you will earn a minimum of a hundred. In this manner, your wealth will continue increasing.

Think of it like this. Allah Ta'ala has granted you what you have so that you may distribute it. You should keep what you need of it and give the rest to others. If you keep the extras without having any use for it, what reply will you give Allah Ta'ala when you die?

Another excellent manner of earning rewards is to send a bit of what you cook to your neighbour. By doing this, mutual love will grow and you will be rewarded for practising the advice of the Ahadees. Rasulullahs said that a woman should throw extra water into her food so that the gravy is increased and some food can be sent to her neighbours.

According to another hadith, the benefit of this gesture is that فإنه ينبت المودة love will grow between the neighbours and ill-feelings and malice will be removed from their hearts.

It is not necessary for you to cook a special dish to send to your neighbour. You should send whatever you are cooking for the day, even though it is not a rarity. Of course your intention should be to please Allah Ta'ala, to carry out the advice of Rasulullahs and to make such a practice common among the Ummah. A friend of mine living in Makkah Mukarramah told me that by Allah Ta'ala's grace, he eats meals from three countries every day. Because his one neighbour is Syrian and the other is Indian, he eats what they prepare together with what his wife prepares as an Egyptian. Whatever he eats he sends to his neighbours and they sent to him whatever they are eating. As a result, they all have at least three dishes every day.

Islam desires that the Muslim society functions like a single family unit. When there is a strong sense of brotherhood among all Muslims in a society and they all have sincere feelings for each other, they will enjoy peace, prosperity, safety and justice. When non-Muslims see such an environment, they will naturally be captivated and this will be a cause for them to accept Islam.

The Rights of Neighbours

Giving due regard to the rights of neighbours is exceptionally important for anyone wishing to give their children a sound upbringing. Who are your neighbours? Your neighbours are everyone living in the forty houses to your right, your left and about your house. Because all these people are you neighbours, there are certain rights that you owe to all of them. This definition of a neighbour is established from a hadith narrated by Ka'b bin Maalik (May Allah be pleased with him/her), which Imam Tabrani (May Allah be Merciful on him/her) has reported in his book. Ka'b bin Maalik (May Allah be pleased with him/her) says that a person once complained to Messenger of Allah (Peace be upon him) that the people closest to him in his neighbourhood are the ones who cause him the most difficulty. Messenger of Allah (Peace be upon him) immediately instructed Abu Bakrr and Umarr to stand at the doors of the Masjid and announce that a neighbour extends up to forty houses away and that a person will not enter Jannah if his neighbours are not safe from his evil.

There are four basic principles concerning the rights of neighbours are as follows:

1. One should not cause any harm or difficulty to one's neighbour.
2. One should protect one's neighbour from people who may harm him.
3. One should be friendly towards one's neighbour.
4. One should repay his rudeness and bad manners with tolerance and good conduct.

BEHAVIOUR WITH ONE'S NEIGHBOURS

The ground rules governing one's behaviour with one's neighbours have been outlined in a hadith which Khir'ati and Tabraani have reported from Abdullah bin Umarr. He says that Rasulullahs said, "That person is not a proper Mu'min who closes the doors of his home to his neighbours and the one whose neighbours are not safe from his evil is also not a true Mu'min. Do you know what the rights of your neighbours are?

You should help him when he requests your help.
You should grant him a loan if he asks you for one.
You should visit him when he is ill.
You should grant him what he needs.
You should console him in his grief.
You should attend his funeral when he passes away.
You should not build your house higher than his without his permission.
You should not cause difficulty for him with the steam of your cooking unless you intend giving him a share of it.
You should give him a share in the fruit you buy. If you cannot afford this, take the fruit secretly into your house and do not allow your child to eat the fruit outside where the neighbour's child may see.

Rasulullahs has also counted good behaviour towards one's neighbours as one of the traits of Imaan. Rasulullahs said,

من كان يؤمن بالله واليوم الأخر فليكرم جاره

"A one who believes in Allah Ta'ala and the Last Day ought to honour his neighbour."
[Bukhari and Muslim]

A GOOD NEIGHBOUR

Abdullah bin Mubarakl had a Jewish neighbour whom he treated so well that when the Jew put his house up for sale, he fixed a price of two thousand Dinaars (gold coins). When people complained that his house was only worth a thousand Dinaars, he told them that while a thousand Dinaars were for the house, the other thousand were for the honour of having a wonderful neighbour like Abdullah bin Mubarak.

A good neighbour is a great treasure. To create a good neighbourhood, we should present an excellent example. If our neighbour is a non-Muslim, we should display the proper Islamic character so that the neighbour will be encouraged to accept Islam. On the other hand, if we are fortunate enough to have a Muslim neighbour, we should make an effort to ensure that the neighbour's entire family becomes pious and righteous Muslims. We should therefore never allow our neighbour to leave our house without hearing some story or lesson in Islam. In fact, as Muslims our concern should be that every person throughout the world becomes righteous and practising Muslims.

OBSERVING HIJAAB IN FRONT OF NEIGHBOURS

There are two important factors to always bear in mind when associating with one's neighbours. Failure to observe these will lead to disastrous consequences for either family. These are as follows:

1. Ensure that there is no contact between the females of your home and the males of your neighbour's home and vice versa. Even your neighbour's twelve-year old son should not enter your home without permission. In fact, children of the opposite gender should not be allowed to play together. When neighbours get friendly and discard the laws of Hijaab, Shaytaan quickly manipulates the situation and involves them in sin.
2. Take every precaution to ensure that your children do not involve themselves in Haraam activities while visiting the neighbours. One such evil is the television. Explain to your children that they should avoid this evil which pollutes society with the immorality of the west that it vomits out. The television is one of the primary causes for the cancer of licentious and indecency that is contaminating society. You should neither have a television in your own home nor should you allow you children to watch television at the homes of others. If your neighbour is the cause of corroding the moral and religious fibre of your family, you will then have to restrict your interaction with her and make du'aa to Allah Ta'ala to guide her.

A Wife With Salah

Abu Hurayrar narrates that Rasulullahs said, "If a woman performs her five daily salah, fasts during Ramadhaan, safeguards her chastity and obeys her husband, she will have a choice of entering Jannah from whichever door she pleases." ["Mishkaat" Pg. 281]

Among the qualities that take a woman to Jannah, Rasulullahs has listed salah as the first priority. When a woman hears the Mu'adhin calling, "Hayya Alas salah" ("Come to salah") and ("Come to success")

حي على الصلاة   حي على الفلاح

she should immediately convince herself that her success lies in performing salah and in nothing else. She should therefore terminate every activity and prepare for salah. Delaying the salah to complete what she is doing will make the task more difficult and cause it to be prolonged. Experience has proven this. When a woman tells herself that she will perform her salah as soon as she completes the task, she ends up delaying the salah for a long time until she eventually performs it during the Makrooh times. She is therefore deprived of the blessings of her salah and also becomes guilty of a sin.

Every woman should therefore make a resolution to perform her salah as soon as the Adhaan is called out so that she can perform it with proper composure and concentration. She should remember that the du'aas made after such a salah is readily accepted and that the salah performed on time is most beloved to Allah Ta'ala. The Ahadees tell us that a du'aa is accepted with every Fardh salah that a person performs. It is really strange that

Muslims should have problems when Allah Ta'ala has granted them salah as a solution to all their problems. When a Muslim performs her salah properly, she will need no Ta'weez or special holy waters. If a woman is experiences with her husband or her in-laws, she should make du'aa to Allah Ta'ala to soften their hearts and to mend their relations.

It should also be remembered that neglecting one's salah is a tremendous loss and the Muslim who neglects her salah will be raised with the Kuffaar on the Day of Qiyamah.

STEALING FROM ONE'S SALAH

Rasulullahs said, "The worst thief is the one who steals from his salah." Astonished, the Companion of the Prophet y asked, "O Messenger of Allah (Peace be upon him) ! How can a person steal from his salah?" Messenger of Allah (Peace be upon him) replied, "By not performing Ruku and Sajdah properly." *[Daarmi]*

There are several Ahadees concerning this matter. Stealing is a dishonourable act and people look down on someone who steals. Apart from this, Rasulullahs added that the person who steals from his salah is not merely a thief like other thieves, but he is the worst of all thieves. One can therefore imagine the gravity of sin.

According to another hadith, Allaht does not even pay any attention to the salah in which Ruku and Sajdah are not performed properly. Yet another hadith states, "A person can be performing salah for sixty years without a single salah being accepted because when he sometimes perform Ruku properly, his Sajdah is not proper and when he performs Sajdah properly, his Ruku is improper."

The great reformer, Mujaddid Alf Sanil had written many letters emphasising the importance of salah. In one of these letters, he writes, "It is extremely important to ensure that the fingers of each hand are kept together in Sajdah and that they are apart during Ruku. The injunctions of the Shari'ah to keep the fingers together and apart are not without good reason. It is therefore very necessary to observe them even though they seem insignificant." He states further, "When standing in salah, the gaze should be fix3d to the place of Sajdah; when performing Ruku, it should be fixed on the feet; in Sajdah, it should be focussed to the nose and when sitting, it should be directed to the hands. By doing this, humility and concentration will be developed in salah. When even this seemingly minor etiquette holds such great importance, one can well imagine how much benefit there is in the more major etiquette and the Sunnah of salah."

OTHER DEFICIENCIES IN OUR SALAH

It is sad to note that while many sisters are performing their salah, they rush with the Ruku and Sajdah. They therefore fail to maintain composure during these two postures whereas composure during all postures of salah is Waajib. In fact, according to certain Ulama, this composure is Fardh and salah will be nullified without it. It is therefore necessary to keep the following factors in mind when performing salah so that your salah can be beautified:

1. Recite Surah Fatiha slowly, ensuring that you pause after every verse. The other Surahs should also be recited slowly.
2. Recite the Tasbeeh of Ruku ("Subhana Rabbiyal Azeem") slowly at least three times. If possible, it is advisable to recite it five, nine, eleven or twenty-one times. The more you recite, the better it is.
3. After getting up from Ruku, slowly recite:

   سمع اللّٰه لمن حمده

   Thereafter, recite:

   ربنا و لك الحمد

   One may also recite:

   ربنا ولك الحمد حمدًا كثيرًا طيبًا مباركًا فيه

   By reciting any of these du'aas, the requirement of composure will be met.
4. In Sajdah, recite the Tasbeeh of Sajdah) at least thrice. Of course, it is best to recite it several times in odd numbers.
5. When sitting in the posture between the two Sajdahs (called Jalsa), you should at least recite:

   However, it is best to recite:

   اللّٰهم إغفرلي وأرحمني وعافني واهدني

   By reciting these du'aas, composure will be achieved in the Jalsa posture as well. You should try to learn these du'aas, which appear in the book

"Hisnul Haseen".

6. It often occurs that while many women regularly perform their salah, they delay its performance. Shaytaan deludes them into thinking that they can perform their salah at leisure after first finishing what they are doing. However, they become engrossed in their activity and manage to perform their salah when the time has almost expired. Many women end up perform Zuhr during the time of Asr and Asr during the time of Maghrib. A woman should perform all her salahs as soon as the Adhaan is called out.

   You should therefore ensure that you do not deprive yourself of the full reward of your salah. Perform your salah on time and at a leisurely pace. Performing salah properly and on time will earn Allah Ta'ala's pleasure and du'aas after such salah is more likely to be accepted. This is therefore the best manner to have all your problems solved.

   Many new brides are shy to perform their salah during the early days of their marriage. However this is the time when she should be especially particular about her salah because this is the beginning of a new life for her. It is rather those women who do not perform their salah who should be ashamed.

7. Many women fail to perform their salah immediately after completing their menstruation cycle, thereby missing a few salahs in the process. It is necessary that a woman begins to perform her salah as soon as she discovers that her menses are complete. However, if the bleeding stops before three days, it is preferable for her to wait until the final hours of the salah time before taking a bath and performing her salah. If three days are over but she has not yet completed her habitual cycle, it is also Mustahab (preferable) for her to wait until the closing hours of the salah before taking a bath and performing the salah. However, the ruling regarding the permissibility of intercourse during this period is a different question. Nevertheless, it is not permissible for a woman to miss any salah after discovering that her menstruation cycle has ended. Every woman should refer to the books of Islamic Fiqh for the details of the rulings pertaining to menstruation.

8. May women wrongly wait for forty days after childbirth before performing salah even though they have stopped bleeding after three days. This practice is incorrect because as soon as a woman stops

bleeding after childbirth, she should take a bath and start performing salah immediately, even though she has bled for a period less than forty days. If a woman missed any salahs in this manner, she has to perform the Qadhaa for all of them.

9. Every woman should do her best to learn to recite the Quran correctly. Even though a woman may not be able to perfect her recitation until she dies, she will Insha Allah Ta'ala be resurrected with those who recited the Quran properly if she sustained the effort to learn proper recitation throughout her life. She should be able to distinguish between a ح and a ہ, a س and a ث, a ق and a ک, etc.
   It is necessary to practise the pronunciation of these letters with some learned Mahram or lady. This is absolutely important because if the letters are not pronounced correctly, the meaning of the Quran will be distorted.
   One should also demonstrate one's salah to a knowledgeable lady or a Mahram so that one's salah can be corrected if there are any failings. One should also read books concerning the salah of a female so that one's salah becomes like the salah that Messenger of Allah (Peace be upon him) taught the Ummah.
10. It is unfortunate that many women fail to perform the Qadhaa salah of the many salahs that they miss after their menstrual period by their delay in taking a bath. If a woman is conscious about the ruling pertaining to menstruation and if she is careful, she will not have to miss any salahs. If she still does miss any of her salahs, she should ensure that she performs the Qadha immediately.

In addition to performing one's own salah, one should ensure that one's daughters who are more than seven years of age also perform their salah regularly. If one has sons of this age, one should send them to the Masjid to perform their salahs with Jama'ah. One should also have a deep concern that one's servants and employees perform their salah regularly. There should not be a soul in one's home who neglects his/her salah. At the same time, one should make sincere du'aa to Allah Ta'ala that He should guide every Muslim on earth to perform salah regularly and correctly.

One should not neglect reciting books of Ahadees like "Fadha'il-e-A'maal", "Riyadhus Saliheen", etc to the entire family. This should be done on a daily basis so that they family can be encouraged to carry out good deeds and to adhere to all the practices of Deen. Of course, non-Mahram men and women should be allowed to sit together.

The guidelines pertaining to salah mentioned above have been extracted from the book "Islahul Khawateen" by Hakeem-ul-Ummah Maulana Ashraf Ali Thanwil. Every woman should make an attempt to read this valuable book.

We shall now quote two incidents from the book "Fadha'il-e-Sadaqat" to illustrate the attachment that women of the past had with salah.

A. It has been reported that after performing her Isha salah, Habeeba Adawiyyae would wrap herself properly and stand on the roof of her home to make du'aa. She would say, "O Allah Ta'ala! He stars have hidden themselves and people have gone to bed. The kings have all closed their doors and people are in solitude with their loved ones. I am now standing before You." She would then perform salah the entire night until dawn.

   When dawn broke, she would make du'aa to Allah Ta'ala saying, "O Allah Ta'ala! The night has departed and the day has arrived. I wish I knew whether You have accepted my night's worship so that I may congratulate myself, or whether You have rejected it so that I may sympathise with myself. I swear by Your honour that if You have to shove me away from Your door, I would never leave it because I am well aware of Your extreme munificence."

B. Ujrae was a blind woman who used to spend the entire night awake in Ibaadah. She would be extremely grieved when the night drew to a close and would say, "O Allah j! Your group of worshippers have spent the hours of darkness running towards You. They have been racing with each other to acquire Your mercy and forgiveness. O Allah Ta'ala! I am begging from You only and have none but You to ask. I beseech You to admit me to the ranks of earliest stalwarts of Islam, to include my record of deeds among those of the highest status and to join me with those who are extremely close to You. You are truly the Most Merciful of those who show mercy, the Highest of all those who have position and the most generous of all those who show generosity. O the Most Kind, shower Your kindness on me." She would then fall into prostration, weep profusely and make du'aa until dawn broke.

The salah of a Woman

You must keep the following guidelines in mind when performing salah.

1. You must ensure that you face the Qiblah.
2. Stand up straight and keep your gazes fixed on the place of Sajdah. It is Makrooh to stand with the head bent forward in a manner that the chin rests on the chest. It is also incorrect to unnecessarily bend the back.
3. Your toes should also face towards the Qiblah. Facing the toes of the right foot towards the right and those of the left foot towards the left is contrary to the Sunnah.
4. Woman should not a space between the feet.
5. Wear a large shawl which covers the entire body from head to feet. Of course, the shawl should not be made of thin material. It is permissible for the face, feet and hands (up to the wrist) to remain uncovered because salah will be correct whether they remain covered or uncovered.
6. Salah will be invalid if you perform salah wearing garments through which the body is visible or which do not conceal the entire body.
7. If during the course of your salah a quarter of any part of your body (besides the face, hands and feet) becomes exposed for the duration in which "Subhana Rabbiyal Azeem" can be recited thrice, your salah will be invalid. If it is exposed for a duration less than this, the salah will be valid but you will be guilty of a sin.
8. It is Makrooh to perform salah wearing clothes that one will not wear in front of people because it is extremely disrespectful for one to appear before the King of all kings wearing clothing that one is ashamed to wear in front of ordinary mortals.

WHEN COMMENCING SALAH

1. Have the intention within your heart that you are performing the salah in question. There will be no harm done if the intention is not recited verbally.
2. Facing the palms towards the Qibla and the fingers up to the sky, raise the hands to the shoulders without taking them out of your head covering. A woman does not raise the hands up to the earlobes as men do.
3. While raising the hands in the above manner, say "Allahu Akbar" and then place the left hand on your chest with the right palm on top of the back of your left hand. Unlike men, a woman will not grasp the wrist of the left hand with the thumb and little finger of the right hand, neither will she fold her hands beneath the navel as men do. This action of saying "Allahu Akbar" while raising the hands is called Takbeer Tahreema.

WHEN STANDING UPRIGHT

1. The standing posture after the Takbeer Tahreema is called Qiyaam. When performing salah by yourself, first recite the Sanah سبحنك اللهم

followed by.

أعوذ بالله من الشيطن الرجيم

And

بسم الله الرحمن الرحيم

Thereafter recite Surah Fatiha,

الحمد لله رب العلمين

Adding the word "*Aameen*" immediately after saying "Wa Lad Duaalleen." Then recite.

بسم الله الرحمن الرحيم

And any Surah of the Quran or at least three verses of any Surah.

2. If you happen to be following an Imam in salah, you should recite

only the Sanah سبحنك اللّٰهم and then listen to his recitation of the Quran. If the Imam is not reciting loudly, then concentrate on the meaning of Surah Fatiha without reciting it.

3. When reciting Surah Fatiha, pause after reciting every verse instead of reciting many verses with a single breath. However, when reciting the Surahs after Surah Fatiha, there is no harm in reciting many verses with a single breath. A woman should recite silently in all salahs.
4. Do not move any limb of the body unnecessarily. Remain as still as possible during salah. You may only scratch a part of your body when the itch is unbearable and when only one hand is used.
5. It is wrong to rest the weight of the body on one leg while the other bends. You may either apply your weight equally to both legs or if you need to take weight off one led, do so in a manner that the other leg does not bend.
6. Do your best to suppress a yawn. If this is not possible, cover your mouth with your hand.
7. To avoid looking about while standing, you should fix your gaze to the place of Sajdah.

WHEN IN RUKU

1. After completing the recitation of a Surah in Qiyaam, say الله أكبر and proceed to bow in Ruku. Commence saying الله أكبر as soon as you start bowing down and complete it once you have settled into the Ruku position.
2. A woman should bow down only until her hands reach her knees and not completely as men do.
3. While in Ruku, a woman should keep her fingers tightly together and not spread them out widely as men do. She should also bend her knees slightly forward and keep her elbows against her sides.
4. Remain in Ruku for as long as it takes to recite the Tasbeeh of Ruku (viz." سبحان ربي العظيم") slowly at least three times. If possible, it is advisable to recite it five times, seven times, nine times, eleven times, etc in odd numbers. The more you recite, the better it is.
5. Fix your gaze on your feet while in Ruku.
6. Balance your weight equally on both legs without leaning on one side.

GETTING UP FROM RUKU

1. After Ruku, stand up completely straight with each joint in place. This posture is called Qaumah.
2. Keep your gaze still fixed on the place of Sajdah.
3. It is noticed that when rising from Ruku, many people do not stand upright and keep their backs bent forward before proceeding into Sajdah. When one does this, the salah has to be repeated. It is therefore imperative that a person exercises composure during the Qaumah posture.
4. You should at least stand for the duration in which you can comfortably recite

   However, it is best to recite:

   ربنا و لك الحمد

   You may also recite:

   ربنا ولك الحمد حمدًا كثيرًا طيبًا مباركًا فيه (بخاري و دابو داؤد)

   By reciting any of these du'aas, the requirement of composure will be met and you will be amply rewarded.

WHEN IN SAJDAH

1. When proceeding from Qaumah into Sajdah, bend the chest forward and first place the knees on the ground. Thereafter, place the hands on the ground, followed by the nose and finally the forehead.
2. A woman in Sajdah should keep her body compressed in a manner that her thighs are against her stomach and her arms are against her sides. Instead of keeping her feet upright in Sajdah as men do, a woman should extend her feet towards her right, keeping them horizontally on the ground. If possible, she should try to face her toes towards the Qibla.
3. In Sajdah, recite the Tasbeeh of Sajdah سبحان ربي الأعلى at least thrice. Of course, it is best to recite it several times in odd numbers. It is not permissible to raise the head out of Sajdah immediately after putting the forehead on the ground. During Nafl salah, you may recite the longer du'aas of Sajdah that have been reported in the Ahadees. These

can be learnt from the book Hisnul Haseen. The easiest of these is

رب إغفرلي

("O my Rabb, forgive me"), which should be recited thrice.

SITTING BETWEEN THE SAJDAHS

1. After completing one Sajdah, one should sit upright for a while before proceeding into the next Sajdah. This sitting posture between the two Sajdahs is called Jalsa. It is sinful to hasten this posture by not sitting upright. Your salah will have to be repeated if you do not sit up straight in the Jalsa position.
2. After getting up from Sajdah, a woman should sit on her left buttock and extend both feet towards her right, keeping the right calf on top of the left calf. The feet should be spread horizontally on the ground. The hands should be on the thighs with the fingers kept tightly together.
3. Your gaze should be on your lap while sitting.
4. You should sit in the Jalsa posture for the duration of at least one Tasbeeh (i.e. for as long as it takes to recite "سبحان اللّٰه" once). However, it is best to recite:

اللّٰهم إغفرلي وارحمني وعافني واهدني وأرزقني

وأجبرني وأرفعني (وابوداؤد، ترمذي، ابن ماجه)

"O Allah Ta'ala! Forgive me, have mercy on me, grant me safety and good health, guide me, provide for me, compensate for my shortcomings and elevate my status."

THE SECOND SAJDAH

1. Just as the first Sajdah, in the second Sajdah, you should also first place the knees on the ground, followed by the hands, the nose and finally the forehead.
2. The second Sajdah should be performed just like the first.
3. When rising from Sajdah, first lift the forehead off the ground, followed by the nose, the hands and then the knees.
4. One should not use the hands to lift oneself from Sajdah into a standing position unless one is overweight or ill.

5. Recite

بسم اللّٰه الرحمن الرحيم

before Surah Fatiha during every Rakah.

IN QA'DAH

1. Every sitting posture in salah besides the Jalsa is called Qa'dah. The method of sitting in the Qa'dah posture is the same as the method of sitting in Jalsa.
2. While reciting the Tashahhud, raise the index finger of the right hand when you reach the part

أشهد أن لا

and then drop it when saying

إلا اللّٰه

3. When raising the index finger, the middle finger and thumb should form a ring while the little finger and the one next to it remain curled. When raising the index finger, do not point it towards the sky, but towards the Qibla.
4. When dropping the index finger as you say, keep the other fingers in the position mentioned above. This position should be maintained up to the end of the salah.

WHEN ENDING THE SALAH WITH SALAM

1. When saying........

السلام عليكم ورحمة اللّٰه

And turning the face to either side, you should turn your face so that someone behind you can see your cheeks.
2. Fix your gaze on your shoulders when turning your head and make the intention that you are greeting all the angels on your right as you turn right and all those on your left as you turn left.

The above is merely a brief discussion of a woman's salah. Refer to books like Behisti Zewar and others for the detailed method of performing salah and the various du'aas to be recited during salah.

Making Du'aa

THE METHOD OF MAKING DU'AA

1. When making du'aa, raise the hands to the level of your chest. There should be a small space between your hands so that the hands are neither touching each other nor very far apart.
2. While making du'aa, you should be looking at your palms.

وصلى الله تعالى على النبي الكريم محمد وآله وأصحابه أجمعين

DU'AA AFTER THE FARDH SALAH

1. Be particular about making du'aa after every Fardh salah because du'aas are readily accepted after the Fardh salah.
2. Begin the du'aa by first praising Allah Ta'alaprofusely. Thereafter, recite Durood followed by du'aa for yourself, your family, and the people of your community and for all the Muslims in the world. Make du'aa that Allah Ta'ala guides the non-Muslims to Islam and that Allah Ta'ala grants safety and comfort to all suffering Muslims.
3. You should spend at least twenty minutes daily making du'aa. If you are unable to make du'aa for twenty consecutive minutes, distribute this time throughout the day. For example, you may make du'aa for five minutes after Fajr, five minutes after Asr and for ten minutes after Isha. If Allah Ta'alagrants you the ability to perform Tahajjud salah, do not pass up this opportunity to engage in du'aa. It is indeed tragic that people have hours to spend in idle chatter and hours to spend in preparing for wedding receptions and other functions, yet they cannot

spare twenty minutes to beg from their Most Merciful Rabb. They fail to realise that even if they get tired of asking from Allah Ta'ala, He is so Generous that He never tires of giving. Whereas people become angry when you keep asking from them, Allah Ta'ala gets pleased as you ask more from Him. You should therefore force yourself to make du'aa for at least twenty minutes until you form a habit of making lengthy du'aas.

4. Make a firm resolution that you will not ask from none besides Allah Ta'ala, not even from your husband, brothers or father. Remember that everyone is dependent on Allah Ta'ala and whatever people have with them has come from Allah Ta'ala. In fact, even if you are thirsty, first ask Allah Ta'ala to quench your thirst before drinking water because the water will be able to slake thirst only by Allah Ta'ala's command. Ask your every desire from Allah Ta'ala, even while walking about.

AN EXCELLENT DU'AA FOR EVERY WOMAN

اللّٰهم أهدني لأحسن الأخلاق والأعمال والأقوال فإنه لا يهدي لأحسنها

إلا أنت وأصرف عني سيئها فإنه لا يصرف عني سيئها إلا أنت

"O Allah Ta'ala! Bless me with splendid character, excellent deeds and fantastic speech because none but You can guide anyone to the best of this. Keep me distant from the evil of all this (i.e. from evil character, evil deeds and evil speech) because none but You can safeguard me from the evil of these things."

If one is unable to memorise the Arabic du'aa, it can be made in English as well.

DU'AA FOR A GOOD PARTNER

When a boy or girl comes of age, the parents, elder brothers and sisters and other family members should encourage him/her to make du'aa for a good partner so that life will be pleasant and comfortable. Allah Ta'ala has mentioned this du'aa in the Quran to convey the message to people that this is the du'aa that they should present in His court. This du'aa is therefore very likely to be accepted. The du'aa is:

﴿ وَالَّذِينَ يَقُولُونَ رَبَّنَا هَبْ لَنَا مِنْ أَزْوَاجِنَا وَذُرِّيَّاتِنَا قُرَّةَ أَعْيُنٍ وَاجْعَلْنَا لِلْمُتَّقِينَ إِمَامًا ﴾ {الفرقان:٦٣}

"O our Rabb! Accord to us the coolness of our eyes from our spouses and children, and make us leaders of the pious (i.e. make our families pious)."

This du'aa should be made throughout one's life, even after marriage. In addition to this, a woman may make other specific du'aas. For example, she may say, "O Allah Ta'ala! Grant me a husband who practises Religion completely and who will assist me to do the same. Make him a soft-hearted person who will appreciate and honour me. Grant us pious children and make us among Your chosen slaves who have a fervour for Jihaad and who are a means of spreading Your Religion throughout the world. Make him a person whose love for You is deeply entrenched in his heart, whose Iman is unshakeable and who places the love for Your Rasulsand the Companion of the Prophet before his love for all other mortals. He should be a person who is averse to the pleasures of this world and whose attention is focussed on the life of the Aakhirah. O Allah Ta'ala! Make him a source of delight, comfort and support for me. *Aameen*."

Another effective du'aa is to recite Durood followed by the following du'aa and again Durood afterwards. The du'aa is:

يا وهاب هب لي زوجًا صالحا

"O the Greatest Giver! Grant me a pious husband."

Because association with other women is often the cause of problems, it is also necessary for a woman to make du'aa to Allah Ta'ala to save her from such problems. For example, she may say, "O Allah Ta'ala! Grant me a comfortable home from my husband's Halaal earnings where I will be able to eat in peace and happily express my gratitude to You. Save me from homes where I shall have to face disputes with my in-laws every day. O Allah Ta'ala! If I have to serve my in-laws, ease the task for me and create the means for me to be able to cook by myself without anyone interfering in my affairs. Make me a good daughter-in-law and grant me a mother-in-law who will appreciate my services and who will ignore the backbiting and slander that others direct at me. O Allah Ta'ala! Grant me a home where I shall be able to easily observe Hijaab from all brothers-in-law and other non-Mahram men. Save me from homes that you have cursed because of the presence of a television or pictures of animate beings. Grant me a home in which I will be able to avoid all major and minor sins and in which I will be instrumental in spreading the Deen. Also grant me the wisdom and diplomacy to be able to save others and myself from sin."

THE DU'AA AFTER MARRIAGE

Together with the du'aas already mentioned, every bride and bride-to-be should recite the following du'aas:

اللَّهم ألف بيني و بين زوجي كما ألفت بين محمد ﷺ وخديجة رضي الله تعالى عنها، اللَّهم ألف بينى وبين زوجي... كما الفت بين محمد ﷺ و عائشة رضي اللَّه تعالى عنها

"O Allah Ta'ala! Create between me and him the love that You created between Muhammads and Khadeja (May Allah be pleased with her). O Allah Ta'ala! Create between us the love that You created between Muhammad (Peace be upon him) and Ayesha (May Allah be pleased with her)."

اللَّهم كما جمعتنا في الدنيا فاجمع بيني وبين زوجي في الجنة .....

[TRANSLATION:"O Allah Ta'ala! Join my husband and I in Jannah as You have joined us in this world."]

اللَّهم إجعلني لزوجي قرة أعين في الدنيا والأخرة

[TRANSLATION: O Allah Ta'ala! Make me a delight to my husband's eyes in this world as well as in the Aakhirah."]

اللَّهم إجعلنى معينة على إيمانه

[TRANSLATION: O Allah Ta'ala! Make me a wife who assists her husband in his faith."]

اللَّهم إجعلني مطيعة وصالحة، وإجعلني ساتر وحافظة للغيب

[TRANSLATION: O Allah Ta'ala! Make me a wife who obeys You as well as my

husband. Make me a pious wife, one who pleases her husband when he looks her and one who safeguards her chastity as well as his possessions and children in his absence."]

آمين يا رب العلمين

Recite the above du'aas after every Fardh salah as well as at the time of Tahajjud. Make these and other du'aas at all times, especially when terminating your fast during the month of Ramadhaan and at the sanctified places when performing Hajj or Umrah. If Allah Ta'ala grants these bounties to a woman, she and her family will enjoy blissful lives in this world as well as in the Aakhirah.

DU'AAS FOR PROTECTION FROM AN EVIL HUSBAND AND A CRUEL MOTHER-IN-LAW

Every girl and her parents should always make du'aa to Allah Ta'ala to safeguard her from an unkind husband, a cruel mother-in-law and an unpleasant family of in-laws. They should also make du'aa to Allah Ta'ala to grant her steadfastness in Deen, Halaal sustenance and everything she requires. The following du'aas are also very beneficial:

اللّٰهم إني أعوذ بك من خليل ماكر عيناه ترياني وقلبه يرعاني إن رأى حسنة دفنها، وإن رأى سيئة إذاعها

[TRANSLATION: "O Allah Ta'ala! I seek Your protection from every plotting friend whose eyes are always watching me and whose heart is always occupied with thinking of me (in search of my faults); who buries any good he sees in me and publicises any evil he sees in me."]

اللّٰهم إني أعوذ بك من كل صاحب يؤذيني

[TRANSLATION: "O Allah Ta'ala! I seek Your protection from a husband who may cause harm to befall me."]

اللّٰهم إني أعوذ بك من كل صاحبة تؤذيني

[TRANSLATION: "O Allah Ta'ala! I seek Your protection from every woman (mother-in-law, sister-in-law) who may cause harm to befall me."]

اللّٰهم لاتسلط علي بذنوبي من لايخافك في ولا يرحمني

[TRANSLATION: "O Allah Ta'ala! Because of my sins do not allow any such person (husband) to govern me who will have no fear for You in matters concerning me and who will not have mercy on me."]

Besides the above du'aas, the Ahadees have reported many other du'aas that are effective to secure a good and pious husband as well as good children. There is no good du'aa that Messenger of Allah (Peace be upon him) has not taught the Ummah and there is nothing harmful from which he has not taught us a du'aa to secure protection. May Allah Ta'ala grant him the highest positions and may He grant us the ability to make all these du'aas. *Aameen.*

These du'aas are extremely valuable because they are like a formatted request that a king's chief minister gives to the subjects of a country, the approval of which is guaranteed. Every woman should also include the recitation of a part of "Munaajaate Maqbool" or "Hizbul A'zam" into her daily routine because the du'aas mentioned in these books are extremely beneficial. Also very useful are the books "Dharee'atul Wusool ilaa Janaabir Rasul s" and "Sattar Istighfaar ki Du'aae", which one should try to read daily as well. If Muslim women read a part of these books daily and sincerely make the du'aas mentioned in them, Muslim homes will be enveloped in Allah j's mercy and the children of these homes will Insha Allah Ta'ala become shining stars of Islam.

WAKING UP AT NIGHT TO MAKE DU'AA

The best formula for creating love between a couple is that each of them should constantly make du'aa to Allah Ta'ala to strengthen their love. By doing this, they will soon notice that their bond will cement in a short while. Just as mortar is needed to join two bricks and glue is required to attach two pieces of paper, Allah Ta'ala's special grace is needed to join two hearts. The external factor needed to acquire this grace is the wife's obedience. She should do whatever her husband asks her to do (provided that his requests do not contradict the Shari'ah) and should apologise for anything that she does against his wishes. This should be done even though it appears to her that he is at fault. In addition to this external factor, the internal factor is also required. The internal factor is the fundamental aspect of du'aa both the husband and the wife should make with open and sincere hearts.

When making du'aa for your husband, think that he is after all the servant of Allah Ta'ala and a member of Prophet (Peace be on him) Ummah. If he is an ill-tempered man, he will only make life miserable for another woman if you leave him. However, if you makes du'aa to Allah Ta'ala, Allah Ta'ala will transform him into a gentle and loving man. Make du'aa to Allah Ta'ala after every Fardh salah and also wake up to make du'aa during the late hours of the night when others are asleep. After performing at least two Rakaahs Tahajjud salah, cry to Allah Ta'ala to guide your husband and the husband of every Muslim woman. We shall now quote the du'aa that a saint used to make to Allah Ta'ala during the still hours of the night.

إلاهي أغلقت الملوك أبوابها وبابك مفتوح للسائلين

إلاهي غارت النجوم ونامت العيون وأنت الحى القيوم الذي لاتاخذه سنة ولا نوم

إلاهي فرشت الفرش وخلا كل حبيب بحبيبه وأنت حبيب المجتهدين وأنيس المستوحشين

إلاهي إن عذبتني فإني مستحق العذاب والنقم وإن عفوت عني فأنت أهل الجود والكرم

إلاهي إن طردتنى عن بابك فإلى باب من التجئ وإن قطعتني عن خدمتك فخدمة من أرتجي، يا جميل العفو أذقني برد عفوك وحلاوة مغفرتک، وان لم اكن أهلا لذلك فأنت أهل التقوى والمغفرة

[TRANSLATION: "O My Allah Ta'ala! The kings and sovereigns have all locked their doors, but Yours are still open for beggars.

O My Allah Ta'ala! The stars have disappeared and people are fast asleep. You are the Living One, the One Who maintains everything. Neither does slumber nor sleep touch You.

O My Allah Ta'ala! Beds have been laid out and every lover is alone with his beloved. However, You are the beloved of those who exert themselves in Ibaadah and You are the companion of those in fear.

O My Allah Ta'ala! If You choose to punish me, I certainly deserve the punishment and if You forgive me then You are undoubtedly Munificent and Forgiving.

O My Allah Ta'ala! If You chase me away from Your door, at whose door shall I find refuge and if You do not accept me for Your service, then whom should I serve and be hopeful? O the Most Forgiving, allow me to taste the coolness of Your clemency and the sweetness of Your mercy even though I am not worthy of it. You are the only One who can rightfully be feared and the Only One from Whom forgiveness can be sought."]

Fater making this du'aa, make du'aa for your husband, your children, your family and for all the Muslims in the world. Experience has shown that du'aas are quickly accepted when one has conviction that they will be accepted. Another excellent du'aa to make is:

اللّٰهم إجعلنا سامعين مطيعين وأولياء مخلصين ورفقاء مصاحبين

[TRANSLATION: O Allah Ta'ala! Make us both (husband and wife) people who hearken to Your commands and who obey You. Make us sincere friends to each other and close companions."]

Ten Practices of Prophet Muhammad

Rasulullahs was a mercy to both men and women. By implementing the Sunnah practices of Rasulullahs, a person's home will be filled with Allah Ta'ala's mercy. As a result of this mercy, love will grow between the members of the household and each person will also develop the love for Allah Ta'ala and His Rasuls. Once the love for Allah Ta'ala and His Rasulshas permeated a person's heart, he will give precedence to the Religion over everyone else. Their hearts will harbour no malice for others because all they will concern themselves with will be pleasing Allah Ta'ala. They will do anything and everything in their power to ensure that Allah Ta'ala is pleased with them regardless of what people say or think.

It is therefore necessary for every woman to learn about the Sunnah practices of Rasulullahsand apply these to her life. Before doing anything, she should ponder how Rasulullahs did the same thing and emulate his manner of doing it. Every deed and every statement of Messenger of Allah (Peace be upon him) should be more valuable to a Muslim than that of any other person or nation. Regardless of what a Muslim has to lose in the process, he will be prepared for the loss rather than compromise on the Sunnah of Rasulullah (Peace be upon him)

We shall now present some Sunnah practices of Rasulullahs so that every reader can introduce them to her life. By doing this, he / she will also attain the pleasure of Allah Ta'ala. (Which is the greatest of all).

وَرِضْوَانٌ مِنَ اللَّهِ أَكْبَرُ {التوبة: ٦١}

1. Brush your teeth regularly with a Miswaak, especially when making wudhu for every salah, before and after eating, at the time of Tahajjud,

before reciting Quran and on every other occasion. If possible, change your Miswak every week, otherwise cut the bristles regularly so that spoilt bristles is not used all the time.

2. Learn and recite the du'as for all occasions e.g. the du'aas for eating, the du'aas for sleeping, the du'aas for the morning and evening, for wearing clothes, for making wudhu, for seeing the new moon, for entering and leaving the house, etc. You should also teach these du'aas to your children and younger brothers and sisters. Insha Allah Ta'ala by reciting all these du'aas, theirs and your tongues will remain pure because they are uttering the same words that the tongue of Rasulullah sspoke. These du'aas will also earn you great rewards in the Aakhirah.

   An important du'aa from among the many du'aas is the du'aa after sneezing viz. "Al Hamdu Lillaahi Rabbil Aalameen Alaa Kulli Haal". When you hear another woman sneezing, recite "Yar Hamu Killaah. If a Mahram sneezes, recite "Yar Hamu KAllah". Whenever anyone gives you anything, ensure that you thank him/her by saying "JazaKAllahu Khayran."

   In addition to this, you should give and take things with the right hand, recite "Bismillaahir Rahmaan nir Raheem" when locking the doors at night and cover all open utensils containing food.

3. Whenever anything breaks, any difficulty occurs or any loss whatsoever takes place, immediately recite,

﴿ إِنَّا لِلَّهِ وَإِنَّا إِلَيْهِ رَاجِعُونَ ﴾ {البقرة:١٥٦}

["To Allah t we belong and to Him shall we return"]. By reciting this, a Muslim acknowledges that nothing belongs to her and that everything she possesses comes from Allah Ta'ala, Who is at liberty to take it back whenever He pleases. Nothing will last forever and we should be prepared to lose things during our lives.

4. When taking your children to the toilet, ensure that they neither face towards the Qibla nor face their backs towards the Qibla. If the toilet faces towards the Qibla, teach them to face somewhat towards the right or the left. Remember that facing towards the Qibla or facing the back towards the Qibla is a grave sin and you should take every precaution to avoid it.

كان إذا حزبه أمر فزع إلى الصلوة

5. It was the practice of Rasulullahs to resort to salah whenever he experienced any difficulty. You should also inculcate the same practice. Therefore, if any of your children fall ill, you should perform two Rakaahs salah and make du'aa to Allah Ta'ala to cure the child. You may say, "O Allah Ta'ala! This illness has come by your command and the cure for all diseases also comes by Your command. I beseech You to cure my child." You should take the child to a doctor for treatment if necessary and also give some Sadaqah.

   In the same manner, if there is a shortage of anything in the home, first perform two Rakaahs salah and make du'aa to Allah Ta'ala before asking your husband. If it is the time of the month when you are unable to perform salah, make wudhu and engage in the Dhikr of "Al Hamdu Lillaah", the third Kalimah, Durood or you may even recite Surah Fatiha. Then recite:

   A hundred times or even more if you can. Thereafter, make du'aa to Allah Ta'ala and ask Him for whatever you need. By always doing this, your relationship with Allah Ta'ala will be greatly strengthened.
6. Always greet other women with "As salamu Alaykum wa Rahmatullaahi wa Barakaatuh" before starting a conversation. It is unfortunate that many women start a conversation with statements like, "How are you?" or "How are the children?" or "I haven't seen for you for such a long time!", etc. All this and more can be said as long as salam is made first. This important Sunnah should also be taught to your children.

The Method of Greeting

Commenting on verse 86 of Surah Nisaa (Surah 4), Mufti Muhammad Shafi l] states, "The verse makes it clear that when someone is greeted, he should reply to the greeting using better words or at least the same words used to greet him. Messenger of Allah (Peace be upon him) explained this verse by his actions when someone greeted him with the words

السلام عليكم يا رسول الله

Messenger of Allah (Peace be upon him) replied by saying,

وعليكم السلام ورحمة الله.

Thereafter, another person arrived and greeted saying,

' السلام عليكم يا رسول الله ورحمة الله'

Messenger of Allah (Peace be upon him) added to his reply when he said,

وعليكم السلام ورحمة الله وبركاته

Another Sahabi (May Allah be pleased with him/her) then greeted Messenger of Allah (Peace be upon him) using all the words of salam when he said,

السلام عليكم يا رسول الله ورحمة الله

To this, Messenger of Allah (Peace be upon him) merely said, عليك (i.e. 'The same to you').Surprised, this Sahabirasked Messenger of Allah (Peace be upon him) why the others received lengthier replies (thus more du'aas from him), whereas he received the briefest reply despite his complete greeting. Messenger of Allah (Peace be upon him) told him, 'You had left nothing for me to add. Because you included all the words of salam in your greeting, I acted according to the Quranic verse and gave you a reply equal to your own greeting.' Ibn Jareer (May Allah be pleased with him/her) and Ibn Abi Hatimr have both narrated this hadith from various narrators."

وعليكم السلام ورحمة اللّٰه وبركاته

The above verse and hadith teach us that our reply to a greeting should include words that are better than those of the person greeting us. We should therefore add extra words of du'aa to our greeting as Rasulullahs did.

THE BENEFITS OF GREETING

A saint one mentioned that if every Muslim from every town and country has to merely make salam to other Muslims of their own towns as well as Muslims from other towns and countries daily, there will be peace and safety throughout the world. One of the main causes for the enmity and strife existing throughout the world is the lack of greeting with the words of salam.

One of the most effective ways to create love between couples and families is for them to regularly greet each other with

السلام عليكم ورحمة اللّٰه وبركاته

The couple and the members of the family should greet each other when they enter the room, when they start conversations, when they meet each other after waking up in the morning and before going to bed. In fact, they should not pass up any opportunity to greet each other.

The status of salam is so great that even in Jannah people will greet each other with salam, the angels will greet them with salam and Allah Ta'ala will Himself greet the people of Jannah with the words of salam. Allah Ta'ala says in verse 58 of Surah Yaaseen (Surah 36),

[سَلَامٌ قَوْلًا مِنْ رَبٍّ رَحِيمٍ] {يس:٥٨}

"They will have a greeting of peace from the Most Merciful Rabb."

Abdullah bin Umarr used to frequent the marketplaces for the express purpose of greeting everyone there, irrespective of who they were or what their purposes were. Remember that you will be greatly rewarded every time you greet a Muslim sister, so the more often you greet, the more you will gain.

THE MEANING OF THE SALAM

The salam is a du'aa that one Muslim makes for another Muslim. The Muslims greeting is really telling the other that she wants her to live in peace and safety and that she wants Allah Ta'ala to shower His mercy and blessings on her. You can well imagine that if a mother greets her children with these words several times, daily the children will be enveloped in Allah Ta'ala's mercy and Shaytan will have no avenue to them.

ANOTHER MEANING OF SALAM

When one Muslim sister greets another with the words السلام عليكم ورحمة الله وبركاته, she is actually reminding the other that she should not forget that Allah Ta'ala is Omnipresent and is watching her at all times. When the other replies with the same words, the first woman is also reminded of the same. In this manner, every person will be cognisant of Allah Ta'ala's presence and they will all avoid sin.

Adults should greet children first so that children may learn the habit of greeting. By doing this, they will also be practising the Sunnah of Messenger of Allah, who always greeted children before they could greet him.

THE ISLAMIC GREETING IS BETTER THAN ANY OTHER FORM OF GREETING

It is common place with every nation and creed that they greet each other in a particular manner to express their love and concern for one another. A study of all forms of greeting will reveal that Islam's manner of greeting is the most comprehensive. In addition to merely expressing love, the salam is a du'aa for the person, invoking Allah Ta'ala's safety from all calamities and difficulties. In addition to this, it is a reminder for the person that we are all in need of Allah Ta'ala and that He is Ever Present and All Powerful. Because of this factor, the salam beco- mes a form of Ibaadah as well.

When the person greeting is desirous for the safety of the one she is greeting (as indicated by the words of salam), it is obvious that the one greeting will not want to harm the one she is greeting. By this token, the salam is also a surety to the one being greeted that s/he need not fear any harm from the one who is greeting. It is for this reason that Ibn Uyayna said,

أتدري ما السلام؟ يقول أنت آمن مني

"Do you know what is salam? The person making salam is really saying, 'You have nothing to fear from me."

In a Nutshell

The greeting of Islam viz. "As salamu Alaykum wa Rahmatullaahi wa Barakaatuh" includes all of the following:

It is the Dhikr of Allah Ta'ala.
It reminds other of Allah Ta'ala.
It is an expression of love and concern.
It is an excellent du'aa.
It is a surety for the person being greeted that she has nothing to fear from the one who is greeting. In fact, Rasulullahs mentioned that.

المسلم من سلم المسلمون من لسانه ويده

A Muslim is one from whose tongue and hands other Muslims have nothing to fear.
[Bukhari Vol. 1 Pg. 6]

If Muslims use the greeting of salam with awareness and appreciation instead of using it as a mere customary salutation, the salam would be sufficient to transform their lives. It is perhaps for this reason that Rasulullahs emphasised that the salam should be popularised among the Muslims. Rasulullahs has also counted making salam among the best of deeds. Besides this, he has enumerated many virtues and benefits of salam.

In a hadith of Muslim, Abu Hurayra (May Allah be pleased with him/ her) narrates that Rasulullahs said, "You will not be able to enter Jannah until you have Imaan and your Imaan will not be complete until you have love for each other. Shall I not inform you of something that will create love between you? Popularise salam among you."

Abdullah bin Umarr reports that a person once asked Rasulullahs what the best of all deeds were. Rasulullahsreplied, "Feed people and make salam to everyone, whether you know a person or not." *[Bukhari and Muslim]*

Anu Umaamahr narrates that Rasulullahs said, "Indeed, the nearest people to Allah Ta'ala are they who are the first to greet." *[Ahmad, Tirmidhi, Abu Dawood]*

Abdullah bin Mas'oodr reports from Rasulullahs that the word "salam" is one of Allah Ta'ala's names, which He has sent to earth. Therefore, people should popularise it among themselves. Whenever a person comes to a gathering and greets the people there with salam, his status is extremely exalted in Allah Ta'ala's estimation because he has reminded them of Allah Ta'ala. If the people do not reply to his greeting, those of a higher calibre than them (viz. the angels) reply to him. *[Bazzaar, Tabraani*]

In another hadith, Rasulullahs stated that the most miserly person is one who is miserly with greeting. *[Bazzaar]*

It is because of these and the numerous other virtues of salam that made Abdullah bin Umarr frequent the marketplace only to greet people with "As salamu Alaykum wa Rahmatullaahi wa Barakaatuh". *[Ma'aariful Quran, Vol. 2 Pg. 503]*

AN IMPORTANT RULING

It is not permissible for a woman to shake hands with or to speak directly with any non-Mahram man even though he is her brother-in-law or her cousin. Doing this will certainly incur Allah Ta'ala's wrath and lead to difficulties in this world as well as in the next.

We shall now continue with the seventh Sunnah in our discussion of ten important Sunnah practices of Rasulullahs.

7. Attribute every occurrence to Allah Ta'ala, saying that it happened by the will of Allah Ta'ala. If a person falls ill, say that the illness is from Allah Ta'ala without attributing it to the heat, cold, food, etc. Similarly, when a person is cured of an illness, say that it was Allah Ta'alawho cured him/her and not that it was some medicine or doctor that provided the cure. One may say that Allah Ta'alaused the cold as a means for one to become ill and that He placed the cure in the

treatment of a certain doctor.

If someone's husband suffered a loss in any way, she should not rebuke him by telling him that he suffered the loss because he did not listen to her. A woman who has trust in Allah Ta'ala would rather console him by saying that everything happens by Allah Ta'ala's command and that they should be patient and hope for reward from Allah Ta'ala.

People are generally accustomed to using the phrase "by chance" and the word "coincidentally" e.g. "I got it quite by chance" or "Coincidentally, my sister happened to visit at the same time that you did". It is incorrect to use these words because nothing happens by chance. Everything that happens happens by the command of Allah Ta'ala and for good reason. Every leaf falling off a tree will fall only with Allah Ta'ala's command just as every drop of rain falls with His command. Everything happening presently and everything that will happen in future is by His command. Therefore, everything you speak about should be attributed to Allah Ta'ala.

Bayazeed Bistaamil was a great saint. After he had passed away, someone saw him in a dream and asked him how he fared in the next life. He said that when Allah Ta'ala asked him what he had brought, he replied that he had brought nothing besides his belief in Tauheed. He did not mention all his many good deeds because he feared that they may be rejected on account of deficiencies found in them. However, Allah Ta'ala reminded him of a particular morning when he suffered pain in his stomach and said, "This is because of the milk I had drunk last night." Allah Ta'ala therefore asked him where his belief in Tauheed had disappeared that morning and whether the stomach pain was result of the milk or Allah Ta'ala's command.

There is of course no harm in saying that the milk had cased stomach pains as long as one believes that the true cause is Allah Ta'ala. However, he was reprimanded for this because of his high status as a saint. This incident is an eye-opener for us all.

We should also guard ourselves against attributing things to ourselves e.g. "The meal that I cooked was very tasty." You should rather say, "Al Hamdu Lillaah! Allah Ta'ala I added great taste to the food I cooked." Everything that happens should be attributed to Allah Ta'ala and to none else.

This lesson should be emphasised to your children as well. When you child asks for something, do not tell him to ask his father to buy it for him. Encourage him to first make wudhu, to perform two Rakaahs salah with devotion and then to make du'aa to Allah Ta'ala. Thereafter, he should ask his father so that his father may attain the reward of fulfilling his desire. Tell the child that his father will then get him what he wants when Allah Ta'alagrants his father the means and the inspiration to do so. In this manner, the child will develop trust in Allah Ta'ala and will not resort to asking from others when s/he grows up. Such a child will not entertain hopes in others and will ask from Allah Ta'ala only. The child will remain pleased with whatever Allah Ta'ala decides and will be able to exercise patience whenever a difficulty arrives.

8. Just as you conceal yourself from strangers, you should also observe Hijaab when associating with your non-Mahram relatives, whether they are your cousins or your brothers-in-law. Failure to do so is a major sin even though there may not be any fear of falling into sin with such as person. If a person truly loves Allah Ta'ala and His Rasuls, she will practise every injunction of the Shari'ah and steer clear of incurring their wrath, which will ultimately destroy her life in this world as well as her life in the Aakhirah.

9. You should be particular about replying to the Adhaan. Rasulullahs has mentioned that the person who replies to the Adhaan with conviction in the heart will certainly enter Jannah. In addition to this, Rasulullahs has also stated that such a person will be forgiven and that he will definitely intercede on behalf of the person who recites the du'aa after the Adhaan. *[Muslim]*

You should therefore ensure that you maintain complete silence when the Adhaan is being called out and that you repeat everything the Mu'adhin says. Of course, when the Mu'adhin calls out حي على الصلاة and حي على الفلاح, you should say لاحول ولا قوة إلا بالله

The du'aa to recite after the Adhaan is:

اللّٰهم رب هذه الدعوة التامة والصلوة القائمة آت محمدا الوسيلة

والفضيلة وأبعثه مقاما محمودا الذي وعدته (مشكوة ص ٦٥)

[TRANSLATION: "O Allah Ta'ala, the Rabb of this perfect call and the Rabb of the forthcoming salah! Grant Muhammads the station of 'Waseela' (an exalted station in the Aakhirah), grant him eminence and the position of 'Maqaam Mahmood' which You have promised him. Verily, You never breach Your promise."] ["Mishkaat" Pg. 65]

Ummu Salma (May Allah be pleased with her) narrates that (in addition to the above du'aa) Messenger of Allahtaught her to recite the following du'aa after the Maghrib Adhaan:

اللّٰهم إن هذ إقبال ليلك وإدبار نهارك وأصوات دعاتك فاغفرلي (مشكوة ٦٦ ج١)

[TRANSLATION: "O Allah Ta'ala! This sounds the arrival of Your night, the departure of Your day and the cries of those making du'aa to You. Please forgive me."]
["Mishkaat" Pg. 66]

Although this verbal reply to the Adhaan is Mustahab, the physical reply to the Adhaan is Waajib (compulsory). For men, this physical reply to the Adhaan entails proceeding to the Masjid for salah and for women; it entails performing salah after the Adhaan. Even if you are at the stove when the Adhaan is called out, switch off the stove and start preparing for salah, thinking that your Rabb has summoned you to prayer and that your success lies in performing your salah. Never allow your Nafs and Shaytaan to deceive you into thinking that you should first complete the work before performing salah. By falling for this guile, your salah will be delayed (maybe even missed) and your work will take more time than it should.

When the Adhaan is called out, you should ensure that all mature males in you household as well as those approaching the age of ten proceed to the Masjid for salah. Use wisdom and diplomacy to encourage them instead of being brusque and harsh. Those children in the house who are between seven and ten years of age should be trained at home to perform their salah.

SIMPLICITY

10. Simplicity is an extremely important Sunnah of Rasulullahs. A hadith mentions that the person who revives a Sunnah of Messenger of Allah (Peace be upon him) after people have discarded it shall earn the reward of a hundred martyrs. You will therefore earn this great reward if you inculcate simplicity in your life. You should therefore resolve to introduce simplicity in your life and make an effort to bring simplicity into the lives of all Muslims. By introducing the Sunnah practices of Rasulullahs into your life, you will have tremendous blessings and mercy in everything you do. When a woman resolves to lead a life of simplicity, the rest of the family will quickly follow suit. There are three specific areas in which simplicity ought to be introduced. These areas are (1) in marriages, (2) in the building of a house and (3) in the finishing and furnishing of a house. When this is done, love will develop in the family and many sins will be avoided. In addition to this, wastage, ostentation, boasting and unnecessary amassing of wealth will be avoided.

Hakeemul Ummah Maulana Ashraf Ali Thanwi (May Allah be Merciful on him) has mentioned, "Women are experts in training men and in confounding their intelligence. When a man asks a woman what he is expected to do after marriage, all she utters is a brief statement i.e. 'Not much. Just do as much as you can.' When a man really decides to do as she says and asks for an explanation of this statement, his ears are filled with thousands of demands which spell disaster for him in both worlds."

["Islaah Khawateen" Pg. 130]

Many men have their heads permanently bowed with the weight of the debts they owe others while others have even committed major sins to satisfy the demands of their wives. It is therefore necessary for women to adopt simplicity in their lives to alleviate the burden on their husbands. By adopting simplicity in especially the three areas mentioned above, the entire family will be relived of unnecessary stress and anxiety.

When building your home, ensure that the design is not elaborate so that additional expenses are not incurred. Think awhile about the homes of the Companion of the Prophet y. The roofs of their homes were made of the fronds of date palms, while the walls were made of mud. There were neither any carpets, nor any expensive beds, cupboards or a large variety of crockery. Despite the absence of these luxuries, their homes were filled with comfort, peace, love, good health and mutual compassion. Neither did a Muslim have fear for a Kaafir nor did a Kaafir fear that a Muslim would harm him.

A wealthy Arab friend of mine has resolved to adopt simplicity in his home for the sole purpose of emulating the Sunnah of Messenger of Allah (Peace be upon him) With the assistance of his wife he has achieved this goal and is enjoying the tranquillity that the Sunnah of Messenger of Allah (Peace be upon him) brings to one's life. When a person truly has love for Messenger of Allah, his every action is more valuable than all the riches and kingdoms of the world.

The second very important matter in which we should endeavour to adopt simplicity is in the finishing and furnishing of our homes. We should have in our homes only what is necessary. What is really a necessity? The true meaning of a necessity can be clearly understood from the nature of the Arabic word for necessity, which is "Dharoorah". This word is derived from the root word "Dharar", which means 'to harm' or 'to cause difficulty'. Necessities have been termed "Dharoorah" because without them, a person will experience great difficulty.

Therefore, if you need to carpet you house, choose the carpet that is the simplest. Similarly, when choosing curtains, choose curtains that are the simplest. In this manner, everything else that is necessary should be simple. Whatever you spend on your house should be well within your husband's budget. Your excess wealth should be spent in charity so that this wealth will be of benefit to you in the Hereafter. Whenever you do something, always stop to think whether Allah Ta'ala will be pleased instead of thinking whether your friends or other people will be pleased. Remember that Allah Ta'ala's pleasure should have precedence over the pleasure of everyone else.

It is also extremely important to adopt simplicity when hosting functions. Whether it is your brother, your sister or any of your children getting married, ensure that the function is as simple as possible. Never ask the opposite party for anything and make it clear to them as well as to everyone else that the Shari'ah has only prescribed the Waleema function, which is hosted by the bridegroom. This function should also be extremely simple. In addition to this, the trousseau should also be simple. Instead of squandering money on elaborate wedding ceremonies and trousseaus, the money should rather be given to the bride to use for her home and future.

Remember that the more simplicity you adopt, the closer you will get to Allah Ta'ala. As a mother, brother, sister or family member you should also exert your influence over others who intend hosting such functions so that they also receive the benefits of the Sunnah and are saved from unnecessary problems in their lives.

A narration of Ahmad reports that Messenger of Allah (Peace be upon him) said,

إن أعظم النكاح بركة أيسره مئونة

(مشكوة ص ٢٦٨) (مسند أحمد، سند الأنصار ٢٣٣٨٨)

"*The marriage with the most blessings is the one that has the least expense.*"

This means that a couple will experience tremendous blessings in their marriage when the expenses from the period of the proposal until the bride's departure to her husband are reduced to a bare minimum. Such a marriage will be a source of contentment and bliss for not only the couple, but for both their families as well. In addition to this, the relationship will also ensure their success in the Aakhirah. The first visible results of these blessings will already become manifest before the marriage when the parties will not be plagued by sleepless nights and the burden of taking debts upon their heads. By adhering to colloquial customs and traditions (such as "Mendhi nights", bridal showers, etc), people will be unnecessarily burdening themselves with anxiety, in addition to suffering the repercussions in the Aakhirah for imitating the lives of the Kuffar.

In trying to impress people by hosting large functions, families only earn insults and abuse instead. After many a large function, people will be heard complaining about the food being too strong, too mild or too oily. Further fuelling disputes, the bride's sister-in-law will be heard grumbling, "She couldn't even show me her wedding outfit at the bridal shower!" Another sister-in-law will say, "She didn't even greet me on the night of the wedding!" In this manner, a barrage of problems will assault the marriage even before the couple can live together.

Messenger of Allah (Peace be upon him) himself married and he also got his daughters married. Every Muslim should learn from the pure examples that he set in this regard.

Messenger of Allah (Peace be upon him) Marries and Hosts a Waleema Function While on Journey

During one of his journeys, Messenger of Allah married Safiyya (May Allah be pleased with her). To celebrate the occasion, Messenger of Allah (Peace be upon him) hosted a Waleema. The Waleema meal comprised of some dates, butter and a few pieces of cheese which were scattered on a tablecloth for the people present to eat. Neither does Islam encourage elaborate feasts nor pompous ceremonies; least of all, the printing of wedding invitations.

If we imitate the practises of Rasulullahs and marry our sons and daughters in this manner, there is every hope that this deed alone will guarantee our salvation in the Aakhirah. When marriages are conducted in the manner that the Shari'ah prescribes, it is not at all farfetched that such marriages will produce gems like salahud Religion Ayyubi (May Allah be Merciful on him/her) and Raabiya Basriyya (May Allah be Merciful on her) who will be responsible for saving thousands of souls from Jahannam. However, these types of delectable fruit will be borne only from trees that can bear the heat of people's insults when assiduously adhering to the Sunnah practices of Messenger of Allah. A poet says:

> "The first condition for following the true Religion is
> love for Muhammad (Peace be upon him)
> Compared to him, everything else is imperfect When you are loyal to Muhammad s, everyone
> is yours

The things of this world are yours, as are the Lowhul Mahfoodh and the pen
Do not be disturbed if the world is upset with you
You do not really need everyone to be pleased with you
When you look at things, decide for yourself
What you ought to do and what you need not do (in conformance with the Shari'ah)
If You are not mine (O Allah) then nothing is mine
When You are mine, everything is mine including
the stars and the earth
Tauheed is that on the Plain of Resurrection,
Allah Ta'ala should say
'It was for My sake that this slave of Mine was angry with the world.'"
[Translated from an Urdu poem]

OPPRESSIVE MOTHERS-IN-LAW

If every woman resolved that she would be kind and gentle when dealing with the innocent lady who will soon be living in her home as her daughter-in-law, life would become pleasant and comfortable for many people. Not only will it be easier for women to marry, but hundreds of parents will not have to lose sleep over the troubled lives of their married daughters. Among the deeper effects that such behaviour will lead to is that immodesty and nudity will be considerably lessened because people will be encouraged to marry.

It is not incorrect to assert that an oppressive mother-in-law together with her daughters who serve as accomplices are among the greatest elements that discourage men and women from marrying. They actively destroy marriages and cause many men to perpetrate major sins. A catalyst in their efforts is the wife of their elder brother who is well-versed in all colloquial customs and traditions. Such women make unnecessary demands from the family of a bride coming to their family. The father of the bride-to-be is then forced to accede to their demands because he fears that they will make his daughter's life a misery if he does not comply. Consequently, he has to bear the burden of incurring debts to pay for the exorbitant expenses.

It is unfortunate that if a man does not host an elaborate wedding function for his daughter, she will have to hear taunts and insults from her mother-in-law for the rest of her life. This will make life unbearable for her and will place undue pressure on her marriage. To avoid this situation, the bride's father has to lower himself to take loans from others. The blistering singe of being refused a loan only aggravates the embarrassment of asking from others. In many cases, the customs of the area demand so much from the father of the bride that he cannot afford them even though he is wealthy. Such burdensome customs include giving elaborate gifts to the groom's family and hosting several functions before the wedding itself. Despite being unable to afford all of this, the bride's father is forced to find the money for it because he knows that after the marriage, his daughter will be unable to bear the stigma that her mother-in-law will attach to her and the insults that will be heaped on her throughout her life. The father is eventually forced to accept any money he can find, whether it is interest, Sadaqah or ill-gotten money.

Mothers-in-law who behave in this manner should beware of Allah Ta'ala's punishment. It has often been noticed that mothers-in-law who have oppressed their daughters-in-law suffer debilitating diseases in the lives. May Allah Ta'ala save us all from such diseases. Problems between mothers-in- law and daughters-in-law are extremely common nowadays because mothers-in-law do not treat their daughters-in-law like their own daughters and daughters-in-law do not treat their mothers-in-law like their own mothers. It is therefore best for a mother-in-law and a daughter-in-law to live separately. If this is not possible, she should at least have her own kitchen.

According to the explicit instruction of Rasulullah s, the bride is not obliged to bring anything to her husband's home, but it the duty of the husband to provide dowry and, of course, the other household necessities. Unfortunately, many of today's mothers-in-law will terrorise their daughters-in-law if they fail to provide something for the house. It is therefore necessary for Muslims to erase these customs from their lives and to make each other understand that they have no right to pressurise the bride's party into providing anything.

The "Jahez"

Although the custom of demanding "Jahez" from the bride's family is disappearing from the lives of many Muslims, there are still many ignorant homes that have failed to see the light. While the groom requires only a wife who is obedient, understanding, loving, attractive and compassionate, his mother, sisters and sisters-in-law also want something from the marriage. It is for this reason that they force the groom to deliver a list to his fiancé's parents with all their demands. These demands are referred to as the "Jahez". Unfortunately, many people have taken this custom so far that they actually specify the make and model of the appliance or furniture they ask for. Such demands are sheer oppression and contrary to the Shari'ah. In fact, when dissecting the Urdu word "Jahez" Ulama have mentioned that each letter is represented as follows:

The first letter "Jeem" (x) stands for "Jurm" i.e. injustice.
The second letter "Haa" (ê) stands for "Hawas" i.e. carnal desires.
The third letter "Yaa" (ð) stands for "Yalghaar" i.e. assault.
The last letter "Zaa" (‹) stands for "Zahar" i.e. poison.

The "Jahez" is really an injustice against the bride's father, a result of the carnal desires of the groom's family, an assault from their side and a poison in the hearts of the bride's parents because it will soon affect their health when they have to bear the disgrace of begging from others.

Whereas people should accept a woman into their homes on the basis of her credentials as a good wife, it has now sadly become the norm in many areas that she is accepted merely on the basis of the quality of the "Jahez" she can bring along. It is therefore not uncommon in such that an excellent woman is looked down upon merely because the "Jahez" she brought for her in-laws was not up to standard. On the other hand, a shrew is regarded as a good woman only because she was able to bring a handsome "Jahez" for her in-laws. Instead of the people of neighbourhood coming to see and congratulate the bride, they now ask whether the washing-machine arrived or whether any other item of the "Jahez" came as requested. When the groom receives everything that was requested as "Jahez", people say that he has been very fortunate.

However, people fail to realise that the most valuable "Jahez" that a groom can hope for is a capable wife who manages the home with dexterity and who has received a sound Islamic education and upbringing. An excellent wife is one who can ably serve her husband and her in-laws and who can raise her children as good Muslims. The best clothing that a woman can bring with her as "Jahez" is the clothing of Islam and obedience. The best jewellery that she can bring are the jewels of Ibaadah, the best perfume she can bring is the perfume of the Sunnah, her best make-up is trust in and fear for Allah Ta'ala. Better than the brand-named appliances and furniture that she can bring as "Jahez" is good character, a smiling face, the knowledge of Deen, modesty and the excellent attributes of the Sahabiyat.

In the past, people were embarrassed to ask others for anything because this entailed begging. However, with customs like "Jahez" and bridal showers, the rich have devised sophisticated methods of begging from people because they asking people to bring them the gifts they want. It seems that the richer people become, the greedier they get. Taking advantage of functions like these, they ask others to bring the most expensive gifts merely to save their own money. This has become an excellent method of dipping one's hands into the pockets of others. It is unfortunate that material possessions are more precious to people than a good wife for their son. It appears that people are auctioning their sons and marrying them to the highest bidder. May Allah Ta'ala guide all Muslims and make them realise the error of their ways before they ruin the lives of others together with their own lives in the Aakhirah.

Insensitive customs such as demanding a "Jahez" will stop only when the wealthy class decide to put an end to it. At least some members of this class should marry their children according to the simple Sunnah method that Messenger of Allahtaught us. In this manner, they will be unshackling the yoke that is suffocating so many poor people. Whereas it is the responsibility of the husband to provide for the wife, the tables have turned to such an extent that nowadays fathers have to part with their most precious daughters as well as thousands of their hard-earned wealth. If this is not oppression on the father, it can be nothing less.

The curse of such customs will not come to an end until the members of a community take decisive action to put an end to it. May Allah Ta'ala assist those who will take the initiative to promote the Sunnah of Messenger of Allah (Peace be upon him) so that people can breathe more easily. *Aameen.*

THE "JAHEZ" IS A HINDU CUSTOM

Allah Ta'ala has given men superiority over women because they have the honour of spending the wealth on women. In addition to this, the Shari'ah has explicitly specified that it is the man's responsibility to ensure that he provides everything necessary in the home. When a marriage takes place, the woman has no financial responsibility whatsoever. The Shari'ah makes it clear that it is the husband who has to spend on his wife and not the other way around. It is only in the upside down world of certain communities that the woman is obliged to make a contribution.

Allah Ta'ala says in the Quran,

﴿ الرِّجَالُ قَوَّامُونَ عَلَى النِّسَاءِ بِمَا فَضَّلَ اللَّهُ بَعْضَهُمْ عَلَى بَعْضٍ وَبِمَا أَنْفَقُوا مِنْ أَمْوَالِهِمْ ﴾ {النساء:٣٤}

"Men are the guardians of women because of the virtue Allah Ta'ala has bestowed some of you over others and because of the wealth that men spend (on women)."

The great commentator of the Quran Imam Razi (May Allah be Merciful on him/her) has mentioned that this verse refers to the dowry that the husband pays to the wife as well as the maintenance that he spends on her. Because the words of this verse are general, it refers to every expense that the husband incurs during the course of his marriage and in preparation for his marriage. Together with providing food and accommodation for his wife, the husband is obliged to provide all the necessities that his wife requires. The Quran and Ahadees do not even make vague reference to the fact that the bride has to contribute the household expenses. Therefore, none of this may be demanded from the bride's parents.

Because Hindu custom dictates that daughters should receive nothing from the estate of their fathers, Hindu fathers spend as much as they can on the "Jahez" of their daughters. The separation from their daughters on the occasion of marriage therefore signifies a permanent separation for them because her share of his estate is given then. With this in mind, Muslims should completely divorce themselves from this Hindu custom and make a concerted effort to prevent other Muslims from it as well.

A MISCONCEPTION

Many Muslims dwell under the misconception that the few items that Messenger of Allah (Peace be upon him) gave his beloved daughter Fatima (May Allah be pleased with him/her) when she married was "Jahez". The reply to this misconception will benefit only those Muslims who really wish to know the truth and who are willing to heed advice. As for those who are bent on exploiting others and who take pleasure in embarrassing others, reading this reply will be an exercise in futility.

The reply is that the things that Messenger of Allahgave for his daughter were actually bought with the dowry that Ali (May Allah be pleased with him/her) had given prior to the marriage. Allaama Zurqaani (May Allah be Merciful on him/her) writes in "Sharh Mawaahib" that Ali (May Allah be pleased with him/her) had a coat of armour which he presented to Rasulullah (Peace be upon him)as dowry. Messenger of Allah (Peace be upon him) sold the armour for 480 Dirhams and used the money to buy a few household items which he sent with Fatima (May Allah be pleased with him/her) after the marriage. Among the items that Messenger of Allah (Peace be upon him) asked Bilal (May Allah be pleased with him/her) to buy with the money was perfume, some clothing, bedding and a pillow. It is therefore clear that the things which Rasulullah (Peace be upon him)gave Fatima (May Allah be pleased with him/her) was not really a "Jahez" as people would call it. If it one insists on calling it "Jahez", it should be borne in mind that it was not paid for by the father but by the son-in-law.

Another factor that disproves the misconception that Rasulullah (Peace be upon him)paid for the "Jahez" of Fatima (May Allah be pleased with him/her) is the fact that he did not do the same for his other daughters. It is not possible for Rasulullah (Peace be upon him) to do something for one daughter which he did not do for the others because he has emphasised that parents deal justly with their children.

سوووابين أولادكم

This reinforces the fact that the so-called "Jahez" was paid for by Ali (May Allah be pleased with him/her) and not by Rasulullah (Peace be upon him).

If the "Jahez" was something important in the Shari'ah, Rasulullah (Peace be upon him) would have certainly given it to all his four daughters. However, the Ahadees do not mention any "Jahez" being given to all his daughters. It is therefore evident that the Shari'ah attaches no significance to the concept of giving "Jahez".

It should also be borne in mind that Ali (May Allah be pleased with him/her) was in the care of Rasulullah sand it was therefore Rasulullahs's duty to see to the marriage and the home of his ward.

Another lesson that we should learn from this incident is that Rasulullah (Peace be upon him) neither gave anything for his son-in-law nor did Ali (May Allah be pleased with him/her) ask Rasulullah (Peace be upon him) for anything. This was the Sunnah practice of Rasulullahs.It is this practice rather than the oppressive practice of "Jahez" that should be implemented. However, it is tragic to note that many Muslims are still adamant to follow the ways of the Hindus. It will not be redundant to reiterate that asking the bride's family for anything is Haraam, whether the asking is done verbally or by hinting.

In his book condemning the custom of "Jahez", Maulana Muhammad Shihaabud Religion Nadwi has mentioned that people who make demands from the bride's party to augment their own luxuries are really stealing from them. They are like thieving parasites, sucking the blood of their relatives.

People who do this and who taunt their daughters-in-law if they did not receive enough "Jahez" should remember that they will have to account for this in the Aakhirah. A woman who asks her son's future in-law to get things for her daughters, for her other sons, for her daughters-in-law and for other members of the family really does not deserve the honourable title of mother which forms part of her description as a mother-in-law. Such people can only be those whose hearts are bereft of fear for Allah Ta'ala. It is indeed unfortunate that they fail to perceive the sin involved in begging. In fact, asking for "Jahez" does not only entail begging, but is also a type of unjust tax. Rasulullah (Peace be upon him) said,

من سئل مسئلة عن ظهر غني أستكثر بها من رضف جهنم قالوا يا رسول

اللّٰه وما ظهر الغني؟ قال عشاء ليلة

"The person who asks for something despite having what he requires is only accumulating the smouldering stones of Jahannam."

When the Companion of the Prophet asked Messenger of Allah (Peace be upon him) what the meaning of "having what he requires" was, he replied, "That he has enough to feed himself for a night."
[Daar Qutni Vol. 2 Pg. 121]

There are many other such Ahadees that make it clear that begging from people is a despised and condemned act in the Shari'ah. What makes matters even worse is that the beggars in this situation actually force people to give them. Those being begged from have no option to refuse because refusal spells either a lifetime of torment for their daughter or her divorce. In fact, there are many people who actually threaten the bride's family in this manner, reminding them that once the fact is publicised that they do not want to pay sufficient "Jahez", no one will propose for any of their daughters in future.

GIVING A GOLD NECKLACE TO THE GROOM'S MOTHER

Another Hindu custom that has crept into Muslim ranks is the attitude that the groom's mother has done a favour to the bride's mother by accepting her daughter into her home. To return the "favour", the bride's mother is expected to buy a gold necklace for the groom's mother. As a result, the poor woman had to beg, borrow or steal the money for this, otherwise she is warned that her name will be spoilt and she will be unable to find husbands for her other daughters. On the other hand, if she obliges, she is assured that her daughter will receive fine treatment and that her other daughters will find matches almost immediately.

Such behaviour is reminiscent of the dark days of ignorance in which the pagan Arabs wallowed in degradation and absurdity. They dreaded having female children and regarded this as a form of disgrace. This is exactly how matters have reverted because many Muslims have adopted the ways of the Hindus who honour sons and look down on daughters.

If you are in an area where this custom is rife, you should remember that your son's mother-in-law will not be happy to part with a gold necklace regardless of how rich she may be. You should therefore never think that it is fine to accept it as a gift because she is happily giving it to you. If you really want to test whether she is giving it happily, tell her that if she does not give you the necklace, you will not retaliate in any manner. Tell her that you will neither harass her daughter nor smear her or her family's name in any way. Add also that if she really feels that she wants to give the necklace, she should give it to her daughter instead. Rest assured that after telling her this, the thankful lady will immediately return home to perform salah as a thanksgiving to Allah Ta'ala and she will also make special du'aa for you for not imposing the tax on her. If her situation is such that she feels obliged to give you the necklace because of social pressure, tell her that if she has so much extra money with her, she may give the necklace privately some months after the wedding without anyone knowing about it. Only time will now tell whether you receive the necklace or not.

If one thinks carefully, one would realise that if anyone deserves a gold necklace as a form of thanks, it is actually the bride's mother who deserves it the most. It was she who invested her money and her priceless time, effort and loves to ensure that her daughter one day becomes capable of being the gem of another person's home. She bore the girl in her womb with great difficulty and then fed and cared for her for many long years. She taught her daughter everything she needed to know to care for her husband and children. After marriage, she has entrusted her precious daughter with her new family and has to bear the pains of separation after so many years of close association. For her sacrifices, she more than deserves even the most jewels on earth.

When it is not permissible for the groom to demand things from his in-laws, how can it be permissible for his mother to do so?

Quoting from canonical books like "Bahrur Ra'iq" and "Shami", the famous book "Fatawa Aalamgeri" has mentioned that if the bride's parents take any money from the groom when he takes their daughter home as his wife, he is at liberty to take the money back because this is a form of bribery. Such money is Haraam even though it is given with a smiling face. This practice has become common in certain area of the Muslim world. However, if it is Haraam for the bride's party to take anything from the groom, it will be even worse if the groom's party take from the bride's family. Demanding the "Jahez" entails oppressive taxation as well as blackmail because the girl is threatened with divorce or unending taunts.

Another important factor to consider is that if the Shari'ah attached importance to giving something to the groom's mother, Rasulullah (Peace be upon him) would have certainly given something to Ali (May Allah be pleased with him)'s mother, whose name was Fatima (May Allah be pleased with him/her) bint Asad (May Allah be pleased with him/her). Neither did she ask for anything, nor was anything given to her. Despite this, she bore no ill-feelings towards her daughter-in -law.

May Allah Ta'ala guide all mothers-in-law to understand the true nature of the Shari'ah. To rid society of this evil, it is also necessary to wage Jihaad against this practice so that women can breath a sigh of relief when they have to get their daughters married.

FEEDING THE BRIDE'S IN-LAWS

No hadith mentions anything about Rasulullah (Peace be upon him) feeding the families of any of his sons-in-law. The Ahadees also do not mention that the responsibility of hosting a Waleema is that of the bride's father. However, the Ahadees do make it clear that the expense of the Waleema celebration has to be borne by the groom.

It is therefore necessary forms to break away from the un-Islamic custom of hosting wedding ceremonies at the expense of the bride's father. You should not host such ceremonies and you should also encourage others to do the same especially if you have an influence over them. Encourage people to rather spend the money on the poor and needy or to at least give it to their daughter in the form of cash, jewellery, property, etc.

Although Rasulullah (Peace be upon him)got four of his daughter married and the Companion of the Prophet y also got their daughters married, there is no proof in any hadith that they hosted functions where the groom's family were fed. Neither did the groom's family ask for such a function nor did the bride's family attach any significance to the act. If this was the practice of Rasulullah (Peace be upon him)and his illustrious Companion of the Prophet, why should today's Muslims demand to do things as the Kuffaar do? Not only do people insist that the groom and his immediately family should be invited to a wedding, but they also go to the extreme of demanding that an additional five hundred to a thousand people should also be invited. Is this not a sophisticated way of begging for food? Is this not wastage of someone's life savings? Is this not opening the door to years of financial struggle for a mere day's entertainment?

One will wonder why there is not a single person from among the five hundred or thousand guests who will oppose the function when they know well that their host is unable to afford the celebration. If the host is a wealthy person, he should realise that by hosting an extravagant feast, he is making life difficult for the poor because they will be forced to either follow his example or to beat it. In this manner, he will be a cause of delaying many marriages, if not preventing them altogether. If there was any significance in hosting a wedding, Rasulullah (Peace be upon him) and the Companion of the Prophet would have certainly set the example. However, it appears as if Muslims prefer following the ways of others and destroying the Sunnah of our beloved Rasulullah (Peace be upon him).

The Marriage and Waleema According to the Sunnah

When the groom is hosting a Walema, it is not necessary for him to serve meat dishes. Even something as simple as dates and juice will suffice because the purpose of the Waleema is to express one's gratitude to Allah Ta'ala. The Ahadees make it clear that a marriage should be as simple as possible and according to what a person can afford. This is necessary because marriage signifies the building of a home and not the destruction of a home (which is the case when people are forced to cater beyond their means).

The manner in which Rasulullahs married the queen of Jannah Fatima (May Allah be pleased with him/her) is a lesson for the world. Ummu Salma (May Allah be pleased with him/her) and Ayesha (May Allah be pleased with him/her) both report that Rasulullah (Peace be upon him) asked the two of them to prepare Fatima (May Allah be pleased with him/her) and take her to her husband Ali (May Allah be pleased with him/her). Consequently, the two of them went to the house where Fatima (May Allah be pleased with him/her) was to reside and spread the soft sand of "Bat'haa" on the ground so that their bedding may be spread on soft ground. They also placed two pillows there, which they personally filled with the bark of a date palm. For the Waleema, they served dates, water and a sweet drink prepared from dates to the people present. When this was over, they placed a stick in the couple's room so that they could hang their clothing or a water bag on it. After narrating this, they added that they never saw a marriage better than that of Fatima (May Allah be pleased with him/her)

[Ibn Majah Pg. 616]

This was the home and marriage of the woman whom Rasulullah (Peace be upon him) described as the queen of Jannah. It was strikingly simple and without stress. However, we have burdened ourselves with the difficulty of hosting elaborate functions, making life difficult for everyone else. Because marriage is one of the necessities of life, it ought to be kept extremely simple so that every person may find it easy.

It is therefore quite obvious that the marriage of Fatima (May Allah be pleased with him/her) did not feature any elaborate feasts coupled with an expensive bridal suite in silk and velvet. The food and the preparation were most simple so that every member of the Ummah until Qiyamah may find it easy to emulate. However, one will scarcely find people today who are prepared to emulate the simplicity of Rasulullahs's life. Instead of being proud to emulate his lifestyle, many wretched people actually feel ashamed to do so. One should bear in mind that if Rasulullah (Peace be upon him) wanted to host an elaborate wedding ceremony for his youngest daughter, he could have easily done so. However, he chose the simplest route for the convenience of his Ummah; so that they do not have to tire themselves in this effort and rather concentrate their wealth and efforts in the propagation of the Deen. It is rather foolish of Muslims to opt for the difficult ways of the Kuffaar instead of the easy way of life that Rasulullah (Peace be upon him) lived.

It is obvious that the pomp and extravagance with which many Muslims host wedding functions is all done for name and show. Allah Ta'ala and His Rasul (Peace be upon him) despise any action done for the purpose of show. Concerning those who behave extravagantly (obviously for show), Allah Ta'alasays in the Quran, "Without doubt, the extravagant ones are the brothers of the shayateen. " When Allah Ta'ala grants a person wealth, this wealth is a test for him and on the Day of Qiyamah, Allah Ta'ala will question him about the avenues in which he spent this wealth. One's wealth should be spend only as the Shari'ah prescribes.

Squandering money on elaborate wedding ceremonies is not condemned only in the eyes of the Shari'ah, but even common society realises that this is an evil and a great wastage. Muslims should realise that it (Peace be upon him) futile to destroy the lives of people merely for a day's frolicking. It is like someone burning the home of another to ashes merely to build a house of his own. He may enjoy the house very much, but will soon have to wake up to reality and find that someone else is burning down his house to build one of his own.

It is therefore the responsibility of every Muslim to follow the lifestyle of Rasulullah (Peace be upon him) and to encourage the world to do the same so that he rot and evils invading society are quickly weeded out. In fact, it has always been the Muslims who have been responsible for bringing the world out of darkness and into the light. The purpose of a Muslim in this world is not to frolic in its pleasures and vanities. What the world needs is for the Muslim Ummah to rise to the occasion and wage Jihaad against the foolish customs and traditions that are plaguing people and making their lives a misery.

TO SUMMARISE

The blessed lifestyle of Rasulullah (Peace be upon him) is long calling to the Muslims, telling them to forsake their false vanities and to adopt the pure practices of Rasulullah (Peace be upon him) because this will ensure their success in both worlds. However, if they insist on following the customs of others, they should understand that nothing will be able to check their downfall. One can either be the slave of Allah Ta'ala or the slave of ignorant customs. If women take the initiative of eradicating these customs from their lives, they can do so quite effectively and will earn tremendous rewards from Allah Ta'ala.

THE RIGHTS WIVES OWE TO THEIR HUSBANDS

1. Obey all his instructions as long as they do not contravene the injunctions of the Shari'ah. Never neglect serving him and always do things that please him if these do not violate the laws of the Shari'ah.
2. Never ask him for more than he can afford.
3. Never allow anyone to enter the house without your husband's permission.
4. Never spend any of his wealth without his permission.
5. Do not leave the house without his permission.
6. Do not observe Nafl (optional) fasts without his permission.
7. When he calls you to bed for intercourse, do not refuse without a valid Shar'ee excuse.

8. Never look down on your husband because of his poverty, nationality, looks, lack of knowledge or for any other reason.
9. Respectfully correct him if you notice him doing anything contrary to the Shari'ah.
10. Never call him by his name because this entails disrespect.
11. Never complain about him to anyone.
12. Never speak to him disrespectfully.
13. Never behave harshly with his relatives because this will hurt him. This applies especially to his parents. Treat them respectfully and kindly.

Parting Advice for the Bride

Remember that marriage is the natural and most honourable course for every woman to take. If there was any better course to follow, then the pure daughter of Abu Bakr (May Allah be pleased with him/her) would have followed it. In fact, the daughter of the best of mankind would have also followed that better course. However, they all took the route of marriage, thereby setting an example for the rest of mankind. Their submission and obedience to their husbands is a source of pride for every Muslim woman and whoever follows their example will surely be treading the path to salvation.

Therefore, the tears you shed upon departure should be tears of joy instead of tears of grief. Blessed are the women who follow the sterling examples of Ayesha (May Allah be pleased with her) and Fatima (May Allah be pleased with her. Blessed also are their husband and their fathers. Marriage is no calamity or punishment but it is a great form of Ibaadah by which a person can attain the pleasure of Allah Ta'ala. Rasulullah (Peace be upon him)said,

النكاح سنة الأنبياء

That marriage was the practice of all the Ambiya (Peace be upon them) because the Ambiya hwere the beloved of Allah Ta'ala, whoever follows in their footsteps must also become Allah Ta'ala's beloved.

Abdullah bin Abbas (May Allah be pleased with him/her) has narrated that Messenger of Allah (Peace be upon him) said,

عن إبن عباس قال قال رسول الله ﷺ لم ير للمتحابين مثل النكاح.

(مشكوة ص ۲۶۸ بحواله ابن ماجه)

"You will not see anything better for two lovers than marriage."

There are various reasons for love to exist between people just as there are various reasons for enmity. This hadith tells us that the factor which best causes hearts to bond is marriage. When a couple marry and devote themselves to each other, the bond of love that is created between them becomes so great that the two become inseparable even though they may be from different nationalities and different cultures."

There are many people who claim to be lovers and who live together. Their association is maintained for ulterior motives even though they claim that it is love that had united them. Once the ulterior motives are removed, they drift very far apart and separate from each other. In fact, their reluctance to marry proves the insincerity of their love.

The objective of marriage is not merely the satiation of carnal passions. It is a commitment to live your life with your spouse and it multiplies a person's status as a man or a woman. After marriage, a man earns the respectable status of being a husband and a father, while his wife is the queen of her home. Each partner becomes a source of comfort and happiness for each other, something that would never have been achieved without marriage. In addition to this, the marriage bonds the families of each partner leading to many social benefits for all concerned. Together with her commitment to make her marriage work, a woman's sacrifice by leaving her homer and family is incentive enough for her to devote herself to the marriage, thereby ensuring the sound and healthy upbringing of her children.

THE DU'AA FOR A MARRIED COUPLE

بارك اللّٰه لك وبارك اللّٰه عليكما وجمع بينكما في خير

(سنن أربعة، إبن حبان، حاكم عن أبي هريرة ، حصن حصين ص ٢٢٨)

"May Allah Ta'ala destine a blessed life for you, may He bless both of you and unite you two with prosperity."

In addition to the above du'aa, the following du'aas should also be made for the couple:

"O Allah Ta'ala! This man and woman have united in marriage and have accepted the responsibility that has been placed on the shoulders of so many before them. This they have undertaken for Your pleasure and following the practice of Your beloved slaves. O Allah! Ta'ala unite their hearts with true love as You had united the hearts of their ancestors Adam (Peace be upon him) and Hawwa (Peace be upon her).

O Allah Ta'ala! Through the blessings of all Your pious servants who have treaded the same path, allow this couple to pass through the trials of life and keep them steadfast through all the adversities that may afflict them. Safeguard them from all evils that may stealthily creep into their souls. Pave the way for them in this world and grant them the best in the Aakhirah. Guide them to emulate the examples that Messenger of Allah, Khadeja (May Allah be pleased with her) and Ayesha (May Allah be pleased with her) set and protect them from the evils of colloquial customs, sins and Bid'ah.

O Allah Ta'ala! Entrench the love for Your Religion deep within their hearts and allow them to serve Your Religion in their youth and even when they are passing the various stages of old-age. When they have married their children as You desire and have started growing white hairs, keep the flame of love burning brightly within their hearts. Even then, keep them steadfast as ambassadors of Your Religion so that they can be instrumental in bringing Your Religion alive in the lives of mankind.

O Allah Ta'ala! Safeguard them as well as their progeny from present and future evils and deceptions regardless of how innocent these may appear to people. Keep their feet from slipping even during the terrible times that Your Prophet (Peace be upon him) predicted; when people will openly ridicule Your Book and Your Religion and when people will lose their Imaan overnight. Keep the armour of Islam on their bodies as long as they remain alive and allow them to pass on from this world wearing the crown of Imaan. Fill their hearts with love for You and make them among those who eagerly await their meeting with You. When they are presented for reckoning on the Plains of Resurrection, do not allow them to be disgraced in front of humanity.

﴿ يَا أَيُّهَا الَّذِينَ آمَنُوا اتَّقُوا اللَّهَ حَقَّ تُقَاتِهِ وَلَا تَمُوتُنَّ إِلَّا وَأَنْتُمْ مُسْلِمُونَ ﴾

{آل عمران: ١٠٢}

O Allah Ta'ala! Even if the world turns traitor, allow us all to remain loyal to Your Religion until our deaths and allow us all to enter Jannah. O Allah Ta'ala! Accept this du'aa of ours. Aameen.

Reply Clearly

Many domestic disputes will be effectively averted if women learnt to express themselves clearly and convincingly. They should explicitly say whatever is in their hearts so that misunderstandings are avoided. We shall present a few guidelines for your benefit that will Insha Allah Ta'ala assist you in a great deal when conversing with your husband and others as well.

1. When your husband asks you a question, do your best to understand what he intends knowing from you before replying.
2. Reply only to the question he asks without adding anything extra. The harm of adding to your reply is that arguments may spring from the additional information and that you may unintentionally disclose a fault of yours, leading to him losing confidence in you. A wise person once said, "Every human errs. However, the wise person is he who successfully conceals his errors while the fool is he who discloses his own errors." It is therefore necessary for you to neither leave an important detail unspoken nor to add more to what has already answered the question.

For example, your husband tells you to make some custard for the night because he is expecting guests in the evening. However, you discover that you have no custard and are unable to get it from anywhere else. Because you understood that your husband's intention was to entertain his guests, you will make something else to serve the purpose. This may be some pudding, cake, etc. Therefore, when the evening arrives and he asks if the custard is ready, you will say, "I could not make the custard but made some pudding instead." He will thank you heartily and feel relieved. However, the incorrect approach will be to not to make anything, thinking that he asked for custard and you were unable to comply because you did not have the means. This will obviously lead to an argument with disastrous consequences.

Another approach to such a situation is to at least inform your husband well before time about your inability to comply with his request. In this manner, he will suggest an alternative or he may buy something like ice-cream to serve to his guests. Whatever the case, you should never wait for your husband to ask you about developments before addressing the problem. Remember that insignificant matters often spark the most serious disputes. If you wait until he arrives home before informing him of the situation, he will find it extremely difficult to go out of the house again to buy something that you need and this will ignite further problems.

If matters are so bad that you were unable to comply with his request until he returned and were unable to inform him earlier, you should perform two Rakaahs salah and ask Allah Ta'ala to mend the situation. When he arrives, gently apologise for not doing as he asked. May Allah Ta'ala guide all Muslim women to always do what is correct. *Aameen.*

Have Mercy on Your Children

A common failing among many women is that they do not respond immediately when their husbands call for them. If a woman wants to earn the pleasure and du'aas of her husband, she should respond as soon as he calls for her. She should not delay in answering with the intention that he will do the work himself. For example, if the husband returns tired from work, immediately lies down to rest and then calls for his wife, she will immediately realise that he wants her to do something minor such as adjusting the speed of the fan, bringing him a glass of water or something else that he can do by himself. She therefore remains silent when he calls with the intention that he should realise that she is busy doing something else and cannot hear him. As a result, he will be forced to do the work himself.

It is such behaviour that often leads to arguments. What aggravates such situations is when the wife responds to the call with an insolent remark such as "I am busy ironing your clothing, you know!" or "Don't you realise that I am busy preparing your supper!"

If you wish to attain your husband's undying love, you will have to ensure that your husband's heart is never tainted with any ill-feelings towards you. You should never give him the opportunity to say that your mother had not taught you well enough or that you cannot compare with the wives of his friends or other women. It is therefore best for you to either stop your work immediately when he calls or you should inform him that you are busy before you start so that he may know that you are busy. For example, you may ask him whether he wants his meals immediately or a little later because you need to perform your Isha salah. Employing a bit of diplomacy is always helpful and will ensure a happy marriage. Among the benefits of deliberated such diplomacy are:

1. Unnecessary disputes will be avoided.
2. He will not burn your heart by comparing you with other women but he will appreciate everything you do for him.
3. You will have no fear that your neighbours or in-laws will hear his shouting and then make a meal of their gossip about you.
4. You will always benefit from the du'aas of your husband both in your lifetime as well as after your death. Your children will also grow up to be pious, capable and resourceful, thereby enabling them to lead their lives successfully.
5. The greatest benefit of such behaviour is that your children will be saved from suffering complexes as a result of the incessant arguments in their home. Enjoying a life of peace and goodwill, they will develop many sterling qualities such as good self-esteem, courage and determination. When a child lives in a home where arguments are common, she will grow up either feeling that her mother is incapable or that her father is a tyrant. She will be plagued with the idea that if her father is always making her mother cry, how will he be able to listen to her? The child's capabilities will also be stifled because she will be living with a mother who is constantly scared of her mother-in-law or sisters-in- law.

By the grace of Allah Ta'ala, I have had the opportunity to teach in both state and private schools and Madrasahs. I have encountered children of all types and I have dealt with them both as an educationalist and a counsellor. In my experiences with children whose homes are the battlefield of their parents, I have noticed the following:

They fail their grades very often.

They are often absent from classes.

They are extremely silent and unreceptive in class.

They are reluctant to participate in games and other activities with other children.

They are unable to answer questions despite knowing the answers.

Such children are the victims of quarrelling couples. The vision of the father slapping the mother and the sound of the mother's sobbing are always in the child's mind. Such a child can never match the confident and happy children in her class.

You should therefore take pity on your innocent children and spare them the grief of your disputes with your husband. Do not give your husband the opportunity to get angry with you. If he does get angry on some account, remain silent and do not provoke a further argument. For the sake of the children you should rather apologise even if he is at fault and make an attempt to change the subject.

May Allah Ta'ala guide all Muslim women to be able to run their homes efficiently without giving anyone an excuse to point a finger at them. *Aameen.*

An Estranged Wife's Letter to her Husband

It was a Friday night and father and brother were gone out to the weekly Friday night gathering at the Masjid. The only man in the house was my brother Bilal because of his studies at the Daarul Uloom. There was no end to my uneasiness and anxiety that night as I lay down to sleep with a disturbed mind. As I fell asleep, I dreamt that Qiyamah had taken place and everyone was being raised from the ground. Everyone was taken to the Plain of Resurrection and they were all concerned with the accounts of their deeds that were due from them.

When I looked to my right, I saw many people entering splendid palaces without any reckoning. They entered beautiful gardens that were filled with the most colourful and exquisite flowers. There was every conceivable pleasure to be found there and a cool breeze blew for them. the men and women entering there were exuberant and carefree. I also hastened to follow them.

As I was about to enter the gate, the gatekeeper stopped me and asked for my entry permit. Surprised, I asked him what ticket he meant. He told me that if I had no permit, I would have to return to the queue of people awaiting their reckoning. Throwing my hands up in the air, I asked him how much the permit would cost. He said, "Respected lady! This permit cannot be bought with money." When I asked him how I could get one, he replied, "For Muslim men, their permit is the pleasure of their parents and for Muslim women it is the pleasure of their husbands. Without this permit, none can enter this Jannah."

"Will the pleasure of my parents not suffice?" I asked him with hope brimming in my heart as I looked at him. Breathing a sigh, he replied, "I am sorry. A married woman has to carry the permit of her husband's pleasure." Despondent, I stared with envy at all the women entering without reckoning. Among them were women whom I recognised, such as my cousins and friends, all of them entering happily with their little children. I felt so embarrassed that I wished that the ground would swallow me up.

Standing there ashamed of myself, some of my friends took pity on me and called me to enter with them. When I did not respond to their call, they came to fetch me. However, when they saw that I did not have the permit of my husband's pleasure, they turned away from me in disappointment. My friend Salma was always a straightforward person. When she saw me like this, she said, "Did we not tell you that the life of the world is very short and that you should keep your husband happy so that you would not have any regrets after death? You did not listen to your husband when he told you not to walk about without Hijaab and not to take videos at weddings. You took no heed when he told you that you should stop missing your salahs and that you should stop preventing him from going out in Allah Ta'ala 's path without an excuse."

I bitterly regretted my deeds and wished that I also had the permit of my husband's pleasure so that could enjoy the bounties of Jannah with the others. My thoughts were interrupted by voices shouting, "Make way! Move out of the way!" I turned to see that a woman was arriving on a conveyance and that her entourage and escort were clearing the way ahead for her. As she arrived at the gate of Jannah, even the gatekeeper greeted her with great respect and honour. When she has dismounted and entered, I asked the gatekeeper who the lady was. He replied, "This lady loved her husband very much and was so obedient to him that he always made du'a for her. She has attained this high status even though she lived with her husband for only eight years."

Upon hearing this reply of the gatekeeper, I began to reflect over my married life. I was at loggerheads with my husband for even the most insignificant matters. I had even left him to come to my parents home, thinking that I am not his slave and that if he does not care me, I will not care for him either. I always thought that I do not need him when my parents can ably look after me. Whereas other women preferred living under their husband's authority, I could not even bear the thought of it. My soul would emerge from my body if I ever heard talk of a woman being subservient to her husband. The times when women served men have passed by. However, although the snake has slithered away, the tracks are still present. I felt that men ought to open their eyes and ears to take a lesson from Europe and America. These were all my misguided thoughts, which I seriously put to question when the gatekeeper told me about the woman who had received such great honour. I was suddenly overcome with envy for her and my emotions were beyond control. I wished that I had also dutifully served my husband as she did so that I could also share her honour. I could bear this no longer and gave a loud scream.

Hearing my scream, my mother and our little sons woke up with a shock. Mother was flustered and asked me what the matter was. Seeing me sit up erect and shivering, mother rushed to my bed and took my head to her chest to comfort me. What could I tell her? As I looked around the room, I saw neither the Day of Qiyamah, nor the beautiful spectacle of Jannah or the gatekeeper. My mother comforted me by telling me that nightmares are from Shaytaan and that I should not worry about them because they will have no effect on my life. I complied as she bade me to sleep, but my mind was now in frenzy. It was not long before I had returned to the realm of dreams.

In another dream, I saw that the scene was set for a wedding to take place. There I saw you looking quite happy as the bridegroom. I ran to you and angrily grabbed hold of your hand asking, "What is happening here?" However, without even looking at me, you coldly shoved me aside. With tears in my eyes and a shattered heart, I returned to my parents home with your words ringing in my ears as you said, "You have caused me tremendous grief and heartache, forcing me to consider remarrying. Before marrying you I was actively serving the Deen, reciting Quran regularly, making Dhikr, etc. However, since you entered my life I have been unable to do this properly." Unable to bear this, I again gave a loud scream and sat upright in my bed.

Although mother consoled my by telling me that matters between you and I were not so bad that you would leave me to marry another woman, I was still not convinced. She again bade me to sleep, but the two dreams had forbidden sleep for me. They had changed the course of my life. I resolved not to disobey you in future. As I seriously considered your complaints against me, I begged Allah Ta'ala for forgiveness. Whereas I was under the impression that you were always pandering to the wishes of your mother and sisters, you maintained that it was I who was causing you grief. After doing some introspection, I realised that I am at fault.

I regretted that you often had to eat take-away foods because I rarely cooked a good meal for you. Whenever you invited people home for meals, you always had to suffer the embarrassment of serving them sloppy dishes. Whereas I always blamed you and your family for having extravagant tastes, I failed to realise that I was at fault for not even making an effort to learn good cooking skills. Although I now became angry with my mother and sisters for not pointing these things out to me, I have also realised that I cannot really blame them because whenever there was a problem, I always put the blame on you without telling them the reason for your anger.

It then occurred to me that your hints about me not maintaining my beauty were spot-on target. I now realised that I have been neglecting myself and rarely beautify myself for you. In addition to this, I also neglect our two children, failing to keep them clean and presentable. They therefore look shabby and unkempt when their father sees them, so you cannot appreciate their appearance either.

I also admit that the times are too often when I behave coldly towards you. I beg your forgiveness for not responding to your sexual advances at times and then waking the children up to throw a spanner in the works. With my mind entangled in such thoughts, I hastily got up to make wudhu and perform Tahajjud salah, begging Allah Ta'ala for forgiveness. The AHadees of Prophet (Peace be upon him) began flooding my mind at that point.

"If I were to command anyone to prostrate to another (human) I would have certainly commanded a wife to prostrate to her husband."

"The angels curse the wife who does not respond when her husband calls her to bed and he spends the night angry with her.

"There are three categories of people whose salah and every good deed is not accepted. The three are: (1) The slave who escapes from his/her master, (2) the woman whose husband is displeased with her and (3) the person who is drunk until he becomes sober."

Because the time of Tahajjud is a time when prayers are accepted, I prayed to Allah Ta'ala to forgive me.

O my beloved husband! Think of all the problems I have given you thusfar as a bad dream and forget it all. Reality is what I have written I this letter. I am now your devoted slave and regret all my previous mistakes. Just as Allah Ta'ala forgives His slaves, you also forgive me and do not deprive me of your large heartedness. Forgive me for coming to my parent's home against your wishes. I am prepared to return home as soon as you would permit me to. Remember that I am always yours.

The children are also missing you terribly and cannot wait to see you again. In conclusion I would like to add that Insha Allah Ta'ala you will never again have cause to be displeased with me in future.

Yours truly,
Your loving wife
XYZ.

THE HUSBAND'S REPLY

No sooner had the husband read his wife's letter when he replied:

My beloved wife your letter reached me after a while. All I can say is that your changed attitude can only be the results of your father's or my father's sincere du'as. I am pleasantly surprised by what you have written and can only thank Allah Ta'ala for it.

Although some time has passed, you have now realised your errors. I was not upset only because you were disobedient to me, but you were also disobedient to Allah Ta'ala and His Rasule. The hurt I felt because of your behaviour is already healing and the future will only do it good. Allah Ta'ala is witness to the fact that my heart is filled with love for you. With the grace of Allah Ta'ala, you have a pious father who will assure you that I have no other woman besides you in my heart. I love you deeply and have definitely forgiven you for your errors.

If the past was a bad dream, then your sweet words and new resolve have dispelled all thoughts of past dreams. I am prepared to forget the past and work for our future. You obviously need no permission to return home because you had none to leave in the first place. This is your home and you are the queen. You may return whenever you please.

It is only Allah Ta'ala Who has made you realise that without pleasing Him, you cannot hope to please anyone else. By performing all your salahs, Allah Ta'ala will be pleased with you and He will ensure that I am also pleased. To keep Allah Ta'ala pleased, we should also avoid weddings and other functions where the laws of Allah Ta'ala are violated. Convey my love and kisses to the children.

Yours truly,

THE STORY AFTERWARDS

Relating her story afterwards, the lady says, "When I returned to my husband, I resolved to be the first to wake up every morning and the last to sleep at night to ensure that my kingdom is in order. The same house that was once a battlefield transformed into a garden of bliss and contentment. Our home now generates an atmosphere of righteousness and is a model for others to emulate. My husband finds happiness whenever he enters the door and has no need to tell me what to do. Everything gets done on time and he is always making du'a for me, his loyal servant. By Allah Ta'ala's grace, we have an abundance of everything we need and people are always praying that our relationship goes from strength to strength. The past has been forgotten.

The two dreams have really transformed my life and people are now full of praises for me instead of insults. The women of the neighbourhood now ask me to give them advice. It is a fact that when a woman practises Islam and treats her husband well, she will become a shining beacon for others to follow. Not only will she have success in this world, but in the Aakhirah as well."

My Advice to My Sisters

"You have read my story. Based on my experiences, I would like to advise my Muslim sisters that she controls the character, the health and the happiness of not only her husband, but her children as well. Every woman should treat her husband as a new bride would and she should always be prepared to make sacrifices for him. She should be his comforting companion and his heroine who rescues him from all worries and anxiety. Like a kind teacher, she should also be there to lovingly protect him from sin.

Remember that a man is not the slave of a beautiful face, but easily becomes the slave of an obedient wife who strives to please him. An obedient wife will capture her husband's heart, thereby having her wishes addressed without even asking. This is the key to her happiness as well.

Another piece of advice to my sisters is that they should always bear in mind the hadith of Prophet (Peace be upon him) that states تحادوأتحابو

"Exchange gifts with each other, you will love each other."

Every wife should therefore buy gifts for her husband. If she is unable to do this, she should get her father or brother to buy it and give it to him as a gift from them. Exchanging gifts develops love and removes malice from the heart.

My final advice is that a wife should ensure that all her domestic chores are complete before her husband returns home from work. This will impress him and win his heart. It is because many women are negligent of this that they have problems with their husbands."

AN EXAMINATION PAPER

Read each question carefully at least three times. If your answer is yes, give yourself five points. Thereafter, add them up to see whether you are a good wife or not. The sum of your points will give you a percentage so that you can gauge your position on a scale of a hundred.

1. Are you awake before your husband and children every morning, encouraging the boys to proceed to the Masjid for the Fajr salah?
2. Do you ensure that your husband's clothes for the next day are ready for him and that everything else he needs for the day are kept together to save him the inconvenience of searching for them?
3. Do you ensure that everything is in order for your husband when he proceeds on a journey; that his bags are packed and that he has all the necessary travel documents, etc?
4. Do you ensure that your children are attending their school and Madrasah classes regularly and that they are completing their homework daily?
5. Do you prepare dishes that your husband likes even though you do not like it or you find it difficult to prepare?
6. Do you encourage your husband to bring his guests home for meals so that he does not feel difficult to ask you to prepare meals for them?
7. Do you ensure that you beautify yourself when he is at home?
8. When he returns from work, do you have something pleasant waiting for him such as some juice or even plain water so that his frustration can be calmed? By doing this, he will feel that there is someone for him after all the trouble he may have experienced at work.
9. If your husband has to tell you that he is inviting his mother or his sisters over for meals and that he is going to give them Zam Zam Publishers latest book releases as a gift, will you welcome the idea with a happy face?
10. When he is sleeping during the day or busy doing something important, do you keep the children occupied so that they do not disturb him?
11. When the children do something dangerous or foolish, do you shout and scream at them or do you rather place your hand lovingly on their heads and explain the wrong to them so that the impression lasts with them that you are concerned about them and not only interested in

venting your anger?

12. When your husband is angry, do you apologise and seek forgiveness even though the fault is not yours?
13. When your husband calls for you once, do you ensure that he does not have to repeat himself?
14. When you are unable to comply with a request he makes, do you inform him beforehand so that he does not learn about it only after asking? For example, if he wants a certain dish prepared and you were unable to prepare it for some good reason, will you tell him this only after he asks for it when sitting down to eat or well before time?
15. Do you place your hand on your children's heads and make du'as for them such as "Abdullah! May Allah Ta'ala make you a Haafidh and an Aalim" or "O Faatima! May Allah Ta'ala use you for the service of His Deen", etc? (Remember that you should never curse your children because this will deprive them of honour and status in people's eyes).
16. When you notice a fault in your husband (such as his failure to tend to the nurturing of the children), do you speak to him kindly instead of rebuking him and do you choose the correct times to speak to him?
17. When you are expecting, do you ensure that you avoid all sins (such as watching television) so that the unborn child is not adversely affected by the spiritual ill effects of sins? (Remember that the good deeds you carry out during this period will have a positive effect on the child by making him/her a good Muslim who will be a valuable asset to the Ummah).
18. When buying toys for your children, do you ensure that the toys are also educational and that they are free of pictures of animate objects? (Remember that the angels of mercy do not enter homes in which pictures of animate objects are displayed).
19. Do you abstain from backbiting and lying about your sisters-in-law (husband's brothers' wives) to earn nearness to your mother-in-law and your other sisters-in-law (your husband's sisters)? (Remember that a person with whom Allah Ta'ala is displeased will not have contentment even though she has all the luxuries of life. Jealousy, carrying tales, lying and making others jealous of one are sins that attract Allah Ta'ala's wrath).
20. (A) Do you respond to your husband's sexual advances?

(B) Do you know who curses the woman who refuses to fulfil her husband's sexual desires without good reason? (Each question here carries 2.5 points).

You now have an idea of where you stand in relation to the ideal wife. If you have done well, make du'a to Allah Ta'ala to keep you steadfast and always improving. Also make du'a to Allah Ta'ala to create such sterling qualities in all Muslim wives. If you have faired miserably in this examination, remember that men actually seek protection from the likes of yourself because you cause them to age before their time. You should therefore resolve to mend your ways and to inculcate the qualities of a good wife. Also make sincere du'a to Allah Ta'ala to assist you with this and to make you among the fortunate women about whom Messenger of Allah (Peace be upon him) gave the glad tidings of entering Jannah.

The Last Will and Testament of a Muslim

The Ahadees have emphasised the necessity of having one's will written especially if a person has missed salahs in her lifetime, has missed her Hajj when it was Fardh on her or when she owes zakaah. When a Muslim fails to write a will under these circumstances, she will be guilty of a sin. The evil of this sin will prevail as long as she does no write the will. You should consult the more detailed books of Islamic jurisprudence to learn the method of writing your last will and testament.

A GOOD HUSBAND'S PARTING WORDS TO HIS WIFE

One of Islam's leading warriors was the Turkish general Anwar Pasha. He devoted his entire life to fighting the enemies of Islam and was blessed with martyrdom while fighting the Bolshevik Russians. A day before his martyrdom, he wrote an affectionate letter to his wife the princess Bakhiyya. The letter was published in Turkish newspapers and was first translated in Indian newspapers on 22 April 1923. The letter contains many lessons and advices for every Muslim. It reads as follows:

To Bakhiyya, my lifelong companion and my source of happiness

Allah Ta'ala is your most Honoured and Esteemed Protector. Your last letter to me is now in front of me. Rest assured, this letter will always remain close to my heart. Although I cannot see you, I can visualise your delicate fingers writing every word; the same fingers that so gently caressed my head when we were together. My eyes are often filled with a vision of your beautiful face in the haze of my tent.

Sadly, your letter suggests that I have forgotten you and have no affection for you anymore. You say that I have broken your heart which is brimming with love merely to play with fire and blood in this far-off land. You say that I have forsaken a lonesome woman who has to spend the nights counting the stars while yearning for my companionship. You say that I love war and swords. However, when writing these words which were obviously motivated by true love, you had no idea of the deep wound it would inflict on my heart. How will I ever be able to convince you that I love nothing in the world more than I love you. You are the goal of all my love. I have loved none besides you because it was you who stole my heart. Then why did I leave you? You may certainly ask this question, my love.

Listen with care! I have not left you in search of wealth and property. Contrary to what my enemies claim, I have also not left you to consolidate my throne. I have left you only because my duty to Allah Ta'ala has brought me here. There is nothing superior to fighting Jihaad in the path of Allah Ta'ala. Jihaad is that great deed the intention of which makes one worthy of Jannatul Firdous. With the grace of Allah Ta'ala, I have not only made the intention of fighting in Jihaad, but I am currently engaged in the same.

My separation from you is the single greatest barrier to my resolve, but this makes me extremely happy because my love for you is proving to be the greatest test of my resolve. I am grateful to Allah Ta'ala for granting me the ability to successfully pass this test by giving precedence to His command and to my love for Him over my personal desires. You should be happy and thankful to Allah Ta'ala that your husband has sacrificed his love for you for the love of Allah Ta'ala.

Although Jihaad with the sword is not compulsory for you, you are still not exempt from Jihaad. In fact, no Muslim male or female is exempt from Jihaad. Your Jihaad is to give precedence to your love for Allah Ta'ala over other desires and over your love for everything else. Together with your love for your husband, you should also develop your love for Him.

Remember that you should never make du'a for your husband to return from Jihaad safely to your lap because this would be selfish. Allah Ta'ala will not be pleased with this. Rather make du'a that Allah Ta'ala should accept your husband's efforts in Jihaad. Make du'a that Allah Ta'ala should either allow him to return victorious or allow the cup of martyrdom to be taken to his lips; the lips that were never polluted with alcohol but always remain moist with the recitation of the Quran and the Dhikr of Allah Ta'ala.

My beloved Bakhiyya! How dear will the moment be when this head which you praised will be separated from the neck. Anwar's greatest desire is to be martyred and raised with Khaalid bin Waleed (May Allah be pleased with him/her) on the Day of Qiyamah. This life is one of a few days and death is inevitable. How can one then fear death? If death is a certainly, why should a person die lying on his bed? Martyrdom is not death but life, an everlasting life!

Dearest Bakhiyya! Listen to my last bequest. After I am martyred I want you to marry your brother-in-law Noori Pasha because he is the closest person to me after you. I desire that after my departure to the Hereafter, he should be the one to loyally serve you.

My second bequest is that you inform all your children about my life and send them all out in Jihaad to defend Islam and their country. I shall be very offended with you in Jannah if you fail to do this.
My third bequest is that you should always treat Mustafa Kamal Pasha well. Assist him in every possible manner because Allah Ta'ala has placed the salvation of the nation in his hands.

I now bid you farewell, my beloved Bakhiyya. I do not know why my heart tells me that I shall not be writing another letter to you after this one. How strange will it be if I am martyred tomorrow; I exhort you to be patient. Instead of being grieved, rejoice over the fact that I was of service to the cause of my Allah Ta'ala.

Bakhiyya, I shall have to go now. In my mind, I am embracing you now.

Insha Allah Ta'ala, we shall meet in Jannah and shall never be again separated.

Yours Anwar

This letter has been extracted from pages 127 to 130 of the book "Turkaan Ahraar", printed in Lahore. It should be borne in mind that at the time when the letter was written, Mustafa Kamal Pasha was only a soldier in the Turkish army. This was long before he took antagonistic steps against Islam as president of Turkey.

A Good Wife's Final Words to Her Husband

When writing her final bequest to her husband, a wife should add the following:

1. She should request him to forgive all her shortcomings and everything that she may have done which has hurt him in any way. She should remember the words of The Prophet (Peace be upon him) who said, "A woman will enter Jannah if she passes away while her husband is pleased with her." She should therefore do her best to obey everything lawful that he asks her to do.
2. If she has the bad habit of applying nail polish, she should remind him in her bequest that this should be removed before her corpse is bathed because the bath will be invalid with the nail polish on.
3. She should advise her sons and grandsons to become Huffaadh of and the Ulama. At the same time, she should also advise her daughters and granddaughters to be righteous Muslims and to learn Arabic. If her sons have grown up and she was unable to make the Huffaadh and Ulama, she should apologise to them and emphasise that they should ensure that their sons become Huffadh, Ulama and sincere callers to Islam.

   If her children are still growing, she should advise them to study Religion and to apply themselves to the service of Islam at all levels. She should stress that they make every effort to ensure that the Religion of Allah Ta'ala dominates all other Religion s, as will happen before the Day of Qiyamah.
4. She should encourage her husband to remarry after her death so that his home will continue running smoothly and so that he may be saved from sin. She should also caution him against allowing another

woman to abuse her children.

5. She should remind him to recite du'as and to do good deeds on her behalf so that she could benefit from the rewards of these deeds.
6. She should instruct him to destroy the photographs of her that appear on her identity document, on her passport or anywhere else so that no photographs of her remain. In this way, her sin of having her photographs taken will not live after her.
7. She should also direct him to look for pious partners for her children once they are ready for marriage. She should issue explicit instructions that the marriage should be simple and contracted only after consultation with elders, Istikhara and the consent of the couple. In addition to this, she must stipulate that her daughter-in-law should be given her own quarters as soon as she marries.

IN CONCLUSION

We request every reader to remember us in their pious du'as for whatever benefit you may have derived from this book. Do not forget to make du'a for all Muslim sisters. Pray to Allah Ta'ala to guide them all to lead their lives as Allah Ta'ala and His Prophet (Peace be upon him) have instructed. It is now your responsibility to raise your children as mentioned in this book and to imbibe the qualities of a good woman in their friends and family. You should also allow other women to read this book so that they can also benefit from it. It should not be allowed to rot in the shelves. After reading this book, recite the following du'a. This du'a should be recited after terminating any gathering so that Allah Ta'ala may forgive any shortcomings.

سبحانك اللّٰهم وبحمدك نشهد أن لا إله إلا أنت نستغفرك ونتوب إليك

O Allah Ta'ala! You are Pure from all defects and all praise belongs to You Alone. We testify that there is none worthy of worship but You. We seek Your pardon, O Allah Ta'ala and turn to You in repentance.

وصلى اللّٰه تعالى على خير خلقه محمد وعلى آله وأصحابه وأزواجه وذريته أجمعين

May Allah Ta'ala bestow His choicest blessings and mercy on the best of His creation Muhammad (Peace be upon him), as well as on his family, his companions, his wives and all his progeny.